S/NVQ Level 3
Working with Children and Young People

YVONNE NOLAN

www.heinemann.co.uk
✓ Free online support
✓ Useful weblinks
✓ 24 hour online ordering

01865 888118

Heinemann is an imprint of Pearson Education Limited, a company incorporated in England and Wales, having its registered office at Edinburgh Gate, Harlow, Essex, CM20 2JE.
Registered company number: 872828

Heinemann is a registered trademark of
Pearson Education Limited

Text © 2007 Yvonne Nolan

Evidence opportunities grid on pages 357–375 © 2007 Rosemary Mitchell

First published 2007
10 09 08
10 9 8 7 6 5 4 3

British Library Cataloguing in Publication Data is available from the British Library on request.

978 0 435 117 04 7

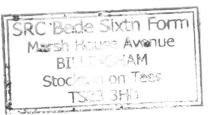

Edited by Sarah Christopher
Typeset and illustrated by Saxon Graphics Ltd, Derby

Original illustrations © Harcourt Education Limited, 2007

Printed in China (RRD/02)
Cover photo © Scott Tysick/Masterfile

Acknowledgements
Every effort has been made to contact copyright holders of material reproduced in this book. Any omissions will be rectified in subsequent printings if notice is given to the publishers.

The publishers and author would like to thank Rosemary Mitchell for her evidence opportunities grid (see pages 357–375) and for referencing the Active knowledge features and Abingdon College (in particular, Michelle Kershaw) for their invaluable assistance.

Photo credits
The authors and publisher would like to thank the following for permission to reproduce photographs:

Alamy: pages 176 (Jon Peters), 184, 197 (Dennis MacDonald)
Corbis: pages 5 (x 2), 123 (Vladimir Pirogov/ Reuters), 129 (David Ashley), 173 (Charles & Josette Lenars)
Digital Vision: page 287
Dreamstime.com: pages 121 (Scrambled), 176 (Nikitu), 179 (Sharply_done), 207 (marmion), 217 (Bmcent1)
Getty Images: pages 86, 92, 246 (Thinkstock)
Harcourt Education Ltd/Gareth Boden: page 218
Harcourt Education Ltd/Jules Selmes: pages 10, 20, 22, 26, 30, 31, 36, 89, 100, 123, 196, 197, 206, 219, 222, 226, 233, 236, 272, 308, 335, 346, 355
Harcourt Education Ltd/Tudor Photography: page 119
iStockphoto.com: pages 160 (digital skillet), 182 (Andrew Ramsey), 190 (Scott Anderson), 233 (Tom De Bruyne), 259 (Don Bayley), 260 (Yvonne Chamberlain), 261 (Ana Abejan), 287 (marmion), 344 (Susan Stevenson)
John Birdsall Social Issues: page 164
Photofusion: pages 22 (Jacky Chapman), 190 (Crispin Hughes), 196 (Paul Doyle)
Richard Smith: pages 53, 70 (x 5), 71 (x 6), 105, 110, 144
Science Photo Library: page 179 (Dr P. Marazzi)
Shutterstock: pages 206, 260

Contents

Introduction

Welcome to Working with Children and Young People. I hope that you will find this book useful whether as a support as you work towards your qualification, or just as a general reference for ideas or to check facts. The book is designed to give you not only information and practical guidance, but also to give you pause for thought and reminders to reflect on your own practice. The child's or young person's voice is included throughout the book, and all of the children's viewpoints are based on actual children and young people and reflect their real-life circumstances.

I have heard working with children and young people described in many ways; 'rewarding', 'challenging', 'frustrating' and 'exhausting' are just a few of them. Of course, it is all of those and more, but most significantly it is a privilege and a huge responsibility to be closely involved with children's and young people's lives in a positive and supportive way. For some children and young people, you may be the first positive influence they have had in their lives, the first person to offer consistent caring, or the first person who has told them 'No' and given them boundaries and structure.

Caring for children and young people is about keeping them healthy and safe from harm, but it is also about preparing them for a future in which they can lead fulfilling lives as fully participating citizens who actively contribute to the communities in which they live. In order to do this, they need to be secure, confident and able to build positive, caring relationships with other people.

For many of the children and young people you meet, this may seem a remote possibility and an unreachable and idealistic dream. However, you have the opportunity to participate in their journey towards these goals and everything you do in your relationship with a child or young person will have an impact on the direction and progress of their journey – that's where the responsibility comes in. The privilege? Just having the chance to be a part of it.

I wish you every success in your qualification and in your future career.

Yvonne Nolan

Acknowledgements

As ever, I owe a huge debt of gratitude to Pen and all the team at Heinemann for their wonderful support and professionalism in turning this from a manuscript into a book. I would also like to thank Rosemary Mitchell at North Devon College for her expert knowledge in creating the evidence grid at the end of this book and for referencing the Active knowledge features.

Dedication

This book is dedicated to the children and young people who find the world a harsh, confusing, unfriendly, scary or challenging place, in the hope that they will find someone who can show them that there can be trust, warmth, love and happiness and that there are people who care about them.

Promote effective communication for and about individuals

Effective Communication is one of the six Common Core areas of skills and knowledge that all those who work with children and young people must be able to demonstrate.

Regardless of the job you do, if you work with children, you have to be able to communicate with them, and with those people who are important to them. Effective communication contributes towards the achievement of all of the outcomes for children and underpins almost all of the work you do.

Communication is all about the way people reach out to one another. It is an essential part of all relationships, and the ability to communicate well with children or young people, young people and their families, colleagues and others is a basic requirement for doing your job.

Communication is not just talking – we use touch, facial expressions and body movements when we are communicating with people face to face; the tone and expression in our voices are the keys when using phone communication; and texts, e-mails and letters all make different demands on our skills as communicators.

It is important that you learn to communicate well even where there are differences in children or young people's abilities and methods of communication; some issues are complex and sensitive and you will need to be able to address these with care and skill.

Recording information clearly and accurately is a key and vital component of being a childcare professional and you need to understand the significance of what you record and how you record it.

This unit is designed to help you to understand how the different aspects of communication combine to build and develop relationships with the children or young people and families you work with.

In this unit you will find 'Active knowledge' features containing activities that will contribute to assessment for your NVQ. Remember that these features only offer the opportunity for partial assessment; you can also refer to the evidence opportunities grid (see pages 357–375) for more ideas to provide suitable evidence for your NVQ.

What you need to learn

- How we communicate
- Listening effectively
- Communicating effectively with children and young people
- Undertaking difficult, complex and sensitive communications
- Offering the right support
- Why we communicate

- Barriers to communication
- The best ways to communicate with a child or young person
- Ways of receiving and passing on information
- Confidentiality
- Looking after information
- Recording information

HSC 31a Identify ways to communicate effectively

How we communicate

(KS 2, 10)

This element is about children and young people communicating. Communication is much more than talking – it is about how we respond to each other in many different ways: touch, facial expression, body movements, dress, not to mention using written communication, the telephone or electronic messages!

Remember

You are the most important tool you have for doing your job. Childcare professionals do not have carefully engineered machinery or complex technology – your own ability to relate to children and to understand them is the key you need!

Reflect

Do this with a friend or colleague.

1) Write the names of several emotions (such as anger, joy, sadness, disappointment, fear) on pieces of paper.

2) One of you picks up a piece of paper. Your task is to communicate the emotion written on the paper to your partner, without saying anything.

3) Your partner then has to decide what the emotion is and say why.

4) Change places and repeat the exercise. Take it in turns, until all the pieces of paper have been used. Make sure that you list all the things that made you aware of the emotion being expressed.

5) Discuss with your partner what you have discovered about communication as a result of this exercise. Think about how you can use this learning in your own practice. Are you sometimes too busy to pick up on signals? Is it sometimes easier to ignore them, even if you notice them? Be honest with yourself about how good you are at picking up on non-verbal communication.

More than talking

Any relationship comes about through communication. In order to be an effective childcare worker, you must learn to be a good communicator. You will have to know how to recognise what is being communicated to you, and to be able to communicate with children and young people and their families, without always having to use words.

When you carried out the exercise in the previous column, you will have found out that there are many things that told you what your partner was trying to communicate. It is not only people's facial expressions that tell you how they feel, but also the way they use the rest of their bodies.

This area of human behaviour is referred to as **non-verbal communication**. It is very important for developing the ability to understand what others are feeling. If you understand the importance of non-verbal communication, you will be able to use it to improve your own skills when you communicate.

Key term

Non-verbal communication: A way of communicating without words, through body language, gestures, facial expression and eye contact.

Signs and signals

When we meet and talk with people, regardless of whether they are adults or children, we will usually be using two language systems: verbal or spoken language, and non-verbal communication or body language.

Effective communication in childcare work requires the ability to analyse your own and others' non-verbal behaviour. Our bodies send messages to other people – often without us meaning to send those messages. Some of the most important body areas that send messages are shown here.

The eyes

We can guess the feelings and thoughts that another person has by looking at their eyes, often called 'the windows of the soul'. We can sometimes understand the thoughts and feelings of another person by eye-to-eye contact. Our eyes get wider when we are excited, or attracted to someone. A fixed stare may send the message that the person is angry. In European cultures, looking away is often interpreted as showing boredom. All children express feeling through their eyes – you can see joy, excitement and wonder, fear and uncertainty, in even the youngest children.

The face

Faces can send very complex messages and we can read them easily.

Our faces often indicate our emotional state. When a child is sad, he or she may look down, there may be tension in the face, and the mouth will be closed. The muscles in the child's shoulders are likely to be relaxed, but his or her face and neck may show tension. A happy person will have wide-open eyes that make contact with you, and will smile.

Voice tone

If adults talk quickly in a loud voice with a fixed tone, people may see them as angry. A calm, slow voice with varying tone may send a message of being friendly. Children's voices talking quickly and loudly can indicate excitement and anticipation, whereas a low whisper can indicate fear and a need for reassurance.

Body movement

The way we walk, move our heads, sit, cross our legs and so on sends messages about whether we are tired, happy, sad or bored.

Posture

Sitting with crossed arms can mean 'I'm not taking any notice'. Leaning back or to one side can send the message that you are relaxed or bored; leaning forward can show interest.

Muscle tension

The tension in our feet, hands and fingers can tell others how relaxed or how tense we are. If people are very tense their shoulders might stiffen, their face muscles might tighten and they might sit or stand rigidly. A tense face might have a firmly closed mouth with lips and jaws clenched tight. A tense person might breathe quickly and become hot.

Gestures

Gestures are hand and arm movements that can help us to understand what a person is saying. Some gestures carry a generally agreed meaning of their own within a culture. When people are excited they may move their arms or hands quickly.

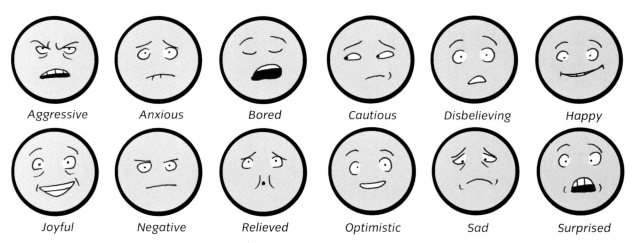

We can read facial expressions easily, even in diagram form

Touch

Touching another adult can send messages of care, affection, power over them, or sexual interest. The social setting and other body language usually help people to understand what touch might mean. As a childcare worker, you should not make assumptions about touch. This is covered in more detail on pages 30–31.

Proximity and personal space

The space between people can sometimes show how friendly or intimate the conversation is. Different cultures have different assumptions about how close people should be (their proximity) when they are talking.

In Britain, when talking to strangers we may keep an arm's length apart. The ritual of shaking hands indicates that you have been introduced – you may come closer. When you are friendly with someone you may accept the person coming even closer to you. Relatives and partners may not be restricted in how close they can come. This is called **proxemics** and was first documented in 1963. Children will behave slightly differently to adults in this respect, simply getting closer to people they are the most familiar with (both carers and playmates). By the time children are in their teens, they will respond in the same way as adults.

Giving out signals

Research shows that people pay far more attention to facial expressions and tone of voice than they do to spoken words. For example, in one study, words contributed only 7 per cent towards the impression of whether or not someone was liked, tone of voice contributed 38 per cent and facial expression 55 per cent. The study also found that if there was a contradiction between facial expression and words, people believed the facial expression.

Face-to-face positions (orientation)

Standing or sitting face to face can send a message of being formal or being angry. A slight angle can create a more relaxed and friendly feeling.

Responding to others

There will be many occasions when you need to communicate effectively with parents and other adults who are important to the children you work

Intimate zone (touching)

Personal zone (less than 1 metre)

Social zone (1–2 metres)

Public zone (2 metres +)

with. How do you work out what another person might be feeling?

- Look at a person's facial expression. Much of what you will see will be in his or her eyes, but the eyebrows and mouth also tell you a lot.
- Notice whether someone is looking at you, or at the floor, or at a point over your shoulder. Lack of eye contact should give a first indication that all may not be well. It may be that the person is feeling unconfident, unhappy, or uneasy. You will need to follow this up.
- Look at how a person sits. Is he or she relaxed and comfortable, or tense and perched on the edge of the seat? Is he or she slumped with the head down? People who are feeling well tend to hold their heads up, and sit in a relaxed and comfortable way. An individual who is tense and nervous, who feels unsure and worried, is likely to reflect that in the way he or she sits or stands.
- Observe hands and gestures carefully. Someone twisting his or her hands, or fiddling with hair or clothes, is signalling worry. Frequent shrugs or spreading of the hands may indicate a feeling of helplessness.

Giving out the signals

Being aware of your own body language is just as important as understanding the person you are talking to; all of the key signs to look for in others also apply to you.

Reflect

Do this with at least one other person – two or three are even better.

1) Think of an incident or situation that is quite important and significant to you. Stand still in the middle of a room and begin to tell your partner about your significant incident.

2) Your partner should start at the edge of the room and slowly move closer and closer to you.

3) At the point where you feel comfortable talking to your partner, say 'Stop'. Mark this point and measure the distance from where you are standing.

4) At the point where you feel that your partner is too close, say 'Stop'. Mark this point and measure the distance from where you are standing.

5) Change places and repeat the exercise.

You may find that you and your partner(s) have different distances at which you feel comfortable, but it is likely to be in the range of 1–1.5 metres (3–5ft).

How do you think each of these people is feeling? What makes you think that?

Keys to good practice: Communication skills

All of the following key points apply whether you are communicating with adults or children, although children are likely to be quicker to let you know if you are giving out inappropriate signals.

✓ You should generally maintain eye contact with the child or young person you are talking to, although you should avoid staring! With children, you sometimes do better to sit beside them, so as not to appear confrontational.

✓ Looking away occasionally is normal, but if your attention wanders when a child is talking to you, they will notice it and you will have lost them: unlike adults, they will not continue talking in the hope that your attention will return.

✓ Sit where you can be comfortably seen. Don't sit where the child has to turn in order to look at you.

✓ Sit near enough to foster a sense of closeness, but not so close that you 'invade their space'.

✓ Make sure you are showing by your gestures that you are listening and interested in what children are saying – sitting half turned away gives the message that you are not fully committed to what is being said.

✓ Folded arms or crossed legs can indicate that you are 'closed' rather than 'open' to what a child or young person is expressing.

✓ Nodding your head will indicate that you are receptive and interested – but be careful not to overdo it and look like a nodding dog!

✓ Lean towards the child to show that you are interested in what they are saying. You can use leaning forwards quite effectively at times when you want to emphasise your interest or support.

✓ Using touch to communicate your caring and concern is often useful and appropriate. Many children find it comforting to have their hand held or stroked, or to have an arm around their shoulders, but remember always to ask the child's permission first.

✓ Be aware of a child's body language, which should tell you if he or she finds touch acceptable.

✓ Always err on the side of caution if you are unsure about what is acceptable to the child.

✓ Think about age and gender in relation to touch. A young child is more likely to expect and want to be comforted using touch – a teenager of a different gender to you may find touching unacceptable.

Remember

- You can often learn as much by observing as by listening.

- Learn to 'listen with your eyes'.

- Your own body sends out as many messages as the person you are talking to.

- Be aware of the messages you give to others.

The risk of stereotyping

It can be very hard to really understand the needs of children and young people. Sometimes it can be tempting to make life easier by relying on standard ideas to explain 'what these children are like'. When a person has a standard picture that he or she uses and regards certain types of children or young people as all being the same, this is called **stereotyping**.

Young people are often stereotyped. Phrases which begin: 'Young people today…' or 'Young people from inner cities…' always continue with a stereotyped view of what 'young people' do or fail to do. Stereotyping fails to recognise and value individuals and assumes that there is a single identity for all 'young people' and that they will all behave in the same way. You will know from your work that nothing is further from the truth. It is common to work with young people from the same street, or from the same gang, who may share some values, but their responses and personalities will be far from identical.

A negative, stereotyped view of young people

Disabled children are often understood as damaged versions of 'normal' children – a negative stereotype that can mean that they may be pitied or ignored. In reality, disabled children are individuals who have different challenges to face, which means that they have different gifts, strengths and experiences to contribute.

Ethical issue

You work for a small charity that does some quite specialist work with children who have been through the justice system and present challenging behaviour. A large corporation with a local support programme offers your organisation a significant sum of money, which will enable you to buy new equipment for the house and organise an activity break the young people are keen on. As part of the donation, the company want to use the slogan 'Globalworld – making your cities safer by solving the problems' and photographs of gangs of predominantly black young people (not the actual young people in your facility) in street fashion. What do you do?

Listening effectively

(KS 2, 10, 12)

Communication is a two-way process. This may sound obvious, but a great deal of communication is wasted because only one of the parties is communicating. Think about setting up communication between two radios – when a link is established, the question is asked, 'Are you receiving me?' and the answer comes back, 'Receiving you loud and clear.' Unfortunately, human beings don't do this exercise before they talk to each other!

You may think that you know how to listen and that it is something you do constantly. After all, you are hearing all sorts of noises all day long – but simply hearing sounds is not the same thing as actively listening.

For most people, feeling that someone is really listening makes a huge difference to how confident they feel about talking. You will need to learn about ways in which you can show children and adults that you are listening to what they are saying.

Reflect

Think about a time you have talked to someone you felt was really interested in what you were saying and listening carefully to you. Try to note down what it was that made you so sure he or she was really listening. Did the fact you thought the person was really listening to you make it easier to talk? When you have worked out why you knew the person was listening to you, think about how you can improve your own practice.

Using body language

You may be surprised to learn that over 80 per cent of what you communicate to others is understood without you speaking a word. Body language, or non-verbal communication, is the way in which we pick up most of the messages people are trying to give us – and some that they're not!

Your body language can let people know that you are really listening to what they are saying. Practise your listening skills in just the same way you would practise any other skill – you can learn to listen well.

Always:

- look at the person who is talking to you
- maintain eye contact, without staring
- nod your head to encourage the person to talk and show that you understand
- use 'aha', 'mm' and similar expressions which indicate that you are still listening
- lean slightly towards the person who is speaking – this indicates interest and concern
- have an open and interested facial expression, which should reflect the tone of the conversation – happy, serious, etc.

What are these people really thinking?

HSC 31b Communicate effectively on difficult, complex and sensitive issues

Communicating effectively with children and young people

(KS 8, 10, 12)

The child or young person and his or her needs should be at the centre of the caring process, and the development of the professional relationship should always be focused on the needs of the child. Effective relationships are the basis of effective communication, and this is even more important when dealing with difficult issues.

Developing relationships

Communication is the basis of all relationships, regardless of whether the relationships are personal or professional. As individuals communicate, a relationship is formed. This is usually a two-way process as each individual involved gets to know the other through a process of communicating and sharing information.

When you work with a child or young person, you will get to know and talk to him or her, and a relationship will grow. This is not always easy. Sometimes it can take a long time before there appears to be even a little communication. However, every communication with a child or young person, no matter how little response you may appear to be getting, will be contributing to building a relationship. It is often surprising, when

relationships are well established, to hear from a child just how important your efforts to communicate were. You may be amazed at how much a child will recall of what you said to him or her, even if the response at the time was to look at the floor and shout an obscenity.

Stages of an interaction

Any communication between people is called an 'interaction'. As you spend time in communication with someone, the nature of the interaction will go through changes.

Stage 1: Introduction, light and general

At first, the content of the communication may be of little significance. This is the stage at which both parties decide whether they want to continue the discussion, and how comfortable they feel. This is the stage at which you chat about minor matters like a new top, the music in the charts or why the rota has changed. Non-verbal communication is very important at this stage, so that it is clear that you are relaxed, interested and ready to listen.

Stage 2: Main contact, significant information

The middle of any interaction is likely to contain the 'meat', and this is where you will need to use active listening skills to ensure that both of you gain something from the interaction. This is where any key issues for the child or young person should come up, either because he or she will want to talk about

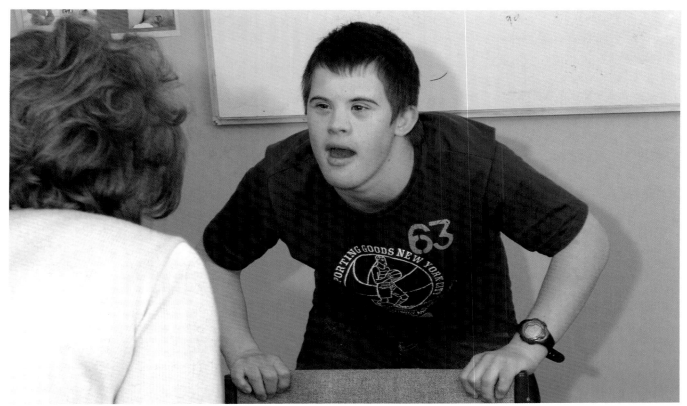

Every communication with a child or young person contributes to building a relationship

something that is bothering or upsetting them, or because you have important, specific issues you need to raise.

Stage 3: Reflect, wind up, end positively

Ending an interaction can often be the most difficult part. Ending in a positive way so that everyone is left feeling that they have benefited from the interaction is very important. You may find that you have to end an interaction because of time restrictions, or you may feel that enough has been covered or you may both need a break! At the end of an interaction you should always try to reflect on the areas you have covered, and offer an encouraging ending, for example: 'I'm glad you've talked about how unhappy you've been feeling. Now we can try to work at making things better.'

Even if the content of an interaction has been fairly negative, you should encourage the child or young person to see the fact that the interaction has taken place as being positive in itself.

Active knowledge   HSC 31 pc 1–9

Think of a difficult interaction you have had with a child, young person or family you have worked with. See if you can identify the stages and think about ways you may have handled it differently.

Making time

If you are called away before you have had a chance to 'wind up' an interaction with a child properly, make a point of returning to end things in a positive way. If you say, 'I'll be back in a minute', make sure that you do go back. One of the key findings when children and young people were asked about the qualities they wanted in the people who worked with them (Children's Workforce Development Council 2006) was that they wanted people to have time for them, and not to be too busy and always having to rush off. Try to remember this, and plan the time you spend with children carefully. Try to make sure that the child knows that you will make time and that they are important to you.

Life stages and development

One of the most significant influences on communication and the way children and young people deal with difficult or stressful issues is the life stage they are at. The chart on the following page will help you to understand the life stages children and young people have already experienced by the time you are working with them. You also need to understand what happens in later stages of development, as one of your key roles is to provide children and young people with a firm foundation for facing the demands and pressures of adult life.

Children are different

It is important to communicate with children or young people in a different way from adults. Children or young people have different emotional, social, intellectual and language needs; they think and converse differently from adults. If you ask a child or young person to tell you about their past life, they might only be able to tell you about very practical, concrete experiences such as a birthday party or where they went on holiday. Adults are more likely to organise their life story into themes about jobs, relationships and aspirations.

Working with children and young people may mean that you have to support them to organise their thoughts. Sometimes it can be useful to find out about a child or young person's past life by doing something practical such as starting a scrapbook. This way, you can begin to find out about complex and difficult areas in a child's life as part of the activity, rather than by making it into a formal 'interview' situation.

Unless you have completed additional training, you will not be expected to undertake any therapeutic work or the casework or counselling which a psychologist or a social worker would do. However, because you will be much closer to the children and young people and see them much more, you will form vitally important relationships with the children and young people you work with, and offering good communication skills will make a major contribution to improving their outcomes.

You may also be asked to support work being undertaken by psychologists or social workers if they are using activity-based approaches to encourage children to talk about their feelings. Children and young people often respond well to using activities to help reveal feelings and emotions about difficult or painful areas. With an older child or a teenager who has an interest in drama, music or art, you could be asked to support work on a play, songs about their life, or a series of paintings. Younger children can often tell you a story using dolls, cars and toy buildings in an imaginative game, and you may be asked to support this and observe and record what happens.

Keys to good practice: Communicating effectively with children and young people

✓ Arrange the immediate environment to ensure privacy, make communication easier and aid understanding.

✓ Check that children and young people who need support to communicate their views and preferences are able to do so.

✓ Use styles and methods of communication that are appropriate to the child or young person and the subject matter.

✓ Give children and young people sufficient time and opportunity to understand the content of the communication.

✓ Observe and respond appropriately to their reactions.

Life stages of children and young people

	Cognitive	Social/emotional	Language	Physical
Infant, birth–1 year	Learns about new things by feeling with hands and mouth objects encountered in immediate environment By 1 year can wave 'bye bye'	Attaches to parent(s), begins to recognise faces and smile; at about 6 months begins to recognise parent(s) and expresses fear of strangers, plays simple interactive games like peekaboo	Vocalises, squeals, and imitates sounds, says 'dada' and 'mama'	Lifts head first then chest, rolls over, pulls to sit, crawls and stands alone. Reaches for objects and rakes up small items, grasps rattle
Toddler, 1–2 years	Extends knowledge by learning words for objects in environment	Learns that self and parent(s) are different or separate from each other, imitates and performs tasks, indicates needs or wants without crying	Says some words other than 'dada' and 'mama', follows simple instructions	Walks well, kicks, stoops and jumps in place, throws balls. Unbuttons clothes, builds tower of 4 cubes, scribbles, uses spoon, picks up very small objects
Pre-school, 2–5 years	Understands concepts such as tired, hungry and other bodily states, recognises colours, becomes aware of numbers and letters	Begins to separate easily from parent(s), dresses with assistance, washes and dries hands, plays interactive games like tag	Names pictures, follows directions, can make simple sentences of two or three words, vocabulary increases	Runs well, hops, pedals tricycle, balances on one foot. Buttons clothes, builds tower of 8 cubes, copies simple figures or letters, for example 0, begins to use scissors
School age, 5–12 years	Develops understanding of numeracy and literacy concepts, learns relationship between objects and feelings, acquires knowledge and understanding	Acts independently, but is emotionally close to parent(s), dresses without assistance, joins same-sex play groups and clubs	Defines words, knows and describes what things are made of, vocabulary increases	Skips, balances on one foot for 10 seconds, overestimates physical abilities. Draws person with 6 parts, copies detailed figures and objects

	Cognitive	Social/emotional	Language	Physical
Adolescent, 12–18 years	Understands abstract concepts like illness and death, develops understanding of complex concepts	Experiences rapidly changing moods and behaviour, interested in peer group almost exclusively, distances from parent(s) emotionally, concerned with body image, experiences falling in and out of love	Uses increased vocabulary, understands more abstract concepts such as grief	May appear awkward and clumsy while learning to deal with rapid increases in size due to growth spurts
Young adult, 18–40 years	Continues to develop the ability to make good decisions and to understand the complexity of human relationships – sometimes called wisdom	Becomes independent from parent(s), develops own lifestyle, selects a career, copes with career, social and economic changes and social expectations, chooses a partner, learns to live co-operatively with partner, becomes a parent	Continues to develop vocabulary and knowledge of different styles of language use	Fully developed
Middle age, 40–65 years	Continues to develop a deeper understanding of life – sometimes called wisdom	Builds social and economic status, is fulfilled by work or family, copes with physical changes of ageing, children or young people grow and leave nest, deals with ageing parents, copes with the death of parents	Vocabulary may continue to develop	Begins to experience physical signs of ageing

	Cognitive	Social/emotional	Language	Physical
Older adult, 65+ years	Ability may be influenced by health factors; some individuals will continue to develop 'wisdom'	Adjusts to retirement, adjusts to loss of friends and relatives, copes with loss of spouse, adjusts to new role in family, copes with dying	Ability may be influenced by health factors; some individuals may continue to develop language skills	Experiences more significant physical changes associated with ageing

Reflect

Think about a child with whom you have been able to form a close and effective relationship. Identify the reasons why this relationship worked. In order to do this, you will need to go right back to the first meeting and go over carefully what was said and how. Think about what it was about the child's response to you that made the relationship work well. A careful analysis over a period of time can help you to see the way you relate to children and how they respond to you. Take the learning from this exercise and use it to improve your practice.

Difficult situations and strong emotions

There are definite and measurable physical effects caused by strong emotional responses. It is useful to be aware of these effects, as they can often be an early indicator of a potentially highly charged or dangerous situation. This is about balancing the obvious pain, anger and hurt which the child is feeling, and your concerns to offer them care and support, with the risk which can be posed to you and other staff by an aggressive and potentially violent young person.

This is less likely to be an issue with younger children as, no matter how out of control they become, they are unlikely to place you in physical danger. The need to offer them care and support in dealing with their emotions is discussed earlier. However, you need to be conscious of the potential risks posed by a young person in the grip of strong emotions. The physical effects of strong emotion can be:

- pupils dilate, the eyelids open wider than usual, and the eyes protrude
- speed and strength of heartbeat is increased
- blood pressure is increased and blood is forced towards the surface of the body; this is clearly noticeable in flushing of the face and neck
- the hair can stand up, causing goose pimples

- breathing patterns will change
- the lung function alters to allow up to 25 per cent more oxygen to be absorbed
- more sweat is produced – this can often be identified as a 'cold sweat'
- the salivary glands are inhibited – resulting in the dry mouth feeling
- the digestive system is affected – the gastric fluids are reduced and blood is withdrawn from the digestive organs
- there is an increase in adrenaline – this reinforces all effects and increases blood clotting.

These responses prepare us for 'fight or flight' – a basic human response to being under threat, in which the body physically prepares us to either fight or run away. Angry children could choose either of these options, so you will need to be prepared.

Children or young people in a highly emotional state will often be highly energised. For example, they don't speak, but shout; they don't sit or stand still, but run or walk about; they will slam doors and possibly throw things.

One apparent effect of strong emotional responses is a temporary lessening of the awareness of pain. Sometimes children and young people in a very emotional state will injure themselves while smashing and throwing objects around, but not seem to notice until everything has calmed down. It is unlikely that you will be able to intervene to deal with an injury whilst a child or young person is in a violent emotional state. You will need to make a judgment about the risks posed by an intervention and the risk to the child from leaving the injury.

For example:

> A young person is smashing furniture in his room and cuts the knuckles on his hand when he punches the dressing table. This is unlikely to justify the risk of an intervention as the injury is minor. However, if he picks up a chair and smashes the window, causing a big gash on the inside of his arm from the sharp shards of glass – then it is likely that you will need to get assistance and intervene to ensure his safety and deal with the injury.

Controlling strong emotions

In growing and developing, most of us learn to control our powerful emotions. The sight of a two-year-old lying on the floor in a supermarket kicking and screaming is not uncommon – it is accepted as normal behaviour for a child of that age. On the other hand, it is not socially acceptable for an adult to do the same thing, however much we may want to on occasions! Adults don't behave in this way in public because we have been socialised into behaviour that is accepted as the norm in society. However, some adults do find it beneficial and therapeutic to have a tantrum in the privacy of their homes, to get relief from the rage they feel.

We can accept children having tantrums in public, but not adults, so a key part of your job is to help children to learn how to control and deal with strong emotions as they grow and develop.

salivary glands are inhibited

breathing patterns will change

lung function alters

goose pimples

digestive system is affected

more sweat is produced

pupils dilate

blood pressure is increased

speed and strength of heartbeat is increased

increase in adrenaline

Physical changes linked with the 'fight or flight' response

We can accept children having tantrums in public, but not adults

Reflect

Think about how you deal with emotions. Think of the occasions when you have felt strong and powerful emotions but managed to keep them under control and not show your distress publicly, and other occasions when you have shown public distress.

Try to identify the difference in circumstances and the factors that caused the two different responses. See if you can apply any of the knowledge you have gained from this to helping young people to control their emotions as they grow and develop.

Undertaking difficult, complex and sensitive communications

(KS 14, 15, 16)

If children are upset as the result of an outside event, such as the death of a close friend or relative, or because they have received some other bad news, such as a parent going to prison, there is probably little you can do to prevent the distress – but the way you communicate with them and the way you handle the situation can often help.

If they are upset because of a row with a friend, or because they are being bullied, or because they can't go to an all-night party on Friday, you may be able to support them to address the issues they are upset about. They still won't get to go to the all-night party, but if you can help them to deal with the reasons, and to agree another alternative activity, you may manage to avoid them simply going anyway!

You must be careful not to pressurise children or young people to discuss more than they want to. You could also offer them a choice of talking to another member of staff or a relative or friend, if they appear to be unwilling to discuss their distress with you.

Unlike adults, children do not have the ability to separate events from themselves: they see that everything that happens is about them and has come about because of them. It is really important to reach children at this point, because otherwise they will develop an explanation for events that fits with this view, and can go through life carrying unnecessary guilt.

A child whose parent dies can often believe that they caused the death through a naughty act.

Young children up to about 7 years old have a clear perception of cause and effect in which they are at the centre of everything; for example, they may feel that their parents divorced because of something they did, and that daddy went away because they were naughty. At this age, everything and everyone is part of their world. This gradually changes until, by the time a child is around 11 years old, they are better able to separate the rest of the world from themselves. Children need reassurance and constant confirmation that they are not responsible for bad things that happen.

As a result of the way children look at the world, their anger may not be directed at others; sometimes children and young people turn it inwards and direct it against themselves. This is a tragedy in waiting because, as a result of a child or young person believing they are the cause of a problem, you may be faced with a distressed, hurt and angry young person who makes it clear that he or she intends to self-harm. In this case you have a responsibility to take immediate action to protect. You should make it clear that you will have to take these steps to prevent harm; the only exception is where you believe that telling the young person will make the risk of self-harm greater. Your primary goal is to stop the young person from harming himself or herself.

Ethical issue

You are faced with a 17-year-old who is very bright, but who has a congenital illness he knows will result in death when he reaches 25. His illness is becoming increasingly painful and he is becoming more and more dependent on others to provide his care. He has told you that he feels he has no dignity left and cannot face the increasing pain. He says he wants to die comfortably in a way and in a place of his own choosing. What do you do?

Just being there can be enough

Your acknowledgement and recognition of distress may be sufficient for some young people who are resilient and well supported by friends, family and other professionals, and they may be able to deal with their distress themselves if they know that they can obtain additional support from you if they need to.

The effects of your interactions

You need to be aware of the ways in which you are using your own communication skills to interact with a child or young person who is distressed in a complex or difficult situation. While you are taking into account the child's body language and the clues of non-verbal communication, you will need to be conscious of the messages your own non-verbal communication is sending. You need to demonstrate openness with an open welcoming position, but don't encroach on a young person's personal space as this often heightens tension. Remember that the need for personal space grows as children develop, so a younger child will want to be closer to you than an adolescent child will. Make eye contact in a way that demonstrates you are willing to listen.

You will need to be calm and non-threatening if a child or young person is angry: if you are aggressive in return, the situation will escalate. If at any point you feel your personal safety is at risk, you should immediately summon help.

You can demonstrate openness with an open, welcoming position

Asking for help

No one is able to deal with every situation with which they are faced, and you may feel that something is beyond your capability. This is nothing to be ashamed of. Knowing your own limitations is important and demonstrates a higher degree of maturity and self-awareness than taking risks and carrying on in a situation in which you are not confident. Contact your manager, other members of your team or other professionals with the experience to deal with the situation – never hesitate to summon help when you feel unsure in dealing with a child, or young person in distress.

 Keys to good practice:
Communicating in complex
or difficult situations

✓ Be aware of your own body language as well as reading that of the child or young person.

✓ Keep an open body posture.

✓ Do not encroach on personal space.

✓ Respond to aggression with calm.

✓ Summon help, or leave if you feel you are at risk.

✓ Never be afraid to ask for help when you are not confident.

Offering the right support

(KS 7, 10)

The level of help and support you should offer is always best decided along with the young people themselves, provided they are old enough. The situation with younger children is different, although you should still find out the child's view of what they want to happen and take it into account when discussing plans with parents or carers.

If you are going to talk to a young person about the sort of support they may need, questions should be clear, and designed to establish the correct level of support, such as, 'I can see you're very upset – do you want to talk to me about it?' or, 'I can see you're very upset – would you like me to find you someone to talk to?'

Broadly, the necessary help you are likely to offer will probably fall into one of three categories, as shown in the following table.

Practical support	Giving information, offering a hug or hand holding, making a telephone call, providing transport or other practical assistance, contacting someone on behalf of the distressed person, or meeting an appropriate professional.
Emotional support	Using listening and communication skills.
Immediate emergency assistance	Summoning immediate help from a colleague, a senior member of staff, an appropriate professional, or the emergency services.

How to offer support

You will need to ensure that you have access to sources of information and the appropriate resources that can be offered in particular circumstances. There are specialist organisations that will offer particular support for children who are bereaved, for children who are being bullied or for those who have survived abuse. You should be sure that you can access all the relevant contact details.

Active knowledge   HSC 31a pc 4b, HSC 31d pc 5b

Check the information stored in your workplace on sources of specialist support for children. If it is inadequate or out of date, create a plan of action for updating it. You might want to research it yourself and keep records for your portfolio.

Using communication skills

When you have identified the best way to provide support, you will need to use your communication skills to the full to begin to establish a supportive relationship. Do not underestimate the support you will be able to provide by using good communication skills and a genuine empathy and care for children and young people – you can build professional relationships which will support the growth and development of the children and young people in your care.

Empathy involves the skill of developing an accurate understanding of the feelings and thoughts of another person. Empathy with a child or young person develops from good active listening, and from understanding the world of childhood and adolescence. It results from a caring attitude, where you can see beyond your own assumptions about the world and can recall and imagine the thoughts and feelings of a child or young person.

Empathy involves the skill of developing an accurate understanding of the feelings and thoughts of another person

How distress can affect you

It can be very upsetting to deal with a child or young person who is displaying powerful emotions. Children's stories or experiences can be so moving and distressing that you may feel very grateful, or perhaps even guilty, for your own happier circumstances.

On the other hand, if you have had difficulties in your own childhood, you could find these echoed or brought to the surface by dealing with a child in distress. In this case it is important to talk to your supervisor as soon as possible to get support for yourself and to arrange for someone else to continue to offer support to the child.

My story

Hi, I'm Lucy and I'm 12. My Mum had me put in care because she said she couldn't cope with me. She didn't need to cope – I was fine, I had my mates, I did stuff to get money if I needed it, I went to school a bit, but it was mostly so boring I wasn't learning anything anyway. I was well angry when I got taken into a children's home – I'm hardly a child, am I? The social workers were right stuck up and just went on about what I should be doing, but there is this one worker at the children's home and she was different, she just sat with me and talked – dead gently. She didn't shout or go on, but she seemed to understand where I was coming from. She said about how angry I must be with my Mum and stuff – like she really knew what it was like. She's the reason I stayed.

Feeling concerned, upset or even angry after a particularly emotional experience with a child or young person is normal. You should not feel that such a response is in any way a reflection on the quality of your work or your ability. After such an experience most people are likely to continue to think about it for some time. One of the best ways to deal with this is to discuss it with your supervisor or with a close friend or relative, always bearing in mind the principles of confidentiality. After a period of time you may come to terms with what happened; but if you find it is interfering with your work, there are plenty of sources of help available to you, both within and outside your workplace. Talk to your supervisor for advice on gaining access to any help you need.

The distress of others, whether in the form of anger, sadness or anxiety, will always be upsetting for the person who works with them. However, if you are able to develop your skills and knowledge so that you can identify distress, work towards reducing it and offer effective help and support to those who are experiencing it, you are making a useful and meaningful contribution to the provision of quality childcare.

My story

Hi, I'm Michelle. I work in a residential special school. I developed a really good relationship with Ella who is 13 years old and has Down's. She was making some progress, we were about a week away from the end of term, she had been asking quite often about how much longer it was until the holidays. I just knew there was something, some reason she didn't want to go home. One evening, it was just the two of us sitting in the kitchen, and she asked me again. I said, 'How do you feel about going home?' and the tears started. Ella disclosed that she was being sexually abused at home by a friend of the family. I did all the right things we learned in the training, so I knew Ella was well supported. I wasn't coping – it all came flooding back. I had been abused by my father and had run away from home when I was fifteen. I couldn't sleep, cried a lot and wasn't much use at work.

My manager was great and I was able to talk to her about it. She put me in touch with a survivors' group, and that made me realise that I could ask for help for myself and that I didn't always have to be strong.

Test yourself

1 How would you prepare to discuss difficult or complex issues with a child?

2 What key factors would indicate that a child is becoming distressed?

3 What steps could you take to reduce a child's distress?

4 What action should be taken if a young person threatens to harm himself or herself?

HSC 31c Support individuals to communicate

Why we communicate

(KS 2, 3)

In general, human beings like to live with other human beings. Most of us are sociable creatures who want to reach out to other people around us. Very few humans lead completely solitary lives. People live and communicate in a range of different groups and communities, for example:

- Families
- Neighbourhoods
- Workplaces
- Schools and colleges
- Interest/activity groups
- Commercial settings
- Users of professional services.

The type and level of communication is very different dependent on the circumstances. Some communications are personal and very intimate; these are usually with people to whom we are very close. Other communications are for a wider audience and are aimed at groups of people.

Communication can be formal...

... or informal.

If you went to a meeting with a child's head teacher, you might expect him or her to greet you with a formal phrase, such as: 'Good morning, pleased to meet you.' An informal greeting you might exchange with the children or young people you work with is more likely to be: 'Hiya – y'OK?'

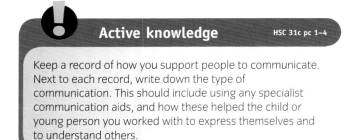

Active knowledge
HSC 31c pc 1–4

Keep a record of how you support people to communicate. Next to each record, write down the type of communication. This should include using any specialist communication aids, and how these helped the child or young person you worked with to express themselves and to understand others.

It is possible that some children or young people might prefer the informal greeting in many situations. An informal greeting can put you at ease; you might feel that the speaker is like you. However, the informal greeting might make children or young people feel that they are not being respected and are being patronised.

Barriers to communication

(KS 1, 2, 3, 6, 7, 8, 9, 10, 13, 14)

There are many factors that can get in the way of good communication. You will need to understand how to recognise these and to learn what you can do to overcome them yourself, and to support children and young people in overcoming them. It is easy to assume that everyone can communicate, and that any failure to respond to you is because of someone's unwillingness rather than inability. There are as many reasons why communication can be difficult as there are ways to make it easier. Never assume that you can be heard and understood and that you can be responded to, without first thinking about the individual child or young person and his or her situation.

Remember

You need to understand the things that can get in the way so you can make sure they don't!

Reflect

Choose two different ways in which you communicate with people, such as talking, writing, telephone. Consider the most important element in each one. For example, for talking it could be language, for the telephone, hearing, and so on. Now think about how you would manage that method of communication without that important element. List the problems you would have and the ways you could try to overcome them. Now be honest about whether or not you have ever really thought about any of this in relation to the children and young people you work with. Look at how you can incorporate this learning into your practice.

Communication differences and how to deal with them

People communicate in all sorts of different ways, so it stands to reason that there will be times when there will be differences in the way that you and a child, young person or family will make contact with each other. Communication differences can include:

- Different styles or ways of speaking
- You speaking a different language to the child or young person or their family
- Either you or the child or young person having a sensory impairment
- Distress, where a child or young person is so upset that he or she is unable to communicate
- An illness or disability which makes communication difficult
- Cultural differences.

There are ways to address all of these differences so that the impact is reduced and none of them should be an insurmountable barrier to good and effective communication.

Styles of speaking

People from different localities, ethnic groups, professions and work cultures all have their own special words, phrases and speech patterns. An older middle-class woman is very unlikely to start a conversation with the words 'Hello mate'; whereas most of the children or young people and young people you work with are equally unlikely to start a conversation with 'Good afternoon, nice to see you again – How are you?' People in both these examples speak in very different ways and have a different level of formality. This does not mean that they are unable to communicate; it just means that everyone has to think about what they do and say and work at it a bit.

People from different localities, ethnic groups, professions and work cultures all have different styles of speaking

Impact of speaking styles

Some children or young people may feel threatened or excluded by the kind of language they encounter from adults they come into contact with. This can be because of what people say or the way they say it. However, merely using informal language will not solve this problem, unless everything else about your communication shows that you genuinely like children or young people, are interested in the child or young person you are talking to and want to make contact.

Professional childcare workers use professional jargon, initials, acronyms and technical terms as a sort of 'shorthand' to communicate with each other. No matter how hard you work at communicating with children or young people, using technical terminology can create barriers, so try to remember not to use it.

 Active knowledge KS 1–3, 6–10, 13, 14

Overheard in the kitchen of a small residential home:

'I need you to help because I'm like "that's my i-Pod" and she's like "so – it's mine now" and she's really doin' my 'ead in and you lot have got to do summink.'

'Well – I think we need to sit down and see if we can't create a positive environment so we engage you both in a really good interaction to explore the resolution opportunities – OK?'

The two statements above use different levels of formality, and include professional jargon.

1) Can you work out what each of them wants from this communication?

2) How do you think the child or young person will feel given such a response?

3) Will she feel respected and valued?

4) What could be an alternative response?

How to reduce the effect of different speaking styles

Being aware is the best route to reducing the impact. As the professional, it is your responsibility to notice where there are differences and to take steps to avoid using confusing or difficult terminology. It is also up to you to adapt your approach as necessary in order to communicate effectively with the child or young person. Adapting your approach does not mean embarrassingly adopting 'street speak' or attempting to sound like one of the children or young people you work with. It does mean using plain, clear language and being prepared to re-phrase and give explanations if you are met with blank looks.

Different languages

It is unlikely that you will go through your career only working with children whose language you can speak. When you and the child or young person or their family speak different languages it can be an isolating and frustrating experience for everyone. Since 2003, British Sign Language (BSL) has been officially recognised as a language. It is a visual language, but has its own structure and grammar.

The child or young person or family may become angry, distressed and frightened at not being able to ask or to have any questions answered. You may become concerned that you are missing vital information, and failing to understand significant parts of a child or young person's life because you cannot communicate either with the child or young person, or with his or her family.

Dealing with language differences

The most effective way of communicating with anyone who speaks a different language is through non-verbal communication. A smile and a friendly face are understood in all languages, as are a concerned facial expression and a warm and welcoming body position.

Children or young people learn new languages very quickly; the younger they are, the quicker they pick it up. Even very recent immigrant children or young people will be speaking English long before their families, so working with children or young people in a different language is not all that common. However, it can be very different with parents and families.

Adults take much longer to acquire language, so you are more likely to be in a position of having to make arrangements to communicate effectively with families. These arrangements can include:

- using non-verbal communication
- using an interpreter
- using pictures, flash cards, etc.

You are likely to use a mix of approaches, depending on the circumstances and the subject of your communication. For example, you would not use pictures to discuss serious concerns about an injury to a child or young person, or to explain what was to happen in relation to an offence the child or young person had been accused of committing. Matters of this importance need an interpreter, but do not be tempted to use the child or young person or family member. This may seem like a simple solution – it isn't, neither is it appropriate. Non-professional interpreters can often allow their own feelings to influence the tone and style of communication, and there may be confidential or personal issues being discussed which should not be shared with others.

On the other hand, you could probably manage to indicate that you are very pleased to meet the family and that their son is doing really well in the local football team by smiling, hand signals and pictures.

Your work setting is likely to be able to access a contact list of interpreters. Social services departments and the police have lists of interpreters, including BSL communicators. The embassy or consulate for the appropriate country will also have a list of qualified interpreters for languages from other countries.

You should be aware that gestures should be used with care. Gestures that are acceptable in one culture may not be acceptable in all. For example, an extended thumb in some cultures would mean 'great, that's fine, OK', but in many cultures it is an extremely offensive gesture. In Britain the hand gesture with palm up and facing forwards means 'Stop, don't do that'. In Greece it can mean 'You are dirt' and is very rude.

If you are unsure which gestures are acceptable in another culture, make sure that you check before using any which may be misinterpreted.

Gestures can mean different things in different cultures

Sensory impairment

Any form of sensory impairment for the child or young person or their family or you, can have a significant impact on communication:

- A loss or reduction of ability to hear clearly can cause major differences in how deaf children or young people communicate and how their speech and language develops.
- A visual impairment can have an impact on how communication is understood and how children or young people's language develops.
- A speech or language impairment can mean that children or young people have difficulty in either using (expressive difficulties) or understanding (receptive difficulties) language.

Communication is a two-way process, and any impairment to key senses can make it difficult for a child or young person to be able to respond and to join in. Most children with a sensory impairment will have this recognised whilst they are quite young, and will have interventions and support from a team of medical, sensory and social care professionals. However, this does not always happen as it should, nor is every child or their family able to engage with support and intervention, so some children and young people can miss out on important treatment and support.

The result can be that, without help to manage any sensory loss, children or young people become withdrawn and feel very isolated and excluded from others around them, which can lead to frustration and anger and some quite challenging behaviour. Being able to reach children and young people in this situation through effective communication is a massive step to improving outcomes.

Deaf children and young people

Hearing loss can now be identified in very young babies and all babies are now screened within a few days of birth. A national screening programme, the NHS newborn screening programme, now ensures that hearing problems are identified early. Of course,

Communication is a two-way process

this is a new programme so babies born from 2006 will benefit, but you will be working with children and young people born long before this, so some may have had their hearing loss recognised later than others.

Children who have been identified as deaf in early childhood are likely to be part of the British deaf community and will use BSL as their first or preferred language. This is a language like any other: it just uses signs, facial and body expressions to communicate rather than sounds. It has a grammatical structure different to English, and anything which can be spoken in English can be translated into BSL. Some children will only communicate in BSL and others will be bilingual, using speech too. Whether children use BSL, speech or are bilingual will depend on the decisions made at the time of the identification of hearing loss.

Other communication approaches and signing systems can be used to communicate with children and young people, such as:

- *Cued speech* – which uses signs alongside the natural mouth movements of speech
- *Paget Gorman signed speech* – a sign system used with speech, used mainly for children with speech and language difficulties
- *Signed English (SE)* – used alongside spoken English with the aim of developing reading and writing skills
- *Fingerspelling* – used, usually alongside BSL, to spell out individual letters for names or places.

The difference between these and BSL is that they are systems of communication that make use of signs rather than languages.

There are other systems and approaches, and you will need to find out about which ones the child or young person uses, but there are some general points about communicating with deaf children and young people:

- Make sure you can be clearly seen.
- Face both the light and the child or young person at all times.
- Include the child or young person in your conversation.
- Do not obscure your mouth.
- Speak clearly and slowly – do not shout; it simply distorts your face and makes your lips difficult to read.
- Try to get away from background noise.
- Use your eyes, facial expressions and hand gestures as much as possible to get your meaning across.

Visual impairment

Visual impairment, including blindness and partial sight, can cause communication problems for children as they develop. Part of a child's development is understanding not only speech and language, but also how humans communicate with each other through signals and non-verbal messages. This includes facial expressions, hand movements and gestures and body position. If a child grows and develops only understanding verbal communication, they may struggle to engage effectively with others. Not only is a child or young person unable to pick up the visual signals that are being given out by others, but they may also fail to give appropriate signals. This can lead to misunderstandings about a child or young person's attitudes and behaviour.

 My story

Hi, I'm Jake and I'm 14. I am deaf and was born that way, so I don't do the whole hearing thing. I sign using BSL. I came into care when my Mum went into hospital with her nerves. They said she's going to be there quite a long time.

It was all a rush when I first came in. It's OK now, but at first I went into this ordinary children's home. No one knew anything about how to talk to me and this plonker of a social worker kept putting her hand on my knee and shouting at me very slowly like I was stupid. Those first few days were a nightmare: it was the holidays, so I wasn't even with proper people who understand the language like when I'm at school. Anyway – it's all sorted now. I'm with brilliant foster carers who can talk to me and I'm going back to school next week – never thought I'd be pleased to go back.

Feedback has been found to be effective in helping blind young people avoid giving inappropriate signals: teachers, support workers, family and friends can all participate in encouraging and giving constructive feedback to help young people be aware of the impact of non-verbal communication signals. Think about it – if a child is congenitally blind (from birth), how will the child know what body language is about unless they are told? Children and young people with partial sight also need extra help in checking the way they respond to others and in picking up the non-verbal messages that are being conveyed to them.

Non-verbal communication is important when you are interpreting the responses of a blind or partially sighted child or young person. Check that you are not misinterpreting behaviour or attitude because you are picking up on non-verbal messages that are not intentional.

Speech, language and communication impairment

Children and young people can experience difficulties in communication due to a range of speech and language impairments.

- Some impairments affect the **speech apparatus** such as the mouth, tongue, nose or breathing. Problems with any part of the speech apparatus can make it difficult for a child or young person to be understood.

- Other impairments centre on **phonology** – which describes problems understanding the sounds that make up language or syntax and grammar, meaning that children and young people struggle with combining words into sentences. Some children with specific language impairments will also have been diagnosed with an autistic spectrum disorder (ASD – see page 29), but not all.

- Some types of language impairment mean that children and young people can have problems with **semantics** – which is about understanding the meaning of words and sentences. Often, words which describe feelings, such as sad, happy and jealous are particularly difficult to understand.

- **Pragmatic difficulties** with language mean that children and young people can have problems in using language appropriately in social situations, for example, constantly interrupting, talking over others, not taking turns to speak, often having an inappropriate conversation, or not recognising when a topic of conversation only needs a short time and when topics need to be expanded.

Studies (Redmond, S.M. & Rice, M.L., Stability of behavioural ratings of children with specific language impairment. *Journal of Speech, Language, and Hearing Research*) have shown that some children with a specific language impairment (SLI) rather than a speech impairment, have social and behavioural problems by school age and these tend to increase as they grow older.

My story

Hi, I'm Danny. I am a support worker for a family with a whole range of needs, but some of them are around Max, who is 10 years old. Max was first identified as presenting challenging behaviour when he was 7 years old – prior to that, he was just regarded as a nuisance I think! Finally, after a whole range of assessments, it became clear that Max had a specific language impairment. He has quite marked pragmatic difficulties with language: he will either talk at length about a subject which seems to have no relevance to any current conversation, or will speak in one- or two-word sentences. He has difficulty with conversations, and does not pick up signals about how to let others join in. His teacher was telling me that the other day there was a class discussion on football. To be fair to Max, he is very interested in football and knows quite a lot – but he just started to speak and went on and on for about ten minutes, shouted louder if anyone else tried to say anything and eventually stormed out of the room when the teacher told him to stop. We are working with the plan and doing the games developed by the Speech and Language Service, and he is improving, but I think the fact that it was football must have got him excited. He and I have been doing lots of games which involve turn taking and he has become quite good. He struggled at first, but he is getting better, the family are joining in as far as they can, but there are a lot of other issues, so capacity is limited sometimes, but they do their best. It is a good feeling when Max and I have a proper conversation, but the report from school was a bit of a downer.

Autistic spectrum disorders (ASD)

Children and young people who are diagnosed as being on the autistic spectrum will have impairments of:

- social interaction
- social communication
- imagination.

Children will only be diagnosed with ASD if they show all three. Children or young people with ASD will have a wide range of behaviours; children will behave in different ways so individual approaches are needed. The levels of functioning can be very different: children and young people with the highest levels of functioning may simply show some behaviours around order and routine and come across as being a bit detached from others, not seeming to recognise or care about the feelings of other people; in other children, ASD can accompany quite severe learning disability and some very challenging behaviour.

You need to be able to recognise how ASD affects communication, such as the inability to recognise that others have thoughts and feelings, and the lack of understanding of the way in which people connect with each other through communication. For a child with ASD, communication is used in order to meet needs or express demands, not to relate to others. The impairment of imagination results in children struggling to participate in imaginative play with other children, or sometimes being unable to distinguish reality from dreams or stories. This can result in repetitive rituals or long rambling tales that seem to have no real basis.

Broadly, it is important to provide a secure structure for children and young people with ASD, not to over-stimulate them, and to make environments and communications as clear and simple as possible. Visual approaches will usually work best, so cards and symbols can often be helpful. You do need to try to see the world from the perspective of the child or young person with ASD and to understand how frustrating it is for them not to be able to make any sense of the world around them.

Find out

You need to find out as much information as you can about any child or young person who has any sort of sensory or communication impairment. The first place to look for information is from the child or young person, but also get as much background as you can from family, colleagues and previous records. You will also need to find out information about the impairment, from specialist organisations or professionals with particular expertise.

You need to be aware of:

- the nature of the impairment
- how it affects the child or young person
- the most effective means of communication
- how you can help.

Reflect

How much do you know about social, communication and language impairments? Do you ever consider the possibility of a child having a language impairment if some behaviour appears inappropriate? Do you know where to go for help to find out more? Think about your own practice and whether or not you always attribute children's behaviour to emotional and psychological causes without giving consideration to other possibilities.

Distress

One of the joys of working with young children is that they usually show their feelings fairly clearly. In fact, when you come across a young child who does not readily cry, laugh or scream and stamp feet – you worry!

Older children and young people are not always as expressive. Some will have learned not to express emotions because of the results it has had in the past; others may be so emotionally damaged that they are unable to recognise or express strong emotions.

Children and young people can become distressed for all sorts of reasons, but some common causes can be identified and you need to be aware of situations and circumstances that can act as triggers. Some are obvious and apply to adults and children; others are age-specific:

- the death or serious illness of someone close
- receiving bad or worrying news – what is worrying to a child or young person is very different to what worries an adult
- there are problems with an important relationship
- being prevented from doing something they want to do
- reacting to the behaviour of others towards them
- a belief that something is unjust
- responding to something that they have heard, seen or read in the media
- being in an environment that they find frustrating or restricting or intensely irritating
- being deprived of information and being scared
- having lots of information and still being scared.

A very distressed child or young person is a challenge to communicate with because:

- they may be screaming or crying so much that they are incomprehensible
- they may withdraw and simply will not talk to you
- a rational conversation may not be possible and they may be abusive, unrealistic or unreasonable – or sometimes all three!

Calming a distressed child or young person so that they are able to communicate with you and take in what you are communicating to them is an essential skill. The response will depend on the type of distress, and the reason for it. A cuddle and a hug will eventually calm most sobbing children: children who are sad, angry or frightened need to feel safe and cared for.

Physical contact issues

It is important to be aware of how physical contact can be interpreted, and of the potential impact, particularly for children who have experienced physical or sexual abuse. The best approach is to get permission – 'Do you want a hug?' will do as the question, and a nod of the head will do as the answer. A shake of the head or a 'no' from the child must be

Being hugged is one of the best ways to feel safe

Active knowledge

HSC 31b
pc 4a, 6, 8

Think about the children and young people you work with and the issues that, your experience tells you, are likely to result in someone getting really upset. Note down as many as you can – at least three general and at least one for each child or young person you work with. Be aware of these potential triggers and discuss ways to address them with your manager and staff team.

My story

Hi, I'm Nadine. I'm 7 years old. I am staying with Annie and Jack. I don't know why. Mum wasn't there when I woke up, it was very cold and I had some bread. Then there was a knock on the door. Mum says I mustn't answer the door, so I didn't and they went away. Then there was a big crash and policemen came in. The lady said that I had to go, I said I had to wait for Mum and she said no. I kicked her and screamed and shouted, but they made me go. Annie gives me a hug when I cry, she wasn't cross that I broke her vase when I kicked the table 'cos I wanted to run away. Mum will be cross that they came in and I'll be in trouble. I don't know what to do, I'm very scared and no one understands so I have to try to get away.

respected absolutely, even if you think a hug is what the child really needs.

Permission is important because of the messages it gives to the child or young person about their rights to say who can and who cannot touch their body. Asking permission shows that you recognise the child as an individual with rights, and that he or she is someone who is valued and treated with respect.

Risks

If you are concerned about the risks you may be taking as a professional, and the possibility of your actions being misunderstood, then you should only have physical contact with children and young people when others are around, and always keep doors open.

These are real risks, and you should not dismiss them lightly. However, you always have to balance the risks to you against the child's need to be comforted and to give and receive affection. The decisions are never easy, have to be made in a split second and can have a big impact. You will need to consider all the key factors:

- the age of the child or young person
- the gender of the child or young person
- the circumstances of the distress
- the quality of your professional relationship with the child or young person
- what you know about how the child or young person is likely to react
- any known history of the child or young person making allegations against staff.

Ethical issue

A teenage girl is very distressed. She has just heard that her Mum has committed suicide. You are a young, single male worker. The girl is known to have demonstrated manipulative behaviour previously, and has made allegations against another male worker in the past, which were found to be untrue. However, she is distraught, you are the only person there and she turns to you with her arms out and tears pouring down her face. What do you do? What are the issues?

There are no absolutes and there is never a 'right' answer. Like so much of working with children and young people, it is about considering the options and responding with what is best for the child or young person – and if they tell you they need a hug, give them a hug!

Illness or disability

A child or young person who is ill or has a physical disability may need special attention paid to communication. You need to be aware that a child or young person who is ill may not respond to you as they would usually do. Similarly, a child or young person with a physical disability may use different non-verbal communication and so you may appear to get a response you were not expecting. Always be conscious that body language can be affected by a physical disability and that you will need to take time to get used to the way a particular child or young person communicates. For example, a child with cerebral palsy will not be able to control body movements, so you will not pick up the non-verbal signals you would expect.

Learning disabilities

A learning disability can mean that a child or young person has a level of understanding which can affect communication. This will vary depending on the extent of the learning disability, but broadly the effect

Using words and phrases which are familiar to the child or young person may make it easier for them to respond

of learning disabilities is to limit the ability of an individual to understand and process information given to him or her. It is also possible that children or young people with a learning disability will have a limited ability to concentrate, so this may mean that communications have to be repeated several times or perhaps paraphrased in a more understandable way. It can be very helpful to use words and phrases which are familiar to the child or young person, so they will be more likely to be able to respond.

Cultural differences

Culture is hugely important to the development of children and young people: their cultural background is where they base their identity and self-image. Children and young people who are removed from, or lose contact with, this cultural base can struggle to work out who they are, and what they believe in. It is because our cultural backgrounds are so important, and make such a great contribution to who we are, that communication difficulties can result when you and the child or young person you are working with come from different cultures.

Culture is about more than race or religion or beliefs; it is about a combination of all of them and also about many other aspects of life such as history, music, food, customs, celebrations and dress. In order to communicate effectively with a child or young person, you need to take time to find out about their cultural background, and what the norms of communication are. Some cultures expect children and young people to be exuberant and to state their needs clearly; others expect them to be quiet and respectful of older people and authority. Particular ways of speaking may be viewed as appropriate in some cultures, and the length of time before reaching the point of what you want to say can vary greatly from culture to culture. As far as you can, you should try to find out the cultural norms relevant to the child or young person's background.

It is important to be able to identify the different interpretations that words and body language can have in different cultures. This is not a straightforward issue; words and signs can mean different things depending on their context. If an older person uses 'wicked' to describe his or her

experience of being mugged by a gang, the phrase would mean 'horrific' or 'terrible'. For a young person 'wicked' could mean something very good or desirable. In a religious context, 'wicked' might relate to the concept of sin.

Communication is always influenced by cultural systems of meaning, and different cultures interpret body language differently. An almost infinite variety of meanings can be given to any type of eye contact, facial expression, posture or gesture. Every culture develops its own special system of meanings. You have to understand and show respect and value for all these different systems of sending messages.

Reflect

Have you really thought about how much you are influenced by your own cultural background? Think honestly about how much you really know about the cultures of the children you work with. How do you feel about other cultures? Do they interest and intrigue you, or do you feel a bit uncomfortable? It's OK to be uncomfortable – you just have to make sure your unease does not impact on how you respond to a child or family.

The best ways to communicate with a child or young person

(KS 2, 10, 11)

The best person to ask how to communicate is, of course, the child or young person! If this is not an option, either because of language differences or because of the particular needs of the child or young person, then ask parents or carers or any other family members, and find out from other professional colleagues who may be involved in working with the child.

By simply observing a child or young person, you can check out a great deal about how he or she communicates and what the differences are between his or her way of communicating and your own.

The more 'homework' you do, the better chance you have of managing to engage with the child or young person. Try not to make assumptions about what you think is going to be acceptable – always do your research and find out.

Making sure you have been understood

Although it is absolutely unacceptable to talk down to children and young people, it is equally pointless trying to communicate using so much jargon and professional terminology that there is no hope of them understanding anything you have said. You must be sure that your communication is being understood. The most straightforward way to do this is to ask the other person to recap on what you have discussed.

You could say something like: 'Can we just double check this so that we are both sure about what is

happening – you tell me what is happening tomorrow.' Alternatively you can rephrase what you have just said and check with the child or young person that he or she has understood. For example:

'The bus is coming earlier than usual tomorrow because of the trip. It will be here at eight o'clock instead of nine – is that OK?'

'Yes.'

'So, you're sure that you can be up and ready by eight o'clock to go on the trip?'

However, never assume that children will retain information, particularly about arrangements – the extent to which they are likely to remember it relates directly to the amount of attention they paid when you told them! The lesson from this is not to give children or young people important information when they are in the middle of doing something more interesting than listening to you, which can include chatting to mates, playing a computer game, listening to music or just lying on the bed staring at the ceiling!

Communication through actions

For many children and young people, it is easier to communicate by actions than by words. You will need to make sure that you respond in an

Keys to good practice: Communicating effectively

✓ Make sure that you know if there are any communication differences between you and a child, young person or family you are working with

✓ Remember, differences can be cultural as well as physical.

✓ Work with children, young people and their families to understand preferred methods of communication and language.

Use all possible sources to obtain information and advice where there are differences in ways of communicating.

appropriate way by recognising the significance of a touch or a sudden movement from a disabled child, or a gesture from someone who speaks a different language. A gesture can indicate what his or her needs are and what sort of response he or she is looking for from you.

You may be faced with a young person who throws something at you. This is a means of communication. It may not be ideal if you are on the receiving end, but nonetheless, it expresses much of the hurt, anger and distress the child or young person is feeling. It is important that you recognise this for what it is and respond to the hurt and anger in the same way you would if the child or young person had been able to express his or her feelings in words. Of course, at the same time, you need to support the child or young person to find ways to express feelings using words, rather than aggressive and violent actions.

Encouraging communication

The best way to ensure that a child or young person is able to communicate effectively is to make him or her feel as comfortable and as relaxed as possible. There are several factors to consider in making people feel confident enough to communicate:

Physical barriers

Communication can be hindered by physical and environmental factors. This may seem obvious, but they need to be considered when planning communication. You need to think about the surroundings. Some young people find it difficult to talk about personal issues in noisy, crowded places, although they will happily communicate with friends regardless of the noise level! A communal lounge

Communication difference	Encouraging actions	
Different language	• Smile • Have a friendly facial expression • Use gestures • Use pictures • Show warmth and encouragement – repeat their words with a smile to check understanding	
Hearing impairment	• Speak clearly, listen carefully, respond to what is said to you • Remove any distractions and other noises • Check out any signs which you can learn • Make sure any aids to hearing are working • Use written communication where appropriate • Use properly trained interpreter if BSL is first language	
Visual impairment	• Use touch if appropriate to communicate concern, sympathy and interest • Use tone of voice rather than facial expressions to communicate mood and response • Do not rely on non-verbal communication, e.g. facial expression or nodding head • Ensure that all visual communication is transferred into something which can be heard, either a tape or somebody reading	

Communication difference	Encouraging actions
Physical disability	• Ensure that surroundings are appropriate and accessible • Allow for difficulties with voice production if necessary • Do not patronise, talk to the child or young person • Remember that some body language may not be appropriate
Learning disability	• Judge appropriate level of understanding • Make sure that you respond at the right level • Remain patient and be prepared to keep covering the same ground • Be prepared to wait and listen carefully to responses

with a television on is not a good place for effective communication, and you need to consider privacy and the importance of keeping personal information confidential.

Remember the temperature – make sure it is comfortable. Think about lighting. Is it too dark or too bright? Children and young people are unlikely to sit in one place to talk to you anyway, but if you are talking with adults, you need to make sure that they are in a comfortable place. Make sure that you do not sit with your face in shadow. It is very disconcerting not to be able to see someone's face when talking to him or her – remember what you have learned about non-verbal communication.

Using the right words

Body language is one key to effective listening, but what you say in reply is also important. You can back up the message that you are interested and listening by checking that you have understood what has been said to you. Using sentences beginning 'So…' to check that you have got it right can be helpful. 'So… it's only since you had the run-in with Casey that you feel worried about going to school.' 'So… you were OK with the house rules before the new ideas about the TV were discussed.'

Remember

- Never take communication for granted.
- Not everyone communicates in the same way.
- It is your responsibility to support the individual to communicate.

You can also use expressions such as 'So what you mean is…' or 'So what you are saying is…'

Short, encouraging phrases used while people are talking can show concern, understanding or sympathy. Phrases such as 'I see', 'Oh dear', 'Yes' or 'Go on' all give the speaker a clear indication that you are listening and want him or her to continue.

Asking the right questions

How you phrase questions to children and young people can make a huge difference to the answers you get. There are essentially two sorts of questions: open and closed. An open question will encourage someone to give a full answer – it cannot be answered in one or two words. This type of question promotes communication and will help towards building a relationship. For example, 'What sort of evening have you planned with Jessica tonight?' will encourage much more conversation than 'Are you going out with Jessica tonight?' Open questions often begin with:

- What
- Why
- How
- When
- Where.

A closed question can be answered with a word or two – usually yes or no. Closed questions are useful if you need to obtain clear information in a short time. For example, 'Did you know Rob was planning to do a runner?', 'Was he wearing his black cap?' or 'Was he there at the end of school?'

Reflect

What type of question is each of the following?

1) 'Are you feeling worried?'

2) 'What sort of things worry you?'

3) 'Do you want to join in the games tonight?'

4) 'What sort of games do you like best?'

5) 'Is your Mum coming to visit?'

6) 'What have you got planned for when your Mum comes to visit?'

7) 'Why were you cross with Charlie this morning?'

8) 'Were you cross with Charlie this morning?'

Think about how often you use each type of question. Consider whether you could make more effective use of different types of questions in your practice.

Electronic communication

Even if you do not use either texting or internet messaging in your professional relationship with children and young people, you need to be aware of the impact it has on the way children and young people communicate with each other and how quickly information will be shared.

Texting

Children and young people communicate very effectively through texting on a mobile phone. You may be among the adults who also find this a cheap and convenient way of passing on information. Texting is quick and direct, and is useful for short information-sharing messages, such as making arrangements, or telling some important news. Texting is not a communication method that lends itself to holding complex or meaningful discussions.

Texting is a popular and effective form of communication for children and young people

Keys to good practice: Supporting individuals to communicate

✓ Support children and young people to express how they want to communicate and to use their preferred methods of communication.

✓ Ensure that any aids to communication, such as hearing aids, are set up and working properly.

✓ Support others who are communicating with children and young people to understand them and use appropriate methods of communication.

✓ Encourage children and young people to respond, to express their feelings and emotions appropriately, and to overcome barriers to communication.

✓ Only use stories about your own experiences to encourage children or young people to talk. Your role is to listen to what children are saying, not to talk about yourself.

✓ Don't ever dismiss fears, worries or concerns by saying, 'That's silly' or 'You shouldn't worry about that.' Children's fears are real and should not be made to sound trivial. You need to acknowledge the fear as real, but also to reassure – so say something like: 'I can see why that would worry you – but…'

Internet messaging

Young people communicate with each other through internet messaging services where they can hold 'conversations' with other contacts who also happen to be online. The advantages to this are that communication is not limited to one country, there are no additional costs to communicating with contacts across the world, and the development of web cams means that people can also have visual communication across continents. The ability to maintain contact in this way has revolutionised the expectations young people have of the speed and frequency of communication.

Test yourself

1 Why is it important to pass on information about children's communication needs and preferences?

2 What steps could you take to improve communication with a deaf child? List three.

3 A 15-year-old boy brought up in an inner city is living in a residential home. One of the staff is the 25-year-old son of an Indian consultant cardiac surgeon. What would you expect to be the cultural differences between them?

4 What factors would you take into account when judging the best way to communicate with someone from a different country?

5 What do you need to do to encourage a child with a visual impairment to feel confident about communicating with you?

6 What is the most important purpose of communication?

HSC 31d Update and maintain records and reports

Updating and maintaining the accuracy of records and reports is vitally important for any childcare setting. The information in records or reports could be:

- about a child or young person who is being looked after
- about a child or young person you are working with in the community
- about a parent or other family member
- about the organisation itself
- about someone who works there
- needed for administrative purposes.

The information could come to you in a range of ways:

- verbally, for example in a conversation either face to face or on the telephone
- on paper, for example in a letter, a child's health record or instructions from a health professional
- electronically, by fax or on a computer.

Whatever the purpose of the information, it is important that you record it accurately. It is also important that you pass on any information correctly, in the right form and to the right person. Recording information is essential in children's services, because the services that are provided are about people rather than objects, so it is vital that information is accurate, accessible and readable.

Ways of receiving and passing on information

(KS 4, 5)

An information-sharing index will be operational in England from 2008. Every child will have a unique identifier and information will include: basic information; whether a common assessment has been carried out and the contact details of any childcare professionals involved; and a flag identifying any professionals who have information to share. This index will mean that children who move around the country are less likely to 'slip through the net' and not be identified as needing help. It will provide children's practitioners in England with a way of finding out if there is any information available about a child they are working with.

In children's services there are many ways in which information is circulated between agencies, colleagues, other team members, children, young people and their families, carers, volunteers and so on. The growth of electronic communication has meant a considerable change in the way that people receive and send information, in comparison to only a few years ago when information sharing was limited to face-to-face meetings, telephone calls or posted letters.

Telephone

One of the commonest means of communication is the telephone. It has advantages because it is instant, straightforward and is a relatively safe and accurate way of communicating and passing on information. However, there are some disadvantages to the telephone in that it can often be difficult to ensure that you have clearly understood what has been said. There can be problems with telephone lines that cause crackling and technical difficulties. It is also possible to misinterpret someone's meaning when you cannot pick up other signals, such as facial expression and body language. If you regularly take or place messages on the telephone, there are some very simple steps that you can take to ensure that you cut down the risk of getting a message wrong.

- Make sure that you check the name of the person who is calling. If necessary, ask the person to spell his or her name and repeat it to make sure you have it right. You may also need to take the person's address, and again it is worthwhile asking him or her to spell the details to ensure that you have written them correctly.
- Always ask for a return telephone number so that the person who receives the message can phone back if necessary. There is nothing more infuriating than receiving a message on which you have some queries and no means of contacting the person who has left it for you. You should read back the message itself to the person who is leaving it to check that you have the correct information and that you have understood his or her meaning.

Incoming post

If it is part of your role to open and check any incoming post, you must make sure that you:

- open it as soon as it arrives
- follow your own workplace procedures for dealing with incoming mail – this is likely to involve stamping it with the date it is received
- pass it on to the appropriate person for it to be dealt with or filed. See pages 39–41 for advice on how to deal with confidential information.

Faxed information

The steps for dealing with an incoming fax message are as follows.

- Take the fax from the machine.
- Read the cover sheet – this will tell you who the fax is for, who it is from (it should include telephone and fax numbers) and how many pages there should be.
- Check that the correct number of pages has been received. If a fax has misprinted or has pages missing, contact the telephone number identified on the cover sheet and ask for the information to be sent again. If there is no telephone number,

send a fax immediately to the sending fax number asking for the fax to be resent.

- Follow your organisation's procedure for dealing with incoming faxes. Make sure the fax is handed to the appropriate person as soon as possible.

E-mail

E-mail is probably the most frequently used means of communication within and between workplaces. It is fast, convenient and easy to use for many people. Large reports and complex information that would be cumbersome to post or fax can be transmitted as an attachment to an e-mail in seconds. However, not everyone in all workplaces has access to e-mail and not all electronic transmission is secure. Be aware of this if you are sending highly sensitive and confidential material. If you do send and receive information by e-mail you should:

- follow the guidelines in your workplace for using e-mail and the transmission of confidential material
- open all your e-mails and respond to them promptly
- save any confidential messages or attachments in an appropriate, password-protected file or folder, and delete them from your inbox, unless that is also protected
- return promptly any e-mails you have received in error
- be careful not to give your password to anyone.

Outgoing post

If you have to write information to send to another organisation, whether it is by letter, fax or e-mail, you should be sure that the contents are clear, cannot be misunderstood and are to the point. Do not write a rambling, long letter that obliges recipients to search for the information they need.

It is likely that you will need to show any faxes or letters to your supervisor before they leave the premises. This safeguard is in place in many workplaces for the good reason that information being sent on behalf of your employer must be accurate and appropriate. As your employer is the person ultimately responsible for any information sent out, he or she will want to have procedures in place to check this.

Confidentiality

(KS 1, 4, 5, 17)

Confidentiality involves keeping information safe and only passing it on where there is a clear right to it and a clear need to do so. Confidentiality is an important right for all children and young people because:

- Children, young people and their families may not trust a care worker who does not keep information confidential
- Children and young people have a right to be valued and not have private and personal information shared with others
- In some situations, the safety of children and their families may be at risk if details of their whereabouts are made available.

A professional service that maintains respect for individuals must keep private information confidential. There are legal requirements under the Data Protection Act 1998 to keep personal records confidential (see page 42).

Boundaries to confidentiality

Children and young people have a right to confidentiality, but also some responsibility in relation to the rights of others. Confidentiality often has to be kept within boundaries and the rights of others have to be balanced to some extent with the children's or young people's rights. As a childcare professional, you may have to tell your supervisor something learned in confidence. The information is not made public, so it is still confidential to the organisation. Information may need to be passed to managers in the following situations:

- A child discloses to you that they have been/are being abused.
- A young person tells you about a crime they are going to commit/have committed with their gang.

- A child or young person tells you that they are being bullied/are bullying others at school.
- You or your family have been threatened by a young person you are working with.
- A child or young person tells you that they intend to harm themselves.

Reflect

Think about the requirements of data protection legislation. Do you comply with it? Do you understand why it is important? Do you know what to do if you find a breach of it? Is your practice up to date?

Confidentiality and the need to know

There are situations where you will need to share information with other professionals. It is important that you are able to do this in the interests of the child or young person, the family or yourself or colleagues. However, in general, children, young people and families should be told clearly what information could be shared and how and why this could happen. You should try to get agreement to share this information.

However, if the seeking of agreement could put that child, young person or others at increased risk of significant harm or an adult at risk of serious harm (perhaps because it would alert the perpetrator of abuse), then you should share the information without seeking consent. Similarly, if seeking agreement would undermine the prevention, detection or prosecution of a serious crime (a crime which could result in serious harm to a child or an adult), including where seeking consent might lead to interference with any potential investigation (perhaps because it would alert a perpetrator who could then destroy evidence or disappear), then you should share information without consent.

The safety and welfare of a child or young person is your first consideration here. Where there is concern that the child may be suffering or is at risk of suffering significant harm, the child's safety and welfare must be what guides your actions.

Having said that, you should, where possible, respect the wishes of children, young people or families who do not consent to share confidential information, provided that there are no risks.

You may still share information if, in your judgement on the facts of the case, there is sufficient need to override that lack of consent. For example, the risk may not be immediate and may not be related to a child's safety, but it may be in the child's interests in the longer term.

You should seek advice from your supervisor where you are unsure, particularly if there is a potential risk to a child or family.

If you do share information, make sure that it is:

- accurate and up to date
- necessary for the purpose for which you are sharing it
- shared only with those people who need to see it
- shared securely.

It is important to record reasons for decisions about information sharing – regardless of the outcome. It may be important in the future for people to understand how decisions were arrived at and what factors were taken into account.

Some examples of people who may have a need to know about work with children, young people and families are:

- supervisors – they may need to help make decisions which affect the child
- colleagues – they may be working with the same child or family
- other professionals – they may also be working with the child or family and need to be kept up to date.

When information is passed to other professionals, it should be on the understanding that they keep it confidential. If you answer the telephone and the caller says he or she is a social worker, speech therapist or other professional, you should explain that you must call back before giving any information. Phoning back enables you to be sure that you are talking to someone from the right organisation. If you meet someone you don't know, you should ask for proof of identity before passing on any information.

Reflect

Think of a time when you told someone something in confidence and later discovered that they had told other people. Try to recall how you felt about it. You may have felt angry or betrayed. Perhaps you were embarrassed and did not want to face anyone. Note down a few of the ways you felt, and then consider the potential impact on vulnerable children and young people of the same thing happening to them.

Who has a right to know

The area of who has a right to know information about children is fraught with difficulty. There comes a stage when children are considered to be able to take competent decisions in relation to their own lives. This can be as late as 16 years, but can also be earlier depending on the circumstances. Relatives will often claim that they have a 'right to know'. The most famous example of this was Victoria Gillick, who went to court in order to try to gain access to her daughter's medical records. She claimed that she had the right to know whether her daughter had been given the contraceptive pill. Her GP had refused to tell her and she took the case all the way to the House of Lords, but the ruling was not changed and she was not given access to her daughter's records. The rules remain the same, but the basis for the Gillick ruling resulted in guidance about children and consent to medical treatment without the involvement of their parents:

- The test is whether the child had sufficient understanding and intelligence to enable him or her to understand fully what is proposed.
- Each child must be assessed separately in relation to each different procedure. It follows that a child may be able to consent to some procedures but not to others.
- There is no specific age at which a child becomes competent to consent. This depends on the particular child and on the seriousness and complexity of whatever treatment or procedure is proposed.

- The Gillick test is about the capacity of the child to make an informed choice, not about making a decision that other people might consider wise.
- A person who has reached the age of 16 years should be regarded as competent to give consent unless there is evidence to the contrary, as in the case of adults. Competence should be assessed in the same way as it is in adults.
- It is good practice to involve families of 16 and 17 year olds in the decision-making process unless the young person specifically requests that this should not happen.
- Attempts should be made to persuade the young person to confide in their family.
- A request from a child under the age of 16 years that the treatment should be kept confidential should be respected unless, in the opinion of the healthcare professional, there are reasonable grounds to suggest that the child is suffering, or is likely to suffer, significant harm as a result.

Competence is not a simple attribute that a child either possesses or does not possess. You can encourage and develop competence by helping children to take decisions about their own care.

Facing the music

It is difficult, however, if you are faced with angry or distressed parents who believe that you have information they are entitled to. The best response is to be clear and assertive (see Unit 34, page 127, for a discussion of assertiveness), but to demonstrate that you understand it is difficult for them: 'I'm sorry. I know you must be angry, but I can't discuss any information unless your daughter agrees', or 'I'm sorry, I can't give out any information about where Jack is living now. But if you would like to leave me a name and contact details, I will pass on the message and he can contact you.'

Looking after information

(KS 4, 5, 19)

Once something is written down, it becomes a permanent record. For this reason, you must be very careful what you do with any files, charts, notes or other written records. They must always be stored somewhere locked and safe. People should be very careful with files that leave the workplace. There are many stories of files being stolen from cars or left on buses!

Records kept on computers must also be kept safe and protected. Your workplace will have policies relating to records on computers, which will include access being restricted by a password, and the computer system being protected, by the use of a firewall, against the possibility of people 'hacking' into it.

Since the Access to Personal Files Act 1987, individuals can see their personal files. The Data Protection Act 1998 gives people a right to see the information recorded about them. This means that people can see their medical records or social services files. Since January 2005 the Freedom of Information Act 2000 has provided people with a right to access general information held by public authorities, including local authorities and the National Health Service. Personal information about individuals cannot be accessed and is protected by the Data Protection Act.

The information you write in files should be clear and useful. Do not include irrelevant information, or opinions that are not backed up by facts, and write only about the individual concerned. Sign and date the information. Anything you write should be true and able to be justified.

All information, however it is stored, is subject to the rules laid down in the Data Protection Act 1998, which covers medical records, social service records, credit information, local authority information – in fact, anything which is personal data (facts and opinions about an individual).

Make sure that you do not give information carelessly.

The principles of data protection

Anyone processing personal data must comply with the eight enforceable principles of good practice. These say that data must be:

Records kept on computers must also be kept safe and protected!

 Keys to good practice:
Recording information

The purpose of a file is to provide an accurate and up-to-date picture of an individual's situation, and an historical record which can be referred to at some point in the future. Some of it may be required to be disclosed to other agencies. Always think about what you write. Make sure it is **ACES**:

✓ **A**ccurate

✓ **C**lear

✓ **E**asy to read

✓ **S**hareable.

- fairly and lawfully processed
- processed for limited purposes
- adequate, relevant and not excessive
- accurate
- not kept for longer than necessary
- processed in accordance with the data subject's rights
- kept secure
- not transferred to countries without adequate protection.

Written records

The confidentiality of written records is extremely important. You will need to make sure that, when you receive information in a written form (perhaps intended for someone's file or a letter concerning someone you are caring for), the information is not left where it could be easily read by others.

Do not leave confidential letters or notes lying in a reception area, or on a desk where visitors or other staff members might see them. You should ensure that the information is filed, or handed to the person it is intended for, or that you follow your agency procedure for handling confidential information as it comes into the organisation.

The dos and don'ts of dealing with information

Type of information	Do	Don't
Telephone calls, incoming	Check the identity of the caller	Give out any information unless you are sure who the caller is
Telephone calls, outgoing	Make sure that you are passing on information to which the caller is entitled	Give out details about an individual that they have not agreed to disclose
Written information	Check that it goes immediately to the person it is intended for	Leave written information lying around where it can be read by anyone
Receiving faxed material	Check your organisation's procedure for dealing with faxed material. Collect it as soon as possible from any central fax point	Leave it in a fax tray where it could be read by unauthorised people
Sending faxed material	Ensure that it is clearly marked 'Confidential' and has the name on it of the person to whom it should be given	Fax confidential material without clearly stating that it is confidential and it is only to be given to a named person. If in doubt, do not use a fax to send confidential information
Receiving e-mailed information	Save any confidential attachments or messages promptly into a password-protected file. Acknowledge safe receipt of confidential information	Leave an e-mail open on your screen
Sending e-mailed information	Ensure that you have the right e-mail address for the person who is receiving the information. Clearly mark the e-mail 'Confidential' if it contains personal information. Ask for the recipient to acknowledge receipt	Leave an e-mail open on your screen. Send confidential information to an address without a named mailbox, e.g. info@…
Photocopying confidential information	Only copy confidential information if absolutely necessary. Copy only as many as you need. Keep track of who has the copies	Leave the original in the photocopier!

You may need to stamp such information with a 'Confidential' stamp so that people handle it correctly.

Choosing the best way to pass on information

Sometimes the method of communication is dictated by the circumstances. If the situation requires an immediate response, or you need to find essential information urgently, then you are unlikely to write a long letter, put it in the post and wait until next week to get a reply! You are far more likely to pick up the telephone and see if you can contact the person you need to speak to, or send a quick e-mail. Or you may choose to fax your request, or fax information in response to a telephone request from someone else. These methods are fast, almost instant, and relatively reliable for getting information accurately from one place to another.

There may be other occasions when, on the grounds of confidentiality, something is sent through the post marked 'Strictly confidential' and only to be opened by the person whose name is on the envelope. This method may be entirely appropriate for information that is too confidential to be sent by fax and would be inappropriate in a telephone conversation or to be sent by e-mail.

The purpose of keeping records

In any organisation records are kept for a variety of purposes. The type of record that you keep is likely to be dictated by the purpose for which it is required. It could be:

- information needed for making decisions
- information to provide background knowledge and understanding for another professional
- information about family and contacts of people who are important to a child or young person

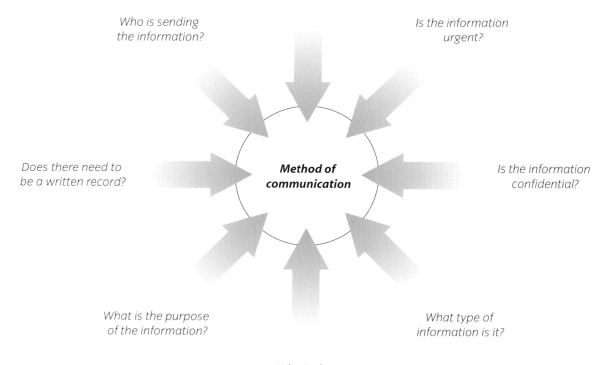

Who is to receive the information?

Who is sending the information?

Is the information urgent?

Does there need to be a written record?

Method of communication

Is the information confidential?

What is the purpose of the information?

What type of information is it?

Who is the information for?

Factors to consider when choosing a method of communication

information to be passed to another professional who is also involved in providing a service

information to be passed from yourself to a colleague over a short space of time to ensure that the care you provide offers an element of continuity

information to help in planning and developing services.

The kind of information that you may record to pass on within your own organisation may well be different from the types of record that you would keep if you were going to send that information to another agency, or if it was going into someone else's filing system.

An informal note like the one below is often used to pass on information which is not appropriate for a formal file or record sheet, but it is nevertheless important for a colleague to take note of. This is different from information that has to go outside the organisation – it would need to be formally written, and word-processed using a more structured format.

Types of record

Information likely to be used in making decisions about a child or young person is very important. It may concern a child who has been the subject of a child protection conference, or a detailed core assessment to decide the best way to provide support for the child or their family.

Where such records are being kept for the purpose of assisting with decision making, it is important that reports are not written in such a way that people have to read through vast amounts of material before finding the key points. It may be necessary to include a significant amount of information in order to make sure that all of the background is there, but a summary at the beginning or the end is always useful.

Recording information

(KS 4, 5, 17, 18, 19)

If you think about the purpose for which the information is to be used, this should help you to decide on the best way to record it. There would be little point in going to the trouble of typing out a piece of information that you were simply going to pass over to a colleague on the next shift. Alternatively, if you were writing something which was to go into someone's case notes or case file and be permanently recorded, then you would need to make sure that the information is likely to be of use to colleagues, or others who may need to have access to the file.

Shona:

Jamie

Please could you make sure that you try to have a chat with Jamie over supper – see if you can find out if anything's bothering him. Nothing I can put my finger on, nothing that could go on the handover record, but he just doesn't seem himself. Please keep an eye on him.

See you tomorrow

Sue

You may need to record and report:

- signs of a change in the needs of a child or young person
- decisions you have made and actions you have taken relating to a child's needs
- difficulties or conflicts that have arisen, and actions taken to resolve them.

How to record information

There would be little point in finding out about the most effective means of communication with a particular child or young person and then not making an accurate record so that other people can also communicate with him or her.

You should find out your employer's policy on where such information is to be recorded – it is likely to be in the child's case notes.

Be sure that you record:

- the nature of the communication differences
- how they show themselves

Keys to good practice: Keeping records

There are certain rules that are likely to be included in any organisation's policy about keeping records and recording information:

✓ All information needs to be clear.

✓ It needs to be legible (particularly if you are writing it by hand) – there is nothing more useless than a piece of information in a record file that cannot be read because someone's handwriting is poor.

✓ It should be to the point, not ramble or contain far more words than necessary.

✓ Any record should cover the important points clearly and logically.

ways which you have found to be effective in overcoming the differences.

Information recorded in notes may look like this:

Communication plan for Janine

Be aware of how language is used with Janine, she will interpret everything literally, e.g. if you tell her to 'chill' she will take off her jumper and go outside. She will become distressed if you talk too fast and do not allow her to follow the links she will make with the words she hears. Try to encourage the others to talk to her rather than just get annoyed. She is using the second set of cards to recognise facial expressions, should be encouraged to look at them whenever possible.

Methods of storing and retrieving records

Imagine going into a record shop which has thousands of CDs stored in racks but in no

Active knowledge · Knowledge evidence only

Look at the following report on K by CS, K's key worker.

K has been bad this week. On Monday he wouldn't go to school. He said he felt ill but he didn't have a temperature or anything. I think he wanted to stay here and see his new girlfriend in the next lodge.

Tuesday 12 noon. After I had just fed him he vomited all over me. I know he can't help throwing up, but he could give me some warning so I didn't have to change all my clothes. I cleaned him up in the usual way. Thursday we had archery in the lounge. K wanted to go in his wheelchair but he's supposed to use his sticks, so I told him he had to try with them. He got really stroppy and refused to go in the end. I think we ought to arrange some other activities for him that he can do in his own lodge. Then we won't have these fights about him getting about. What do you think?

1) What is your opinion of this report? Consider the factual detail, the attitude shown towards K by his key worker, and the practical suggestions made.

2) List the improvements that you would make to this report.

3) What problems could be caused by report writing like this example?

4) If you were CS's manager, how would you respond to receiving a report like this?

recognisable order; they are not filed by the name of the artist, nor by the title of the album. Imagine how much time it would take to trace the particular album that you are looking for. Anything from Greenday to Abba to Mantovani would be all jumbled together! This is exactly what it is like with a filing system – unless there is a system that is easily recognisable and allows people to trace files quickly and accurately, it is impossible to use.

Records are stored in filing systems, which may be manual or computerised. All organisations will have a filing system, and one of the first jobs you must undertake is to learn how to use it.

Some organisations have people who deal specifically with filing, and they do not allow untrained people to access the files. This is likely to be the case if you work for a large organisation, such as a local authority. Smaller agencies are likely to have a general filing system to which everyone in the organisation has access. This is exactly the kind of situation where files and records are likely to go missing and to be misplaced.

If you learn to appreciate the importance of records and the different systems that can be used for their storage, then you can assist rather than hinder the process of keeping records up to date, in the right place and readily accessible when people need them.

Computerised systems

Most organisations use a computerised system, with very clear procedures to be followed by everyone who accesses the system. The procedures will vary, but usually involve accessing files through a special programme, which may well have been written especially for your organisation, or specifically for record-keeping in children's services.

You may not be able to delete or alter any information that is in someone's file on a computer, depending on your level of access. It is possible that you will only be able to add information in very specific places, or it could be that files are 'read only' and you cannot add any information to them. This process, because it will not allow people to change or alter files, does have the advantage that information

is likely to remain in a clear format. It is less likely to become lost or damaged in the way that manual files are. After all, it is really not possible to leave a computer system on a bus!

A computerised system enables organisations to keep a great deal more information in much less space, and they can link into other parts of children's services and enable access to information. Although they can be expensive to install and to set up, the advantages outweigh the disadvantages in the long run. It also means that everyone in the organisation has to learn how to operate the system and how to use the computer – this is a new skill for many people. It is, however, a skill worth learning if it enables you to record and use information more accurately and effectively.

Manual systems

Some organisations still use manual systems. The types of file used can vary: the most usual type is a brown manila folder with a series of documents fastened inside; other types include ring binders, lever arch files and bound copies of computer printouts.

All of the files have to be organised (indexed) and stored in a way that makes them easily accessible whenever they are required.

Alphabetical system

If there are not too many files, they can be kept in an alphabetical system in a simple filing cabinet or cupboard. In this sort of system, files are simply placed according to the surname of the person they are about. They are put in the same order as you would see names in a telephone directory, starting with A and working through to the end of the alphabet, with names beginning *Mc* being filed as *Mac* and *St* being filed as *Saint*. GPs' patient records are usually kept using an alphabetical system.

Numerical systems

Where there are large numbers of files, an alphabetical system would not work. Imagine the numbers of M. Johnsons or P. Williamses who would appear as patients in a large hospital! In that situation an alphabetical filing system would become impossible to manage, so large organisations give their files numbers, and they are stored in number order. Clearly, a numerical system needs to have an index system so that a person's name can be attached to the appropriate number.

A hospital is likely to give a patient a number that will appear on all relevant documentation so that it is always possible to trace his or her medical notes. However, there still needs to be an overall record to attach that person's name and address to the particular set of case notes, and these days this is normally kept on a central computer.

Other indexing systems

It could be that, instead of files being organised alphabetically, they may be organised according to the different services an agency offers. For example, they could be kept under 'Mental health services', 'Care in the community services', 'Services for children or young people' and so on. Within these categories files would be kept in alphabetical order. In a similar way, files may be organised under geographical areas.

Other types of records

Most organisations maintain electronic records for accounts, suppliers, personnel and all essential business records. There will be a back-up for any electronically held information; this may be a paper system or more likely an off-site electronic back-up.

Useful information about advice and support services in the area could be maintained in a resource area or filing system, so that helpful leaflets and information packs are not left in a heap on a shelf or a window sill! An electronic index of useful websites, with links, can be very valuable for children, young people and their families if they have computer access and are comfortable accessing information in this way.

Remember

Filing systems can work extremely well if they are properly run. They work efficiently and effectively in most organisations, as long as everyone who uses them follows a few basic rules (see the following table).

Some basic rules about filing

Do	Don't
Enter information clearly and precisely	Alter or move around the contents of a file, or take out or replace documents which are part of someone's file
Be sure that you access electronic files strictly within your permitted level of access	Make any changes to files unless permitted to do so
Make sure you log in and out correctly	Copy any part of an electronic record system Forget to log out
Leave a note or card (or something similar) when you borrow a file from a manual filing system	Remove an index card from a system
Return files as soon as possible	Keep files lying around after you have finished with them

1 Name four reasons for keeping records about children and young people.

2 Name three advantages and three disadvantages of a computerised filing system.

3 Why is it important to record and report changes in needs of children and young people?

4 What might be the consequences of mismanaging records?

5 What are the key principles of data protection?

HSC 31 UNIT TEST

1 What signals would tell you if someone is relaxed and confident?

2 When may physical contact be helpful in communication?

3 What could you do to show a child or young person that you are interested in what he or she is saying?

4 List three physical factors you would consider when planning good communication on a difficult or sensitive issue.

5 You have to tell five people that there has been a change in time for a meeting next week – a colleague from a similar workplace to yours, the child's social worker, the child's GP, an officer-in-charge from another residential home, the child's mother who has poor literacy skills.

   a How would you contact each person?

   b How would you record your contacts?

   c Why would you record your contacts?

6 You receive a telephone call from someone who says she is a child's aunt. She asks for details about her niece's condition and well-being. You have never heard the child mention an aunt, and to your knowledge she has never visited the child. How would you deal with this telephone call? Give reasons for your answer.

Don't forget to refer to the evidence opportunities grid (see pages 357–375) for more ideas for suitable evidence for your NVQ.

Promote, monitor and maintain health, safety and security in the working environment

This unit is about the way you can contribute to making your workplace a safe, secure and healthy place – for the children, young people and families who use it, for those who work alongside you, and for yourself. Your workplace may be a family home, a school, a residential home, a children's hospice, a hospital, a day centre or your own home. Whichever it is, as a childcare professional, you have a responsibility for safety and security.

You have a duty to contribute to ensuring the safety of the children and young people you work with, and the first part of this unit looks at ways to make the environment safer and more secure.

Your own working practices also impact on the risks to children and young people, and you will look at how the way you work makes a major contribution to ensuring health and safety.

The third element in this unit enables you to look at how to respond to children and young people in an emergency, the sort of emergencies you may have to deal with and how to deal with the aftermath.

Caring for children and young people is not just about relationships and active working; it is also about safeguarding and creating safe places for children and young people to be in. Even though the work you do in this unit may directly contribute towards the outcomes of 'being healthy' and 'being safe', it is also an important part of enabling children and young people to achieve other outcomes that improve their lives.

Safeguarding children is everyone's responsibility, and safeguarding is not just about protection from abuse, it is also about keeping children and young people safe in their day-to-day lives as they play, study and enjoy life.

In this unit you will find 'Active knowledge' features containing activities that will contribute to assessment for your NVQ. Remember that these features only offer the opportunity for partial assessment; you can also refer to the evidence opportunities grid (see pages 357–375) for more ideas to provide suitable evidence for your NVQ.

What you need to learn

- What is safety?
- How to maintain security
- The legal framework
- Dealing with hazardous waste
- How to promote a safe work environment
- Safe manual handling
- How to contribute to infection control
- Challenging inappropriate practice
- How to maintain personal safety
- Fire safety
- Health emergencies

HSC 32a Monitor and maintain the safety and security of the working environment

What is safety?

(KS 10, 11, 12, 13)

It sounds very simple and straightforward: help to make sure that the place in which you work is safe and secure. However, when you start to think about it – safe for whom or from whom? Safe from drugs? From hazardous fumes? From infection? From intruders? From child abusers? From work-related injuries? Health and safety impacts on many areas of your work and, while you are not expected to be an expert, you do need to know what your responsibilities are.

Responsibilities for safety and security in the workplace

Employer's responsibilities	Employee's responsibilities	Shared responsibilities
Planning safety and security, e.g.: • making sure that equipment is provided • carrying out risk assessments • developing systems for checking visitors • ensuring proper storage available for hazardous substances, food, medicines	Using the systems and procedures correctly, e.g.: • if you have to lift – use the equipment according to instructions • follow the risk assessment and make safety checks • be vigilant about who comes and goes • follow the procedures for storage and hygiene	Safety of children and young people using the facilities, e.g.: • employer provides a hoist and the training on how to use it; you must use it properly and safely
Providing information about safety and security, e.g.: • providing training for lifting and handling, food hygiene, etc. • providing information about hazardous substances in a COSHH file	Reporting flaws or gaps in the systems, equipment or procedures in use, e.g.: • reporting if a wheelchair has a loose brake • reporting that the visitor recording system is not being used • passing on that the lone working protocol is not really effective because the mobile phone contract has run out	Safety of the environment, e.g.: • Employer must provide 'wet floor' notices; you must use them • Employer must replace a worn carpet – but only if you report it

Updating systems and procedures:
• All systems and processes must be regularly reviewed, e.g.:
  – Risk assessments for visitor recording
  – COSHH procedures
  – Lifting and handling risk assessments
  – Lone working procedures		

Safety in the workplace

You share responsibility with your employer for the safety of everyone who uses your service. There are many different hazards that can cause injury to children and young people, especially if they are excited, hyperactive or distressed. You will need to take specific steps and be particularly vigilant if you work with children and young people with a disability or a sensory impairment.

Think about the sorts of **environmental and equipment** hazards you may come across, such as:

- stairways which will need to be gated if there are young children
- needles or other sharps which may be around in the garden or playing area
- windows which need to be restricted from opening too far
- electrical sockets which will need protecting if there are young children
- playing surfaces which should be made from appropriate safety materials
- worn electrical flexes on lamps or audio equipment which will need to be replaced
- wet or slippery floors, particularly in bathrooms and kitchens
- fires or heaters which will need to be protected if there are young children
- clothes and belongings on the floor in rooms and corridors, creating a tripping hazard
- toys and play equipment which must be checked to see if they are faulty, dirty or damaged
- equipment for moving and lifting children and young people which must be checked for faults and immediately withdrawn from use if found
- hazardous substances such as cleaning fluids or medicines which must be clearly labelled.

There are also hazards connected with people such as: moving and handling techniques if you work with disabled or very young children; checking on visitors and making sure that people who do not have CRB checks are not left alone with children; keeping the premises safe against potential intruders; managing challenging behaviour; and making sure that workers are safe if they are working alone.

Your role

Your responsibility to contribute to a safe environment means more than simply being aware of these potential hazards. You must take steps to check and deal with any sources of risk. If you are supervising a team, you must also ensure that they are aware of the possible risks and hazards and know how to deal with them, or how to ask for help or advice. Although it is ultimately your employer's responsibility, you have a duty to contribute to the safety of children and young people and any staff you supervise.

You can fulfil your role in two ways: you can deal directly with the hazard, or you can report it to your line manager – if you have one.

Dealing directly with the hazard

This means that you have taken individual responsibility. It will probably apply to obvious hazards such as:

- wet floors – you can dry them as far as possible and put out warning signs
- open flights of stairs – you can put up a stair gate
- needles and sharps – you can check gardens and playing areas before children and young people use them
- unguarded fires – you can put up a fire guard
- belongings all over the floor, such as clothes, books and CDs – these can be picked up and tidied away, depending on the age of the children and young people – a system of personal responsibility for possessions should apply!
- visitors to the building – challenge anyone you do not recognise; asking 'Can I help you?' is usually enough to establish whether a person has a good reason to be there
- fire – follow the correct procedures to raise the alarm and assist with evacuation.

Key terms

Hazard: Something that could possibly cause harm.

Risk: The likelihood of a hazard causing harm.

After washing floors, dry them as much as possible and set out warning signs

Informing your manager

When you inform your manager, the hazard becomes an organisational responsibility. You should report hazards that are beyond your role and competence, such as:

- faulty equipment – fires, kettles, computers, etc.
- worn floor coverings
- loose or damaged fittings or furniture
- obstructions too heavy for you to move safely
- damaged or faulty games or play equipment or toys
- people acting suspiciously on the premises.

How to maintain security

(KS 2, 4, 9)

Most places where children are looked after are not under lock and key, with some obvious exceptions such as **secure units**. Children are able to come and go and cannot be locked in, but children and young people also have a right to be secure in the places where they live, study or play. Security in a children and young people's environment is about:

- security against intruders
- security in respect of children's privacy and decisions about unwanted visitors
- security against being abused
- security of possessions.

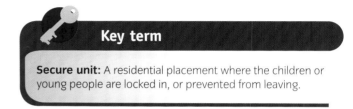

Key term

Secure unit: A residential placement where the children or young people are locked in, or prevented from leaving.

Security against intruders

Children and young people are not usually very good at noticing new people: they can be careless or simply be listening to music, texting a friend or daydreaming and just not notice who is around. They are also less likely than an adult to question someone about reasons for being where they are. It is your job to safeguard and protect children and young people and keep them safe from people who have no right to be with them.

If you work for a large organisation, such as a local authority children's services department, it may be that all employees are easily identifiable through identity badges with photographs. In a smaller organisation, there may be a system of issuing visitors' badges to visitors who have reasons to be there, or security may simply rely on the vigilance of the staff.

Some workplaces operate electronic security systems, like those in the NHS where cards are 'swiped' to open doors. Less sophisticated systems in small workplaces may use a keypad with a code number known only to staff and those who are legitimately on the premises. It is often difficult to maintain security with such systems, as codes will be forgotten or become widely known. In order to maintain security, it is necessary to change the codes regularly, and to make sure everyone is aware of the change.

Small residential children's homes are typical of places where it is difficult to maintain security and still make it feel like home. Foster carers have to address health and safety issues as far as possible whilst still maintaining a home for all children in their care.

Challenge anyone you do not recognise

A few children's facilities still operate with keys. If mechanical keys are used, there will be a list of named keyholders and there may be a system of handover of keys at shift change (in a small unit, all staff may have keys). Some of the old buildings once used as massive children's homes, with literally hundreds of beds, are still standing, although now used for other purposes. It is easy to imagine the staff with large bunches of keys on a belt, but thankfully this is now only a reminder of the suffering of children past and a marker of how far we have progressed in understanding and meeting the needs of children and young people.

Remember

If you find an intruder on the premises, don't tackle him or her – raise the alarm.

Protecting independent young people

Young people who are being supported to live in their own homes can be exposed to considerable risks. You must try to impress on them the importance of finding out who people are before letting them in. Local police and fire services will provide security advice and items such as smoke alarms and door chains to vulnerable young people.

Keys to good practice: Protecting against intruders

✓ Be aware of everyone you come across. Get into the habit of noticing people and thinking, 'Do I know that person?'

✓ Challenge anyone you do not recognise. The challenge should be polite. 'Can I help you?' is usually enough to find out if a visitor has a reason to be on the premises.

✓ If a person says that he or she is there to see a child or young person, first check with the child or young person that he or she is expecting a visitor, and that they know the person and want to see them. In the case of a young child, check that the person is someone that the family has indicated can visit the child. If not, advise the person to contact the family and arrange with them to see the child. Do not give any contact details for the family; if they are genuine, they will have the contact details.

✓ Never allow anyone to take a child out, or be with a child unsupervised unless this has been agreed with the family, or whoever has parental responsibility.

Restricting access

Young people have a right to choose who they see. If there are relatives or friends who wish to visit and a young person does not want to see them, you may have to make this clear. It is difficult to do, but you can only be effective if you are clear and assertive. You should not make excuses or invent reasons why visitors cannot see the young person concerned. You could say something like: 'I'm sorry, Ricky has told us that he does not want to see you. I realise that this is hard for you, but it is his choice. If he does change his mind we will contact you. Do we have your phone number?'

Do not allow yourself to be drawn into passing on messages or attempting to persuade – that is not your role. Your job is to respect the wishes of the young person you are working with. If you are asked to intervene or to pass on a message, you must refuse politely but firmly.

Part of making sure that children and young people are protected is maintaining the security of the premises and the people who have access.

Only people who have been checked and cleared by the Criminal Records Bureau (CRB) may be left unsupervised with children. This includes families and visitors: if they have not been CRB cleared, they can only be unsupervised with the child they are visiting, not with any other children or young people in the house.

You must ensure that a visitors' book, which records all visitors to the premises, is maintained and is always used, regardless of the identity of the visitor.

There may also be occasions when access to a particular child or young person is restricted for other reasons, such as a court order. This should be clearly recorded on the child's record, with information included about the restrictions and how they are to be applied. Your line manager should have further details if there is not enough information in the records. If you are working in a supervisory capacity, it will be part of your role to ensure that all the team are aware of these restrictions.

Protecting children and young people from abuse is dealt with in depth in Unit HSC 34, but it can never be repeated too often that children and young people have a right to be protected from harm and abuse. You have a duty to protect them and you must report immediately any abuse you see or suspect.

Active knowledge

HSC 32a
pc 2, 3

You need a colleague or friend for this activity. One of you should be the person who has come to visit, the other the childcare professional who has to say that the young person will not see him or her. Try using different scenarios – angry, upset, aggressive, and so on. By the time you have practised a few times, you may feel better equipped to deal with the situation when it happens in reality.

It is possible to do a similar exercise on your own by imagining different scenarios and writing down the words you would say in each of the situations.

How does your workplace ensure that only people with the right to enter are on the premises?

How would you deal with someone who should not be there?

My story

Hi, I'm Ricky. I'm 15 and I'm in a rehab unit for people with spinal injuries. I was in a car driven by my brother. He picked me up from town this night and I didn't realise he'd been at the pub first. His driving was even worse than usual and he ended up rolling the car after hitting the kerb. Thanks to him, I'm paralysed and I'm going to be stuck in a wheelchair. Mum keeps coming in and saying how he didn't mean to hurt me and how he's sorry. Well he didn't look sorry when he swaggered in here: he just went on and on about how he was going to have to go to court and how his brief is going to make sure that he doesn't go to prison if I say that someone ran across the road so he had to swerve. Well, I hope he does go to prison – he's a complete t*****. I said I didn't want to see him again and I wasn't going to lie for him. He keeps trying to visit me to persuade me to go to court…

The staff promised me that they wouldn't let him in if I didn't want to see him, so every time he comes they ask me and I say 'no' and they tell him to push off. They've told Mum to stop going on about him as well, I think, because she's shut up about him too. I really feel that the staff here understand how I feel. They make it clear that it's what I want that matters to them, not what anyone else thinks is 'the right thing to do'.

B0009446

Security of property

Property and valuables belonging to children who are looked after should be safeguarded. Often possessions that may appear worthless are hugely important: they may represent emotional security, hold many memories or be an important link to someone significant in the child's life. Some children, who have missed out on the loving they should have had, can become very focused on possessions. Similarly, some children with ASD (Autistic Spectrum Disorders – see Unit 31, page 29) can become very attached to something and become distraught if it goes missing.

Your employer will have a property book in which records of all personal possessions are entered. There may be particular policies within your organisation, but as a general rule you are likely to need to:

- make a record of all possessions if children are admitted to a residential establishment
- record valuable items separately
- describe items of jewellery by their colour, for example, 'yellow metal' not 'gold'
- inform your manager if you become aware that a young person is keeping valuables or a significant amount of money.

Active knowledge

Links to HSC 32a pc 1

Find out where the property book is in your workplace, and how it is filled in. Check who has the responsibility to complete it. If you are likely to have to use it, make sure you know exactly what your role is. Do you have to enter the property in the book? Do you have to make sure the valuables are safe? Do you have to give the child or young person or family a copy of the entry? Ask the questions in advance – don't leave it until you have to do it.

It is always difficult when items go missing in a childcare setting, particularly if they are valuable or of particular significance to the child or young person. It is important that you check all possibilities before calling the police.

Action stages when property goes missing

Health and safety out and about

There are always additional health and safety considerations when you are looking after children outside the usual environment. For example, if you are planning a visit or holiday trip, you may need to consider the following:

- accessibility
- safety of premises and potential hazards
- accessibility and safety of transport
- security of children, property and travel documents
- medications for the children
- safety checks on any toys or play or sports equipment
- instructions for using any unfamiliar equipment
- provision for special dietary arrangements
- insurance.

All of the UK countries have National Minimum Standards used by inspectors. These cover the extra steps necessary for outings, visits and holidays.

The legal framework

(KS 1, 2, 3, 4, 6, 14, 15, 16)

The settings in which you look after children and young people are generally covered by the Health and Safety at Work Act 1974 (HASAWA). This Act has been supplemented by many sets of regulations and guidelines, which extend it, support it or explain it. The regulations most likely to affect your workplace are listed in this section. You will also have to comply with the National Minimum Standards of the UK country and the sector you work in. Regardless of whether you work in care, education or health, the relevant standards will be the basis for the Inspection Framework for your country. The Standards contain requirements in relation to health, safety and security, and your service will be inspected to see if it complies.

You and the law

There are many regulations, laws and guidelines dealing with health and safety. You do not need to know the detail, but you do need to know where your responsibilities begin and end.

The laws place certain responsibilities on both employers and employees. For example, it is up to the employer to provide a safe place in which to work, but the employee also has to show reasonable care for his or her own safety.

Broadly, employers have to:

- provide a safe workplace
- ensure that there is safe access to and from the workplace
- provide information on health and safety
- provide health and safety training
- undertake risk assessment for all hazards.

You must:

- take reasonable care for your own safety and that of others
- co-operate with your employer in respect of health and safety matters
- not intentionally damage any health and safety equipment or materials provided by your employer.

Both the employee and employer are jointly responsible for safeguarding the health and safety of anyone using the premises.

Each workplace where there are five or more workers must have a written statement of health and safety policy. The policy must include:

- a statement of intention to provide a safe workplace
- the name of the person responsible for implementing the policy
- the names of any other individuals responsible for particular health and safety hazards
- a list of identified health and safety hazards and the procedures to be followed in relation to them
- procedures for recording accidents at work
- details for evacuation of the premises.

Active knowledge

Find out where the health and safety policies which relate to your workplace are and show you understand how they benefit the children, young people and staff. With careful thought this could produce evidence for HSC 32a or HSC 32c.

The Health and Safety Executive

Britain's Health and Safety Commission (HSC) and the Health and Safety Executive (HSE) are responsible for the regulation of almost all the risks to health and safety arising from work activity in Britain. The HSC is sponsored by the Department of Work and Pensions and is accountable to the Minister of State for Work. The HSE's job is to help the HSC ensure that risks to people's health and safety from work activities are properly controlled.

The Health and Safety Executive (www.hse.gov.uk) states:

Our mission is to protect people's health and safety by ensuring risks in the changing workplace are properly controlled.

The HSC believes that prevention is better than cure, so two of its key roles are 1) providing information and support to ensure that workplaces are safe, and 2) enforcement in order to ensure that legislation is adhered to. The HSE has the power to prosecute employers who fail in any way to safeguard the health and safety of people who use their premises.

An employee has to show reasonable care for his or her own safety

Risk assessment

Risk assessment is designed for employers and self-employed people, who are required by law to identify and assess risks in the workplace. This includes any situations where potential harm may be caused. There are many regulations that require risks to be assessed, some covered by European Union directives. These include:

- *Management of Health and Safety at Work Regulations 1999*
- *Manual Handling Operations Regulations 1992 (amended 2002)*
- *Personal Protective Equipment at Work Regulations 1992*

- *Health and Safety (Display Screen Equipment) Regulations 1992 (amended 2002)*
- *Noise at Work Regulations 1989*
- *Control of Substances Hazardous to Health Regulations 2002 (COSHH)*
- *Control of Asbestos at Work Regulations 2002*
- *Control of Lead at Work Regulations 2002.*

There are five key stages to undertaking a risk assessment, which involve answering the following questions.

- What is the purpose of the risk assessment?
- Who has to assess the risk?
- Whose risk should be assessed?
- What should be assessed?
- When should the risk be assessed?

The Management of Health and Safety at Work Regulations 1999 state that employers have to assess any risks which are associated with the workplace and work activities. This means all activities, from walking on wet floors to dealing with violence. Having carried out a risk assessment, the employer must consider any mitigating factors – in other words, anything that may compensate for the risk. The employer must then apply **risk control measures** – actions that must be taken to reduce the risks. For example, alarm buzzers may need to be installed or extra staff employed, as well as steps such as providing extra training for staff. Each workplace is likely to have its own risk assessment documentation, but it may look like the table below.

Risk assessments are vital in protecting the health and safety of both you and the children and young

Hazard	People at risk	Measures to reduce risk
Intruder gaining access	Children, staff	• Security of doors and windows to be checked. Encourage everyone to remember to lock doors. • Install alarm and personal alarms for staff • Staff and children to be advised not to tackle any intruder
Injury from lifting disabled children	Children, staff	• Install hoists • Staff to be trained in use
Tripping risk from belongings left on floors	Children, staff	• Staff to remove any belongings to 'tidy box' regularly each day • Young people to be encouraged to take responsibility • Charity 'fine' to reclaim removed belongings from 'tidy box'

people. You should always check that a risk assessment has been carried out before you undertake any potentially risky task, and follow the steps identified to reduce the risk.

However, do not forget that you must reach a balance between the individual wishes of each child or young person you work with, and your own safety and the safety of others. Some examples of this principle are discussed in the section on manual handling starting on page 67.

The risk assessments carried out in relation to health and safety in the workplace are similar to those in relation to children and young people – but the content and the focus is different. Here we are looking at the employer's responsibilities in making sure that the workforce is not exposed to risks at work. When you undertake a risk assessment for a particular child, you are assessing the risk and resilience factors in the current circumstances and how likely it is that the child will suffer significant harm.

Key term

Risk control measures: Actions taken in order to reduce an identified risk.

Risks in someone's home

Of course, the situation is somewhat different if you are a foster carer and work in your own home, or if you work in a child or young person's own home to support the whole family. Your employer can still carry out risk assessments and put risk-control measures in place, such as a procedure for working in pairs in a situation where there is a risk of violence. What cannot be done is to remove environmental hazards such as worn electrical flexes, worn patches on carpets or old equipment. All you can do is advise the family of the risks, and suggest how things could be improved.

Obviously, if you feel that home conditions are so poor as to present a serious risk of significant harm to the child or young person, you must immediately report your concerns in order that you can take the necessary action to protect the child or young person.

However, if you are looking at untidiness, broken toys and some worn carpets, then advice and encouragement to improve matters is all you can do. You also need to take care!

Remember

It may be your workplace, but it is the child and family's home. If you work in a child's home or long-term residential children's home, you have to balance the need for safety with the rights of people to live as they wish. Both you and the children using the service are entitled to expect a safe place in which to live and work, but remember their rights to choose how they want to live.

Control of Substances Hazardous to Health (COSHH)

There are many substances hazardous to health – nicotine, many drugs, too much alcohol, etc. – but the COSHH Regulations apply to substances that have been identified as toxic, corrosive or irritant. This includes cleaning materials, pesticides, acids, disinfectants and bleaches, and naturally occurring substances such as blood, bacteria, etc. Workplaces may have other hazardous substances that are particular to the nature of the work carried out.

The Health and Safety Executive states that employers must take the following steps to protect employees from hazardous substances.

Step 1

Find out what hazardous substances are used in the workplace and the risks these substances pose to people's health.

What might this mean for you?

It is likely that the most hazardous substances in your workplace will be cleaning fluids: bleach, caustic cleaners for ovens, and so on. Depending on where you work, there may also be anti-bacterial, disinfecting fluids. You could also be regularly exposed to bodily fluids such as vomit, urine, faeces, blood and sweat – again, this will depend on your workplace, although most work with children and young people will involve coming into contact with a range of bodily fluids at some point!

Step 2

Decide what precautions are needed before any work starts with hazardous substances.

What does this mean for you?

This means that any cleaning fluids, bleaches or caustic fluids must be clearly labelled and only stored in the proper containers. All hazardous substances must be properly stored, and information about how to deal with any emergency relating to them must be readily available to you.

Your employer must have a process in place for dealing with bodily fluids and must make sure that you know what to do and have any necessary protective clothing such as gloves, aprons and glasses.

Step 3

Prevent people being exposed to hazardous substances, but where this is not reasonably practicable, control the exposure.

What does this mean for you?

This stage applies far more to people who work in industrial environments such as petrochemicals or pharmaceuticals. However, it is not really practical to prevent people who work with children from using cleaning materials or dealing with body fluids, so employers have to control exposure by ensuring that you have the necessary protective clothing.

Step 4

Make sure control measures are used and maintained properly, and that safety procedures are followed.

What does this mean for you?

Short of standing over you, it is difficult for employers to make absolutely sure that you follow procedures. However, you will be trained and will understand why the procedures are there. Most employers will make deliberately ignoring safety procedures a disciplinary offence.

Step 5

If required, monitor exposure of employees to hazardous substances.

What does this mean for you?

This stage doesn't really apply to work with children and young people. It is unlikely that you would be exposed to harmful chemicals or other substances so regularly or in such large quantities as to make monitoring necessary.

Step 6

Carry out health surveillance where assessment has shown that this is necessary, or COSHH makes specific requirements.

What does this mean for you?

It means that an employer must check if people are regularly exposed to substances known to be hazardous. For some people who work with children and young people who are ill or disabled, it may mean that an employer has to regularly check that people are not risking back injuries from moving and handling.

Step 7

If required, prepare plans and procedures to deal with accidents, incidents and emergencies.

What does this mean for you?

Again, this is aimed at large chemical works or power stations where any major incident or accident could cause serious damage to large numbers of people. In most places where children and young people live, study or play there is sufficient information to deal with accidents contained in the COSHH file. Every workplace must have a COSHH file, which should be easily accessible to all staff. This file lists all the hazardous substances used in the workplace. It should detail:

- where they are kept
- how they are labelled
- their effects

- the maximum amount of time it is safe to be exposed to them
- how to deal with an emergency involving one of them.

Step 8

Make sure employees are properly informed, trained and supervised.

What does this mean for you?

This means exactly what it says!

Remember

Hazardous substances are not just things like poisons and radioactive material – they are also substances such as cleaning fluids and bleach.

If you have to work with hazardous substances, make sure that you take the precautions detailed in the COSHH file. This may be wearing gloves or protective goggles, or may involve limiting the time you are exposed to the substance or only using it in certain circumstances.

The COSHH file should also give you information about how to store hazardous substances using the

Active knowledge

You must ensure that you and all your staff know the location of the COSHH file in your workplace. Read the contents of the file, especially information about the substances you use or come into contact with and what the maximum exposure limits are. You do not have to know the detail of each substance, but the information you need should be contained in the COSHH file, which must be kept up to date.

correct containers as supplied by the manufacturer. All containers must have safety lids and caps, and must be correctly labelled.

Never use the container of one substance for storing another, and *never* change the labels.

There are set symbols used to indicate hazardous substances. Before you use *any* substance, whether it is liquid, powder, spray, cream or aerosol, take the following simple steps:

- Check the container for the hazard symbol.
- If there is a hazard symbol, go to the COSHH file.
- Look up the precautions you need to take with the substance.
- Make sure you follow the procedures, which are intended to protect you.

**DANGER
Highly flammable
material**

**DANGEROUS
CHEMICALS**

**DANGER
POISON**

**DANGEROUS
CHEMICALS**

**DANGER
Caustic**

**DANGER
CORROSIVE
SUBSTANCE**

These symbols, which warn you of hazardous substances, are always yellow

If you are concerned about a substance being used in your workplace that is not in the COSHH file, or if you notice incorrect containers or labels being used, report this to your manager; it then becomes his or her responsibility to act to correct the problem.

Reporting of Injuries, Diseases and Dangerous Occurrences (RIDDOR)

Reporting accidents and ill health at work is a legal requirement. All accidents, diseases and dangerous occurrences should be reported to the Incident Contact Centre. The Centre was established on 1 April 2001 as a single point of contact for all incidents in the UK. Reporting is important because it means that risks and causes of accidents, incidents and diseases can be identified. All notifications are passed on to either the local authority Environmental Health department, or the Health and Safety Executive, as appropriate.

Your employer needs to report:

- deaths
- major injuries (see the table below)
- accidents resulting in more than three days off work
- diseases
- dangerous occurrences.

Dangerous occurrences

If something happens which does not result in a reportable injury, but which clearly could have done, then it may be a dangerous occurrence and must be reported immediately.

Accidents at work

If accidents or injuries occur at work, either to you, to other staff or to an individual you are caring for, the details must be recorded. You must record the incident regardless of whether there was an injury.

Reportable injuries and diseases

Your employer should have procedures in place for making a record of accidents, either in an accident book or on an accident report form. This is required

Reportable injuries
fracture other than to fingers, thumbs or toes
amputation
dislocation of the shoulder, hip, knee or spine
loss of sight (temporary or permanent)
chemical or hot metal burn to the eye or any penetrating injury to the eye
injury resulting from an electric shock or electrical burn leading to unconsciousness or requiring resuscitation or admittance to hospital for more than 24 hours

Reportable diseases
certain poisonings
some skin diseases such as occupational dermatitis, skin cancer, chrome ulcer, oil folliculitis acne
lung diseases including occupational asthma, farmer's lung, pneumoconiosis, asbestosis, mesothelioma

Reportable injuries

any other injury which leads to hypothermia (getting too cold), heat-induced illness, or unconsciousness; requires resuscitation; or requires admittance to hospital for more than 24 hours
unconsciousness caused by asphyxia (suffocation) or exposure to a harmful substance or biological agent
acute illness requiring medical treatment, or leading to loss of consciousness, arising from absorption of any substance by inhalation, ingestion or through the skin
acute illness requiring medical treatment where there is reason to believe that this resulted from exposure to a biological agent or its toxins or infected material

Reportable diseases

infections such as leptospirosis, hepatitis, tuberculosis, anthrax, legionellosis (Legionnaires' disease) and tetanus
other conditions such as occupational cancer, certain musculoskeletal disorders, decompression illness and hand-arm vibration syndrome

Reportable major injuries and diseases

not only by the RIDDOR regulations, but also, if you work in a residential setting, by the inspectors.

Any accident book or report form must comply with the requirements of the Data Protection Act 1998 by making sure that the personal details of those involved cannot be read by others. This can be ensured by recording personal details on a tear-off part of the form so that only an anonymous description of the accident is left, or by using individual, numbered and recorded forms that are then logged at a central point. However it is done, it is a legal requirement that personal details are not available for others to see unless consent has been given.

Make sure you know where the accident report forms or accident book are kept, and who is responsible for

---

Date: 24.8.07   **Time:** 14.30 **hrs**   **Location:** Main lounge
Description of accident:

Jack was watching TV in the lounge with Pete and Maria, they started play fighting and Jack tripped over the coffee table and fell heavily, banging his head on a footstool.

He was very shaken and although he said that he was not hurt, there was a large bump/bruise developing on his head. Jack appeared pale and shaky. Terry McD was senior staff on duty and the first aider. He checked Jack over and sent for GP.

Locum GP arrived after about 45 mins and said that Jack was bruised and shaken, but did not seem to have any evidence of any injuries.

Jack appeared fine and did not want any fuss.

Incident was witness by two young people who were in the lounge at the time: Pete and Maria.

Signed: *Shona Smith*   **Name:** Shona Smith

---

recording accidents (this is likely to be your manager).

You must report any accident in which you are involved, or which you have witnessed, to your manager or supervisor. It may be useful to make notes, as in the example on the previous page, as soon as possible after the incident so that details on the accident report form can be complete and accurate.

Dealing with hazardous waste

(KS 11, 12)

As part of providing a safe working environment, employers have to put procedures in place to deal with waste materials and spillages. The types of hazardous waste you are most likely to come across are shown in the following table, alongside a list of the ways in which each is usually dealt with.

Waste can be a source of infection, so it is very important that you follow your employer's procedures. Keeping yourself and your colleagues safe is obviously important and your employer will be following the legislation and guidelines designed to do this. However, your concern is for the children and young people you work with and a safe working environment for you is a safe living, learning or recreational environment for them.

Type of waste	Method of disposal
Clinical waste – used dressings	Yellow bags, clearly labelled with contents and location. This waste is incinerated.
Needles, syringes, cannulas ('sharps')	Yellow sharps box. Never put sharps into anything other than a hard plastic box. This is sealed and incinerated.
Body fluids and waste – urine, vomit, blood, sputum, faeces	Cleared and flushed down sluice drain or toilet. Area to be cleaned and disinfected.
Soiled linen	Red bags, direct into laundry; disintegrate in wash. If handled, gloves must be worn.

Ways of dealing with waste

Test yourself

1 **a** How many possible hazards and risks can you find in the illustration below? List at least six.

   b Which of these are the responsibility of the employer?

   c Which are the responsibility of the staff?

2 Why is it important to check someone's right to enter the premises?

3 What should you do if you see someone you do not recognise in your workplace?

4 What are the employer's responsibilities in respect of hazardous substances?

5 What are the employee's responsibilities for hazardous substances?

6 Name three reportable diseases and describe the process for reporting them in your workplace.

HSC 32b Promote health and safety in the working environment

In the previous element, you looked at the procedures and policies that have to be put in place to protect workers and people who use the service, and the laws that govern health and safety. Now you need to learn about the steps you should be following to ensure that the laws and policies work in practice.

Active knowledge
HSC 32a pc 5b, 9, HSC 32c pc 7. Also links to HSC 31 and HSC 34.

Look at the incident/accident report form for your workplace. Does the form provide enough information? The purpose of the form is to provide sufficient information to:

- ensure the child or young person receives the proper medical attention
- provide information for treatment at a later date, in case of delayed reactions
- give information to any inspector who may need to see the records
- identify any gaps or need for improvements in safety procedures
- provide information about the circumstances in case of any future legal action.

Think about how you would re-design the report form if necessary, and what further headings you would include. Make sure that the accident form complies with the requirements of the Data Protection Act 1998.

How to promote a safe work environment

(KS 6, 8, 11, 14, 18)

Childcare environments are places where accidents can quite often happen, not because staff are careless or fail to check hazards, but because children and young people can be boisterous, and some have little sense of danger.

Checklist for a safe work environment

It is important that you are always aware of any risks in any situation you are in. It helps to get into the habit of making a mental checklist. The checklist will vary from one workplace to another, but could look like the one on the next page.

One of the factors to consider in your checklist may be what your colleagues do about health and safety issues. It is very difficult if you are the only person following good practice. You may be able to encourage others by trying some of the following options:

- always showing a good example yourself
- explaining why you are following procedures
- getting some health and safety leaflets from your trade union or environmental health office and leaving them in the staffroom for people to see
- bringing in any information you can about courses or safety lectures
- asking your manager if he or she can arrange a talk on health and safety.

What you should do in a situation where a colleague is behaving inappropriately or using unsafe practices is covered in Challenging inappropriate practice on page 73.

What you wear

Generally, uniforms are not appropriate when working with children and young people. However, staff providing personal care for children and young people may need to use protective clothing to minimise the possibility of spreading infection.

Clothes worn for work should be comfortable and well fitting with plenty of room for movement. Inappropriate clothing can be restrictive and prevent free movement.

High-heeled or poorly supporting shoes are a risk to you in terms of foot injuries and very sore feet! They also present a risk to children if you are involved in

Area of risk	Hazards	Check
Environment	Floors	Are they dry?
	Carpets and rugs	Are they worn or curled at the edges?
	Doorways and corridors	Are they clear of obstacles?
	Electrical flexes	Are they trailing?
Equipment	Beds	Are the brakes on? Are the beds high enough?
	Electrical or gas appliances	Are they worn? Have they been safety-checked?
	Lifting equipment	Is it worn or damaged?
	Mobility aids	Are they worn or damaged?
	Substances such as cleaning fluids	Are they correctly labelled?
	Containers	Are they leaking or damaged?
	Waste disposal equipment	Is it faulty?
People	Visitors to the building	Should they be there? Have they been CRB checked?
	Handling procedures	Have they been assessed for risk?
	Intruders	Have the police been called?
	Violent and aggressive behaviour	Has it been dealt with?

Checklist for a safe working environment

lifting and handling or supporting movement, because if you overbalance or stumble, so will the child.

Staff should be encouraged to tie up long hair. Hair can contain substantial amounts of bacteria, which could cause infection. In addition, loose long hair could be a safety hazard, and easy to grab in a difficult situation.

There may be restrictions on wearing jewellery or carrying things in your pocket that could cause injury to a child or young person. These can also pose a risk to you – you could stab yourself in the chest with a pair of scissors or ballpoint pen!

Wristwatches should not be worn if you are involved in providing personal care to children and young people. Apart from the possibility of scratching the child or young person when providing personal care, wearing a watch can prevent good hand-washing practice.

Many workplaces do not allow the wearing of rings with stones. Not only are they a possible source of infection, but they can also scratch children or tear protective gloves.

Safe manual handling

(KS 4, 13)

You may be involved in lifting and handling if you provide personal care to children and young people

The Manual Handling Operations Regulations 1992 require employers to avoid all manual handling where there is a risk of injury 'so far as it is reasonably practical'. Everyone from the European Commission to the Royal College of Nursing has issued policies and directives about avoiding lifting. Make sure you check out the policies in use in your workplace and that you understand them.

Lifting Operations and Lifting Equipment Regulations (1992) (LOLER)

These regulations came into effect on 5 December 1998 and apply to all workplaces. An employee does not have any responsibilities under LOLER, but under the Management of Health and Safety at Work Regulations, employees have a duty to ensure that they take reasonable care of themselves and others who may be affected by the actions that they undertake.

Key to good practice: Reducing risk

✓ Simple precautions can often be the most effective in reducing the risk. Always look for the risk and take steps to reduce it.

THINK RISK → ASSESS → REDUCE → AVOID

Employers do have duties under LOLER. They must ensure that all equipment provided for use at work is:

- sufficiently strong and stable for the particular use and marked to indicate safe working loads
- positioned and installed to minimise any risks
- used safely – i.e. the work is planned, organised and performed by competent people
- subject to ongoing thorough examination and, where appropriate, inspection by competent people.

In addition employers must ensure that:

- lifting operations are planned, supervised and carried out in a safe way by competent people
- equipment for lifting people is safe
- lifting equipment and accessories are thoroughly examined
- a report is submitted by a competent person following a thorough examination or inspection.

Lifting equipment designed for moving loads must be inspected at least annually, but any equipment designed for lifting and handling people – even if provided by employees – must be inspected at least every six months. A nominated competent person may draw up an examination scheme for this purpose.

Remember

Lifting and handling individuals is the single largest cause of injuries at work in health and care settings.

Manual lifting

There is almost no situation in which manual lifting and handling could be considered acceptable, but the views and rights of the child or young person being lifted must be taken into account and a balance achieved.

On the rare occasions when it is still absolutely necessary for manual lifting to be done, the employer has to make a risk assessment and put procedures in place to reduce the risk of injury to the employee. This could involve ensuring that sufficient staff are available to lift or handle someone safely, which can often mean that four people are needed.

Your employer should arrange for all staff to attend a moving and handling course. You must attend one each year, so that you are up to date with the safest possible practices.

If you do have to lift, what should you do?

Encourage all children and young people to help themselves. You would be surprised how much 'learned helplessness' exists: this can occur when childcare workers find it is easier to take over rather than encouraging the child or young person to do things for themselves. This may stop them making the effort to maintain their independence – in short, they learn how to become helpless.

Remember

Always use lifting and handling aids.
There is no such thing as a safe lift.

Use the aids which your employer is obliged to provide

It is also essential that the views of the child or young person being moved are taken into account. While you and your employer need to make sure that you and other staff are not put at risk by moving or lifting, it is also important that the child or young person needing assistance is not caused pain, distress or humiliation. Groups representing disabled people have pointed out that blanket policies excluding any lifting may infringe the human rights of an individual needing mobility assistance. For example, children and young people may, in effect, be confined to bed unnecessarily and against their will by a lack of lifting assistance. A High Court judgment (A & B vs East Sussex County Council, 2003) found in favour of two disabled women who had been denied access to lifting because the local authority had a blanket ban on lifting regardless of circumstances. Such a ban was deemed unlawful. It is likely that similar cases will be brought under the Human Rights Act 1998, which gives people protection against humiliating or degrading treatment.

The Disability Discrimination Act 1995 came fully into force in October 2004. It was introduced in several stages to take account of the time needed to meet its requirements, including time for service providers to consider making reasonable changes to their premises so that they could be accessed by disabled users.

Since October 1999, service providers have had to consider making reasonable adjustments to the way they deliver their services so that disabled people can use them. The new duties will apply to service providers where physical features make access to their services impossible or unreasonably difficult for disabled people.

Remember

Your employer has a statutory duty to install lifting equipment, but it is your responsibility to use the equipment that is provided.

Ethical issue

As a new member of staff at a residential facility for disabled children, you are told: 'Oh, we don't bother with the hoist. None of the children are very heavy. It's much better to just lift them yourself: that way they get to feel they are doing more for themselves because they can help a bit. Anyway, I don't think the hoist works any more.'

1 What would you do next?

2 If the hoist does not work, what would you do?

3 What could be the consequences of lifting incorrectly

  a to the staff?

  b to the children they are attempting to lift?

4 What training and safety procedures would you recommend?

Reflect

Are you confident that your own moving and handling skills are up to date? If not, what steps are you taking to improve them?

How to contribute to infection control

(KS 11)

The very nature of work in some childcare settings means that great care must be taken to control the spread of infection. This is particularly important if your work involves providing personal care to children, but any residential setting where even small numbers of children or young people live together is at risk of passing on infections.

There are various steps you can take to help prevent the spread of infection.

You do not know what viruses or bacteria may be present in any child or young person, so it is important that you take precautions when providing personal care for anyone. The precautions are called 'standard precautions' precisely because you need to take them with every child you provide personal care for.

Prevention of infection is everyone's responsibility, so you must ensure that colleagues follow the appropriate guidelines.

Wear gloves

When	Any occasion when you will have contact with body fluids (including body waste, blood, mucus, sputum, sweat or vomit), or when you have any contact with anyone with a rash, pressure sore, wound, bleeding or any broken skin. You must also wear gloves when you clear up spills of blood or body fluids or have to deal with soiled linen or dressings.
Why	Because gloves act as a protective barrier against infection.
How	See instructions below.

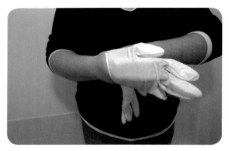

1 Check gloves before putting them on. Never use gloves with holes or tears. Check that they are not cracked or faded.

2 Pull gloves on, making sure that they fit properly. If you are wearing a gown, pull them over the cuffs.

3 Take them off by pulling from the cuff – this turns the glove inside out.

4 Pull off the second glove while still holding the first so that the two gloves are folded together inside out.

5 Dispose of them in the correct waste disposal container and wash your hands.

Wash your hands

When	Before and after carrying out any procedure which has involved contact with a child or young person, or with any body fluids, soiled linen or clinical waste. You must wash your hands even though you have worn gloves. You must also wash your hands before you start and after you finish your shift, before and after eating, after using the toilet and after coughing, sneezing or blowing your nose.
Why	Because hands are a major route to spreading infection. When tests have been carried out on people's hands, an enormous number of bacteria have been found.
How	Wash hands in running water, in a basin deep enough to hold the splashes and with either foot pedals or elbow bars rather than taps, because you can re-infect your hands from still water in a basin, or from touching taps with your hands once they have been washed. Use the soaps and disinfectants supplied. Make sure that you wash thoroughly, including between your fingers. This should take between 10 and 20 seconds. See instructions below.

1 Wet your hands thoroughly under warm running water and squirt liquid soap onto the palm of one hand.

2 Rub your hands together to make a lather.

3 Rub the palm of one hand along the back of the other and along the fingers. Then repeat with the other hand.

4 Rub in between each of your fingers on both hands and round your thumbs.

5 Rinse off the soap with clean water.

6 Dry hands thoroughly on a disposable towel.

Alcohol hand rub

Alcohol hand rubs can be useful when hands are **socially clean** and if you are not near a source of water. A small amount should be used and rubbed into the hands using the same technique as for washing with water. The hand rub should be rubbed in until the hands are completely dry.

Key term

Socially clean: Clean enough to be acceptable socially, but not 'clinically clean', i.e. you could not carry out any sort of clinical contact in this condition. For hands, it means you could shake hands with someone, but not operate on them! There are three levels of clean: socially clean, clean and sterile.

Wear protective clothing

When	You should always wear a gown or plastic apron for any procedure that involves bodily contact or is likely to deal with body waste or fluids. An apron is preferable, unless it is likely to be very messy, as gowns can be frightening for the children you are working with.
Why	Because it will reduce the spread of infection by preventing infection getting on your clothes and spreading to the next child you come into contact with.
How	The plastic apron should be disposable and thrown away at the end of each procedure. You should use a new apron for each child or young person you come into contact with.

Tie up hair

Why	Because if it hangs over your face, it is more likely to come into contact with the child or young person you are working with and could spread infection. It could also become entangled in equipment and cause a serious injury.

Clean equipment

Why	Because infection can spread from one child to another on instruments, linen and equipment just as easily as on hands or hair.
How	By washing large items like trolleys with antiseptic solution. Small instruments must be sterilised. Do not shake soiled linen or dump it on the floor. Keep it held away from you. Place linen in the proper bags or hampers for laundering.

Deal with waste

Why	Because it can then be processed correctly, and the risk to others working further along the line in the disposal process is reduced as far as possible.
How	By placing it in the proper bags. Make sure that you know the system in your workplace. It is usually: clinical waste – yellow soiled linen – red recyclable instruments and equipment – blue.

Take special precautions

When	There may be occasions when you have to deal with a child or young person who has a particular type of infection that requires special handling. This can involve things like hepatitis, some types of food poisoning or highly infectious diseases.
How	Your workplace will have special procedures to follow. They may include such measures as gowning, double gloving or wearing masks. Follow the procedures strictly. They are there for your benefit and for the benefit of the other individuals you care for.

Active knowledge HSC 32a pc 4

Make notes of three ways in which infection can be spread. Then note down three effective ways to reduce the possibility of cross-infection.

Reflect

Think about how well you challenge inappropriate practice. Do you always challenge – or do you sometimes leave it rather than face resistance or argument?

Challenging inappropriate practice

(KS 18)

You may have to deal with a situation where one of your colleagues is misusing equipment or behaving in an inappropriate way towards children and young people or other care workers – a way that fails to minimise risks to health, safety or security.

Depending on the severity of the problem, you should:

- challenge the behaviour, or the source of the bad practice
- have a one-to-one discussion with the colleague in question
- act as a mentor with whom your colleague can share problems and difficulties
- act as a role model of good practice.

How to maintain personal safety

(KS 3, 8, 10, 16, 17)

There is always an element of risk in working with children and young people. There is little doubt that there is an increase in the level of personal abuse suffered by workers in children's services. There is also the element of personal risk encountered by workers who visit families in the community, and have to deal with homes in poor states of repair and with an assortment of domestic animals.

However, there are some steps you can take to assist with your own safety.

Keys to good practice: Steps to personal safety

✓ If you work alone in the community, always leave details of where you are going and what time you expect to return. This is important in case of accidents or other emergencies, so that you can be found.

✓ Carry a personal alarm, and use it if necessary.

✓ Ask your employer to provide training in techniques to combat aggression and violence. It is foolish and potentially dangerous to go into risky situations without any training.

✓ Try to defuse potentially aggressive situations by being as calm as possible and by talking quietly and reasonably; if this is not effective, leave.

✓ If you work in a residential or hospital setting, raise the alarm if you find you are in a threatening situation.

✓ Do not tackle aggressors, whoever they are – raise the alarm.

✓ Use an alarm or panic button if you have it – otherwise yell, very loudly.

✓ You could discuss with your employer the possibility of drafting a written 'lone-working' policy that identifies steps to be taken to protect staff working alone.

Test yourself

1 Note down some safe techniques for moving and handling.

2 What steps would you take to encourage others to identify and report health and safety risks?

3 What are the most effective methods of infection control, and why are they effective?

4 What are the different ways of disposing of waste?

5 What are the steps involved in carrying out a risk assessment?

HSC 32c Minimise risks arising from incidents and emergencies

Working with children and young people is always unpredictable, and you could have to deal with any type of emergency. It is unlikely that you would ever have to be totally responsible in an emergency situation, but you may need to be the first to respond, or be the one to contact expert help; to do this effectively, you must have some basic knowledge about the emergencies which can arise and what you can usefully do to protect the children and young people as far as possible.

Fire safety

(KS 2, 3, 4, 15, 16, 17)

Your workplace will have procedures that must be followed in the case of an emergency. All workplaces must display information about what action to take in case of fire. The fire procedure is likely to be similar to the one shown on this page.

Remember

Don't be a hero! Never attempt to tackle a fire unless you are confident that you can do so safely, for example, when:

● you have already raised the alarm

● you have a clear, unobstructed route away from the fire in case it grows larger

● you have the correct type of extinguisher and are confident of your ability to operate it.

Fire Safety Procedure

1 Raise the alarm.

2 Inform the receptionist or dial 999.

3 Ensure that everyone is safe and out of the danger area.

4 If it is safe to do so, attack the fire with the correct extinguisher.

5 Go to the fire assembly point (this should be specified for the particular work setting).

6 Do not return to the building for any reason.

Your employer will have installed fire doors to comply with regulations – never prop them open.

Your employer must provide fire lectures each year. All staff must attend and make sure that they are up to date with the procedures to be followed.

The Fire Precautions (Workplace) (Amendment) Regulations 1999 require that all workplaces should be inspected by the fire authority to check means of escape, firefighting equipment and warnings, and that a fire certificate must be issued.

Which extinguisher?

There are specific fire extinguishers for fighting different types of fire. You do not have to memorise them as each one has clear instructions on it, but it is important that you are aware that there are different types and make sure that you read the instructions before use.

Extinguisher type and patch colour	Use for	Danger points	How to use	How it works
Red Water	Wood, cloth, paper, plastics, coal, etc. Fires involving solids.	Do **not** use on burning fat or oil, or on electrical appliances.	Point the jet at the base of the flames and keep it moving across the area of the fire. Ensure that all areas of the fire are out.	Mainly by cooling burning material.
Blue Multi-purpose dry powder	Wood, cloth, paper, plastics, coal, etc. Fires involving solids. Liquids such as grease, fats, oil, paint, petrol, etc. but **not** on chip or fat pan fires.	Safe on live electrical equipment, although the fire may re-ignite because this type of extinguisher does not cool the fire very well. Do **not** use on chip or fat pan fires.	Point the jet or discharge horn at the base of the flames and, with a rapid sweeping motion, drive the fire towards the far edge until all the flames are out.	Knocks down flames and, on burning solids, melts to form a skin smothering the fire. Provides some cooling effect.
Blue Standard dry powder	Liquids such as grease, fats, oil, paint, petrol, etc. but **not** on chip or fat pan fires.	Safe on live electrical equipment, although does not penetrate the spaces in equipment easily and the fire may re-ignite. This type of extinguisher does not cool the fire very well. Do **not** use on chip or fat pan fires.	Point the jet or discharge horn at the base of the flames and, with a rapid sweeping motion, drive the fire towards the far edge until all the flames are out.	Knocks down flames.

Extinguisher type and patch colour	Use for	Danger points	How to use	How it works
Cream AFFF (Aqueous film-forming foam) (multi-purpose)	Wood, cloth, paper, plastics, coal, etc. Fires involving solids. Liquids such as grease, fats, oil, paint, petrol, etc. but **not** on chip or fat pan fires.	Do **not** use on chip or fat pan fires.	For fires involving solids, point the jet at the base of the flames and keep it moving across the area of the fire. Ensure that all areas of the fire are out. For fires involving liquids, do not aim the jet straight into the liquid. Where the liquid on fire is in a container, point the jet at the inside edge of the container or on a nearby surface above the burning liquid. Allow the foam to build up and flow across the liquid.	Forms a fire-extinguishing film on the surface of a burning liquid. Has a cooling action with a wider extinguishing application than water on solid combustible materials.
Cream Foam	Limited number of liquid fires.	Do **not** use on chip or fat pan fires. Check manufacturer's instructions for suitability for use on other fires involving liquids.	Do not aim jet straight into the liquid. Where the liquid on fire is in a container, point the jet at the inside edge of the container or on a nearby surface above the burning liquid. Allow the foam to build up and flow across the liquid.	

Extinguisher type and patch colour	Use for	Danger points	How to use	How it works
Black Carbon dioxide CO_2	Liquids such as grease, fats, oil, paint, petrol, etc. but **not** on chip or fat pan fires.	Do **not** use on chip or fat pan fires. This type of extinguisher does not cool the fire very well. Fumes from CO_2 extinguishers can be harmful if used in confined spaces: ventilate the area as soon as the fire has been controlled.	Direct the discharge horn at the base of the flames and keep the jet moving across the area of the fire.	Vaporising liquid gas smothers the flames by displacing oxygen in the air.
Fire blanket	Fires involving both solids and liquids. Particularly good for small fires in clothing and for chip and fat pan fires, provided the blanket **completely** covers the fire.	If the blanket does not completely cover the fire, it will not be extinguished.	Place carefully over the fire. Keep your hands shielded from the fire. Take care not to waft the fire towards you.	Smothers the fire.

Evacuating buildings

In an extreme case it may be necessary to help evacuate buildings if there is a fire, or for other security reasons, such as:

- a bomb scare
- the building having become structurally unsafe
- an explosion
- a leak of dangerous chemicals or fumes.

The evacuation procedure you need to follow will be laid down by your workplace, with the same information whatever the emergency is: the same exits will be used and the same assembly point. It is likely to be along the following lines:

- Stay calm, do not shout or run.
- Do not allow children and young people to run.
- Organise people quickly and firmly without panic.
- Direct those who can move themselves and assist those who cannot.
- Use wheelchairs to move disabled children quickly.

Health emergencies

(KS 5, 7, 15, 16, 17)

You need to understand the actions you should take if a health emergency arises, such as a child becoming ill or being injured. The advice that follows is not a substitute for a first aid course, and will only give you an outline of the steps you need to take. Unless you have been on a first aid course, you should be careful about what you do, because the wrong action can cause more harm to the casualty. It may be better to summon help.

If any child or young person is injured or taken ill while you are caring for them, the parents or those with parental responsibility must be informed as soon as possible, unless there is a clear legal basis for not doing so.

What you can safely do

Most people have a useful role to play in a health emergency, even if it is not dealing directly with the ill or injured child. It is also vital that someone:

- summons help as quickly as possible
- offers assistance to the competent person who is dealing with the emergency
- clears the immediate environment and makes it safe – for example, if someone has fallen through a glass door, the glass must be removed as soon as possible before there are any more injuries
- informs the child or young person's parents/carers as soon as possible
- offers help and support to other people who have witnessed the illness or injury and may have been upset by it.

Active knowledge
HSC 31a KS 4c, HSC 32c pc 1 (environmental emergency)

1 Where are the main evacuation points in your workplace?

2 Which children and young people use each one?

3 Do any children or young people need assistance to reach evacuation points? If so, of what kind?

4 Who is responsible for checking your workplace is cleared in an emergency?

5 What are your personal responsibilities in an emergency situation?

Remember

Do not attempt something you are not sure of: you could do further damage to the ill or injured child and lay yourself and your employer open to being sued. Instead, summon help and wait for it to arrive.

How you can help the casualty in a health emergency

It is important that you are aware of the initial steps to take when dealing with the most common health emergencies. You may be involved with any of these emergencies when you are at work, whether in a residential, hospital or community setting.

If you are working in a hospital where skilled assistance is always immediately available, the likelihood of your having to act in an emergency, other than to summon help, is remote.

In a residential setting, help is more likely to be readily available, although it may not necessarily be the professional medical expertise of a hospital.

In the community, you may have to summon help and take action to support a casualty until the help arrives. It is in this setting that you are most likely to need some knowledge of how to respond to a health emergency.

This section gives a guide to recognising and taking initial action in a number of health emergencies:

- severe bleeding
- cardiac arrest
- shock
- loss of consciousness
- epileptic seizure
- choking and difficulty with breathing
- fractures and suspected fractures
- burns and scalds
- poisoning
- electrical injuries.

Severe bleeding

Severe bleeding can be the result of a fall or injury. The most common causes of severe cuts are glass – as the result of a fall into a window, or fighting using broken bottles – or knives from accidents in the kitchen.

Symptoms

There will be apparently large quantities of blood from the wound. In some very serious cases, the blood may be pumping out. Even small amounts of blood can be very frightening, both for you and the child. Remember that a small amount of blood goes a long way, and things may look worse than they are. However, severe bleeding requires urgent medical attention in hospital. Children can literally bleed to death and extensive bleeding can cause shock and loss of consciousness.

Aims

- To bring the bleeding under control
- To limit the possibility of infection
- To arrange urgent medical or paramedic attention.

Action for severe bleeding

1   You will need to apply pressure to a wound that is bleeding. If possible, use a sterile dressing; otherwise, use any absorbent material, or even your hand. Do not forget the precautions (see 'Protect yourself' below). You will need to apply direct pressure over the wound for 10 minutes (this can seem like a very long time) to allow the blood to clot.

2   If there is any object in the wound, such as a piece of glass, *do not* try to remove it. Simply apply pressure to the sides of the wound.

3   Lay the child down and raise the affected part if possible.

4   Make the child comfortable and secure.

5   Summon medical assistance.

Protect yourself

You should take steps to protect yourself when you are dealing with casualties who are bleeding. Your skin provides an excellent barrier to infections, but you must take care if you have any broken skin. Seek medical advice if blood comes into contact with your mouth, nose or gets into your eyes. Blood-borne viruses (such as HIV or hepatitis) can be passed on only if the blood of someone who is already infected comes into contact with broken skin or gets into your system.

- If possible, wear disposable gloves.

- If this is not possible, cover any areas of broken skin with a waterproof dressing.
- If possible, wash your hands thoroughly in soap and water before and after treatment.
- Take care with any needles or broken glass in the area.
- Use a mask for mouth-to-mouth resuscitation if the child's nose or mouth is bleeding.

Cardiac arrest

Cardiac arrest occurs when a person's heart stops. Cardiac arrest can happen for various reasons, the most common of which is a heart attack, but a person's heart can also stop as a result of shock, electric shock, a convulsion or other illness or injury.

Symptoms
- No pulse
- No breathing.

Aims
- To obtain medical or paramedic help as a matter of urgency
- It is important to give oxygen, using mouth-to-mouth resuscitation, and to stimulate the heart, using chest compressions. This procedure is called cardiopulmonary resuscitation – CPR. You will need to attend a first aid course to learn how to resuscitate – you cannot learn how to do this from a book. On the first aid course you will be able to practise on a special dummy.

Action for cardiac arrest

1   Check whether the child or young person has a pulse and whether he or she is breathing.

2   If not, call for urgent help from a qualified medical practitioner or the emergency services.

3   Start age-appropriate methods of resuscitation if you have been taught how. There are different approaches to cardiopulmonary resuscitation (CPR) for babies under one year, young people up to puberty and adults.

4   Keep up resuscitation until help arrives.

Shock

Shock occurs because blood is not being pumped around the body efficiently. This can be the result of loss of body fluids through bleeding, burns, severe vomiting or diarrhoea, or of a sudden drop in blood pressure or a heart attack.

Symptoms

The signs of shock are easily recognised. The child or young person:

- will look very pale, almost grey
- will be very sweaty, and the skin will be cold and clammy
- will have a very fast pulse
- may feel sick and may vomit
- may be breathing very quickly.

Aims

- To obtain medical help as a matter of urgency
- To improve blood supply to heart, lungs and brain.

Action for shock

1   Summon expert emergency medical, nursing or paramedic assistance.

2   Lay the child or young person down on the floor. Try to raise the feet off the ground to help the blood supply to the important organs.

3   Loosen any tight clothing.

4   Watch the child carefully. Check the pulse and breathing regularly.

5   Keep them warm and comfortable, but *do not* warm with direct heat, such as a hot water bottle.

Do not:

- allow the child to eat or drink
- leave the child alone, unless it is essential to do so briefly in order to summon help.

Loss of consciousness

Loss of consciousness can happen for many reasons, from a straightforward faint to unconsciousness following a serious injury or illness.

Symptom

A reduced level of response and awareness: this can range from being vague and 'woozy' to total unconsciousness.

Aims

- To summon expert medical or paramedic help as a matter of urgency
- To keep the airway open
- To note any information which may help to find the cause of the unconsciousness.

Action for loss of consciousness

1   Make sure that the child or young person is breathing and has a clear airway.

2   Maintain the airway by lifting the chin and tilting the head backwards.

3   Look for any obvious reasons why the child or young person may be unconscious, such as a wound or an ID band telling you of any condition he or she may have. For example, many children who have medical conditions that may cause unconsciousness, such as epilepsy or diabetes, wear special bracelets or necklaces giving information about their condition.

4   Place the child in the recovery position (see page 81), *but not if you suspect a back or neck injury*, until expert medical or nursing help or the emergency services arrive.

Do not:

- attempt to give anything by mouth
- attempt to make the child sit or stand
- leave the child alone, unless it is essential to do so briefly in order to summon help.

The recovery position

Many of the actions you need to take to deal with health emergencies will involve you placing someone in the recovery position. In this position a child has the best chance of keeping a clear airway, not inhaling vomit and remaining as safe as possible until help arrives. This position should not be attempted if you think someone has back or neck injuries, and it may not be possible if there are fractures of limbs. These instructions **do not** apply to babies under one year – if you need to place a baby in the recovery position, you should cradle the child in your arms with the head tilted downwards so they cannot choke or inhale vomit.

1   Kneel at one side of the child, at about waist level.

2   Tilt back the child's head – this opens the airway. With the child on his/her back, make sure that limbs are straight.

3   Bend the child's near arm as in a wave (so it is at right angles to the body). Pull the arm on the far side over the chest and place the back of the hand against the opposite cheek (**a** in the diagram below).

4   Use your other hand to roll the child towards you by pulling on the far leg, just above the knee (**b** in the diagram). The child should now be on his or her side.

5   Once the child is rolled over, bend the leg at right angles to the body. Make sure the head is tilted well back to keep the airway open (**c** in the diagram).

Epileptic seizure

Epilepsy is a medical condition that causes disturbances in the brain resulting in sufferers becoming unconscious and having involuntary contractions of their muscles, which produces the fit or seizure. Children and young people who have epilepsy do not have any control over their seizures, and may do themselves harm by falling when they have a seizure.

Aims
- To ensure that the child or young person is safe and does not injure himself or herself during the fit
- To offer any help needed following the fit.

Action for epileptic seizure

1   Try to make sure that the area in which the child or young person has fallen is safe.

2   Loosen all clothing.

3   Once the seizure has ended, make sure that the child or young person has a clear airway and place in the recovery position.

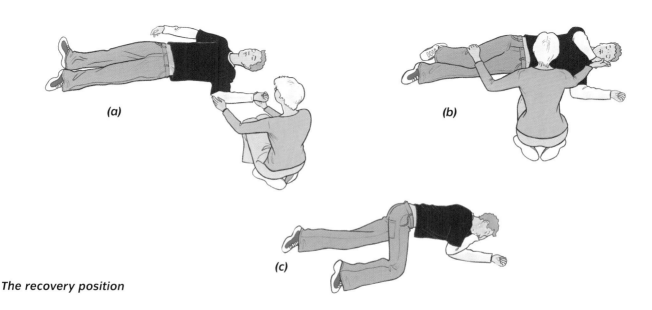

(a)

(b)

(c)

The recovery position

4 Make sure that the child or young person is comfortable and safe. Particularly try to prevent head injury.

5 Call an ambulance unless you are familiar with the child or young person's condition and deal with his or her seizures regularly.

Do not:

- attempt to hold the child down, or put anything in the mouth
- move the child until he or she is fully conscious, unless there is a risk of injury in the place where he or she has fallen.

Choking and difficulty with breathing (in adults and children over 8 years)

This is caused by something (usually a piece of food) stuck at the back of the throat. It is a situation that must be dealt with, as people can quickly stop breathing if the obstruction is not removed.

Symptoms

- Red, congested face at first, later turning grey
- Unable to speak or breathe, may gasp and indicate throat or neck.

Aims

- To remove obstruction as quickly as possible
- To summon medical or paramedic assistance as a matter of urgency if the obstruction cannot be removed

Action for choking

1 Ensure any non-fixed braces, dentures or loose tooth crowns are removed. Sweep the mouth with one gloved finger to clear any food, vomit or anything else from the mouth.

2 Try to get the child to cough. If that is not immediately effective, move on to step 3.

3 Bend the child forwards. Slap sharply on the back between the shoulder blades up to five times (**a** in the diagram above right).

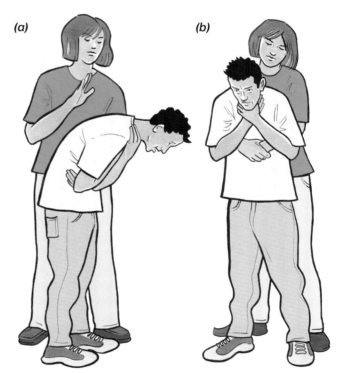

(a)   *(b)*

Dealing with a child or young person who is choking

4 If this fails, use the Heimlich manoeuvre *if you have been trained to do so*:

i) Stand behind the child or young person with your arms around him/her. Join your hands just below the breastbone. One hand should be in a fist and the other holding it (**b** in the diagram).

ii) Sharply pull your joined hands upwards and into the child or young person's body at the same time. The force should expel the obstruction.

iii) Alternate backslaps and abdominal thrusts until you clear the obstruction.

Fractures and suspected fractures

Fractures are breaks or cracks in bones, usually caused by a fall or other type of injury. The casualty will need to go to a hospital as soon as possible to have a fracture diagnosed correctly.

Symptoms

- Acute pain around the site of the injury
- Swelling and discoloration around the affected area
- Limbs or joints may be in odd positions
- Broken bones may protrude through the skin.

Action for fractures

1   The important thing is to support the affected part. Help the child to find the most comfortable position.

2   Support the injured limb in that position with as much padding as necessary – towels, cushions or clothing will do.

3   Take the child or young person to hospital or call an ambulance.

Do not:

- try to bandage or splint the injury
- allow the casualty to have anything to eat or drink.

Burns and scalds

There are several different types of burn: the most usual are caused by heat or flame, while scalds are caused by hot liquids. Children and young people can also be burned by chemicals or by electrical currents.

Symptoms

- Depending on the type and severity of the burn, skin may be red, swollen and tender, blistered and raw or charred
- Usually severe pain and possibly shock.

Aims

- To obtain immediate medical assistance if the burn is over a large area (as big as the child's hand or more) or is deep – remember, it is the size of the child's hand, not yours
- To send for an ambulance if the burn is severe or extensive. If the burn or scald is over a smaller area, the child could be transported to hospital by car
- To stop the burning and reduce pain
- To minimise the possibility of infection.

Action for burns and scalds

1   For major burns, summon immediate medical assistance.

2   Cool the burn down. Keep it flooded with cold water for 10 minutes or, for a chemical burn, for 20 minutes. Ensure that the contaminated water used to cool a chemical burn is disposed of safely.

3   Remove any jewellery, watches or clothing not sticking to the burn.

4   If possible, cover the burn, unless it is a facial burn, with a sterile or at least clean non-adhesive dressing. For a burn on a hand or foot, a clean plastic bag will protect it from infection until an expert can treat it.

If clothing is on fire, remember the basics: *stop, drop, wrap* and *roll* the child or young person on the ground.

Do not:

- remove anything which is stuck to a burn
- touch a burn, or use any ointment or cream
- cover facial burns – keep pouring water on until help arrives.

Remember

If a child or young person's clothing is on fire, STOP – DROP – WRAP – ROLL:

- Stop him or her from running around.
- Get him/her to drop to the ground – push him/her if you have to and can do so safely.
- Wrap him/her in something to smother the flames – a blanket or coat, anything to hand. This is better if it is soaked in water.
- Roll him/her on the ground to put out the flames.

Poisoning

Children and young people can be poisoned by many substances, drugs, plants, chemicals, fumes or alcohol.

Symptoms

Symptoms will vary depending on the poison.

- The child or young person could be unconscious
- There may be acute abdominal pain
- There may be blistering of the mouth and lips.

Aims

- To remove the child to a safe area if he/she is at risk, and it is safe for you to move him/her
- To summon medical assistance as a matter of urgency
- To gather any information which will identify the poison
- To maintain a clear airway and breathing until help arrives.

Action for poisoning

1 If the child is unconscious, place him/her in the recovery position (see page 81) to ensure that the airway is clear, and that he/she cannot choke on any vomit.

2 Dial 999 for an ambulance.

3 Try to find out what the poison is and how much has been taken. This information could be vital in saving a life.

4 If a conscious child has burned mouth or lips, he or she can be given small frequent sips of water or cold milk.

Do not

- try to make the child vomit.

Active knowledge   HSC 32ca pc 1–6 (health emergency)

Provide proof that you have a good basic understanding of what to do in health emergencies.

Electrical injuries

Electrocution occurs when an electrical current passes though the body.

Symptoms

- Electrocution can cause cardiac arrest and burns where the electrical current enters and leaves the body.

Aims

- To remove the child from the current when you can safely do so
- To obtain medical assistance as a matter of urgency
- To maintain a clear airway and breathing until help arrives
- To treat any burns.

Action for electrical injuries

There are different procedures to follow depending on whether the injury has been caused by a high or low voltage current.

Injury caused by high voltage current

This type of injury may be caused by overhead power cables or rail lines, for example.

1 Contact the emergency services immediately.

2 *Do not* touch the child or young person until all electricity has been cut off.

3 If he or she is unconscious, clear the airway.

4 Treat any other injuries present, such as burns.

5 Place in the recovery position (see page 81) until help arrives.

Injury caused by low voltage current

This type of injury may be caused by electric kettles, computers, drills, lawnmowers, hairdryers, etc.

1 Break the contact with the current by switching off the electricity, at the mains if possible.

Move the casualty away from the current

2   It is vital to break the contact as soon as possible, but if you touch a person who is 'live' (still in contact with the current) you too will be injured. If you are unable to switch off the electricity, then you must stand on something dry which can insulate you, such as a telephone directory, rubber mat or a pile of newspapers, and then move the child away from the current as described below.

3   Do not use anything made of metal, or anything wet, to move the child from the current. Try to move him/her with a wooden pole or broom-handle, even a wooden chair.

4   Alternatively, drag him/her with a rope or cord or, as a last resort, pull by holding any of the child's dry clothing *not* in contact with his/her body.

5   Once the child is no longer in contact with the current, you should follow the same steps as with a high voltage injury.

Other ways to help

Summon assistance

In the majority of cases this will mean telephoning 999 and requesting an ambulance. It will depend on the setting in which you work and clearly is not required if you work in a hospital! But it may mean calling for a colleague with medical qualifications, who will then be able to make an assessment of the need for further assistance. Similarly, if you work in the residential sector, there may be a medically qualified colleague available. If you are the first on the scene at an emergency in the community, you may need to summon an ambulance for urgent assistance.

If you need to call an ambulance, try to keep calm. Do not attempt to give information until it is asked for – this wastes time. Emergency service operators are trained to find out the necessary information, so let them ask the questions, then answer calmly and clearly.

Follow the action steps outlined in the previous section while you are waiting for help to arrive.

Assist the person dealing with the emergency

A second pair of hands is invaluable when dealing with an emergency. If you are assisting someone with first aid or medical expertise, follow all his or her instructions, even if you don't understand why. An emergency situation is not the time for a discussion or debate – that can happen later. You may be needed to help to move a casualty, or to fetch water, blankets or dressings, or to reassure and comfort the child or young person during treatment.

Make the area safe

An accident or injury may have occurred in an unsafe area (it was probably for precisely that reason that the accident occurred there) and may have made the area unsafe for others. For example, if someone has tripped over an electric flex, there may be exposed wires. Alternatively, a fall against a window may have left shards of broken glass, or there may be blood or other body fluids on the floor. You may need to make the area safe by turning off the power, clearing broken glass or dealing with a spillage.

It may be necessary to redirect people away from the area of the accident in order to avoid further casualties.

Maintain the privacy of the casualty

You may need to act to provide some privacy for the casualty by asking onlookers to move away or stand back. If you can erect a temporary screen with coats or blankets, this may help to offer some privacy. It may not matter to the casualty at the time, but he or she has a right to privacy if possible.

Make accurate reports

You may be responsible for making a report on an emergency situation you have witnessed, or for filling in records later. Concentrate on the most important aspects of the incident and record the actions of yourself and others in an accurate, legible and complete manner.

How to deal with witnesses' distress – and your own

Children and young people who have witnessed accidents, especially accidents causing injury to other children, can often be very distressed by what they have seen. The distress may be as a result of the nature of the injury, or the blood loss. It could be because the child is a friend or relative or simply because seeing accidents is traumatic. Some people can become upset because they do not know how to assist, or they may have been afraid and feel guilty later.

You may need to reassure children and young people about the injured child and the fact that he or she is being cared for appropriately. However, do not give false reassurance about things you may not be sure of.

You may need to allow children to talk about what they saw. One of the most common effects of witnessing a trauma is that people need to repeat over and over again what they saw.

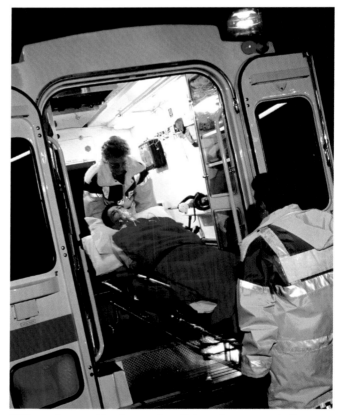

Witnessing accidents can be distressing, especially when they involve children or young people

What about you?

You may feel very distressed by the experience you have gone through. You may find that you need to talk about what has happened, and that you need to look again at the role you played. You may feel that you could have done more, or be angry with yourself for not having a greater knowledge about what to do.

There is a whole range of emotions you may experience; Unit HSC 34 covers in detail the different emotions that may arise in similarly difficult circumstances involving abuse, and describes ways to cope with such feelings. You should be able to discuss them with your supervisor and use any support provided by your employer.

If you have followed the basic guidelines in this element, you will have done as much as could be expected of anyone at the scene of an emergency who is not a trained first aider.

Test yourself

1   In which conditions would it be safe for you to attempt to tackle a fire?

2   In what situations should you attempt first aid?

3   What is the single most important thing for an untrained person to do in a health emergency?

4   List three tasks you can carry out at the scene of a health emergency which do not necessarily involve first aid.

5   How would you talk to an ill or injured child or young person while you waited for help?

6   How would you support others who had witnessed an incident or accident?

HSC 32 UNIT TEST

1   What kind of substances would you expect to see in the COSHH file in your workplace?

2   Which tasks would you expect to find in the risk assessment file?

3   Is any specialised equipment in use in your workplace? If so, what sort of equipment? What basic precautions would you expect to follow when using it?

4   Describe your workplace rules about staff dress. What are the reasons for these rules?

5   What health and safety training would you expect staff in your workplace to undertake?

6   List at least three security precautions taken in your workplace.

Don't forget to refer to the evidence opportunities grid (see pages 357–375) for more ideas for suitable evidence for your NVQ.

Unit HSC 33

Reflect on and develop your practice

The knowledge and skills addressed in this unit are the key to working effectively in all aspects of your practice. In order to work effectively, it is essential to know how to evaluate your work and improve on what you do, and to understand the factors that have influenced your attitudes and beliefs.

The children's services sector is constantly benefiting from new research, developments, policies and guidelines. You need to make sure that you are up to date with work practices and knowledge, and aware of current thinking. It is the right of children, young people and their families to expect the best possible quality of care from those who provide it, and high-quality care requires all practitioners to regularly reflect on their own practice and look at ways of improving.

Each organisation and each individual owes a duty of care to children and young people: this means that it is your responsibility to make sure that the service provided is the best it can possibly be. This is not an option, but a duty, which you accept when you choose to become a professional childcare worker. The information in this unit will help you to identify the best ways to develop and update your own knowledge and skills.

This unit makes a major contribution to all five of the outcomes for children, because it is aimed at improving the practice of all those working with children and young people. Similarly, the skills and knowledge contained in this unit are a vital part of being able to develop all the skills and knowledge necessary across all the areas of the Common Core.

In this unit you will find 'Active knowledge' features containing activities that will contribute to assessment for your NVQ. Remember that these features only offer the opportunity for partial assessment; you can also refer to the evidence opportunities grid (see pages 357–375) for more ideas to provide suitable evidence for your NVQ.

What you need to learn

- Knowing your role
- How to explore your own values, interests and beliefs
- How your values, interests and beliefs influence your practice
- Reflective practice
- Support networks
- Learning from work practice
- Making good use of training/development opportunities
- Developing your own personal effectiveness
- Understanding new information
- How to ensure your practice is current and up to date
- Preparing a development plan

HSC 33a Reflect on your practice

Knowing your role

(KS 1, 3, 6)

The changes and developments in how children's services are delivered across the whole of the UK have resulted in slightly different models in each country, but generally, there is now a focus on delivering integrated services and on making the *outcomes* for the child (the *end result*s) the centre of the way you work, rather than the *service* (*how* you work with the child or young person).

In England and Wales, the Green Paper *Every Child Matters* and the following Children Act 2004 had two main impacts: the integration of education and children's social services; and major changes in processes such as assessment and information sharing. This ensured that all children's practitioners would work together in the best interests of the child. All work with children now has to contribute towards ensuring that these five outcomes for the child or young person are improved:

- Be healthy
- Stay safe
- Enjoy and achieve
- Make a positive contribution
- Achieve economic well-being.

The Isle of Man, which is not part of the UK, has adopted the same outcomes, with the exception of the final one, which is replaced by 'Prosper' (which may well be a clearer description).

The vision for children and young people in Scotland is that they should be valued by ensuring that they are:

- Safe: Children and young people should be protected from abuse, neglect and harm by others at home, at school and in the community.
- Nurtured: Children and young people should live within a supportive family setting, with additional assistance if required, or, where this is not possible, within another caring setting, ensuring a positive and rewarding childhood experience.

- Healthy: Children and young people should enjoy the highest attainable standards of physical and mental health, with access to suitable healthcare and support for safe and healthy lifestyle choices.
- Achieving: Children and young people should have access to positive learning environments and opportunities to develop their skills, confidence and self-esteem to the fullest potential.
- Active: Children and young people should be active, with opportunities and encouragement to participate in play and recreation, including sport.
- Respected and responsible: Children, young people and their carers should be involved in decisions that affect them, should have their voices heard and should be encouraged to play an active and responsible role in their communities.

All children's practitioners work together in the best interests of the child

In Northern Ireland, the vision of the ten-year strategy is that children and young people will be:

- Healthy
- Enjoying, learning and achieving
- Living in safety and with stability
- Experiencing economic and environmental well-being
- Contributing positively to community and society
- Living in a society which respects their rights.

The child at the centre

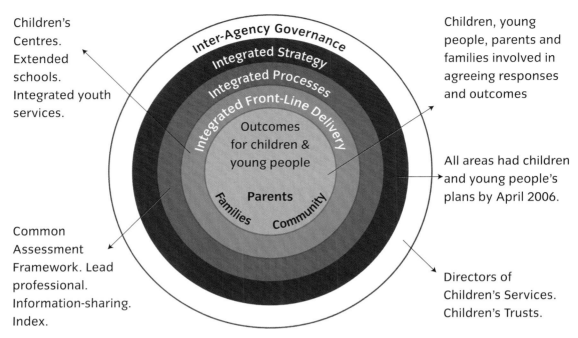

Children's Centres. Extended schools. Integrated youth services.

Common Assessment Framework. Lead professional. Information-sharing. Index.

Children, young people, parents and families involved in agreeing responses and outcomes

All areas had children and young people's plans by April 2006.

Directors of Children's Services. Children's Trusts.

This diagram, which is used to show how children's services work in England, is similar but not identical in other countries. However, significantly, it shows how the children and their families are at the centre, while all the necessary components for delivery surround them

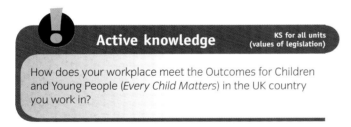

Active knowledge
KS for all units (values of legislation)

How does your workplace meet the Outcomes for Children and Young People (*Every Child Matters*) in the UK country you work in?

Common skills and knowledge

Whatever your job, whether you work in residential care, in a special school, a children's hospice, as a foster carer or supporting children and families in the community, you need to consider how the work you do has an impact on achieving important outcomes for children and young people. Your skills in working with colleagues and in putting children first are key areas of expertise you will need to develop.

As part of changing children's services in England, a Common Core of skills and knowledge has been identified. Although this is England-based, the knowledge and skills identified are valuable wherever you work. This covers the basic requirements for anyone who works with children, in whatever capacity, whether as a classroom assistant, a residential care worker, a clinical psychologist, social worker, GP, school nurse, health visitor, family support worker, nursery nurse, childminder or foster carer. Even those volunteering to run the local sports team, Brownies or playgroup need to be sufficiently competent in all areas of the Common Core in order to do their job.

Looking at the six Common Core areas of skills and knowledge is a good starting point for thinking about your own practice and identifying where you need to increase your knowledge or develop your skills:

Area	Skills	Knowledge
Effective communication and engagement	• Listen, empathise • Summarise, explain • Consult and negotiate	• How communication works • Confidentiality and ethics • Sources of support • Importance of respect
Child and young person development	• Observation and judgement • Empathy and understanding	• Understand context • Understand how babies, children and young people develop • Be clear about your own job role • Know how to reflect and improve
Safeguarding and promoting the welfare of the child	• Relate, recognise and take considered action • Communication, recording and reporting • Personal skills	• Legal and procedural frameworks • Wider context of services • Self knowledge
Supporting transitions	• Identify transitions • Provide support	• How children and young people respond to change • When and how to intervene
Multi-agency working	• Communication and teamwork • Assertiveness	• Your role and remit • Know how to make queries • Procedures and working methods • The law, policies and procedures
Sharing information	• Information handling • Clear communication • Engagement	• Importance of information sharing • Role and responsibilities • Awareness of complexities • Awareness of laws and legislation

Common Core areas of skills and knowledge

 My story

Hi, I'm Sandra and I'm the support worker for Laura. I first started to work with Laura when she was 5 and first started school. It's been wonderful to see her grow and develop. She always was determined, happy and confident even when she was little. Her family are great too. I know there have been times when her mum, Debbie, has really struggled to cope, not with Laura, but with all the bureaucracy and conflicting advice from everyone who was involved. She would come to pick Laura up and often be almost in tears because Social Services had organised something, but it needed information from the hospital before it could go ahead, or the hospital said they were waiting for Social Services – or whatever. *Every Child Matters* has meant that the team of people working with Laura now have to work together, and there is just one person who organises everything. I was a bit daunted when Debbie asked me to do it – I'm just a support worker, and I think the social worker had just assumed it should be her. Anyway, after lots of discussion at the review meeting, Debbie was really insistent and the hospital consultant backed her up and it was decided that I would be the Lead Professional for Laura. This means that I am the person Debbie comes to for anything to do with Laura. I arrange appointments, meetings and reviews, and make sure that things happen in the right order. I follow up and check that the whole team, including Laura and Debbie, are up to speed with what's happening. I thought it would be hard, but it's OK, and the Head has given me some extra time to do it properly. They're talking about letting the Lead Professionals hold the budgets for the child – then we could really start doing some interesting things!

My story

Hi, I'm Laura and I'm 15. I have spina bifida and hydracephalus. I live at home and go to a special school. There's been lots of stuff around about all the changes in services, but I've not really seen all that much, because I've known most of the people who help me for years. I have noticed, though, that I get to say a lot more about what happens and how stuff gets done. People seem to listen more to what I'm saying. Mum says it's much better now, because there's just one person who kind of organises everything, instead of her having to chase up loads of different people. We got to say who was going to be the main person – they're called a Lead Professional. We asked for my support worker – Sandra – to do it, because she knows us really well. So now Sandra does all the organising of meetings and passing on information to everyone else like the doctor, the consultant, the physiotherapist and the mobility guy, and Mum just contacts her if she wants to know anything. It seems to work better... to be honest, I'd much rather tell you about the holiday that I'm going on with my mates from school. Sandra helped to organise all that too.

Regardless of the country you work in, these areas of skills and knowledge will give you a good reference point for your practice, and will help you to focus your plans for your personal and professional development.

How to explore your own values, interests and beliefs

(KS 1, 3, 6, 7, 11)

Before you can think about how you will improve and develop your practice, you need to understand the influences on the way you work, and whether or not any of your own values and beliefs are having an impact on how you interact with children, young people and their families.

Everyone has his or her own values, beliefs and preferences. What you believe in, what you see as important and what you see as acceptable or desirable are as much a part of your personality as whether you are shy, outgoing, funny, serious, friendly or reserved.

The way in which you respond to others is linked to what you believe in, what you consider important and the things that interest you. You may find you react positively to people who share your values and less warmly to those who have different priorities.

Choosing your friends and meeting with others who share your interests is one of life's joys and pleasures; however, the professional relationships you develop with the children, young people and families you

work with are another matter. As a childcare professional you are required to provide the same quality of care for all children, not just for those whom you like. This may seem obvious, but knowing what you need to do and achieving it successfully are not the same thing.

If you allow your own preferences to dominate your work you may fail to perform to the standards of the General Social Care Council's Code of Practice for Social Care Workers or the Codes of Practice of the Scottish Social Care Council, Care Council for Wales or Northern Ireland Social Care, which apply to all those who work in Children's Social Care. The Council codes require that workers must respect and promote the individual views and wishes of service users, which means children, young people and families. But how do you manage to make the right responses when there is a clash between your views and those of the people you are working with? The first step may be to identify and understand your own views and values.

Your friendships reflect your own values, interests and beliefs

Being aware of the factors that have influenced the development of your personality is not as easy as it sounds. You may feel you know yourself very well, but knowing *who* you are is not the same as understanding how your beliefs are influencing your reactions – understanding *how* you got to be you.

Unravelling these influences is never easy, and you are not being asked to carry out an in-depth analysis of yourself – simply to begin to realise how your development has been influenced by a series of factors. Be honest with yourself and look at the potential ways these influences could affect the way you think about the children, young people and families you work with. Knowing what may happen makes you more alert to making sure it doesn't.

Reflect

Step 1

Take a range of items from a newspaper, about six or seven. Make a note of your views on each of them: say what your feelings are on each one – does it shock or disgust you, make you sad, or angry, or grateful that it hasn't happened to you?

Step 2

Try to think about why you reacted in the way you did to each of the items in the newspaper. Think about what may have influenced you. The answers are likely to lie in a complex range of factors, including your upbringing and background, experiences you had as a child and as an adult, and relationships you have shared with others.

Factors which influence our development

Everyone's values and beliefs are affected to different degrees by the same range of factors. (See the diagram below.)

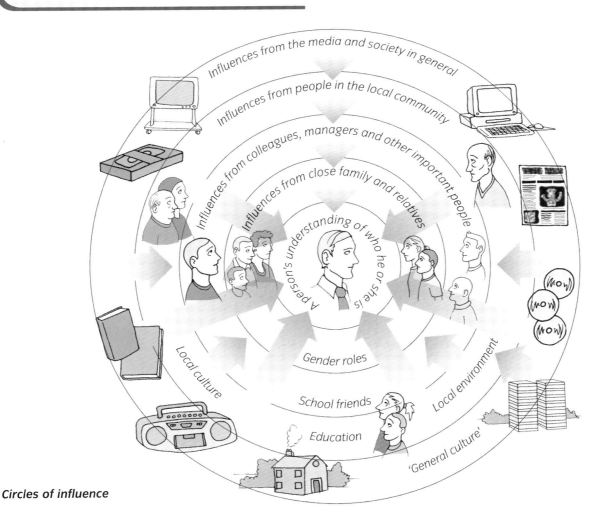

Circles of influence

Each of us will be influenced to a greater or lesser degree by these layers of influence. The extent of the influences will be different for each person. It is therefore important that you have considered and reflected on the influences on your development so that you understand how you became the person you are.

Reflect

Look at the circles in the diagram on the previous page. Try to think about the factors in each of the circles that have influenced your own development, and the values and beliefs that you now hold. Note down at least three from each circle. Now see if you can answer the following questions: Which factors have had the strongest effect in making you who you are? Which factors continue to influence you? Try to imagine how you might have been different if you had lived in a different family or in a different community. Can you imagine how different life experiences create different belief systems? Can you see why it is vitally important not to make assumptions about what is right and wrong in different people's lives?

Key influences on development

The table on page 95 shows some of the key factors associated with differences between people – the factors that can result in different people having different values.

You should be able to begin to trace some of the influences from your past environment on the development of your own attitudes and values.

We are strongly influenced by our contact with other people, but different people live very different lives and mix with communities that have very different beliefs. People have different cultures, family values, religions, social class backgrounds, and so on. Men often grow up with very different expectations and experiences of life from women. Older people are likely to have had different life experiences from those of younger people. The diagram below shows some of the factors that influence our personal beliefs.

Some of the ideas and influences that help form our beliefs

Age	People may be classified as being children, teenagers, young adults, middle-aged or old. Discrimination can creep into our thinking if we see some age groups as being 'the best', or if we make assumptions about the abilities of different age groups.
Gender	In the past, men often had more rights and were seen as more important than women. Assumptions about gender such as what is women's or men's work can still result in mistakes and discrimination.
Race	People understand themselves in terms of ethnic categories such as being black or white, as European, African or Asian. Many people have specific national identities such as Polish, Nigerian, English or Welsh. Assumptions about racial characteristics and beliefs, or thinking that some groups are superior to others, result in discrimination.
Class	People differ in their upbringing, the kind of work they do and the money they earn. People also differ in lifestyle and the views and values that go with different levels of income and spending habits. People may discriminate against others because their class or lifestyle is different.
Religion	People grow up in different traditions of religion. For some people, spiritual beliefs are at the centre of their understanding of life. For others, religion influences the cultural traditions that they celebrate; for example, many Europeans celebrate Christmas even though they might not see themselves as practising Christians. Discrimination can take place when people assume that their customs or beliefs should apply to everyone else.
Sexuality	Many people see their sexual orientation as very important to understanding who they are. Gay and lesbian relationships are often discriminated against. People sometimes judge other relationships as 'wrong' or abnormal.
Ability	People may make assumptions about what is 'normal'. People with physical disabilities or learning difficulties may become labelled, stereotyped and discriminated against as damaged versions of 'normal' people.
Relationships	People choose many different lifestyles and emotional commitments, such as marriage, having children, living in a large family, living a single lifestyle but having sexual partners, or being single and not being sexually active. People live within different family and friendship groups. Discrimination can happen if people start to judge that one lifestyle is 'right' or best.
Politics	People can develop different views as to how a government should act, how welfare provision should be organised and so on. Disagreement and debate are necessary; but it is important not to judge people as bad or stupid because their views are different from ours.

Some of the ways in which people are different from each other

Problems arise because our own culture and life experience may lead us to make assumptions as to what is right or normal. When we meet people who are different it can be easy to see them as 'not right' or 'not normal'. Different people see the world in different ways.

Our culture may lead us to think that some habits are more 'normal' than others, but in a multicultural, multi-faith society such as the UK it is more difficult to define what 'normal' is. What is normal for one person is not for another. For instance, taking off your shoes when entering a holy place is normal for many people, but would be an unusual experience for others. Having a whole extended family sharing a house is normal in some cultures and definitely not in others. Normality can only ever be 'your normal' –

Reflect

Think about the following scenario, first used by Vic Finkelstein in 1991. Does it make you think differently? Discuss it with colleagues – how should you change the way you work?

Several thousand disabled people have all gathered together in their own village. Everything in the village is designed for wheelchair users. One thing the wheelchair architects quickly discovered was that there was no need to have ceilings at 8ft 6ins or door heights at 6ft 6ins. These heights could be lowered considerably.

A few able-bodied people came to live in the village. Soon all were suffering from dark bruises on their heads and acute backache. Soon, a number of reports were produced by social workers, doctors and so on and eventually a number of aids were produced to help the able-bodied. These included toughened helmets to wear at all times to guard against the knocks from the low ceilings and doorframes. The able-bodied were also given special braces that gave support whilst they moved around bent double.

These people were unable to find employment.

One who tried to get a job as a television interviewer was told that the village society would find the helmet wearing distressing and unacceptable.

Charities were organised and the logo was a figure bent double, staring at the ground, carrying a collection box.

One day the able-bodied people got together and said that if the buildings in the village were adapted by raising door and ceiling heights, then their problems would be solved. However, after much discussion, the villagers decided that this was unreasonable, as it would cause great expense and disruption. They were very sympathetic to the problems of the able-bodied, but felt that such extreme demands simply showed that able-bodied people were unable to accept the limitations of their condition.

there is no such thing as a 'normal for everyone'. The idea of normality has to be within a particular set of circumstances.

How your values, interests and beliefs influence your practice

(KS 2, 11)

Once you have begun to identify the major factors that have influenced your development, the next stage is to look at how they have affected the way in which you work and relate, both to service users and colleagues. This is the basis of developing into a 'reflective practitioner' – someone who evaluates and thinks about what he or she does.

Working in childcare requires that, in order to be effective and to provide the best possible service for the children and young people you work with, you can think about and evaluate what you do and the way you work, and identify your strengths and weaknesses. Reflection and evaluation should not undermine your confidence in your own work; rather you should use them in a constructive way to identify areas that require improvement.

The ability to do this is an indication of mature and thoughtful practice. Any workers in childcare who believe that they have no need to improve their practice or to develop and add to their skills and understanding are not demonstrating good and competent practice, but rather an arrogant and potentially dangerous lack of understanding of the nature of work in the childcare sector.

A useful tool in learning to become a reflective practitioner is to develop a checklist which you can use, either after you have dealt with a difficult situation or at the end of each shift or day's work, to look at your own performance. There is an example checklist on the next page.

Is it ethical for you to go ahead with some work, even though you know that you are not very good at it?

For example: you work for a small, charitable organisation that runs activity programmes for young people at risk of exclusion. The manager in your local area has gone on maternity leave, and the organisation really cannot afford to employ someone on a short-term contract. You are asked to 'act up' and manage the six programmes currently running in your area. You know that you are not good at management, you do not have organisational skills, are not very assertive and the manager has to do some tough negotiating with the local authority. If you don't do it, the organisation will have to spend money it can't afford to employ someone, but if you do, you are likely to make a mess of it and not deliver what the organisation needs. What do you do?

Checklist to evaluate practice

1   How did I approach my work?

2   Was my approach positive?

3   How did the way I worked affect the children and/or young people?

4   How did the way I worked affect my colleagues?

5   Did I give my work 100 per cent?

6   Which was the best aspect of the work I did?

7   Which was the worst aspect of the work I did?

8   Was this work the best I could do?

9   Are there any areas in which I could improve?

10 What are they, and how will I tackle them?

Reflective practice

(KS 11)

What is reflection and what do you need to be able to do in order to improve your practice? Reflection involves thinking things over; you could visualise reflection as reflecting ideas inside the mind like light bouncing between mirrors. Reflection involves complex mental processing that discovers new ideas or new ways of looking at events. Reflection helps us to realise new ideas and make new sense of practice issues.

Imagine that every morning a young person who lives in a children's home comes to breakfast and complains. The complaints might be about anything: sinks that don't drain quickly enough, someone's nicked his T-shirt, the food, going to school, etc. Naturally this behaviour is annoying for everyone else having breakfast. It is not significantly different from the grumbles of all the young people – it's just that he does it every morning, and never seems to be able to start an ordinary conversation, which all the others do (most of the time). But why does this young person only ever complain?

Reflecting on the situation might enable you to come up with some answers. But reflection can involve different levels of thinking.

Reflective practice involves thinking things over

Just noticing what happens

Perhaps the interaction with this young person always follows a pattern. He will wait for a short period and then launch into a verbal outburst about what is wrong, completely unresponsive to the reactions of others. Having completed the outburst, he looks for a reaction and then storms off.

Just noticing these details is a good start to the reflective process. It would be so easy to label him as 'difficult' or 'challenging', and then use this label as if it were an explanation – no further thinking required. Noticing and thinking about the detail of what happens may help to avoid labelling this young man.

Reflection in order to make sense of a situation

What does the young person's pattern of behaviour mean? Perhaps this confrontational exchange represents a release of tension. Perhaps he does not have the emotional skills to engage in more sociable conversations. Perhaps he is trying to create a sense of belonging within the home, and he uses confrontation because it is the only way he knows to communicate.

This may be completely wrong – reflection may not always give you the correct answer, but trying to make sense of a situation helps you to be open to new ideas.

Going deeper – trying to understand feelings

What does the young person feel like when he comes to complain? He may feel a little isolated – a little insecure. Perhaps he is thinking, 'If I don't feel good, then someone else is to blame.' Perhaps these emotions become focused on trivia such as what's for breakfast or who has his T-shirt.

Thinking about feelings might help to generate extra ideas about what could be happening.

Going deeper – reflecting on wider issues

Thinking about the problems that young people experience might reflect on the significance of these feelings. There are people who always search for other people to blame whenever anything is perceived to be less than perfect – many young people have grown up in a 'victim culture' where there is always someone to blame. This is convenient because if it is someone else's fault, you don't have to take responsibility. But maybe we all tend to do this! Maybe we feel that 'they' should do something about climate change, about house prices, or about holes in the road. Perhaps we all like to retreat into a childlike state, expecting a kind parent to make the world comfortable and perfect for us.

Reflection that takes a wide view can involve new thoughts that could, for example, help us to understand ourselves better. Perhaps the difference between the young person's behaviour in the example above and our own behaviour is simply that we are more skilled at knowing how, when and where it is safe to 'have a moan'.

Reflection that results in new ways of thinking

How far do we take responsibility for our own emotions? If you were a person who assumed your emotions were all caused by outside events, it could be a major shock to find that your own thinking can directly influence your feelings. Many of the assumptions we make about life are hard to change. Abandoning the belief that someone else should make your life better and deciding that you are responsible for your life could represent a huge, and perhaps frightening, shift in thinking.

Reflection on your own assumptions is not something that can happen overnight. This kind of reflection involves an extreme shift in thinking that can change people's lives.

How deeply does your own reflective thinking need to go? You may not want to dramatically change the way you think; you may be comfortable with who you are and how you think. The important thing is that you recognise the values, beliefs and assumptions that influence your behaviour and responses, and that you use reflection to identify areas of practice that need to be developed and improved.

Learning

When you have identified skills you would like to improve, the next step is to set about learning them. One of the best-known theories about the way in which people learn is the Lewin/Kolb cycle of experiential learning.

Basically, this cycle means the following.

Something happens to you or you do something; it can be an unusual event or something you do every day (**concrete experience**).

You think about it (**reflective observation**).

You work out some general rules about it, or you realise that it fits into a theory or pattern you already know about (**abstract conceptualisation**).

Next time the same situation occurs, you apply your rules or theories (**active experimentation**).

This will make your experience different from the first time, so you will have different factors to think about and different things to learn – so the cycle continues. You never stop learning.

For example, you decide that having an evening with board games would be really good for the young people in a small group home. You tell everyone at

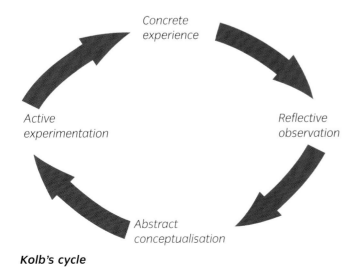

Kolb's cycle

breakfast; no one looks very enthusiastic, but one or two young people make polite comments. In the evening, everyone makes an excuse and goes out.

Within Kolb's learning cycle you have had a concrete experience.

Stage 1

Stage 1 of the learning cycle is the experience that the young people have rejected your idea of a games evening. But why have they reacted in this way?

Stage 2

Stage 2 involves thinking through some possible reasons for the reaction. Perhaps they don't like board games. Perhaps they don't like you deciding what they will do with their evening. Perhaps they think that board games are childish. Perhaps they have no experience of playing board games. Perhaps they all really did have other plans.

Stage 3

Kolb's third stage involves trying to make sense of your reflections. What do you know about different cultural responses to being organised? Is it possible that your announcement about the evening's activity has been taken as an attempt to impose your views? Is it possible that the young people felt that their image was at risk – that board games were not 'cool'? You need to try to find an explanation that uses the knowledge you have about young people's behaviour.

Stage 4

Kolb's fourth stage involves 'experimenting', or checking out your ideas and explanations. You could try asking if people would like to do stuff together one evening. Or you could ask people if they have any favourite games.

You may have to go round this 'learning cycle' a number of times before you can understand and interpret the needs of a group of young people.

How quickly can you work through these four stages? Would you be able to think through these issues while working with the young people, or would you need to go away and reflect on your practice? The answer to this question might depend on the amount of experience you have had in similar situations.

An evening playing board games: is it a great bonding opportunity – or a damp squib?

What is your learning style?

Everyone learns in a different way. Honey and Mumford (1982) developed a theory based on this idea of a four-stage process of learning from experience. They theorised that some people develop a preference for a particular part of the learning cycle. Some people enjoy the activity of meeting new people and having new experiences, but these 'activists' may not get so much pleasure from reflecting, theorising and finding answers to individual needs. Some people mainly enjoy sitting down and thinking things through: these are 'reflectors'. Some people enjoy analysing issues in terms of established theoretical principles: these are 'theorists'. Finally, some people prefer trying out new ideas in practice: these are 'pragmatists'.

Reflect

Think about the ways in which you learn new things. Do you tend to use one part of the learning cycle more than others? Does that cause any problems? Are there some areas of learning you miss out on because of it? Think about ways in which you could develop your skills in other parts of the cycle.

Honey and Mumford have argued that the ideal way to approach practical learning is to balance all the components of the learning cycle. Some people can achieve this more holistic approach. For other people it might be important to recognise their own biases and try to compensate for an over-reliance on one style.

You can test your own learning style preference or obtain further details of tests based on this theory at www.peterhoney.com.

One approach is to adopt this four-stage model of learning from experience and to actively monitor personal problem solving at work. For example, you might make records about an issue and records of practical action taken in an attempt to meet service user needs or to solve other practical problems.

The 'four-stage' or 'cycle' theory of learning from experience is just one model of learning. This model may be useful in practice, especially as a way of approaching complicated, non-routine problem

Reflect

Keep a reflective diary for a week; note down your feelings about the events and look back on how you handled them, and what you could do to improve.

At the end of each working day, spend a few moments writing down one or two key issues that concerned you or irritated you – or even that you did well! How did you respond to these issues? How could you learn from this experience to take your own practice forward?

Examples might include noticing a trailing lead from someone's headphones, failing to move it, then tripping over the lead yourself and spilling something! The result might be that you had to spend much more time cleaning up your spill than it would have taken to move the headphones in the first place. Or perhaps there was a difficult interaction with a family you don't get along with very easily – perhaps nothing significant, but a niggling feeling that you could have done better.

At the end of the week, see if there are issues that crop up regularly. It may be helpful to ask your manager to check it over: sometimes an objective viewer can notice more than you can. If you identify repeated issues – for example, a problem in dealing with confrontation, or difficulties because your IT skills are not good – then look with your manager at what you can do to improve.

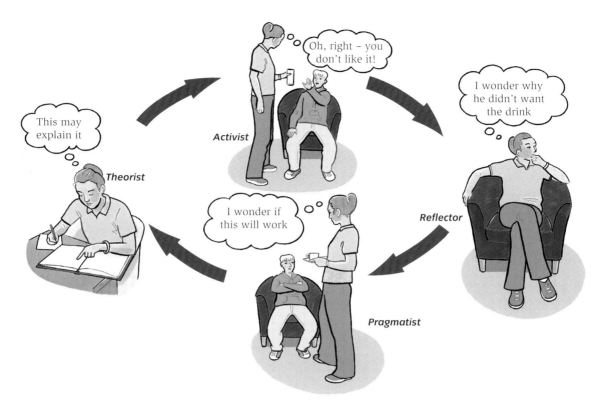

The 'four-stage' or 'cycle' theory of learning from experience

solving. There are many other ways in which care workers might undertake personal development.

Which of these stages do you enjoy most, or do you enjoy each of these stages equally?

You can see how reflecting is closely connected with learning: you do something, then you reflect on it and learn from it, so that the next time you perform the same task you will be able to do it better and more effectively.

Different ways of learning

Formal training and development are not the only ways you can learn and expand your knowledge and understanding. There are plenty of other ways to keep up progress towards the goals you have set yourself.

Not everyone learns best from formal training. Other ways people learn are from:

- being shown by more experienced colleagues – this is known as 'sitting next to Nellie'!
- working and discussing issues as a team or group
- reading textbooks, journals and articles

- following up information on the internet
- making use of local library facilities or learning resource centres
- asking questions and holding professional discussions with colleagues and managers.

Active knowledge

HSC 33 KS 6 (part)

Write down the different ways of learning that you have experienced. Have you, for example, studied a course at college, completed a distance-learning programme or attended hands-on training sessions? Tick the ways of learning that have been the most enjoyable and most successful for you.

Here is a checklist of ways of learning that you might find useful:

- watching other people
- asking questions and listening to the answers
- finding things out for yourself
- going to college and attending training courses
- studying a distance-learning course or a course on the internet.

How could you use this information about how you like to learn to update your workplace skills?

Support networks

(KS 4, 5, 8, 9)

Undertaking reflection alone is very difficult, so it is important to make use of your manager to get feedback. Support networks, whether formal or informal, are one of the most effective means of identifying areas of your own practice that need development. They will also help you to deal with any dilemmas or conflicts that you have identified.

Formal networks

These are usually put in place by your employer, and include your immediate line manager and possibly other more senior members of staff. You are likely to have a regular system of feedback and support meetings, or appraisal sessions with your line manager. These could be at differing intervals, and organised on a local or regional basis. Taking part will give you the chance to meet with colleagues working with other organisations and to share ideas, issues and good practice.

Informal networks

Informal support networks develop among work colleagues. These can be major sources of support and assistance. Working in a team means being concerned for your colleagues and offering support where you can. Part of the effectiveness of many teams is their ability to provide useful ideas for improving practice, and support when things go badly.

Some staff teams provide a completely informal and ad-hoc support system, where people give you advice, guidance and support as and when necessary. Other teams will organise this on a more regular basis, and they may get together to discuss specific situations or problems that have arisen for members of the team. You need to be sure that you are making maximum use of all opportunities to gain support, advice and feedback on your practice.

Getting the most out of supervision

Supervision is a long-established, vital part of working in childcare. The opportunity to receive feedback on your practice is a key part of your personal and professional development. Your line manager, or professional lead, if you are working in an integrated team, should be fully aware of the work you have been doing. He or she should be able to identify difficult situations and look at ways to work effectively with particular children, young people or families where you may be struggling, as well as identifying areas of practice which you may need to improve and areas in which you have demonstrated strengths and ability.

Make sure that you are well prepared for sessions with your line manager so that you can get maximum benefit from them. This will mean bringing together your reflections on your practice, using examples and case notes where appropriate. You will need to demonstrate that you have reflected on your practice and that you have begun identifying areas for development. If you can provide evidence through case notes and records to support this, it will assist your line manager greatly.

Informal networks can be major sources of support and assistance

You will also need to be prepared to receive feedback. While feedback is likely to be given in a positive way, this does not mean that it will be uncritical. Many people have difficulty accepting criticism in any form, even where it is intended to be supportive and constructive. If you are aware that you are likely to have difficulty accepting criticism, try to prepare yourself to view feedback as valuable and useful information that can add to your ability to reflect effectively on the work you are doing.

Your response to negative feedback should not be to defend your actions or to reject the feedback. You must try to accept and value it. A useful reply would be: 'Thank you, that's very helpful. I can use that next time to improve.' If you are able to achieve this, you are likely to make the maximum use of opportunities to improve your practice.

On the other hand, if criticism of any kind undermines your confidence and makes it difficult for you to value your own strengths, you should ask your line manager to identify areas in which you did well, and use the positive feedback to help you respond more constructively to the negative feedback. You should receive supervision at least monthly.

Line manager's role

Your line manager's role is to support and advise you in your work and to make sure that you know and understand:

- your rights and responsibilities as an employee
- what your job involves and the procedures your employer has in place to help you carry out your job properly

- the philosophy of care where you work – that is, the beliefs, values and attitudes of your employer regarding the way that children and young people are cared for – and how you can demonstrate values of care in the way you do your work
- your career development needs – the education and training requirements for the job roles you may progress into, as well as for your current job.

Mentoring

Some employers (and some courses) will provide you with a mentor. This is usually, but not necessarily, someone from your own workplace. The role of a mentor is not quite the same as a line manager; mentoring is about supporting and encouraging you as you learn and develop. Mentors will advise you about the best ways to develop your thinking or the most effective ways to extend your experience or make best use of a newly acquired skill. A mentor will not supervise your work, but will help you with your personal and professional development, and will be there to give you advice and to help you to move ahead with how you think about your work and your learning.

Appraisal

Appraisal and supervision are different: while supervision focuses on your professional practice, appraisal is about all aspects of your performance as a professional. Many different appraisal systems are in use, but they are broadly similar. Appraisal may be undertaken by your line manager, who may not be your professional manager if you are in an integrated team, or your organisation may have specific managers who undertake appraisals throughout the organisation. Appraisals usually take place annually, and you are likely to be given a document in advance in order to prepare for it. Each workplace will have its own documents, but the checklist below may help you to review your performance and be ready to participate in an appraisal meeting.

During your appraisal, you will have the opportunity to review your performance over the period since your last appraisal. You will look at the goals you set last time and whether or not you have achieved them. If not, you will look at why not, and if they should be changed. If you have achieved the goals, you will be

able to discuss what your professional goals will be for the next period. This could include specific training or achieving qualifications or changing your job role.

Training and development sessions

One of the other formal and organised ways of reflecting on your own practice and identifying strengths, weaknesses and areas for development is during training opportunities. On a course, or at a training day, aspects of your practice and areas of knowledge that are new to you will be discussed, and this will often open up avenues that you had not previously considered. You should take every opportunity to go on training days or courses. Sometimes it may be hard to fit everything in when you are really busy at work, but if you can possibly make the time, you can really benefit.

General

1 What do you enjoy about your work?

2 Do you feel you are valued in your working environment? Why?

3 Is there anything about your work that is worrying/ concerning you? What?

4 What do you think you do well?

5 What do you think needs improving? How?

6 How do you think you have contributed to the organisation in the past year?

7 How has the organisation contributed to your development?

8 What is your goal for the next year?

Checklist to help review your performance

Active knowledge

Identify the formal and informal support networks in your workplace. Think about the ways in which you use the different types of network and how they support your development. Do you think you could make more use of networks than you currently do? Speak to your line manager if you have problems identifying networks in your workplace.

Test yourself

1 List at least three factors that can influence the way you work.

2 What is the key difference between working in childcare and working in most other jobs?

3 Describe some of the different learning styles that people may use. Explain how each would be appropriate for different types of skills.

4 Describe the advantages that learning to be a thoughtful and reflective practitioner brings a) to the care worker, and b) to the individuals he or she cares for.

HSC 33b Take action to enhance your practice

Learning from work practice

(KS 2, 5, 8, 9, 10)

Everything you do at work is part of a process of learning. Even with regular tasks there is always something new each time you do them. A simple task like making a child a sandwich may result in a lesson – if, for example, the child tells you she would prefer ham today, even though she has only ever wanted cheese in the past – you will have learned a lesson about never making assumptions that everything will always be the same.

Of course, you also learn from more serious events: dealing with a situation where a child discloses to you about previous abuse, or where you support a child and their family through a serious illness, or work with a young person to deal with bullying – all of these will provide you with huge opportunities to learn. What matters is that you make the most of the opportunities. Whenever you are dealing with a new situation, make sure that you ask questions of more experienced and senior colleagues about why things are being done in a particular way. Try to find the time to research the area of practice and always try to link theoretical knowledge to real situations.

Learning from working is also about making good use of the skills and experience of your colleagues and line manager. Not only does this mean they will be able to pass on knowledge and advice to you, but you have the perfect opportunity to discuss ideas and talk about day-to-day practice in the service you are delivering.

Finding time to discuss work with colleagues is never easy; everyone is busy and you may feel that you should not make demands on their time. You may be in a position where you have to prioritise your time to provide supervision for others, and your manager has to prioritise time for your supervision.

Most supervision will take place at scheduled times but you may also be able to discuss issues in the

Talking about day-to-day practice with your colleagues is an ideal way to learn

course of handover meetings or team meetings and other day-to-day activities. Use supervision time or quiet periods to discuss situations which have arisen, problems you have come across or new approaches that other colleagues are using.

Active knowledge

You have already begun the process of keeping a reflective diary. Build on this to enhance your practice. Plan a feedback session with your line manager. You may have straightforward questions, or more complicated issues, such as 'How did you make the decision that it was safe enough for James to go out to the shops by himself, when there are obvious risks?'

Try discussing such issues with different experienced colleagues – you may be surprised at what you learn.

Using your mistakes

Everyone makes mistakes – they are one way of learning. It is important not to waste your mistakes, so if something has gone wrong, make sure you learn from it. Discuss problems and mistakes with your line manager, and work out how to do things differently next time. It is important to reflect on both success and failure and you can use reflective skills in order to learn from situations that have not worked out the way you had planned.

In some jobs the results of mistakes may be a file in the wrong place, or a crop of beans which doesn't grow, a letter which is not delivered or a till which doesn't balance. Other jobs carry a far greater responsibility when things go wrong: for example, air traffic controllers, surgeons, pilots – and people who work with children and young people. Real children and young people are on the receiving end of our mistakes in childcare, so learning how not to do it again is vital.

Using your successes

It is just as important to reflect on why something worked, so that you can repeat it. Don't simply pat yourself on the back! Explore why your work went well. Use your supervision time and opportunities to talk with experienced colleagues.

Organisations need to learn too – learning from near misses

Looking at practice and learning from it is not only important to the individual practitioner – organisational learning is also vital. 'Near misses' is a term used to describe situations where something could have gone wrong but didn't, or something did go wrong, but no serious harm was caused. The important result is that learning is gained from it.

This may be learning about your own practice and performance, but it could also be learning for the organisation about any systems and processes that need to be improved: organisational learning is an essential part of reducing the risks to children and young people.

The importance of this type of review is that it is carried out by colleagues, which is why it is called a 'peer review'. It is not about the quality of the work of individuals, but it is about looking at what went wrong and how the systems and processes of the organisation allowed that to happen. It is also a key component in the development of a 'no blame' culture, where staff are confident in identifying and reporting areas of concern without feeling that this will be viewed as an individual failing.

Each organisation will have its own way of organising peer reviews, but they are likely to cover the following questions.

- What happened?
- How did it affect the child/family?
- How did it affect the team/organisation?
- Could it have been avoided and, if so, how?
- How might it be stopped from happening again?
- What learning or development needs has this highlighted?

Making good use of training/development opportunities

(KS 4, 7, 8, 9, 11)

Personal development is to do with developing the personal qualities and skills that everyone needs in order to live and work with others, such as understanding, empathy, patience, communication and relationship building. It is also to do with the development of self-confidence, self-esteem and self-respect.

If you look back over the past five years, you are likely to find that you have changed in quite a few ways. Most people change as they mature and gain more life experience. Important experiences such as changing jobs, moving home, illness or bereavement can change people. It is inevitable that your personal development and your professional development are linked – your personality and the way you relate to others are the major tools you use to do your job. Taking advantage of every opportunity to train and develop your working skills will also have an impact on you as a person.

Professional development is to do with developing the qualities and skills that are necessary for the workplace. Examples are teamwork, the ability to communicate with different types of people, time management, organisation, problem solving, decision making and, of course, the skills specific to the job.

Continuous professional development involves regularly updating the skills and knowledge you need for work. You can achieve this by attending training sessions both on and off the job, and, when you are given training opportunities, by making the most of them with careful planning and preparation.

Key terms

Personal development: Developing the personal qualities and skills needed to live and work with others.

Professional development: Developing the qualities and skills necessary for the workforce.

Legal requirements for training

National Minimum Standards now lay down the number of trained and qualified staff which all residential establishments, including residential schools, for children must have, and they are periodically inspected by the inspectors for each country within the UK.

Acts of Parliament have resulted in the establishment of clear sets of standards for inspectors to use. These include standards relating to staff training and personal and professional development. All staff are required to undertake induction and foundation training when they first start working in childcare. There is also a requirement in England and Wales that at least 80 per cent of staff working with children must be qualified to, or working towards, at least NVQ level 3. The standards also require that staff receive supervision and are given a Personal Development Plan for ongoing training. Paid training days must be provided, and an annual appraisal must take place. There is also an age requirement: any staff with sole responsibility for children must be at least 21, and all staff must be at least four years older than the oldest child in the establishment.

In Scotland, all staff with management responsibility must hold an L4 qualification and a management qualification, line managers must hold an L4 and all residential childcare workers must hold at least an SVQ L3 qualification along with an academic qualification such as an HNC.

The National Minimum Standards

The National Minimum Standards (NMS) are the minimum standards a service is expected to provide to meet an individual's needs. They are published by the Secretary of State under section 23(1) of the Care Standards Act 2000. They are service specific – in other words, there are particular sections about caring for young people, caring for older people, caring in the home, and so on. It is important that you know the standards relevant to the service you provide. Copies of the NMS appropriate to your service should be available at your workplace, and can also be found on the Ofsted website at www.ofsted.gov.uk and on the Department of Health website at www.doh.gov.uk/ncsc.

Many different types of training opportunities will be open to you

How to get the best out of training

Your line manager will work with you to decide on the types of training that will benefit you most. This will depend on the stage you have reached with your skills and experience. There would be little point, for example, in doing a course in advanced micro-surgery techniques if you were at the stage of having just achieved your First Aid certificate! It may be that not all the training you want to do is appropriate for the work you are currently assigned to – you may think that a course in advanced therapeutic activities sounds fascinating, but your line manager may suggest that a course in basic moving and handling is what you need right now. There will be opportunities for training throughout your career. You will only get the best out of training and development opportunities if they are the right ones for you at the time.

How to use training and development

You should work with your line manager to prepare for any training you receive, and to review it afterwards. You may want to prepare for a training session by:

- reading any materials which have been provided in advance
- talking to your line manager, or a colleague who has attended similar training, about what to expect
- thinking about what you want to achieve as a result of attending the training.

Reflect

Think about the last training or development session you took part in.

Did you make adequate preparations beforehand so that you could benefit fully from it?

What and how did you contribute, and what did you learn? Do you have a set of notes?

How did you follow up the session? Did you review the goals you had set yourself, or discuss the session with your line manager?

Think about how/if you have used what you learned at the session. For example, how has the way you work changed, and how have your service users and colleagues benefited from your learning?

Developing your own personal effectiveness

(KS 1, 4, 5, 6, 8, 9, 11)

The children's sector constantly changes and moves on. The focus on integrated delivery of services for children and young people, and the importance of all the work we do supporting the achievement of improved outcomes for children, has been one of the largest and most significant changes ever. In order to work effectively in this way, you will need to be sure that you are working in a team with other colleagues, and that all your work is focused on the child or young person and the path towards achieving the outcomes for them.

Keys to good practice: Training

Make the most of training by:

✓ preparing well

✓ taking full part in the training and asking questions about anything you don't understand

✓ collecting any handouts and keeping your own notes of the training.

Think about how to apply what you have learned to your work by discussing the training with your line manager later. Review the ways in which you have benefited from the training.

Many of the old ways of working have now moved on, and the benefits to children and families of integrated working are enormous. Families are now able to engage with support for their child and have just one point of contact; the team of professionals providing support will work together and there will be a lead professional co-ordinating the work.

Legislation and the resulting changes have, sadly, come from enquiries into appalling tragedies, where lessons have been learned and major changes and improvements have resulted.

Despite all this, much of what we do in the children's sector will remain the same: the basic principles of protecting, safeguarding, treating children and young people with respect, ensuring they are empowered, that they reach their full potential and, most importantly, caring, will continue.

Being aware of new developments

There are many ways in which you can ensure that you keep up to date with new developments in the children's sector. You should not assume that your workplace will automatically inform you about new developments, changes and updates – you must be prepared to actively maintain your own knowledge base and ensure that your practice is in line with current thinking and new theories. The best way to do this is to incorporate an awareness of the need to constantly update your knowledge into all of your work activities. If you restrict yourself to specific times, such as a monthly visit to the library, or a training course every six months, you are likely to miss out on a lot of information.

Sources of information

The media

The area of childcare is always in the news, so it is relatively easy to find out information about new studies and research. You will need to pay attention when watching television and listening to radio news bulletins to find out about new developments, legislation, guidelines and reports relating to children and young people and the childcare workforce.

Active knowledge

For one week keep a record of every item relating to children and young people which you hear on the radio, see on television or read in a newspaper. You may be surprised at the large number of references you manage to find.

Reports and reviews

You can read the findings of enquiries into the failures experienced within children's services, and this might provide you with a focus for reflection. In the past there have been many cases where children have been neglected or abused and there has been a professional failure to protect them adequately. While you may not be involved in policy-making decisions with respect to these services, there may be many principles such as **whistle blowing** that are relevant in your own work setting. Many past serious failings might have been prevented if people had been able to identify the issues and take action earlier.

It will also be important to reflect on positive practice. The inspectorates in each of the countries of the UK, on their websites and in some of the documents designed for the public, include brief anecdotes and case studies that help to explain the positive role of standards and inspection in improving the quality of care and education for children and young people.

Conferences

Professional journals also carry advertisements for conferences and training opportunities. You may also find such information in your workplace. There is often a cost involved, so the restrictions of the training budget in your workplace may mean that you cannot attend. However, it may be possible for one person to attend and pass on the information gained to others in the workplace, or to obtain conference papers and handouts without attending.

The internet

The development of information technology, and in particular the internet, has provided a vast resource of information, views and research.

The internet provides a vast amount of information

There are clearly some limitations to using the internet: for example, some people are not confident about using computers. However, the use of computers in the children's sector is becoming increasingly widespread and important. If you have access to a computer, using the internet is a simple process that you could easily learn.

Another 'health warning' is to be wary of the information you obtain on the internet, unless it is from **accredited** sources such as a government department, a reputable university or college, or an established research centre. Make every effort to check the validity of what you are reading. The world wide web provides free access to vast amounts of information, but it is an unregulated environment – anyone can publish information, and there is no requirement for it to be checked or approved. People can publish their own views and opinions, which may not be based on fact. Be careful that you do not assume anything to be factually correct unless it is from a reliable source.

Treated with care, the internet can prove to be one of the speediest and most useful tools in obtaining up-to-date information.

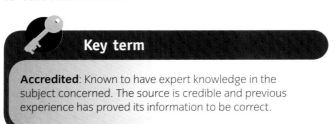

Key term

Accredited: Known to have expert knowledge in the subject concerned. The source is credible and previous experience has proved its information to be correct.

Your line manager and colleagues

One of the sources of information that may be most useful to you is close at hand – your own line manager and colleagues. They may have many years of experience and accumulated knowledge, which they will be happy to share with you. They may also be updating their own practice and ideas, and have information that they would be willing to share.

Understanding new information

(KS 6, 11)

Reading and hearing about new studies and research is all very well, but you must also understand what it is that you are reading. It is important that you know how new theories are developed and how research is carried out. Research can have a big impact for children and young people – think about the results of the controversy over the MMR vaccine, or the changes made to the school curriculum following research into literacy levels.

Research can influence government policy at local, regional and national levels. It also influences professional practice by providing the basis and justification for action. Good practice should always be based on evidence. This approach, now developing in social care and social work, has been the basis of health care practice for many years and practice has changed as a result of research. For example, there are sometimes controversies over new drugs because they will only be prescribed to groups of patients for whom research evidence has shown that they work. It is precisely because the results of research provide the evidence to change practice, that you should know how it is conducted and how the results are tested.

Reliability and validity

There are specific methods of carrying out research to ensure the results are both **reliable** and **valid**. If research is reliable, it is trustworthy – it can be depended on and gives solid facts; if research is valid, it has been properly carried out and properly interpreted – anyone looking at the research would draw the same conclusions. Research is judged on both of these factors, and you need to be able to satisfy yourself that the reports you read are based on reliable and valid research.

Key terms

Reliability: A piece of research shows *reliability* when the results would be repeated if someone else were to carry out the same piece of research in exactly the same way, so the research can be depended on and trusted.

Validity: A piece of research shows *validity* when the conclusions drawn from it are consistent with the results, consistent with the way in which the research was carried out and consistent with the way in which the information has been interpreted.

The research process

You will need to understand some of the basic terms used when discussing research in any field.

Primary research refers to information or data obtained directly from the research carried out, not from books or previously published work.

Secondary research refers to information obtained from books, previously published research and reports, CD-ROMs, the internet, etc. – any information obtained from work carried out by others. For example, if you were asked to write an assignment, you are most likely to find the information from secondary sources such as textbooks or the internet, rather than carry out a research project yourself in order to establish the information you need.

The result obtained from research is referred to as **data**, regardless of whether it is in numbers or words. It does not become 'information' until you do something with it to set it into context, compare it with other data, explain why it is important, or explain what it means – then it becomes 'information' rather than just 'raw data'.

There are two broad approaches to research – **quantitative** and **qualitative** research – and they

determine both the way in which the research is carried out and the type of results that are obtained.

Quantitative research

This approach has developed from the way in which scientists carry out laboratory experiments. The method produces statistical and numerical information. It provides hard facts and figures, and uses statistics and numbers to draw conclusions and make an analysis.

Many researchers in the field of health and care use quantitative approaches and produce quantitative data. They may carry out 'experiments' using many of the rules of scientific investigation. In general, if you are reading research that provides statistics and numerical information and is based purely on facts, it is likely to have used a quantitative approach.

Many government publications are good examples of quantitative research – they give statistics in relation to the National Health Service, for example, such as the numbers of patients on waiting lists, or the numbers of children being looked after throughout the country.

Qualitative research

A qualitative approach looks at the 'quality' rather than the 'quantity' of something. It would be used to investigate the feelings of people who have remained on the waiting list for treatment, or children and young people's attitudes towards being in care, or the relationships between those in care and those who work with them. Generally, qualitative data is produced in words rather than figures and will consist of descriptions and information about people's lives, experiences and attitudes.

Active knowledge

HSC 33 KS 6, 10

By using any of the methods for finding up-to-date information, such as newspapers, journals, reports, television, the internet or textbooks, find two pieces of research carried out within the past two years. One should be quantitative and one qualitative. Read the results of both pieces of research and make a note of the differences in the type of information provided.

> ## Keys to good practice: Applying new skills and knowledge in practice
>
> ✓ Plan out how you will adapt your practice on a day-to-day basis, adding one new aspect each day. Do this until you have covered all the aspects of the new information you have learned.
>
> ✓ Discuss with your line manager and colleagues what you have learned and how you intend to change your practice, and ask for feedback.
>
> ✓ Write a checklist for yourself and check it at the end of each day.
>
> ✓ Give yourself a set period of time, for example, one month, to alter or improve your practice, and review it at the end of that time.
>
> ✓ New knowledge is not only about the most exciting emerging theories. It is also often about mundane and day-to-day aspects of your practice, which are just as important and can make just as much difference to the quality of care you provide for your service users. It is also about taking your practice forward by developing your knowledge across a range of situations.

How to ensure your practice is current and up to date

(KS 11)

There is little point in reading articles, watching TV programmes and attending training days if your work practice is not updated and improved as a result. It is often difficult to find time to keep up to date and to change the practices you are used to; and any form of change takes time and can be a little unusual to begin with. So when we are under pressure, it is only normal that we tend to rely on ways of working which are comfortable, familiar and can be done efficiently.

You need to make a conscious effort and allocate time to updating your knowledge and incorporating it into your practice. You could try using the 'Keys to good practice' list above to ensure that you are using the new knowledge you have gained.

Reflect

Think about whether you have ever changed your practice as a result of learning something new. If you have, think about how often this has happened. Also be honest with yourself about when you have learned about new ways of working, but have carried on doing things as you have always done.

Preparing a development plan

(KS 3, 4, 5, 11)

It is a requirement of many organisations that their staff have Personal Development Plans. A Personal Development Plan is a very important document as it identifies a worker's training and development needs and provides a record of participation.

A Personal Development Plan should be worked out with your line manager, but it is essentially your plan for your career. You need to think about what you want to achieve, and discuss with your line manager the best ways of achieving your goals.

There is no single right way to prepare a Personal Development Plan, and each organisation is likely to have its own way. However, it should include different development areas – such as practical skills and communication skills – the goals or targets you have set – such as learning to manage a team – and a timescale for achieving them. Timescales must be realistic. For example, if you had never managed a team before, but decided that you needed to achieve competence in managing a team in six months, this would be unrealistic and unachievable. But if your target was to attend a training and development programme on team building during the next six months and to lead perhaps two team meetings by the end of the six months, those goals and targets would be realistic and you would be likely to achieve them.

When you have set your targets, you need to review how you are progressing towards achieving them, and update your plan. This should happen every six months or so.

Development plans can take many forms, but the best ones are likely to be developed in conjunction with your line manager. You need to carefully consider the 'areas of competence' and understand which ones you need to develop for your work role. Identify each as either an area in which you feel fully confident, one where there is room for development, or one where you have limited current ability. The headings in the table below are suggestions only.

Once you have completed your plan you can identify the areas on which you need to concentrate. You should set some goals and targets, and your line manager should be able to help you ensure they are realistic. Only you and your line manager can examine the areas of competence and skills you need to achieve. This is a personal development programme for you and you must be sure that it reflects not only the objectives of your organisation and the job roles they may want you to fulfil, but also your personal ambitions and aspirations.

When you have identified the areas in which you feel competent and chosen your target areas for development, you will need to design a personal development log which will enable you to keep a record of your progress. This can be put together in any way that you find effective.

In your plan you may wish to include things as varied as learning sign language, learning a particular technique for working with children with challenging behaviour, or developing your potential as a manager by learning organisational and human resources skills. You could also include areas such as time management and stress management. All of these are legitimate areas for inclusion.

Development plan		
Area of competence	Goals	Action plan
Time management and workload organisation	Learn to use computer recording and information systems	Attend 2-day training and use study pack. Attend follow-up training days. Use computer instead of writing reports by hand
Review date: 3 months		
Professional development priorities My priorities for training and development in the next 6 months are:	IT and computerised record systems	
My priorities for training and development in the next 6–12 months are:	As above and NVQ assessor training	

Repeat this exercise in: 6 months
and review the areas of competence and priorities.

Active knowledge

Your task is to prepare a Personal Development Plan. You should use a computer to do this, even if you print out a hard copy in order to keep a personal portfolio.

Step 1

Use the model on this page and the next to prepare your plan.

Step 2

Complete the plan as far as you can at the present time. Note where you want your career to be in the short, medium and long term. You should also note down the training you want to complete and the skills you want to gain. You should do this on a computer if possible; otherwise, complete a hard copy and keep it in a file.

Step 3

Update the plan regularly. Keep on reviewing it with your line manager.

Personal Development Plan

Name:

Workplace:

Line manager:

Long-term goals (1–5 years)

Medium-term goals (6–12 months)

Short-term goals (next 6 months)

Areas of strength

Areas of weakness

Training and development

This section of your plan helps you to look at what you need to do in order to reach the goals you recorded in the first section. You should make a note of the training and development you need to undertake in order to achieve what you have identified.

Short-term goals	Development needed
Medium-term goals	Development needed
Long-term goals	Development needed

Milestones and timescales

In this section you should look at the development you have identified in the previous section and plan some timescales. Decide what the 'milestones' will be on the way to achieving your goal. Make sure that your timescales are realistic.

Development	Milestone	By when

Reviews and updates

This section helps you to stay on track and to make the changes that are inevitable as you progress. Not all your milestones will be achieved on target – some will be later, some earlier. All these changes will affect your overall plan, and you need to keep up to date and make any alterations as you go along.

Milestone	Target date	Actual achievement/revised target

Test yourself

1. Why are Personal Development Plans important?

2. Who would you ask to help you to prepare a Personal Development Plan?

3. Do you agree with the requirements in the National Minimum Standards for training? Give reasons for your answer.

4. Name three ways of finding out current and up-to-date information about practice.

5. Why does it matter that you keep your practice up to date?

6. How could you make sure that you get the most benefit from new knowledge after a training session?

HSC 33 UNIT TEST

1   What is the value of reflection as part of your development as a childcare practitioner?

2   What do you understand by the term 'constructive feedback'?

3   Describe the differences between formal and informal support networks.

4   How would you ensure that you gain the maximum benefit from a supervision session?

5   Name five sources where you could find new information to improve your practice.

6   Name three ways your practice has changed in the past two years because of new knowledge you have gained.

Don't forget to refer to the evidence opportunities grid (see pages 357–375) for more ideas for suitable evidence for your NVQ.

Promote the well-being and protection of children and young people

Working to prepare children and young people for a full, happy and satisfying life is a privilege, but it also carries a huge responsibility. Nowhere is this responsibility clearer than in the work you will do to achieve this unit. Children have rights, but these are not just a repeat of those of adults – children's rights recognise the fact that they are often in a position of having no power to protect themselves or to fight for their rights.

Depending on where you work, you may be with children who have already been treated in a way that has infringed their rights, or you may work with children who struggle to recognise that they also have responsibilities to people around them, or you could be working with children who, because of illness or disability, are vulnerable and need special protection.

Looking after the well-being of children and young people, and doing everything possible to safeguard and protect them, underpins most of the work you are doing. The issues of rights, well-being and protection are interlinked and, during your work for this unit, you will see how they all come together to create the right environment to give children and young people the best possible life chances.

In this unit you will find 'Active knowledge' features containing activities that will contribute to assessment for your NVQ. Remember that these features only offer the opportunity for partial assessment; you can also refer to the evidence opportunities grid (see pages 357–375) for more ideas to provide suitable evidence for your NVQ.

What you need to learn

- Children's rights: the UN Convention on the Rights of the Child
- Making the challenge
- Meeting needs
- Working together to safeguard children
- Types of abuse
- Responding to abuse
- Signs and symptoms of abuse
- The effects of abuse
- The laws to protect children

HSC 34a Work with children and young people in ways that promote their rights and responsibilities

If you are going to promote children and young people's rights and responsibilities effectively, you need to be clear about what these are and how they link into your work. Your work involves you in promoting and protecting the rights of the individual children you work with, but their rights are also promoted and protected on different levels: nationally by the Children's Commissioner, and globally by the United Nations. The rights children and young people have are identified in the UN Convention on the Rights of the Child, and all services and provision for children and young people should be based on the articles of the Convention. Responsibility for making sure each country follows the agreements of the Convention rests with The Committee for the Rights of the Child, an international body made up of experts on children's rights. The Committee last reviewed the UK governments' records in 2002.

The UN Convention on the Rights of the Child

(KS 1, 2, 3, 7, 8, 9, 10, 14, 15, 22, 23)

The Convention on the Rights of the Child is the first legally binding international instrument to incorporate the full range of human rights – these are civil, cultural, economic, political and social rights. In 1989, world leaders decided that children needed a special convention just for them because people under 18 years old often need special care and protection that adults do not. The leaders also wanted to make sure that the world recognised that children have human rights too. The key instrument identifying children's rights is the Convention, agreed by 192 of the 194 countries in the world (the two countries which have not signed up are Somalia and the United States of America).

The Convention has 54 articles that define and explain the rights which children have – remember, these are binding on all the countries that agreed, including the UK.

Previously, you have looked at the outcomes for children from each of the UK countries to focus and guide the work you do. As you go through the Articles of the Convention, you should be able to see how the rights link into the legislation, regulations, guidelines and outcomes for work with children and young people which govern provision for children in the UK.

At the same time, it is impossible not to think of the millions of children throughout the world who cannot even imagine many of these rights as they struggle to find shelter and enough to eat.

Children's Commissioners

Each of the countries of the UK has a Commissioner for Children and Young People; the titles vary slightly, as do the powers and responsibilities of the jobs. All Commissioners have to promote and champion the rights of children and young people. Commissioners in Scotland, Wales and Northern Ireland also have the role of safeguarding and defending Children's Rights, whereas the Commissioner in England only has the power to promote awareness of the rights of children (see the table opposite).

The four groups of Articles

There are four headings that group the Articles of the Convention: *Guiding Principles, Survival and Development Rights, Protection Rights* and *Participation Rights*. They are easier to look at if they are grouped so that you can see the key themes running through the thinking behind the rights. You will see that some rights appear in more than one group.

Commissioner independence *	Wales	Northern Ireland	Scotland	England
Secretary of State can direct Commissioner to carry out an inquiry	NO	NO	NO	YES
Commissioner must consult Secretary of State before holding an independent inquiry	NO	NO	NO	YES
Commissioner's annual report goes directly to Parliament/Assembly	YES	YES	YES	NO
Legislation ties Commissioner to Government policy	NO	NO	NO	YES

* 'The State of Children's Rights in England', Children's Rights Alliance for England 2005

Guiding principles: general requirements for all rights

Definition of the child (Article 1): The Convention defines a 'child' as a person below the age of 18.

Non-discrimination (Article 2): The Convention applies to all children, whatever their race, religion or abilities; whatever they think or say, whatever type of family they come from. It doesn't matter where children live, what language they speak, what their parents do, whether they are boys or girls, what their culture is, whether they have a disability or whether they are rich or poor. No child should be treated unfairly on any basis.

Best interests of the child (Article 3): The best interests of children must be the primary concern in making decisions that may affect them. All adults should do what is best for children. When adults make decisions, they should think about how their decisions will affect children. This particularly applies to budget, policy and law makers.

The Convention applies to all children

Right to life, survival and development (Article 6): Children have the right to live. Governments should ensure that children survive and develop healthily.

Respect for the views of the child (Article 12): When adults are making decisions that affect children, children have the right to say what they think should happen and have their opinions taken into account. This does not mean that children can now tell their parents what to do. The Convention encourages adults to listen to the opinions of children and involve them in decision making – not give children authority over adults. Article 12 does not interfere with the right and responsibility of parents to express their views on matters affecting their children. Moreover, the Convention recognises that the level of a child's participation in decisions must be appropriate to the child's level of maturity. Children's ability to form and express their opinions develops with age and most adults will naturally give the views of teenagers greater weight than those of a pre-schooler, whether in family, legal or administrative decisions.

What happens in practice

Children's Commissioners are one way in which governments make sure that children and young people's views are taken into account. There is a Youth Parliament, which started in 1999. It has Youth Members of Parliament aged from 11 to 18 years old, and represents the views of many children and young people. There are many children's organisations that arrange consultations and seek out the views of young people.

National and local bodies consult with children and young people more than ever before, and you must remember that this is an essential part of what you do for individual children. You should always involve children and young people in decisions that affect them – the little decisions as well as the big ones.

Survival and development rights: the basic rights to life, survival and development of one's full potential

Article 4 (Protection of rights): Governments have a responsibility to take all available measures to make sure children's rights are respected, protected and fulfilled. When countries ratify the Convention, they agree to review their laws relating to children. This involves assessing their social services, legal, health and educational systems, as well as levels of funding for these services. Governments are then obliged to take all necessary steps to ensure that the minimum standards set by the Convention in these areas are being met. They must help families protect children's rights and create an environment in which they can grow and reach their potential.

Article 5 (Parental guidance): Governments should respect the rights and responsibilities of families to direct and guide their children so that, as they grow, they learn to use their rights properly. Helping children to understand their rights does not mean pushing them to make choices with consequences that they are too young to handle. Article 5 encourages parents to deal with rights issues "in a manner consistent with the evolving capacities of the child". The Convention does not take responsibility for children away from their parents and give more authority to governments. It does place on governments the responsibility to protect and assist families in fulfilling their essential role as nurturers of children.

What happens in practice

All UK governments have developed parenting support programmes, through which highly skilled and qualified practitioners provide Parent Education. Sometimes parents will ask for this type of support when they know that they are struggling with a difficult relationship with their child; at other times, participation in Parent Education can be compulsory,

ordered by the courts when it appears that parents are unable to support their children to attend school or to keep away from anti-social behaviour or criminal activity.

Active knowledge

Find out about Parent Education. Find out what goes on, how parents are supported and where the nearest group is. Check out what the links are between your workplace and Parent Education – do you signpost people to Parent Education groups? Are the parents of any of the children you work with receiving parenting support?

Article 6 (Survival and development): Children have the right to live. Governments should ensure that children survive and develop healthily.

What this means in practice

Everyone who works with children has an absolute duty to safeguard and protect them – all of the UK governments have the health of children as one of the main outcomes to be achieved.

Article 7 (Registration, name, nationality, care): All children have the right to a legally registered name, officially recognised by the government. Children have the right to a nationality (to belong to a country). Children also have the right to know and, as far as possible, to be cared for by their parents.

Article 8 (Preservation of identity): Children have the right to an identity – an official record of who they are. Governments should respect children's right to a name, a nationality and family ties.

What this means in practice

This is only partly about records – birth certificates, passports, national insurance and NHS numbers. All of these are important ways of providing children with an identity that can be proved, but these rights are also about belonging to a country and feeling that there is somewhere that is 'home'. These rights can often be an issue for children of asylum seekers, who may be in a situation of uncertainty, often for many months.

Article 9 (Separation from parents): Children have the right to live with their parent(s), unless it is bad for them. Children whose parents do not live together have the right to stay in contact with both parents, unless this might hurt the child.

Article 10 (Family reunification): Families whose members live in different countries should be allowed to move between those countries so that parents and children can stay in contact, or get back together as a family.

Article 14 (Freedom of thought, conscience and religion): Children have the right to think and believe what they want and to practise their religion, as long as they are not stopping other people from enjoying their rights. Parents should help guide their children in these matters. At the same time, the Convention recognises that as children mature and are able to form their own views, some may question certain religious practices or cultural traditions. The Convention supports children's right to examine their beliefs, but it also states that their right to express their beliefs implies respect for the rights and freedoms of others.

Article 18 (Parental responsibilities; state assistance): Both parents share responsibility for bringing up their children, and should always consider what is best for each child. Governments must respect the responsibility of parents for providing appropriate guidance to their children – the Convention does not take responsibility for children away from their parents and give more authority to governments. It places a responsibility on governments to provide support services to parents, especially if both parents work outside the home.

What this means in practice

This is about the importance of families to children. Wherever humanly possible, you work to keep families and children together and to give whatever support is needed. This can include:

- practical help, such as support workers, transport, aids and adaptations, health support
- financial help, such as benefits, direct payments, child support, grants and additional payments
- emotional help, such as social workers, psychologists, group support, parent education.

Article 20 (Children deprived of family environment): Children who cannot be looked after by their own family have a right to special care and must be looked after properly, by people who respect their ethnic group, religion, culture and language.

Article 22 (Refugee children): Children have the right to special protection and help if they are refugees (if they have been forced to leave their home and live in another country), as well as all the other rights in the Convention.

My story

Hi, I'm Darren and I'm 5 – I'm nearly 6 and I'm bigger than Clay Wilson who lives next door. I'm 6 on the 17th of June, which is on Tuesday, and I'm having a party – I've never had a party before. My dad went away, a few weeks ago, I think, but it was Christmas. Mum says he isn't coming back. Policemen came, I was in bed, it was very loud and I was frightened and Dad went away with them. Mum cried a lot and I was hungry – Jenny, Clay's mum, made my tea a lot. A lady came and said I could go and stay with nice people because my mum wasn't well, but I didn't want to go and I ran and hid and I promised to be good if I could stay with Mum. Then the lady went away and Mum said I didn't have to go. The next day Christine came. She comes a lot and makes lovely things for tea. It's nice when Christine is there, and our house is nice too – I think it's different from before.

My story

Hi, I'm Christine. I was asked to come in as an emergency to support this family. Dad – Joseph – is on remand, but he's a dealer, so he's going down for a long time. Katrina – Mum – just fell apart when he was arrested. She was quite vulnerable anyway: she had a history of mental health problems from the days when she had a habit, and she's had lots of depressive episodes. Neighbours were good and very supportive, but the children were not being fed, conditions in the house were getting pretty bad, and the children were not getting to school. Darren was the biggest concern. The other children are older: they seemed to spend most of their time with friends. Certainly neither of them was able to look out for Darren. At one point it looked as if Darren was going to have to go to foster parents for a while to give Katrina a break but, when it was discussed, he was so distressed that she decided that she couldn't do it. And this is where I came in. I started doing five days, but Katrina has really moved on and now I just do three. The older ones, Marcus and Alisha, are around more now, and Katrina is coping amazingly well – best of all, little Darren seems really happy. And I'll do anything for one of his fabulous smiles!

Article 23 (Children with disabilities): Children who have any kind of disability have the right to special care and support, as well as all the rights in the Convention, so that they can live full and independent lives.

What this means in practice

These articles reflect the values and codes of practice that underpin your work, and are also the basis of the learning and skills you need to do your job. All children and young people need care and protection,

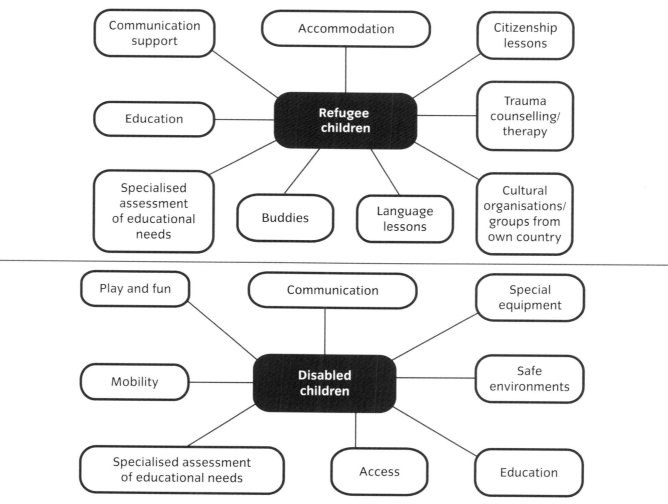

Special care and protection

but there will always be some more vulnerable ones who need particular special attention.

Article 24 (Health and health services): Children have the right to good-quality health care – the best health care possible – to safe drinking water, nutritious food, a clean and safe environment, and information to help them stay healthy. Rich countries should help poorer countries achieve this.

Article 25 (Review of treatment in care): Children who are looked after by their local authorities, rather than their parents, have the right to have these living arrangements looked at regularly to see if they are the most appropriate. Their care and treatment should always be based on "the best interests of the child". (See Guiding Principles, Article 3 on page 119.)

Article 26 (Social security): Children – either through their guardians or directly – have the right to help from the government if they are poor or in need.

Article 27 (Adequate standard of living): Children have the right to a standard of living that is good enough to meet their physical and mental needs. Governments should help families and guardians who cannot afford to provide this, particularly with regard to food, clothing and housing.

What this means in practice

This group of articles is about meeting children's basic needs. Everyone has some basic needs, for food, shelter and warmth – if these needs are not met, children cannot move on to meeting other emotional and intellectual needs. The services provided for children looked after by local authorities are reviewed on a regular basis. This legal requirement in the UK upholds a key right for looked-after children.

Article 28: (Right to education): All children have the right to a primary education, which should be free. Wealthy countries should help poorer countries achieve this right. Discipline in schools should respect children's dignity. For children to benefit from education, schools must be run in an orderly way – without the use of violence. Any form of school discipline should take into account the child's human dignity. Therefore, governments must ensure that school administrators review their discipline policies and eliminate any discipline practices involving physical or mental violence, abuse or neglect. The Convention places a high value on education. Young people should be encouraged to reach the highest level of education of which they are capable.

If basic needs are not met, children's emotional and intellectual needs cannot be met

Article 29 (Goals of education): Children's education should develop each child's personality, talents and abilities to the fullest. It should encourage children to respect others' human rights and their own and other cultures. It should also help them learn to live peacefully, protect the environment and respect other people, in particular their parents.

What this means in practice

Corporal punishment is not allowed in schools in the UK, nor in any early education setting or provision for looked-after children. All children in school have an individual education plan – or programme in Scotland – which they should have participated in designing, so that they can learn in the best way and at the pace which is right for them. The plan should contain information about: the short-term targets set for, or by, the child; the teaching strategies to be used; the provision to be put in place; the review date; the success and/or exit criteria; and the outcomes (recorded at the review).

Article 30 (Children of minorities/indigenous groups): Minority or indigenous children have the right to learn about and practice their own culture, language and religion. The right to practise one's own culture, language and religion applies to everyone; the Convention here highlights this right in instances where the practices are not shared by the majority of people in the country.

Article 31 (Leisure, play and culture): Children have the right to relax and play, and to join in a wide range of cultural, artistic and other recreational activities.

Article 42 (Knowledge of rights): Governments should make the Convention known to adults and children. Adults should help children learn about their rights, too. (See Protection of rights, Article 4 on this page.)

What this means in practice

Part of the important outcomes about children enjoying life and achieving, and those about children making a contribution or taking part in society, is reflected here in the Articles about taking part in recreational activities. It is important that all children, no matter what their interest or level of ability, should be supported to take part in activities.

There is little point in children and young people having rights if they are not aware of them. You cannot assume that they will know, or will find out; you should make sure that you actively promote their rights to children and young people, and tell them where they can find out more information.

Active knowledge
HSC 34 KS 1 (part)

Find out how to access information about the Children's Commissioner in the country where you work, and about any other sources where children and young people can find out about their rights. Websites can be a good way for children and young people to find out, so look for web-based information as a priority.

Protection rights: keeping safe from harm

Article 4 (Protection of rights): Governments have a responsibility to take all available measures to make sure children's rights are respected, protected and fulfilled. When countries ratify the Convention, they agree to review their laws relating to children. This involves assessing their social services, legal, health and educational systems, as well as levels of funding for these services. Governments are then obliged to take all necessary steps to ensure that the minimum standards set by the Convention in these areas are being met. They must help families protect children's rights and create an environment in which they can grow and reach their potential. In some instances, this may involve changing existing laws or creating new ones.

Article 11 (Kidnapping): Governments should take steps to stop children being taken out of their own country illegally. This article is particularly concerned with parental abductions. The Convention's Optional Protocol on the sale of children, child prostitution and child pornography has a provision that concerns abduction for financial gain.

Article 19 (Protection from all forms of violence): Children have the right to be protected from being hurt and mistreated, physically or mentally. Governments should ensure that children are properly cared for and protect them from violence, abuse and neglect by their parents, or anyone else who looks after them. In terms of discipline, the Convention does not specify what forms of punishment parents should use. However any form of discipline involving violence is unacceptable. There are ways to discipline children that are effective in helping children learn about family and social expectations for their behaviour – ones that are non-violent, are appropriate to the child's level of development and take the best interests of the child into consideration. In most countries, laws already define what sorts of punishments are considered excessive or abusive. It is up to each government to review these laws in light of the Convention.

What this means in practice

In the UK, the only people who are allowed to hit children are parents! Twelve countries in Europe have already banned corporal punishment and others are considering it. In the UK, the Children Act 2004 would have brought England and Wales into line with the UN Convention, but an amendment in the House of Lords meant that physical punishment of children was still allowed, provided that it did not leave a mark on the skin or cause 'mental harm'. The Children's Commissioners are all calling for a total ban on physical punishment.

Article 20 (Children deprived of family environment): Children who cannot be looked after by their own family have a right to special care and must be looked after properly, by people who respect their ethnic group, religion, culture and language.

Article 21 (Adoption): Children have the right to care and protection if they are adopted or in foster care. The first concern must be what is best for them. The same rules should apply whether they are adopted in the country where they were born, or if they are taken to live in another country.

Article 22 (Refugee children): Children have the right to special protection and help if they are refugees (if they have been forced to leave their home and live in another country), as well as all the other rights in the Convention.

Article 32 (Child labour): The government should protect children from work that is dangerous or might harm their health or their education. While the Convention protects children from harmful and exploitative work, there is nothing in it that prohibits parents from expecting their children to help out at home in ways that are safe and appropriate to their age. If children help out in a family farm or business, the tasks they do must be safe and suited to their level of development and comply with national labour laws. Children's work should not jeopardise any of their other rights, including the right to education, or the right to relaxation and play.

Participation rights: having an active voice

Article 4 (Protection of rights): Governments have a responsibility to take all available measures to make sure children's rights are respected, protected and fulfilled. When countries ratify the Convention, they agree to review their laws relating to children. This involves assessing their social services, legal, health and educational systems, as well as levels of funding for these services. Governments are then obliged to take all necessary steps to ensure that the minimum standards set by the Convention in these areas are being met. They must help families protect children's rights and create an environment in which they can grow and reach their potential. In some instances, this may involve changing existing laws or creating new ones. Such legislative changes are not imposed, but come about through the same process by which any law is created or reformed within a country. Article 41 of the Convention points out that when a country already has higher legal standards than those seen in the Convention, the higher standards always prevail.

Article 12 (Respect for the views of the child): When adults are making decisions that affect children, children have the right to say what they think should happen and have their opinions taken into account.

Article 13 (Freedom of expression): Children have the right to get and share information, as long as the information is not damaging to them or others. In exercising the right to freedom of expression, children have the responsibility to also respect the rights, freedoms and reputations of others. The freedom of expression includes the right to share information in any way they choose, including by talking, drawing or writing.

Reflect

'I suppose that the chief thing about being a child is being in the power of grown ups. Everything comes from them – food, law, treats, and punishments. They have the power to give and to withhold. Some of them make up the rules as they go along to suit their convenience, and the child, who would like the chance to make up a few rules himself, knows it.'

Stolen Childhood, Anuradha Vittachi, Polity Press, 1991

Can you remember what it felt like to be powerless? Consider your own practice – how often do you consider if what you do takes power from children? How will you know if you are making children feel like the child described in the comment above? What will you do about it?

Article 14 (Freedom of thought, conscience and religion):
Children have the right to think and believe what they want and to practise their religion, as long as they are not stopping other people from enjoying their rights. Parents should help guide their children in these matters. The Convention respects the rights and duties of parents in providing religious and moral guidance to their children. Religious groups around the world have expressed support for the Convention, which indicates that it in no way prevents parents from bringing their children up within a religious tradition. At the same time, the Convention recognises that as children mature and are able to form their own views, some may question certain religious practices or cultural traditions. The Convention supports children's right to examine their beliefs, but it also states that their right to express their beliefs implies respect for the rights and freedoms of others.

Article 15 (Freedom of association):
Children have the right to meet together and to join groups and organisations, as long as it does not stop other people from enjoying their rights. In exercising their rights, children have the responsibility to respect the rights, freedoms and reputations of others.

Article 16 (Right to privacy):
Children have a right to privacy. The law should protect them from attacks against their way of life, their good name, their families and their homes.

Article 17 (Access to information; mass media):
Children have the right to get information that is important to their health and well-being. Governments should encourage mass media – radio, television, newspapers and internet content sources – to provide information that children can understand and not to promote materials that could harm children. Mass media should particularly be encouraged to supply information in languages that minority and indigenous children can understand. Children should also have access to children's books.

What this means in practice

Much of the content of these articles relates to making sure children and young people know what is going on, not only in their own lives, but also in the wider world. It is also about the importance of children thinking about key issues, and considering and discussing them with others. In working with children, you may need to promote and facilitate discussion and thinking about issues: this could be around the dinner table, if you work in a residential setting; or it could be in a classroom or a club-based group; or you could just share ideas on a one-to-one basis with a child or young person. You may find, however, that particular groups of children and young people need no intervention from adults and are more than willing to argue, discuss and consider all kinds of issues and information. Access to information is essential and a vital human right but, as Article 17 highlights, children are also vulnerable so it is important to be aware of the risks to children of accessing some kinds of information. The most obvious example is the exercising of parental control over the internet, something you will have a policy on in your workplace. This is an important part of safeguarding children and making sure that they are protected from exploitation by people who contact them on the internet.

Active knowledge

Describe your workplace policy on accessing the internet. What level of 'parental control' is used on computers? Who sets it? Who is responsible for checking that it has not been changed? Are the children and young people involved in deciding what to access? If not, why not?

Making challenges

(KS 4, 5, 6, 7, 9, 11, 12, 13)

Children's rights are not always respected, and it is an important part of your work to challenge on behalf of children when you feel that this is not happening. Making challenges can be difficult, especially if it involves a senior colleague, or the management of your organisation. For example:

You are in a staff meeting and your manager announces that children's records are now being transferred to the integrated children's system, so that everything will be compatible when the time comes to upload records into the Information Sharing Index. You ask if the children have been informed and consulted about this. Your manager says that they are sure that the government must have consulted children when they decided to do this, but there is little point in talking to children here about it because it is going to happen anyway … and to be honest, children aren't very interested in stuff about records.

You need to challenge this. Children have a right to know and express a view about anything about them – and records certainly are. They also have a right to privacy. They need to be informed about who will have access to these records, where they will be kept and the purpose of keeping records in this way.

Challenges do not have to be aggressive or confrontational: you can challenge calmly and assertively by using positive language that does not appear to criticise or undermine people. Something like: *'I agree that having a new system for records is essential and I think it's really great that the government have consulted children on the idea. I think we can reinforce the work we do here as champions for children by being up-front and transparent, and by making sure all their rights are observed.'*

If all else fails, you may have to resort to: *'Well, I'm going to talk to the children about it so that they know what is going on.'* If this is blocked, you may have to 'blow the whistle', an issue which is dealt with later in this unit (see page 149).

Making sure that children and young people's rights are respected is also an integral part of the Code of Practice, developed by all the UK registration bodies, for social care workers – as a professional you will need to adhere to this. Social care professionals are

The children don't need to be consulted – they won't be interested.

I think we can reinforce the work we do here as champions for children by making sure all their rights are observed.

You can challenge calmly and assertively by using positive language

being registered on a 'rolling programme' and, once registered, compliance with the Code is mandatory: breach of it can result in disciplinary proceedings and possibly being struck off the professional register for the region in which you live.

Test yourself

1 Which two countries have not signed up to the UN Convention on the Rights of the Child?

2 How are children's rights promoted and protected in the UK?

3 Why are rights for children important?

4 How is the performance of countries monitored in respect of children's rights?

5 Where can children go to find out about their rights?

HSC 34b Support children and young people to express their views and preferences about health and well-being

Children and young people have the right to have their views considered about anything that concerns them. This is particularly important when it comes to their health and well-being. You need to be clear about the concepts of health and well-being.

Health is not just about the absence of illness, although that is a key part of it. There is also something about being healthy which is positive, so health is about being 'positively well', rather than just 'not ill'.

Well-being is different to health: it is broader and health is included, but only as a part.

Meeting needs

(KS 2, 3, 4, 5, 8, 16, 17, 18, 21)

Generally, well-being is about a child or young person having their needs met. This can include physical, social, emotional and intellectual needs. Some people may describe well-being as 'happiness', which it is to some extent; but happiness can be a very brief state, whereas well-being is a deeper, more underlying condition, more like 'contentment' or 'fulfilment'. However, happiness can be a useful starting point for thinking about well-being.

One of the key aspects of well-being is having needs met. Although all children are different, everyone shares some basic needs as human beings. Additionally, some children and young people have individual needs because of experiences and circumstances. The basic, shared human needs can be broadly split into:

- **P**hysical
- **I**ntellectual
- **E**motional
- **S**ocial.

A simple acronym is **PIES**.

Physical needs

These are things like food and drink, warmth, shelter, sleep and excercise.

Physical needs are usually very basic, and it is impossible to survive without them. Of course, the needs will vary with the age of the child but, generally, human beings have a greater range of physical needs at the start of their lives and in old age.

Views and preferences

All children should be able to say how they want to have their physical needs met. They should be encouraged and supported to think about what they eat, how they live and how they take care of their health. It is also important to give children and young people information on which to base their views about what they want. You cannot expect children to decide that they will, for example, eat more vegetables and fruit and less chips and ice-cream unless they have some good reasons backed up by hard facts.

Intellectual needs

This is not about being clever! Intellectual needs are about mental stimulation and having varied interests. Like physical needs, intellectual needs change at different life stages: for example, a baby needs stimulation by colours and simple shapes or by new sounds. Learning through formal education is important, but intellectual needs are met in many other ways too, such as finding out new information, arts, music, debate and discussion, games and contests (yes – even computer games!).

All children and young people benefit from having interests and outlets which offer a challenge and a new perspective

Views and preferences

The view that 'I'm not going to school any more 'cos I learn much more by lying here and watching the telly' is not quite what is meant by encouraging children to express their views about education! However, children should not be passive receivers of learning. Education is an interactive process and children should be encouraged to see it in this way. They should also be encouraged to have clear views about what they want to achieve and the best way to do it. Encouraging children to question information and to form opinions about what they are learning is an important part of developing a two-way process of education where children are able to share and contribute.

Emotional needs

The keys to emotional fulfilment are being clear about who you are, and liking who you are. If people are confused about their own identity or are unhappy with themselves, it will always be difficult to reach out to others and develop good relationships. Most people like to be liked; most people like to love and be loved. At the various stages of our lives, the needs will be different, but basically everyone needs to feel secure, nurtured and loved. As children grow, they need love and care, as well as boundaries and routines, in order to feel safe and secure. As children develop into adolescence and then into adulthood, close friendships and loving sexual relationships provide emotional fulfilment.

Views and preferences

One of the tragic consequences for children who are emotionally deprived is that they are the least capable of being able to talk about feelings and to express their needs. It is heartbreaking to see a neglected child who doesn't cry; they don't cry any more because no one ever came when they did. It is vital for all children that they are able to demand and expect safety and security. They also have a right to be understood, so regardless of how the views are expressed – and that could well be by throwing something at you, or by shouting and swearing – you need to show that you have understood the message, and that you have supported parents and others in learning how to understand what is being said.

Social needs

Social needs are about relationships with other people. No one lives in a vacuum, and most human beings like to relate to other human beings! Children learn about relating to others as they grow and develop: toddlers learn about how to share and take turns; pre-school children learn to play co-operatively with others; children make friends. As they develop, children also learn how to behave in a way which is socially acceptable, so that they are not excluded or regarded with disapproval.

Views and preferences

Generally children and young people should be able to meet and socialise with whoever they want, but there may be occasions when this is not possible. It could be that there are legal restrictions in respect of some family members or friends that children cannot see, or can only see in specified circumstances. There may also be concerns about particular associates who are known to have a negative influence. You will need to be able to discuss this with parents if appropriate, and involve the child or young person so that they are a part of any decisions.

Self-esteem

Oscar Wilde said:

> To love oneself is the beginning of a life-long romance.

Feeling good about yourself has a great deal to do with the level of confidence that you developed as you grew up. Everyone needs to feel that they have a valuable place and a valuable contribution to make within society.

The reasons people have different levels of self-esteem are complex. The way people feel about themselves is laid down during childhood. A child who is

Reflect

How much do you like yourself? How confident are you? Are there areas of your life in which you are more confident and comfortable than others? How important do you feel in different areas of your life? How much do you value yourself?

These are difficult questions and, if you take the time and trouble (it could take many days) to think them through carefully, you should make notes of what you discover – even if you don't like some of the answers. You should also try to think about some of the reasons why you feel as you do: any events in your past that have had an impact, or the way in which you were treated by others as a child.

If you don't have the time to spend thinking about yourself, ask the following question: 'Why am I not important enough to have some time for me?'

Finally ask yourself: 'If I disappeared tomorrow, what would I be remembered for?'

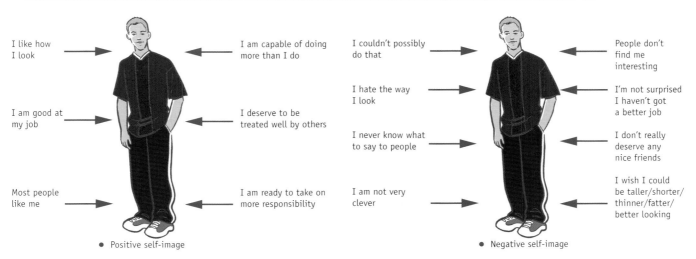

- Positive self-image
- Negative self-image

The way people feel about themselves is laid down during childhood

encouraged and given a lot of positive feedback is the sort of person who is likely to feel that he or she can make a useful contribution to any situation. But a child who is constantly blamed or belittled is likely to grow into an adult who lacks self-belief, or finds it difficult to accept new challenges.

Promoting self-esteem

Children must be at the centre of everything you do. If they are to develop into confident adults who like themselves and have confidence in their own ability, they need a firm base to start from. Depending on the work you do, many of the children and young people you work with will have had a challenging start in life, and some may have been seriously damaged by previous experience. Your job may involve you in providing full-time care for children and young people, or you may see them on a regular basis. Regardless of how and where you interact with children and young people, they must know that they are central to everything you do.

Child-centred practice

You can show this by always giving them the opportunity to comment and put forward their own views about what they want to do with you. This does not mean that children and young people get to run the show and do everything they want!

Making sure that children and young people are able to have some control over clearly defined areas is very important. Whether you only see individual children or young people once or twice a month, or if you work with a whole group at a time, or work in a busy unit and never seem to see the same child twice, letting them know that they are the focus of your practice, your concern and your attention is vital.

Feeling confident

Children and young people will find it easier to express their views if they have the confidence that comes from believing that people value what they have to say. From birth, children are very effective communicators: not

Children and young people should be given the opportunity to comment and put forward their own views about what they want to do with you – within reason!

only do they communicate what they want, but they pick up what is being communicated to them, so children know if you genuinely like them and if you really care about what happens to them.

If you are working with a baby or with a child or young person who uses unspoken communication, you will need to ensure that you know how to understand the message that he or she is sending. Older children and young people are likely to have an established means of communication, and you will be able to find out what you need to do from the child or young person, family or carers. Communicating with babies is fascinating, right from birth: body language expresses what a baby wants – and what it doesn't! In recent years there has been a recognition that babies can be taught to sign using similar signs to the communication systems designed to be used with speech. The development of 'baby signing' has further improved the way in which parents, carers and professionals can understand and meet the needs of very young babies.

What do you want to do... next?

All of us can remember being asked the favourite question of most adults: 'What do you want to do when you grow up?' This question is really just a way of saying: 'What are your hopes, dreams, ambitions and goals for your life?' It is important for children that you are able to support them to express hopes,

plans, dreams and wishes, and to work alongside them and their families to make plans. How you go about this will vary according to your job. If you work in a school or in a supporting service for young people such as Connexions, the Youth Service or CAMHS, you may be supporting young people to set goals and targets and make plans to achieve them as part of your day-to-day work. The key of any goal or target is that it has to be achievable and realistic. One of the best-known ways of setting up goals and targets is to make them SMART: specific, measurable, achievable, realistic and time-related (see below).

If you work in residential settings where you are very involved in the day-to-day lives of the children and young people, you are likely to be involved with the planning and achieving of their hopes and dreams. Getting children to think and talk about what they want and how they feel is the first stage of helping them realise that so much is possible if they set out clear plans for how they will get there.

Setting the boundaries

Encouraging and supporting children and young people to express views and preferences is an essential part of your practice as a professional, but it is never a substitute for your responsibility to safeguard their welfare. Many of the preferences that young people express may have levels of risk which mean that they are unrealistic and need to be 'redirected'! The skills

SPECIFIC	Specific: they say exactly what you mean with no vague, general statements like 'I will do better'.
MEASURABLE	Measurable: you can prove that you've reached them. For example: 'I will be able to play all the chords and songs in the level 4 guitar book', rather than 'I will get better at playing the guitar'.
ACHIEVABLE	Achievable: you can reach them in the foreseeable future. The plan may be to be a famous footballer, but planning to get into the school first team is more achievable in the short term.
REALISTIC	Realistic: they are about action you can take. 'I will buy that huge white house with the veranda for my mum' is a wonderful goal, but 'I am going to work to make sure I get at least all my predicted grades in my GCSEs' is probably a more realistic start.
TIME-RELATED	Time-related: they have deadlines. Goals and targets should always state 'by (date)'. If not, they can easily drift and end up not being achieved.

A good way to set goals is to make them SMART

involved in getting a child or young person to accept that something they want to do – or something they don't want to do – has risks attached are important ones to learn.

Regardless of the age or apparent level of understanding of the child or young person, they must be involved in assessing and considering risks involved in their expressed preferences. Risks could be about an activity which has dangers, about financial commitments or about behaviour, or risks to others. A choice not to do something – 'I'm not having that needle!' – may also have risks attached.

Explanations are the key to getting children to accept and understand boundaries. All children and young people need boundaries: children without boundaries are insecure, frightened and often very angry. They may not present in that way, but all of the developmental research shows that children like the security provided by knowing where the boundaries are and knowing that someone will exercise control to enforce them.

Families

Many children you are working with will have grown up with either very few boundaries, inconsistent ones or overly rigid and punitive ones. A clear explanation about why they can't do what they want in the way

My story

Hi, I'm Hassan. I'm 17 and I have a social worker because I was into cars and driving and so ended up in court and have got to be supervised by the Youth Justice Team. I've had her as my social worker for about two years now. That's a long time – most of them last about six months, then you never see them again. Actually, her name's Savita and she's OK. She's been on at me about working out what I want to do and all that, so I heard about this base jumping where you jump off cliffs and tall buildings with a parachute. I found out all about it and it is the ultimate in extreme sports – I think you can only do it in Norway. Anyway, I told her when I saw her last week that I knew what I wanted to do and that I was going to make it one of my targets – she was not happy! But, to be fair, she was OK. The best way to explain is to let you hear the conversation.

S.   Yes, I appreciate that extreme sports are a better way of getting an adrenalin rush than nicking cars – and I am so impressed that you are being so positive and coming up with ideas.

H.   So I can go base jumping then?

S.   Well – I do think that jumping from the top of a cliff with a parachute is a risky way to get an adrenalin high. What other options are there?

H.   Well, I could do the Cresta run on a tea tray!

S.   Very funny!

H.   Well there aren't any other options as good as that. I mean, you just have to jump – other stuff you have to train for, or be good at.

S.   I expect you have to train for base jumping – what other stuff?

H.   Climbing and white water rafting and paragliding – all that stuff.

S.   You are amazing. I don't know how you manage to find out so much information about everything – you are always so thorough in your research.

H.   Same as everyone else, nothing special.

S.   Oh no, it's not the same. Loads of people don't take half as much time to find out about things and ask questions as you do. You'd make a fabulous journalist! You know, I think the guys who run the outdoor centre also do the whitewater rafting and climbing courses.

H.   Now who's being funny! You know that the outdoor centre stuff isn't my thing – can't really see me in an anorak.

S.   Agreed, but I don't mean the stuff they do for the kids. I mean the stuff they do for themselves – those guys are serious adrenalin junkies!

H.   Well, if it's the real thing – I mean I'm not interested in girly stuff. Could be worth checking out – and that'd be OK then to do that?

S.   Sounds good to me – here's the mobile for Steve at the centre. Give him a call. I'll tell him to expect to hear from you.

H.   Do you really think I'd make a good journalist?

they want to and a rapid move to look at alternatives is usually the best way.

You may also be in the position of working with families to support them to learn about how to establish boundaries and how to listen to the views of children and young people. Many parents struggle to listen to their children, usually because no one ever listened to them as they grew up and they have no idea how to do it. Parent Education can help many parents: they will be able to attend groups or individual sessions with skilled parenting practioners and share their concerns and worries with other parents.

Active knowledge

HSC 34b pc 1d, 6

Find out what support is available for the parents of children and young people you work with.

Test yourself

1   Which of the following are important for well-being? Why?

- Having somewhere decent to live
- Having enough to eat
- Having friends
- Being loved
- Buying nice clothes
- Being interested in things
- Having a nice car
- Not having an illness or disease.

2   How can you help children and young people to explain what they want?

3   What is your primary duty in relation to what children want?

HSC 34c Contribute to the protection of children and young people

Working together to safeguard children

(KS 7, 8, 9, 19)

The elected councillors of each local authority have the responsibility as 'Corporate Parents' to look after children in their care as if they were their own children, but they have far wider responsibilities too.

One of those is to safeguard and promote the welfare of children. To do so, each local authority must work in partnership with other agencies, children and young people and their families, the voluntary sector and the wider community.

Safeguarding is about the ways in which risks to children can be identified and minimised. This is not just the responsibility of one agency or one department within a local authority, but of everyone who works, volunteers or comes into contact with children and young people.

It is not just children's services that have a responsibility to safeguard and protect children. Consider the other services that need to be involved: child and adolescent mental health services, housing, youth services, health services, sport, leisure, art galleries and museums, police, Connexions, the probation service, youth offending teams, drug and alcohol teams and voluntary sector providers of services for children and young people. The list is long!

The responsibility for saying how all these organisations should co-operate in England and Wales and for making sure that it happens effectively lies with the Local Safeguarding Children Board (the LSCB). Each local LSCB is made up of senior managers from all the different agencies, and they have to develop policies and procedures for all agencies to follow in order to protect children. Child safeguarding and protection in Scotland is governed by the Children (Scotland) Act 1995.

Safeguarding and promoting welfare

There are many ways in which the welfare of children and young people needs to be safeguarded. For example:

- work in schools to reduce bullying
- informing children and young people about the risks of using the internet
- taking steps to minimise risks from internet access
- educating and minimising harm and risks from drugs and alcohol abuse
- tackling teenage pregnancy and sexually transmitted disease among young people
- educating children, young people and their families about healthy eating and lifestyles and providing healthy food in schools
- promoting children and young people's health through public health programmes, e.g. immunisation, screening
- tackling high-risk accident areas on roads and public transport
- providing safe play areas and places to play sport and exercise.

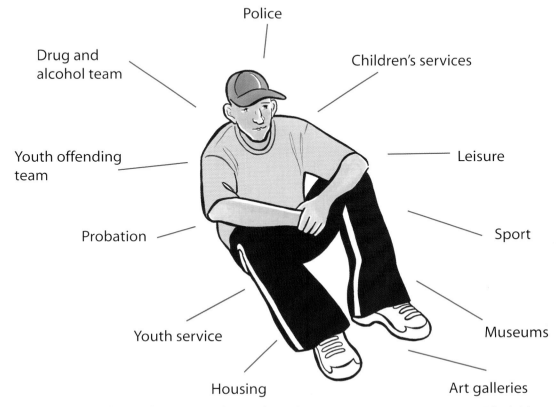

Safeguarding is the responsibility of everyone who works, volunteers or comes into contact with children and young people

The concept of safeguarding and promoting the welfare of children and young people is about looking at all the potential risks, and recognising that we all have a responsibility to be aware of these and to minimise them as far as possible.

Your role in child protection

In this section, you will look at some of the most difficult issues that you will face as a childcare professional. For many people, starting work with children and young people means coming to terms for the first time with the fact that some children and young people are subjected to abuse by those who are supposed to care for them. For others, it will not be the first time that they have been close to an abuse situation, either through personal experience of surviving abuse or being in a family where abuse was happening.

Regardless of previous experience, coming face to face with abusive situations is difficult and emotionally demanding. In order to protect children effectively, you must know how to recognise abuse and what to do about it. It is a tragic fact that almost all disclosures of abuse are true – and you will have to learn to *think the unthinkable*.

You need to be aware of the different types of abuse: abusers can be parents, informal carers, childcare professionals and even the policies and practices of the care setting itself.

You need always to consider abuse as a possibility, always to be alert to potentially abusive situations and always to *listen and believe* when you are told about abuse, if you want to provide the best possible protection for the children and young people you work with.

This standard is not about abuse by strangers, which needs to be dealt with in the same way as any other crime.

Types of abuse

(KS 16, 24)

Abuse can take many forms. These are usually classified under four main headings:

- physical
- sexual
- emotional
- neglect.

There is one further category:

- institutional.

This is categorised separately because the perpetrator is an organisation and not an individual. The types of abuse which result from institutional abuse will fall into one of the four types above it.

> Abuse is a deliberate act: no one accidentally abuses a child.

Physical abuse

Any abuse involving the use of force is classified as physical abuse. This can mean:

- punching, hitting, slapping, pinching, kicking – in fact any form of physical attack
- burning or scalding
- restraint, such as tying up or tying children to beds or furniture
- deliberate starvation or force feeding
- excessive or inappropriate use of medication
- fabricated or induced illness, where perpetrators will cause illness or injury to a child in order to gain attention for themselves.

Sexual abuse

Sexual abuse of children is about abuse of a position of power. Children can never give informed consent to any sexual activity of any description. Sexual activity is abusive because it exploits children and young people and happens for the personal gratification of the perpetrator.

Sexual abuse can consist of:

- full sexual penetration of any part of the body with a penis, finger or any other object
- touching inappropriate parts of the body, or any other form of sexual contact
- sexual exploitation through prostitution or pornography or any other sexual involvement
- exposure to, or involvement in, pornographic or erotic material
- exposure to, or involvement in, sexual rituals
- making sexually related comments or references which provide sexual gratification for the abuser
- making threats about sexual activities
- exposure to the sexual activity of others.

Emotional abuse

All the other forms of abuse also have an element of emotional abuse. Any situation where a child becomes a victim of abuse at the hands of someone they trusted is, inevitably, going to cause extensive emotional distress. However, some abuse is purely emotional: there are no physical or sexual elements involved. This abuse can take the form of:

- humiliation, belittling, putting down
- withdrawing or refusing affection
- bullying
- making threats
- shouting, swearing
- making insulting or abusive remarks
- racial abuse
- constant teasing and poking fun
- placing a child in a state of fear.

Neglect

Neglect is very different from other forms of abuse. Whereas most abuse involves a deliberate act, neglect happens when care is not given and a child suffers as a result. Of course, as children get older there are many tasks that they can, and should, do for themselves. However, many children still need some level of care until they reach adulthood.

Neglect can happen because those responsible for providing the care do not realise its importance or because they cannot be bothered or choose not to provide it. As the result of neglect, children can become ill, hungry, cold, dirty, injured or deprived of their rights. Neglecting a child can mean:

- not providing sufficient nutritious food
- not providing assistance with eating food if necessary
- not keeping a child warm
- not keeping a child clean and changing nappies if necessary
- not providing clothing for a child for the appropriate weather conditions e.g. wet, cold, sun, etc.
- leaving a child alone without a responsible carer
- living in dirty, unhygienic and potentially hazardous conditions
- not seeking necessary medical/health care support
- not making sure that a child receives an education.

Institutional abuse

Institutional abuse is not confined to large-scale physical or sexual abuse scandals of the type which are well publicised. Of course, this type of systematic and organised abuse can go on in residential, school, sport, leisure or church-based settings, and must be recognised and dealt with appropriately and the children must be protected. However, children can be abused when they are in places where they could expect to be cared for and protected, in many other ways. Here are some possible scenarios.

- Children in residential settings are put in a state of fear by the staff.
- A child or young person is given no involvement or consultation about plans that affect them.
- A child or young person's freedom to go out is limited unreasonably.
- A child or young person's privacy and dignity are not respected.
- Personal correspondence is opened by staff.
- Children are threatened with emotional punishment, such as not being able to see family or friends.
- The setting is run for the convenience of staff, not children.

- Staff use sedation or medication excessively or inappropriately.
- Children are not given access to advice and advocacy.
- Complaints procedures are deliberately made unavailable to a child or young person.

Responding to abuse

(KS 2, 20, 25)

If you suspect abuse

One of the most difficult aspects of dealing with abuse is to admit that it is happening. If you have never encountered deliberate abuse before, it is hard to make the mental leap to admitting and recognising it. However, abuse does happen, and is relatively common: the evidence from people who have survived abuse is that one in ten children experience some form of abuse whilst growing up. You should always consider abuse as the *first option* when a child has an unexplained injury or a change in behaviour with no obvious cause. You may be wrong, and further investigations may prove that there has not been any abuse, but it is worse to be wrong if a child is being abused and you have done nothing.

Abuse happens and children do not disclose it for a range of reasons:

- they are too young
- they do not have the level of understanding to realise what is happening to them
- they are ashamed and believe that it is their own fault
- they have been threatened by the perpetrator or are afraid
- they do not think that they will be believed
- they do not believe that anyone has the power to stop the abuse.

Relatively few children disclose abuse without support, so it is essential you are alert to the possibility of abuse and are able to recognise possible signs and symptoms. If you believe that you have seen signs of abuse, you have an absolute duty to take action by following the procedures in your workplace.

These are likely to involve you in making a referral to the responsible agency, or maybe in reporting your concerns to the responsible person in your workplace. You must discuss your concerns with your line manager, who will work with you to decide the next steps.

What to do if a child or young person discloses abuse

If abuse is disclosed to you by a child or young person you are working with, first you must *listen and believe*. Make sure that you communicate, both by words and by body language, that you believe the child.

Do not ask any questions that could possibly be leading questions, for example: 'And then did he hit you again?' The only questions you should ask should be to prompt the child to continue his or her disclosure, such as, 'And then what happened?' You have to be very careful about this – if you ask any leading questions of the child, then it may damage the evidence, which can later be used to secure a conviction in court. Try to leave the questioning to expert social workers and police officers who have had special training to carry out this type of interview.

You may well be asked to promise not to tell anyone – *never make that promise,* as it is not one you can keep. If you are asked, 'If I tell you something, will you promise not to tell anyone?' you must always make it clear that you cannot make that promise. You must say something like, 'I can't say that until I know what you are going to tell me.'

Following disclosure, you must make it clear that you have to tell others about what you have been told, but that the information is confidential within the group of people who need to know in order to protect. The answer to 'I don't want you to tell people' is to say something like, 'The only people I will tell are those who will help me to make you safe.'

Signs and symptoms of possible abuse

(KS 8, 16, 20, 24)

Information on signs and symptoms comes with a warning – not every sign or symptom is the result of abuse, and not all abuse produces these signs and symptoms. They are a general indicator that abuse should be considered as an explanation. You and your colleagues will need to use other skills such as observation and communication with other professionals in order to build up a complete picture.

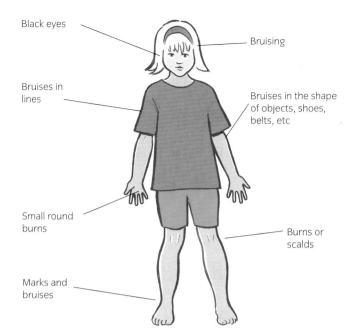

Physical signs of abuse in children

The signs and symptoms in the table could never be a comprehensive list; nor does the existence of one of these signs mean that abuse has definitely taken place. Each is an *indicator* that abuse *may* be happening.

Sign/symptom	Could indicate
• Any bruising, especially on upper arms, ears, inside eye socket or on any part of the chest, abdomen or back • Any injuries which parents cannot explain and child seems unwilling to explain • Burns, particularly small round burns which could have come from a cigarette A child who is or becomes: • aggressive or abusive • bullying other children or being bullied themselves • watchful, cautious or wary of adults • unable to concentrate • avoiding activities that involve removal of clothes, e.g. sports • reluctant to play and be spontaneous • having temper tantrums • lying, stealing, truanting from school	Physical abuse

Sign/symptom	Could indicate
• Bleeding, soreness or infections in the genital/anal area • Frequent abdominal pain • Suddenly behaving differently when the abuse starts • Showing very low self-esteem • Starting to wet or soil themselves • Inappropriate sexual references or ideas during play • Self-harming • Running away • Sleeping problems or nightmares • Starting to behave in an inappropriate sexual way • Suddenly withdrawn and secretive • Suddenly changing in achievement at school • Afraid of physical contact • Starting to behave promiscuously • Starting to abuse alcohol or substances • Making excuses not to go home	Sexual abuse
A child who is or becomes: • very passive and unable to be spontaneous • having feeding problems and failing to thrive • finding it hard to develop close relationships • being over-friendly with strangers • delayed in his or her social development • unable to be creative or imaginative	Emotional abuse or neglect

Assessing the risk

In order to safeguard and protect children effectively you must be able to make a judgement about the risks of their situation. Formal risk assessments are usually carried out by the social work team to whom an initial child protection or child in need referral is made. Most teams will have a risk assessment tool that they use to consider all the factors. The process is not dissimilar from any other risk assessment: look at the risks and consider what is, or could be, in place to minimise the risk.

In assessing risks to children and young people, you need to consider the risk, but also the resilience, sometimes called 'protecting' factors. For example, a drug-using mother working as a prostitute to fund her habit may have a chaotic lifestyle which presents a risk to her child, but there may be a very supportive and capable grandmother who is very involved – thus providing the child with resilience to risk. Think about it like the risk of falling from the top of a three-storey building. If you walk around with no safety rail, the risk is very serious, but the resilience factor is that there is a huge air-filled balloon at the base of the building, thus reducing the risk considerably. The following sections deal with the various areas of risk. Who can abuse? Why does it happen? All of this information gives you risk factors to look out for, but you have to be aware of the resilience factors too.

Where abuse can happen

Abuse can take place at home, in school or in a childcare setting. At home, it could be parent or another carer or relative who is the abuser, although

My story

Hi, I'm Ahmed. I work as a support worker for children and their families. I've been supporting Jason and his two children – Romeo, who is 4, and Chardonnay, who is 6. Jason was left with the children when his long-term partner Casey died from a drug overdose two years ago. He has coped OK with a lot of help from his Auntie Hyacinth who lives just around the corner. Jason has a fairly messy life, he is still doing some dealing and is using probably more than he should. One of the areas I've worked hard with him on is being organised and having routines and he's got quite good at all the domestic stuff. I've also spent a long time showing him how to play with his children. Now he'll do things with them when they come in from school and at weekends – not all the time, but it's getting there. Jason had no idea about any of this. He was abused by his mother's boyfriend, his mother had a chaotic lifestyle and Jason went in and out of care from the age of 10. The fact that he has been able to do as much as he has is a credit to him.

Hyacinth is great. She calls in every day and will always pick up on stuff if there's a problem. The children just go round to hers if Jason isn't home: if he gets involved in stuff, he just forgets to come home. It doesn't happen often, but it has the potential to go horribly wrong when it does.

Today Hyacinth told me she has advanced cervical cancer. The prognosis is not hopeful. Her main concern is Jason and the children. She thinks that Jason is not reliable enough to have sole responsibility for the children and that they will need to come into care. She is distraught at the prospect, which is why she put off seeking medical treatment for so long. She also knows that Jason will be devastated because of his own experiences in the care system.

There will have to be a serious re-assessment of the risks to these children.

---

it could also be a neighbour or regular visitor. It can also be a professional care worker or other person who has regular contact with a child, such as a teacher, priest, sports coach, youth leader, etc., who is perpetrating the abuse. This situation can mean that abuse goes undetected for some time because of the nature of the contact abusers may have.

In a residential or day-care setting, abuse may be more likely to be noticed, although some of the more subtle forms of abuse, such as humiliation, can sometimes be so commonplace that it is not recognised as abusive behaviour.

Who abuses?

Abuse is not only carried out by individuals: groups or even organisations can also create abusive situations. There have been well-publicised cases where groups of professional childcare workers in residential settings have abused children in their care, and the same is true in residential school situations. Authority figures such as priests and teachers have also been found to have abused children with whose care they were entrusted. Often people will act in a different way in a group to how they would act alone. Think about teenage 'gangs', which exist because people are prepared to do things jointly which they would not think to do if they were by themselves.

There is also abuse that comes about because of the way in which an establishment is run, where the basis for planning the systems, rules and regulations is not the welfare, rights and well-being of the children or young people, but the convenience of the staff and management. This is the sort of situation where children can have their letters opened, be given communal clothing, only allowed visits at set times and not allowed to express views about their own lives. This is now recognised as 'institutional abuse'. It is rare that such behaviour is found, but this was common practice only 30 years ago – and there are some staff whose views do not seem to have changed much since those days!

Childcare settings can also be the setting for bullying and abuse by other children or young people.

Remember

Abusers might be:

- individuals
- groups
- organisations.

Where are the high risks?

It is not possible accurately to predict situations where abuse will take place. It is possible, though, to identify some factors that seem to make it more likely that abuse could occur. This does not mean that abuse will definitely happen – neither should you assume that all people in these circumstances are abusers – but it does mean that you should be aware of the possibility when you are dealing with these situations.

High-risk situations

Child abuse can happen in situations where:

- parents have many unmet needs of their own
- parents or carers need to show dominance over others
- parents or carers have been poorly parented themselves
- parents or carers were abused themselves as children
- families are living in poverty and deprivation
- families have a history of poor or violent relationships
- children place many demands and stresses on parents/carers because of illness or disability and there is inadequate support.

Active knowledge

Find out the answers to all of these questions – if you can't find out any answers, ask your line manager. How does your workplace make assessments of risk to children? What factors are considered? Is a special tool used? How are risks discussed? How are plans made to reduce risks? Where is this recorded? How often do you re-assess risks?

High risks in care settings

Abuse can happen in a care setting when:

- staff are poorly trained or untrained
- there is little or no management supervision or support
- staff work in isolation

- there are inadequate numbers of staff to cope with the workload
- there are inadequate security arrangements
- there is no key worker system and good relationships are not formed between staff and the children and young people.

Reflect

Look at your workplace. Do any of the above points apply? If any of these are the case in your workplace, you need to be aware that people can be put under so much stress that they behave abusively. Remember that abuse is not just about physical cruelty. If none of these things happen in your workplace, then try to imagine what work would be like if they did. Sit down, with a colleague if possible, and think or talk through the effects of any two of the items in the list. Think about how you need to adapt your practice to take account of any risks you have identified.

What if a professional carer abuses?

There are special procedures in place for investigating abuse inflicted by childcare workers or foster carers. It is investigated by an outside agency and immediate steps are taken to remove the alleged perpetrator from contact with the children or young people until the investigation has been completed.

The Child Protection Register

The Child Protection Register is a record of all the children for whom there are concerns that they are at risk of, or have suffered, significant harm. The Register is held and maintained by the local authority, but the information can be shared with other relevant professionals. There are four main categories in the Register: physical abuse, sexual abuse, neglect and emotional abuse. The decision to place the name of a child or young person on the Register is taken by a Child Protection Conference. This must be followed by a child protection plan, which is reviewed regularly. You may well be working with children who are 'on the Register' and so will be involved in regular reviews and planning for the future.

Keys to good practice: Dealing with abuse

If you want to be effective in helping to stop abuse you will need to:

✓ believe that abuse happens

✓ recognise abusive behaviour

✓ be aware of when abuse can happen

✓ understand who abusers can be

✓ know the policies and procedures for handling abuse

✓ recognise likely abusive situations

✓ report any concerns or suspicions.

Your most important contribution will be to be *alert*. For example, a child's care plan or your organisational policy should specify how you will keep a check on whereabouts – if you are alert to where a child or young person is, and who he or she is with, it is a contribution to minimising risks.

Compensation

Anyone, including a child, who has been abused by someone who has been tried in court and found guilty, can receive Criminal Injuries compensation. It is also possible for cases to be brought even where there is no criminal trial. It is vital that any child or young person who has been abused in any way should have a solicitor to act in his or her interests.

Many factors are involved in building protection against abuse

The effects of abuse

(KS 16, 19)

Abuse devastates those who suffer it. It causes people to lose their self-esteem and their confidence. Many children and young people become withdrawn and struggle to communicate, and anger is common amongst those who have been abused. This anger may be directed against the perpetrator, or at those people around them who failed to recognise the abuse and stop it happening, or at the world in general. One of the greatest tragedies is when children and young people who have been abused turn their anger against themselves. Children and young people may deliberately self-harm or may 'self-destruct' through behaviour or lifestyle. These are situations that require expert help. You may be involved as part of a team working with a child who has survived abuse; if so, there will be an agreed plan that will be reviewed regularly.

The perpetrator of the abuse also requires expert help, and this should be available through various agencies depending on the type and seriousness of the abuse. People who abuse children receive very little sympathy or understanding from society. There is no public recognition that some abusers may have been under tremendous strain and pressure, and may have themselves been abused as children. Abusers may find that they have no support from friends or family. Many abusers will face the consequences of their actions alone.

Effects on you

Childcare professionals who have to deal with abusive situations react in different ways. There is no 'right way' to react. Everyone is different. If you have to deal with abuse, these are some of the ways you may feel, and some steps you can take which may help.

- If this is the first time you have dealt with abuse, or if you are more involved than previously, you may feel quite traumatised by an abusive incident. It is quite normal to find that you cannot get the incident off your mind, that you have difficulty concentrating on other things, or that you keep having 'flashbacks'. You may also feel that you need to keep talking about what happened.

- Talking can be very beneficial, but if you are discussing an incident outside your workplace, you must remember rules of confidentiality and never use names. You will find that you can talk about the circumstances just as well by referring to 'the boy' or 'the father' or 'the daughter'. This way of talking does become second nature, and is useful because it allows you to tell others about things which have happened at work whilst maintaining confidentiality.

- These feelings are likely to last for a fairly short time, and are a natural reaction. If at any time you feel that you are having difficulty, you must talk to your manager or line manager, who should be able to help.

- Alternatively, the situation may have made you feel very angry, and you may have an overwhelming urge to inflict some serious damage on the perpetrator of the abuse. Whilst this is understandable, it is not professional and you will have to find other ways of dealing with your anger. Again, your line manager should help you.

- Everyone has different ways of dealing with anger, such as taking physical exercise, punching a cushion, writing feelings down, crying or telling their best friend. Whatever you do with your anger in ordinary situations, you should do the same in this situation (just remember to respect confidentiality if you need to tell your best friend).

You should talk to your line manager if you are having difficulties with your feelings

It is perfectly legitimate to be angry, but you cannot bring this anger into the professional relationship.

- The situation may have made you distressed, and you may want to go home and have a good cry, or give your own children an extra hug. This is a perfectly normal reaction. No matter how many years you work, or how many times it happens, you may still feel the same way.

- Some workplaces will have arrangements where workers are able to share difficult situations and get support from each other. Elsewhere, colleagues may offer each other support and advice in an informal way. You may find that work colleagues who have had similar experiences are the best people with whom to share this type of experience.

- There is, of course, the possibility that the situation may have brought back painful memories for you of abuse you have suffered in your own past. This is often the most difficult situation to deal with, because you may feel as if you should be able to help because you know how it feels, but your own experience has left you without any room to deal with the feelings of others. There are many avenues of support now available to survivors of abuse. You can find out about the nearest support confidentially, if you do not want your workplace colleagues or line manager to know.

- There is no doubt that dealing with abuse is one of the most stressful aspects of working with children and young people. There is nothing odd or abnormal about feeling that you need to share what you have experienced and looking for support from others. In fact, most experienced line managers would be far more concerned about a worker who appears quite unaffected by dealing with abuse, than about one who comes looking for guidance and reassurance.

Remember

- Feeling upset is normal.
- Talk about the incident if that helps.
- Being angry is OK, but deal with it sensibly – take physical exercise, do the housework, cry.
- Do not be unprofessional with the abuser.
- If you are a survivor of abuse and you find it hard to deal with your feelings, ask for help.

The laws to protect children

(KS 1, 7, 8, 9, 15, 26, 27)

Ultimately, the responsibility for child protection in England and Wales lies with the Department for Children, Schools and Families (DCSF). The DCSF issues both statutory (compulsory) and non-statutory (advisory) guidance to local councils, although the National Assembly for Wales also produces guidance for Welsh authorities. Children's services departments are then responsible for making sure that they have policies and procedures in place which follow the guidance.

The Scottish Executive provides guidance to local councils in Scotland. In Northern Ireland, the Department of Health, Social Services and Public Safety issues guidance to the four local health and social services boards.

On the following pages are some of the most important pieces of legislation and guidelines with an impact on the safeguarding and protection of children and young people.

Legislation and guidelines	Key impacts
Children and Young Persons Act 1933	Mostly overtaken by subsequent legislation, but some key provisions still apply:
	Power to the police to force an entry where there is reason to believe that a child is at risk
	List of acts which are sexual offences, these are listed in Schedule 1 of the Act – thus sex offenders are described as 'Schedule 1 offenders'
	This Act also deals with children's employment in entertainment
Children and Young Persons Act 1989	(covers England and Wales) This is the basis for current practice in child protection
	Paramountcy principle – the child's interests must come first
	Views of child must be considered
	Concept of parental responsibility
	S17 identified 'children in need'
	S47 placed a duty on local authorities to investigate where there is 'reasonable cause to believe that a child is suffering, or is likely to suffer, significant harm'
Children (Northern Ireland) Order 1995	Similar provisions to above
Children (Scotland) Act 1995	Similar provisions to above
Sex Offenders Act 1997	Created sex offenders register and offenders must notify police of changes of address
Human Rights Act 1998	Sets out rights that also apply to children. Gives right not to be subjected to torture or inhuman and degrading treatment
Working Together to Safeguard Children (1999)	Statutory guidance about the systems and processes to be implemented to safeguard and protect children
	Subsequently updated 2006
Protection of Children Act 1999 Protection of Children (Scotland) Act 2003	Created list of people unsuitable to work with children (PoCA), which must be checked before employment
	Also requirement to run check through Criminal Records Bureau before employment
	Employers must inform list if anyone dismissed because of abuse

Legislation and guidelines	Key impacts
Children's Commissioner for Wales Act 2001 Commissioner for Children and young people (NI) Order 2003 Commissioner for Children and Young People (Scotland) Act 2003	Created Children's Commissioners with remit to promote and uphold children's rights
Education Act 2002	Required local education authorities, school and college governing bodies to safeguard and protect the welfare of children
Adoption and Children Act 2002	Extended definition of 'harm' from 1989 Act to include 'witnessing domestic violence'
Sexual Offences Act 2003	Updated offences against children to include grooming, trafficking and abuse of position of trust (which includes childcare professionals) Also includes offences committed by British citizens when abroad
Children Act 2004	Followed from the Laming enquiry into the death of Victoria Climbie. *Every Child Matters* was the Green Paper. This Act has separate sections for England and Wales. All local authorities must bring children's social services and education into one children's services department with a director and a lead elected member. Services to be integrated around five outcomes to benefit children. Local Safeguarding Children's Boards to take responsibility for child protection policy and procedures in each local authority Makes it an offence to hit a child if it leaves a mark on the skin or causes mental harm Established the Children's Commissioner in England
Domestic Violence Crime and Victims Act 2004	Made it an offence for anyone to 'allow' the death of a child, so all members of a household where a child is being abused can be held responsible

What happens in an emergency?

All countries have legal procedures where police, social workers or sometimes the NSPCC can take immediate steps to protect children in an emergency. This is only a short-term measure and must then be followed by proper assessments and investigations.

The flow chart on the next page gives a good picture of the processes followed.

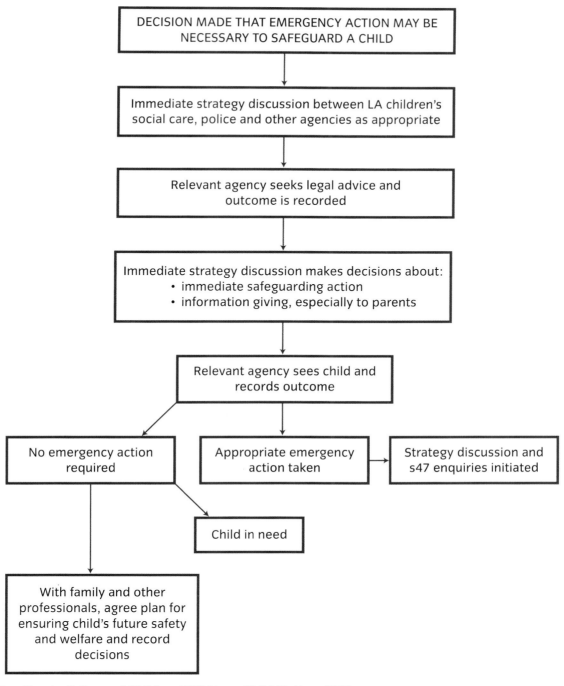

Working Together to Safeguard Children DfES Every Child Matters 2006

Working in partnership

Work to protect children is always done in partnership with the child or young person and with the parent(s) if possible.

There are circumstances where this cannot happen, for example:

- A baby, or very young child, has been abandoned

- A child has been injured and it is not clear if either or both of the parents are the perpetrator
- A child has disclosed abuse but the non-abusing parent does not believe the child
- A child has been severely neglected by parent(s).

Even in these circumstances, parents should be informed of actions and any plans.

What to do if you suspect abuse in your own workplace

Blowing the whistle

One of the most difficult situations to deal with is when you believe that abuse is happening in your workplace. It is often hard to accept that the people you work with would abuse children and young people, but if you have evidence or good grounds for concern, then you will have to take action.

- The first step is to report the abuse to your line manager.
- If you suspect that your line manager is involved, or will not take action, you must refer it to the most senior manager who is likely to be impartial.
- If you do not believe that it is possible to report the abuse to anyone within your workplace, you should contact your local Director of Children's Services (or the NSPCC, if you prefer).
- If you work for the NSPCC, Children's Services or the health service and you are concerned about abuse, you should still follow the same steps, although you will need to contact a senior manager who is not directly involved with your workplace.

If you do not believe that there is anyone within your workplace or organisation who would take action on any concerns, or if you have reported concerns and nothing has been done, you should contact the inspectorate for your country. In England, this should be Ofsted; in Scotland, Her Majesty's inspectorate of Education (HMIE) and/or the Care Commission; in Wales, The Social Services Inspectorate for Wales (SSIW) and/or the Care Standards Inspectorate for Wales (CSIW); and in Northern Ireland, the Northern Ireland Social Services Inspectorate.

Reporting and recording information

Where there are injuries, or the possibility of physical evidence, as in sexual abuse, a medical examination must be carried out. The parents must consent if they have parental responsibility, unless they are the suspected abusers, in which case they should be informed but their consent is not required. If there is a risk to other children by the parents being made aware of the examination – for example, the family may disappear, thus placing any other children at risk and abandoning the child concerned – a decision can be made not to inform them at that stage. The examination must be carried out by a paediatrician with specialist training and must be done in a suitable child-friendly environment. This usually means a children's hospital or a specialist examination suite. Examinations of children should not take place in a general hospital A&E or in a police station.

It is also important that you write a report of the incident as soon as possible. You may think that you will never forget what you saw or heard, but details do become blurred with time and repetition. Your workplace may have a special form or you may have to write a report. If there is a reason why writing a report is not possible, then you should record your evidence on audiotape. It is not acceptable practice to pass on the information verbally – there must be a record that can be referred to. Your evidence may be needed by the social workers and police officers who will investigate the situation. It may be useful for a doctor who will conduct an examination, or it may be needed for the case conference or court proceedings.

How to write the report

You must record information clearly, which must be dated and timed, and make sure that you only record what you saw and heard and what you know from your own experience. Do not record what others have told you. Recording it does not mean that it is over, but it does help in enabling you to gather your thoughts. Sometimes it can help if you have to organise yourself by writing things down.

Protecting children and young people

Protecting and safeguarding the welfare of children is what you do – it is why you go to work each day. Supporting children and their families to achieve the best possible outcomes to improve their own life chances is what working with children is all about.

Test yourself

1 What is the difference between abuse and neglect?

2 What are the categories under which children can be placed on the child protection register?

3 List four factors that may lead you to suspect that a child has been sexually abused.

4 List four factors that may lead you to suspect that a child has been physically abused.

5 What is the difference between risk and resilience?

HSC 34 UNIT TEST

1 Who are the guardians of children's rights?

2 List at least five children's rights that you consider to be of key importance. Why do you think this?

3 How well do you think the UK does at promoting children's rights?

4 What factors contribute to well-being?

5 Identify three key areas in which children and young people should be encouraged to express views and preferences.

6 What is the difference between safeguarding and child protection?

7 Why is safeguarding important?

8 Who are your main partners in working with children and young people?

Don't forget to refer to the evidence opportunities grid (see pages 357–375) for more ideas for suitable evidence for your NVQ.

Contribute to the assessment of children and young people's needs and the development of care plans

In simple terms, this unit is about finding out what children and young people's needs are and then planning how to meet them. However, that does not mean that this is a simple task. In order to make an effective assessment, you need to know a great deal of information – including information about the child's history, family, education, relationships and health – but you also have to know the basis for the assessment: what are the criteria against which you are assessing. You have to know what you need to find out and you have to know what you don't know – so that you can see where the gaps are.

You also have to find out what the child or young person and his or her family want to result from the involvement and intervention of childcare professionals – these will be the outcomes. Then you need to be able to work with the child or young person and family to find out the best way to achieve the outcomes they have identified.

Accurate and thorough assessments are the best hope any child has of being able to identify and achieve outcomes to improve well-being and life chances.

In this unit you will find 'Active knowledge' features containing activities that will contribute to assessment for your NVQ. Remember that these features only offer the opportunity for partial assessment; you can also refer to the evidence opportunities grid (see pages 357–375) for more ideas to provide suitable evidence for your NVQ.

What you need to learn

- Assessments
- Needs
- Making an assessment
- Children's development
- Family and social relationships
- Analysing the information and making a judgement
- How care plans are agreed
- Involving the child and family
- Recording the decisions about care plans
- Plans
- Implementing care plans
- Care plans for looked-after children
- Care plans for children who are not looked after
- Recording and informing

HSC 36a Contribute to the assessment of children and young people's needs, wishes and preferences

Assessments

(KS 1, 2, 7, 8)

Children and young people can be assessed for all sorts of reasons, and you will become involved in different types of assessment depending on the job you do.

However, this unit is about assessing children's needs for the purpose of developing care plans, so it will essentially be about assessing and planning for children in need and children who are looked after. If your job involves working with disabled children, you may also be involved in developmental assessments relating to a child's disability. If you work in a health setting, you could be involved in assessments of a child's progress or responses to treatments or palliative care programmes. Working in an education setting may mean that you are involved in assessments of a child's potential and progress, or their behaviour or attendance. The purposes of the assessments may be different, but the processes of carrying them out and the underlying principles remain largely the same. Any assessment should:

- have the child as its centre
- be based on child development
- consider the child in the context of family and environment
- be rooted in ensuring equality of opportunity for all children
- be undertaken in co-operation and partnership with parents and family
- identify strengths and look to build on them, not just list problems
- involve all other relevant agencies as partners
- be recognised as a 'process', not an 'event'
- be evidence-based.

Key term

Palliative care: Care given to those with conditions that cannot be cured, usually terminal illnesses. The care aims to improve quality of life and lessen symptoms, but cannot actually combat the condition itself.

An assessment following the principles above will involve the child and the family, and will be about the child or young person. This may sound obvious, but it is easy to lose the focus on the child and end up producing an assessment about the family, or about the capacity of the school, or about the needs of the support team – instead, the child must always be front and centre of any assessment. An assessment will also recognise the context in which a child or young person lives; this could be about living accommodation or the family dynamics or the nature and type of a disability, and it could take into account any inequalities faced by the child or young person. Good assessments seek for the 'positives' in the life of the child or young person and look to see how they can be built on and become a key part of future planning. There is a danger in only looking at the problems that you focus on them and miss the opportunities to look for positive outcomes for the child's future.

The legal basis for assessment

Part III of the Children Act 1989 is the legal basis for the provision of local services to children in need. The Act defines a child as being anyone under the age of 18 years.

The key principles underpinning the Children Act 1989 are to both safeguard and promote the welfare of vulnerable children:

It shall be the general duty of every local authority to safeguard and promote the welfare of children within their area who are in need; and so far as is consistent with that duty, to promote the upbringing of such children by their families, by providing a range and level of services appropriate to those children's needs.

Children Act 1989 s17(1)

The definition of a child in need is also in the 1989 Act:

A child shall be taken to be in need if –

a. he is unlikely to achieve or maintain or to have the opportunity of achieving or maintaining a reasonable standard of health or development without the provision for him of services by a local authority …

b. his health or development is likely to be significantly impaired, or further impaired, without the provision for him of such services; or

c. he is disabled,

And 'family' in relation to such a child includes any person who has parental responsibility for the child and any other person with whom he has been living.

Children Act 1989 s17(10)

There are similar provisions for Scotland under the Children (Scotland) Act 1995.

Needs

(KS 1, 2, 14, 15, 18)

In Unit 34 you learned about the different needs that all children and young people have. These are broadly split into PIES:

- physical – food, warmth, sleep, exercise, etc.
- intellectual – mental stimulation, challenges, learning
- emotional – feeling secure, being loved, giving love, self-esteem
- social – relationships with others, friendship, interacting with others.

Of course, these needs take a wide range of forms, but all of them will fall into one or more of these categories.

Maslow's Hierarchy of Needs

Not all needs are at the same level. A widely accepted view from psychologist Abraham Maslow is that there is a 'hierarchy of needs' and that we must meet the needs at the lower levels before we are able to develop and progress to higher-level needs.

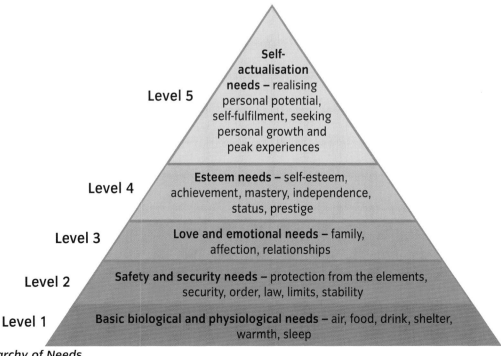

Level 5 — Self-actualisation needs – realising personal potential, self-fulfilment, seeking personal growth and peak experiences

Level 4 — Esteem needs – self-esteem, achievement, mastery, independence, status, prestige

Level 3 — Love and emotional needs – family, affection, relationships

Level 2 — Safety and security needs – protection from the elements, security, order, law, limits, stability

Level 1 — Basic biological and physiological needs – air, food, drink, shelter, warmth, sleep

Maslow's Hierarchy of Needs

As you look at the levels, you can see that there is a progression from basic physical needs to more complex needs relating to relationships, self-esteem and fufilment. Maslow's argument, put simply, is that someone cannot enter into a positive and happy relationship if they are starving, nor can they go on to extend themselves and achieve to their full potential if they are not content with who they are.

Basic physical needs

People will do whatever is necessary to meet their basic physical needs. These needs rank as the most important when people are placed under threat. Most people are fortunate enough to be able to take the basic physical needs for granted, but all human beings, if they are deprived of them, will go to great lengths to satisfy those needs. For example, if a person is starving it becomes his or her overriding priority to find food. All of the higher-level needs fade into insignificance when compared to needs like food, warmth and shelter. For children the needs are the same, but the ability to meet them is often dependent on others. For example, a hungry baby will cry until someone provides food, a freezing toddler does not have the means to get warm and a young child locked out of his or her home has no means of finding shelter.

Safety and security needs

These are the needs which people will try to satisfy once they have met their basic needs. When they have sufficient food, some heat and a shelter, they will look to feel safe and secure. Children need to be safe and secure from harm in order to develop. Sufficient food and warmth may keep a child alive, but a child who grows up in an atmosphere of violence, abuse, fear and anxiety is unlikely to become a well-adjusted adult.

Love and emotional needs

Children need to be loved. They need to grow up in a loving and caring environment, and be able to form a strong emotional attachment with an adult who will care for them. This is usually the mother, but can be another figure: the father or a grandparent or a foster carer. Regardless of who the person is, they must remain permanent and constant in the child's life. There has been a great deal of research into attachment and bonding, and the issues are not all straightforward, but early attachment with a mother-figure is thought to form the basis for the future emotional well-being of the child as he or she progresses into adulthood (John Bowlby 1958, 1969, 1973, 1980). Without this attachment, it is difficult for any child to relate to and form relationships with others. The lack of an early attachment has a serious impact on the self-esteem of children and young people as they grow and develop. This need to form relationships with other human beings only becomes important after basic needs and safety and security needs have been achieved.

Esteem needs

Self-esteem is about the way children and young people feel about themselves. The child who feels confident and positive as they grow will be more likely to become a happy and confident adult. It is vital that children's achievements are recognised and praised so that they understand that they are respected and have a valuable and useful contribution to make.

Self-actualisation needs

This is about every human being's need to reach his or her maximum potential. This might be through setting out to achieve new goals or meeting new challenges, or through developing existing talents. Abraham Maslow suggests that if our other needs have not been met (from the most basic needs up to self-esteem needs), these needs will never be met, because people will continue to try to achieve the needs lower down the hierarchy: they will never attempt self-fulfilment and will never reach their full potential. If children and young people are encouraged to develop interests, attempt challenges and always do the best they can, they are far more likely to develop into adults who achieve their full potential. Children who are discouraged or constantly

Hi, I'm Alex, I'm 8 and I go to school; the bus comes to pick me up and I go with my friends. The bus takes Emily's wheelchair on a lift. I am very, very clever. My helper in school says that I do the best drawings she has ever seen and that my blue jumper makes her smile and that I am funny. My drawings are on the wall in the classroom. Our teacher asked for people to talk to the visitors about the drawings, and I said that I would. The visitors were very interested – she was a very nice lady and I told her that I liked her and she smiled and said thank you. I was on the telly. The lady was called Queen.

My story

Hi, I'm Mathilde. I work particularly with Alex, but with the rest of the class too. He is such a lovely little boy and so full of confidence. His parents spend a lot of time with him and he is the key focus of the family. I believe in making sure that everything the children do receives a positive comment. I make sure I speak to all of the children each day and always say something – even if it is just 'Thank you for wearing such a lovely blue jumper – that has really cheered me up' or 'That is the best smile I have seen all day.' Even small comments like these can make a difference if children have them reinforced constantly.

told 'Be careful' or 'No, you can't do that' or 'That's too hard for you' are far less likely to be contented and fulfilled adults than those who are encouraged with 'Give it a try', 'Do your best' or 'You can do it'.

Making an assessment

(KS 4, 8, 17)

An assessment is a two-stage process: first you gather information, then you make a judgement using the information you have. One of the most common

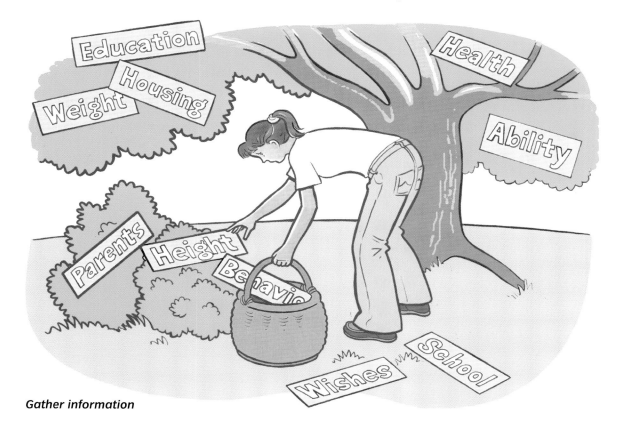

Gather information

Make a judgement

failings in the assessment process is that people gather huge amounts of information and don't draw any conclusions.

Gathering information

You need information *about* a child in order to make an assessment, but the key to doing it well is to gather it *with* the child or young person. He or she is the focus of the assessment and is your first port of call for information. Do not assume that there is any reason why you cannot gather information directly from a child or young person: the information is there for the asking; you just have to go about getting it in a different way.

If you are not able to speak directly to a child in a way which they can understand, or if you are not able to hear and understand what a child is communicating to you, you will have to get basic factual information from the child's parents or carers. Do not mix this up with finding out the views of parents or carers – this is information about the child or young person.

A great deal of the information you gather for an assessment does not have to be spoken: you can observe the behaviour of children, which will tell you a great deal about likes, dislikes and what a child wants. Observing the behaviour of children with whom you do not have spoken communication is invaluable in making an assessment. If you do not know the child well, you will need to ask parents, carers or colleagues to interpret some behaviour or communications that you observe.

Reflect

Remember that only 7 per cent of what we communicate is through spoken language – the rest is understood from body language. Babies communicate very well, even though they don't actually speak. Gestures, facial expressions, body movements and sounds enable babies to make their needs, wishes and views very clear! How good are you at understanding what children and young people are really communicating? Do you really listen to everything you are being told – or only to what children say? Take some time to reflect about how good you are at 'listening with your eyes'.

What information to gather

The assessment framework used in England and Wales has a useful diagram illustrating the different aspects of a child's life you need to consider when you are making an assessment. Regardless of where you work, this is a useful reminder of what you need to think about when gathering information for an assessment. However, there are limits to the amount of information you may want to gather depending on the circumstances. Sometimes even the basic referral information cannot be obtained in an emergency situation in which steps need to be taken quickly to protect a child or young person. In this case, emergency procedures take over: sufficient information is gathered to enable the child to be made safe, and this will be followed later with an in-depth assessment. Sometimes an initial assessment will be undertaken to establish the need for more in-depth and ongoing work, as not all children will need to have long-term involvement. However, this unit is looking at assessments which lead to a care plan, which means that as much information as possible should be brought together so that the most effective plan can be developed.

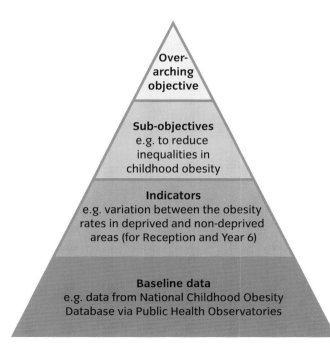

Hierarchy of objectives (Department of Health)

Children's development

(KS 8, 12, 15, 19)

You must know and understand the key milestones for children as they grow and develop: if you do not know where children should be at any point in their development, how will you know if a child is developing and progressing as they should? However, you need to make sure that you also give careful consideration to which areas of a child's development you are going to assess and be sure that you know how you are going to measure the development. If you do not have the expertise to use developmental charts and scales, work with a colleague who does. You also need to think about the factors that may have had an impact on how a child has progressed, which could include:

- physical or learning disability
- sensory impairment
- emotional trauma
- harm or abuse
- family circumstances
- living environment.

Do not underestimate the effect that any of these factors can have on a child's progress through expected developmental milestones (for the stages in a child's development, see the chart in Unit 31, pages 12–14).

Health

The health of children and young people is not just about developmental milestones, although they are important and you should make sure that a child has had all the appropriate developmental checks. It is also about well-being and physical health. You will need to make an assessment of the child's general health, and whether or not he or she is receiving appropriate health care – not just care if the child is ill, but also preventive health measures such as vaccinations, dental and optical care. For some children, there may be genetic factors to consider, such as hereditary illnesses or disabilities; it is important that you establish whether or not there is proper recognition of the implications of any hereditary conditions and that any necessary steps for treatment or care are being taken. When you are finding out information about a child or young person's health, you also need to find out about diet, exercise and the understanding of the child about how to maintain a healthy lifestyle. In older children and young people, it is also important to find out about health-related issues such as substance misuse.

Education

Children's education is about much more than school, so do not fall into the trap of thinking that you only need to find out information about education if a child is of school age. Education begins from birth, and all early education is through play. In order to undertake an effective assessment, you will need to consider aspects such as whether or not the child or young person has the chance to socialise and interact with other children, and whether there is a

parent or carer who is actively involved and who is supportive of the child's **cognitive development**. Remember that if the child or young person is receiving education, whether in a nursery, with a child minder, in a playgroup or in school, then you should involve the education provider in the assessment.

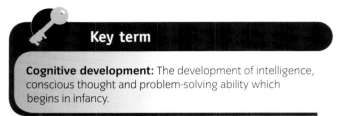

Key term

Cognitive development: The development of intelligence, conscious thought and problem-solving ability which begins in infancy.

Emotional and behavioural development

The information you need to know about a child's emotional development concerns how they relate to others, the early attachments they had and any serious disruptions they experienced. As children grow, they develop the ability to empathise and put themselves in the position of someone else. A child who has experienced emotionally damaging experiences may not be able to do this. You also need to consider how the child or young person copes under stress and pressure and how well they deal with anger and rage. This is where you need to look at how children present themselves to the world. Are they shy or outgoing? Are they chatty and friendly or rude and sullen? Are they angry and intimidating or kind and thoughtful?

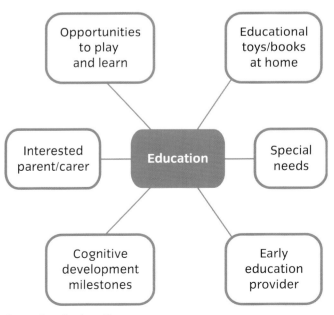

Aspects of education

Emotional and behavioural development

Identity

As children grow and develop, they begin to see themselves as separate individuals and will start to develop a sense of who they are. Self-image or self-concept is about how children and young people see themselves. Overall it can be a positive image or a negative one, but a great many factors contribute to an individual sense of identity. These will include:

- gender
- race
- language/accent
- values and beliefs
- religion
- sexual orientation.

All of these aspects will contribute to a greater or lesser extent, depending on the age and the circumstances of the child concerned.

Self-esteem is about how children and young people value themselves. A child who is encouraged and regularly told how good he or she is and given a lot of positive feelings is the sort of person who is likely to feel that he or she has something to offer, and can make a useful contribution to any situation. However, a child who is shouted at, blamed or belittled constantly is likely to grow into an adult who lacks belief in himself or herself, or finds it difficult to go into new situations and to accept new challenges.

Family and social relationships

(KS 3, 5, 14, 16, 17, 18, 19)

In making an assessment, you need to know about how a child or young person relates to others. Even in very young children, it is possible to observe how they interact with other children and to gather information about how they relate to other family members. What is the attitude to siblings? For example, is the child caring and loving or bullying and aggressive? As children reach around 10 years old, they are able to empathise – to see the point of view of others and to 'put themselves in someone else's shoes'. You also need to find out about friendships and how well the child or young person is able to make age-appropriate relationships with his or her peers.

Social presentation

The age at which a child becomes aware of how they present to the outside world varies depending on the child, but many aspects of modern society seem to have combined to make this earlier than even 20 or 30 years ago. An assessment should look at the extent to which a child or young person recognises that the clothes they wear, their appearance and their personal hygiene, as well as their behaviour, have an impact and an effect on others. It is also important to

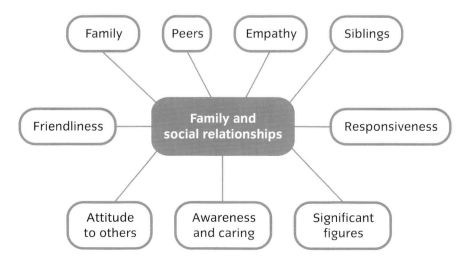

Family and social relationships

consider whether a child or young person is prepared to modify behaviour in order to make it socially acceptable.

Self-care skills

This part of an assessment is really about how well a child or young person is moving towards independence. Remember that when a young person has a disability or impairment, you need to consider independence as relative to the ability of the child or young person. There are many tasks that children begin to do for themselves as they grow: the obvious ones are washing, personal hygiene and dressing, but there are other self-care skills such as the ability to make arrangements and solve problems – for example, planning to travel somewhere on public transport, or being able to prepare a meal or go shopping. Clearly, many self-care skills are relative to age and ability.

Parents and the ability to parent effectively

Any assessment must consider the capacity of parents. In order to provide effective parenting, the family should be living in a stable environment where all-important early attachment relationships are not disrupted and where life is not chaotic, but has some sense of order and routine.

Children should also receive love, warmth and affection from their parents. You should look for the touches and physical contact that are so important for children as signals of love and affection. Demonstrable love and affection must be present alongside guidance and clear boundaries, so that children know the limits of what they can and cannot do. Children need to be able to see and understand what is expected of them – so the old saying of 'don't do what I do, do what I say' is not an effective way to parent children. Parents should be able to model the behaviour that is expected from children and be able to explain boundaries and the reasons for them. Boundaries should never be reinforced with physical punishment, hitting or bullying in order to get someone weaker and smaller than you to do what

you want – this is not the kind of behaviour which parents should be modelling.

Parents are a child's first and most important educators, and they should provide stimulation and opportunities for children to develop and learn. They also need to support a child to communicate and relate to others, to play and to go to school as appropriate.

Equally essential is basic physical care: children need to be kept warm, fed and clean, as well as to have somewhere warm and comfortable to sleep. They also need to be safe from harm and from danger, both inside and outside the home.

Make sure that you think about all of the following areas in so far as they are relevant to the particular child or young person you are assessing:

- keeping safe
- setting boundaries
- modelling behaviour
- providing stimulation
- providing stability
- providing physical care
- providing love, warmth and affection.

Family and environment

Children and young people do not live and grow up in a vacuum. In general they live with a family in a

Children or young people should be living in a stable environment

particular area. During the assessment process it is important to take all this into account. You will need to find out about the way the family functions and behaves, check out the history of the family and whether there have been any major changes or significant events. You need to know who lives with the child and how they relate. You also need to find out some medical background and history, particularly any genetic factors that could have an impact on the child's development.

The area in which the family lives can be influential in a child's life, so you need to include what you know and can find out about the prevailing culture of the area, and to what extent the family are a part of the local community. Be careful, though, not to make assumptions about how someone may behave just based on the area they live in.

There is often more to families that just the main members; often the wider family network can be important and may have a great influence, or provide significant support for a family. The social and economic circumstances of a family, including employment history and financial situation, can have a significant effect on a child or young person, so you will need to find out as much as you can about the history of family circumstances.

Analysing the information and making a judgement

(KS 2, 3, 4, 6, 16, 17)

Once you have gathered all the necessary information, you need to collate it in some kind of order under each of these three areas: child development, parenting capacity and family and environment. At this stage, it may be that more than one professional is contributing to the analysis and there will need to be careful consideration of the importance and significance of the different areas of information that have been gathered. The key factor throughout is always the needs of the child and these must outweigh everything else when you are supporting the analysis of information.

If you are in a position of contributing to the analysis, you must do so from a position of knowing the key developmental milestones, understanding the minimum requirements for 'good enough' parenting and understanding the potential impact of family behaviour and local, environmental influences.

There is a range of potential judgements about future action in relation to any particular child, but any plan must be based on the analysis of the information and supported by evidence. In practice, this means being able to show, by making reference to the information you have gathered and any relevant research, that any action plan is likely to be effective and is appropriate for the child.

With the child and family

None of this is an isolated activity. The child and, where possible, the parents must be involved in the process of assessment and should be encouraged to make a contribution and give comments. An assessment and care plan conducted without the

Ethical issue

You are gathering information for an assessment of Kieran, a 12-year-old boy who has, over the last 12 months, been displaying very aggressive and disruptive behaviour in school. He has also begun to be involved in criminal activity and his behaviour is causing concern to his family and school. He has been arrested a few times but has, so far, only been cautioned. During the assessment process, his mother tells you that when he was born, he was one of twins, but she has never told Kieran about this. His twin brother Gareth was seriously disabled with a rare genetic syndrome. Gareth was cared for in a special unit until he died a couple of months before his 11th birthday. Kieran's mother had not had any contact with Gareth following his birth; her marriage had broken down and she had moved to a new town with Kieran. Neither she nor Kieran have any contact with extended family. She has given you the information because she is concerned that Kieran's 'bad behaviour' is a result of something 'in the blood'. She is adamant that Kieran should not be told about his sibling. What are the issues for you?

co-operation and involvement of the child and family has little chance of success and fails to reflect the rights of children to be informed and to contribute to decisions which affect them.

Test yourself

1　What are the key areas for assessment?

2　Why is it important to involve children and families?

3　List three areas you would take into account when gathering information about a child's development.

4　List three areas you would take into account when gathering information about parenting capacity.

5　List three areas you would take into account when gathering information about family and environment.

HSC 36b Support the development and implementation of care plans

How care plans are agreed

(KS 6, 7, 10, 13, 16, 17, 21)

Many, but not all, care plans are agreed at family group conferences where all the key agencies will be involved. If there have been concerns about a child or young person suffering significant harm, this will be dealt with through a child protection conference following the procedures from *Working Together to Safeguard Children* or the relevant procedures for the country you work in.

If there is only one agency involved, there may not be a conference as such, but there is likely to be communication and contact between any other agencies and the key worker who will be involved and the child and his or her family.

You may be involved in developing and planning the care for a child or young person either because your agency is the commissioner of services for the particular child and family, and you have been involved in collecting information and making the initial assessment of needs, or because your agency will be a provider of services for the child and family.

If you have been involved in carrying out the information gathering for the assessment of needs, and are contributing to a family group conference, you must make sure that you provide all of the information to the participants in the meeting as early as possible. People need time to read and consider background information before coming to a meeting. The key people who must have all of the information and must be involved in the decisions about care plans are the child or young person and his or her family. This way, clear decisions about how to best meet the needs of the child or young person are most likely to be made. If people only receive information when they arrive at the meeting, or if the child and family have not shared in the information and any recommendations, it may not be possible for a decision to be made on the spot. This can result in delays, causing frustration and disappointment for the child and family and may, depending on their circumstances, increase risk.

Involving the child and family

(KS 2, 3, 4, 5, 13, 16, 17, 21)

Meetings that are held between childcare professionals can be very intimidating for children or young people and families and they may feel that they do not have the confidence to participate. It is important that you work to encourage the child or young person and his or her family to feel able to make an active and effective contribution to the meeting. The meeting is about them, and they are the most important people. It is easy to lose sight of this and to allow the child and family to feel that their role is a purely passive one. In order to make the process more accessible, there are certain things you should do.

- Go through the procedure of the meeting with them so that they know exactly who will be there, what will happen, the order in which matters will be discussed and the type of contributions that all of those present at the meeting will make.
- Help them to decide what they actually want to say and to work out the best way to present it. This could be in a written form or they could prepare some notes in advance to ensure that they cover all of the points they are wanting to make.
- Make sure that they know the different results that could come from the meeting so that they will not be surprised by any of the decisions that could be taken. Explain to them that there could be a range of options for the meeting to consider and that they need to think about what they want to happen.
- Where necessary make practical arrangements for them to attend. This could include ensuring accessibility to the meeting, providing transport where necessary, or providing any necessary translation interpretation or other communication assistance.

The child or young person's view

It may be that the child or young person and his or her family feel confident and well able to put across their own point of view. If so, your role is simply to support and encourage them in doing so; but if this is not the case, or if they have expressed views and there is either a misunderstanding or a difference of opinion within the planning meeting as to how this child's needs are best met, your role is to ensure that the child's views are clearly represented and understood. This is particularly important where the child or young person may not be able to communicate directly to the meeting, either because they are too young or because of communication difficulties.

Getting the balance right

There is a fine balance between representing the child or family's point of view and putting across your own views about what you think may be best for them. You will need to be careful that it is the child or family's viewpoint that you represent and not your own, even if you consider that their views are not necessarily the most appropriate. When you are making contributions at the meeting, you should always ensure that you begin with 'X has told me

Reflect

Try to remember a situation where you have felt that you were not in control and that other people in the situation held the power. This may have involved a medical situation, for example, where you were a patient and you felt that you were unable to ask all of the questions that you wanted to because the doctor did not seem to have time to answer your questions; it may have been a situation involving lawyers or other professionals; it could have been your child's teacher or head teacher who made you feel that you were lacking in the skill and ability to put across what you really wanted to say. Remember how you felt in those situations, and use the situation you have chosen as your 'trigger' to recall those feelings whenever you are in a care planning meeting, or any other situation with a child and their family and encouraging them to put their views across. Think how much easier it might have been in your own circumstance if you had had somebody acting as a support for you. Once you have identified your trigger, it will always be easy to recall your feelings.

Be clear on whether the views you express are your own or those of the child and family you are representing

that…' or 'Mrs Y has explained to me that she would prefer…', rather than 'I think that…' or 'In my opinion, the best course of action would be…' It is important not only for the accuracy of the views, but also to make sure that the child and family know that it is their views which are being represented and not your own, and that they are able to exercise some control over the outcome.

Difficult situations

You can find yourself in a difficult position when the child or young person and family's views of the outcomes to meet their needs are different from the views of the other professionals at the conference. Your role is very clearly to represent the interests of the child or young person. However, you should not get drawn into the role of attempting to manipulate the meeting to ensure that a child or their family achieves their desired outcome, nor should you allow yourself to be involved in arguments with other professionals. You should simply ensure that the child or young person's views are clearly expressed. However, if you do not agree with this view, the child or young person and family should already know this and should be aware of what you are going to contribute to the conference.

Recording decisions about care plans

(KS 3, 6, 9, 13, 19, 21)

This is essential in order to eliminate the possibility of confusion and misunderstanding. It is likely that your agency will have a specific format for recording decisions, or that minutes will be taken of the meeting and all of the conclusions reached must be recorded. It is important that the discussions which were undertaken at the meeting are briefly recorded – this enables the people who have taken part in the meeting to check that their contributions and views have been noted – but the key is to have a clear record of all final decisions.

It will be important to make sure, either through you directly or through whoever organises it within your agency, that the information recorded from the meeting is circulated to all of those who were present. The most important people who must receive a copy of this information are the child or young person and his or her family, regardless of whether or not they were present at the care-planning meeting.

Reaching decisions

Whether decisions about care plans are made in a family group conference or by the social worker and the child and family, there are some key factors that should guide the process:

- ensuring that the child is safe
- children must have their needs met within a reasonable period of time
- children and young people must be able to continue with education with the minimum interruption.

Within these parameters, decisions must be made on the best ways to meet the child or young person's needs by carefully all the information and how positives and strengths can be built on. It is also important to think about what the child and family can cope with – a series of complex interventions can overwhelm some families and produce unsatisfactory outcomes. Decisions must be based on evidence, so that it is clear that the interventions agreed for the care plan are known to be the most effective in the particular circumstances of the child or young person. There may have to be an alternative plan for interventions if the first choice is not available, because waiting may not be an option, depending on the circumstances. Even if the ideal resource is not available, the information needs to be passed to the commissioners, so that gaps in provision can be acted on.

Plans

(KS 2, 6, 8, 17)

All plans need to be clear about several main points; if there is no possibility of confusion on key issues, it is more likely that the plan will be clearly understood and followed by all those involved. The following aspects of a plan need to be clear:

- the objective of the plan: for example, to provide therapy and to evaluate its effectiveness
- what services will be provided by which professional group or designated agency
- the timing and nature of contact between the professional workers and the family
- the purpose of services and professional contact
- specific commitments to be met by the family: for example, attendance at a family centre
- specific commitments to be met by the professional workers: for example, the provision of culturally sensitive services or special assistance for those with disabilities
- which components of the plan are negotiable in the light of experience and which are not
- what needs to change and the goals to be achieved: for example, the child's weight to increase by a specific amount in a particular period, regular and appropriate stimulation for the child in keeping with his or her development and age
- what is unacceptable care of the child
- what sanctions will be used if the child is placed in danger or in renewed danger.

In England, the Integrated Children's System provides a range of assessment and progress records and plans depending on the age of the child and nature of the assessment (this will have slight variations depending on the country you work in). Any relevant aspect of a child's life should have a plan, so a child may have an overall care plan but also an education plan and a health plan.

If you work as a provider of services for children and young people, you need to make sure that you understand the requirements of the plans for the child. A well-written plan should have a clear set of 'outcomes' – these are the end results that the plan is designed to achieve. They should be clear and measurable, not vague statements of intent. For example:

Not:

✗ Jamie's well-being will be improved

But:

✓ Jamie will improve school attendance by 50 per cent

✓ Jamie wants to learn to swim: swimming lessons will be provided through school

✓ Jamie will be encouraged to socialise with peers: the aim is for him to undertake one extra activity each week with other young people of his age

✓ Jamie's mother will prepare a family meal at least three nights each week and she and Jamie will eat together and spend time talking.

When things don't go to plan

Not all plans run smoothly, and it is important that you feed back to the responsible key worker, likely to be the child's social worker, if you are experiencing problems in delivering the plan as agreed. Plans can go wrong for all sorts of reasons. It may be that the child or family has had a change of heart or a change of circumstances. It may be that you are no longer able to provide the service as agreed initially. Whatever the reasons, any problems must be recognised and discussed immediately so that the child does not have an interruption in service provision.

My story

Hi, I'm Jamie and I'm 14 years old. I live with my mum. I don't remember my dad; he cleared off years ago. Mum used to have blokes, but not recently, probably because she's getting a bit old now. There was a load of hassle because school was a real pain. They got one of these new heads, she thought she was something special. Loads of us never went to school and nobody seemed to mind, but this new woman came and lots of people started going again. Don't know why – people said it was better, more interesting and that – but I don't know, I didn't think so – but I must admit I didn't go that often.

I don't know what happened really, I just didn't want to go anywhere. It was easier to stay in my room and do stuff on the computer and do games and that. Mum wasn't bothered as long as I wasn't in her way – so I stayed there. Then this social worker came and asked loads of questions, but to be fair, she did seem to be interested in the answers. She talked to Mum loads as well, then there was a meeting, so now I have a 'mentor' called Paul. He's OK, we have quite a laugh. He sees me at school, and at the project where I can do games with mates. It's really good because Paul has arranged for me to learn to swim: I've always wanted to swim. I get lessons after school – so it's worth going just for that. Mum's started being OK too. She keeps cooking tea for me and I tell her about what I've been doing and she's dead interested… she seems different somehow.

Implementing care plans

(KS 2, 3, 4, 16, 17)

An assessment is not a 'snapshot' and a care plan is not set in stone. It is a flexible document, which may need to be adapted as the child progresses or circumstances change. If you are providing services for a child, you will need to observe and carefully record how children are responding to the interventions in the care plan, and you will need to maintain discussions with the social worker and other agencies about any changes that may need to be introduced. For example: the care plan includes an arrangement for 'time out' for a young person where family arguments have been a serious problem. Relationships at home have improved significantly because of other interventions in the plan, so the 'time out' provision has not been used for several months, and it is thought to be no longer necessary.

Complaints

The child or young person and their family should be made aware of the complaints system and the steps they can take if they are unhappy with the way in which the care plan is working. Do not assume that they are aware of the complaints system – it may be well publicised and there may be leaflets in the foyer, but you do need to check that they know about the system and how to use it. If you become aware that the child or family is unhappy with the way the care

plan is being delivered, and the issues cannot be resolved, then you must remind them about the complaints system and advise them how to get help and support to use it if necessary.

Providing information

One of your key roles at the start of this process is to provide information to the child or young person and their family about the interventions and activities that are proposed. It is not reasonable to expect, for example, a young person to agree to 'attendance at a community project' unless they have full information to make a choice. This will include information about:

- the exact nature of the project
- the location of the project
- the type of activities
- the general atmosphere and ethos of the project
- the number of young people who attend
- what the transport arrangements will be.

These are just a few of the questions a young person or his or her family may have about what will be provided. Truly informed choices can only be made when the young person or family have all the information.

All of us have the right to make informed choices about all aspects of our lives. For example, you would not buy a pair of shoes simply because the shop assistant said, 'Oh, I have got a great pair of shoes for you.' You would want to try the shoes on, see if you

liked the colour and the style and see if they were comfortable before you made the decision to buy. Similarly, you would not buy a holiday or a car simply because somebody said to you, 'I have got a nice holiday here that I am sure would suit you.' You would want to ask questions about where, when, how much, what type of accommodation, and so on.

When it is not possible to obtain agreement

Of course, not all provision is undertaken with the agreement of the young person. Sometimes interventions are as the result of a court order, so there is no choice on the part of the young person.

Where this is the case, it can be considerably more difficult to work with the child or young person and to help them to feel that they do have a contribution to make to the planning process. Clearly, because of the compulsory nature of the service provision, there are some aspects over which they have no choice. However, where this is the case, you should encourage

All of us have the right to make informed choices about all aspects of our lives

 Keys to good practice: Enabling children and young people to exercise choice

✓ Communicate all information to children, young people and their families clearly and in a way that can be understood.

✓ Make sure that their views are clearly represented to any forum where decisions are being taken or proposals being formulated.

✓ Support the child or young person to put forward their own views wherever possible.

✓ Clearly record information and planning proposals and ensure that all of the relevant people involved receive them.

✓ Make sure that children, young people and their families and those involved with them receive the plan in a form that they can access and understand.

✓ Ensure that the child or young person has the opportunity to comment on the plan in his or her own time and in an atmosphere in which he or she feels able to make adverse comments if necessary.

✓ Always provide children and young people with the information they need to make informed choices, even if that is restricted by their circumstances.

✓ Ensure that all of those involved with the process are kept informed of any changes and updates made to the proposals.

the child or young person to exercise choice in the areas where it is possible for them to do so. Simply because they are living in a particular setting or involved in a particular service as a result of compulsion, this does not remove their rights to exercise choice within the limitations of the circumstances. You should ensure that, where possible, children and young people are able to exercise choice, however limited their options may be.

Active knowledge

HSC 36a pc 3, 4, 6, 7 (part)

How do you ensure that the children and young people with whom you work are given informed choices? How do you ensure that they have the information they need to make an informed choice in relation to their needs, wishes and preferences?

Test yourself

1   Why is it important to plan?

2   Which aspects of a child's life may have a plan attached?

3   How does planning take place when a child is at risk of significant harm?

4   How can you ensure that children and young people are involved in planning?

5   How does planning link to assessment?

HSC 36c Contribute to reviewing care plans for children and young people

The purpose of reviewing care plans is twofold: first, it is part of an ongoing process of monitoring and review so that a child's circumstances are constantly being checked and reassessed and updates are made as needed; second, it provides an 'event' or 'snapshot' of a child's situation on a regular basis, when the plan may be reconsidered and either reconfirmed or changed.

Reflect

Then take a much shorter period, for example, the last year, and look at much smaller changes that may have happened to you during that time. They could be financial changes; changes in your job role; the fact that you are now undertaking a qualification; you may be driving a different car, or have acquired digital television… any number of small changes will have affected the way in which you are living your life. Again, make a list of these changes and consider the impact that each of them has had. Although the second list may have had a smaller impact than some of the big changes you listed in your first reflection, these changes will nonetheless have combined to illustrate some quite large changes in your lifestyle. Consider the results of this exercise when you are thinking about how you will monitor and review the care plans that are in place for the children and young people you work with.

Reflect

Look at yourself and your circumstances over the last ten years and make a list of the ways in which your circumstances have changed. For example, you may have more children than you had ten years ago, or you may have some children who have left home and moved away; members of your family may have died or been born in the last ten years; you could be living in a larger house or a smaller house; you could have more money or less money; you could be doing the same job or a different job. All of these are major changes that have taken place in your life in just the short period of ten years. Your list will help you to see the sorts of situations which change and which affect people's lives.

All care plans should be reviewed regularly. For children and young people the nature of the review depends on their legal status.

Care plans for looked-after children

(KS 7, 20, 21)

Children who are looked after by the local authority, whether through a court order or on a voluntary basis, must have their plans reviewed by an independent person, called an Independent Review Officer (IRO). The role of the IRO is to ensure that the child's views are taken into account and to monitor the work of the local authority.

Care plans should be made, if possible, before a child comes into care, or otherwise within 14 days. The next review is after 4 weeks, then after 3 months and then at least every 6 months.

The IRO must chair the meeting to review the child or young person's progress and then complete a form recording the outcomes of the review.

Guiding principles

Regardless of the nature or purpose of the review, the same guiding principles apply.

- What have been the outcomes of the last review?
- Is a new assessment of need called for?
- Has the care plan been called into question by developments?
- Do its objectives need to be reformulated? Or is it a question of choosing new means to achieve the same ends?
- How integrated does the care plan now appear?
- How is the principle of sensitive, open and shared planning being upheld?
- How **cogent** is the planning process?
- How is the current planning process being recorded so that it can be monitored as part of a flexible but continuous long-term process?

Key term

Cogent: Clear, logical and convincing.

The child's views should be taken into account

Care plans for children who are not looked after

(KS 2, 3, 6, 16, 21)

Where children or young people are not looked after by the local authority, reviews must still take place, and will follow the same guiding principles, but they are not undertaken by an IRO. As much information as possible should be gathered ahead of the review, so that the number of people who actually need to be there is as few as possible. This makes the review process less threatening for the child or young person and his or her family. It is important that the child or young person participates in the review if at all possible; this can be done in writing if the child or young person has decided not to attend.

All steps should be taken to enable all children and families to participate, including any necessary arrangements to support communication or make physical access possible. If you are working with the child or family, you may be the person responsible for enabling children and young people to access reviews.

Recording and informing

(KS 2, 6, 16)

All review decisions, whether to continue with the present plan or to adopt some new interventions or a change of approach, must be recorded, and you should check that the child or young person and their family understands any decisions that have been made. Where children are looked after, the IRO will explain any changes, but you may have to do so for other children and young people.

Test yourself

1   Why is it important to provide information at each stage of the process to the child or young person and to his or her family?

2   What is the value of including all agencies and professionals who may be involved with a child or young person in a care review meeting?

3   What is the purpose of a review?

4   Why are reviews important?

5   What is the role of an IRO?

1   Carry out a 'mock' initial assessment on a child (real or imaginary) and record all the information on the assessment form. How easy did you find it? Were you able to get the information you needed? How useful was the form that you used?

2   What do you think is the most important information that you get from an assessment?

3   Who do you think gains the most benefit from an assessment: the child/young person, the service provider or the service commissioner?

4   What are some of the potential consequences of a poor-quality assessment?

5   What is your response if a parent says that you are just being nosy and invading their privacy by asking all these questions?

Don't forget to refer to the evidence opportunities grid (see pages 357–375) for more ideas for suitable evidence for your NVQ.

Support children and young people to manage their lives

This unit covers much of the 'fun' part of working with children and young people! It is about the ways in which you help and support children and young people to develop and express themselves through activities, appearance, hobbies and interests.

As well as being undoubtedly enjoyable and good fun to help young people with their clothes and appearance and to encourage new activities and interests, it is also a really important part of children and young people's development. The skill with which you handle these areas can make a significant difference to the children and young people you work with.

You will need to develop an awareness and understanding of the issues surrounding appearance for many disabled children and young people or those – for example, many refugees – for whom cultural identity is particularly important.

Interests and hobbies are important for children and young people, but they can also carry risks, and you will need to be able to judge the risk in relation to the benefits each brings. However, although there are potentially serious implications for some of the work in this area – it is still the fun bit!

In this unit you will find 'Active knowledge' features containing activities that will contribute to assessment for your NVQ. Remember that these features only offer the opportunity for partial assessment; you can also refer to the evidence opportunities grid (see pages 357–375) for more ideas to provide suitable evidence for your NVQ.

What you need to learn

- Clothes and society
- Why clothes matter to children and young people
- Your role with clothes
- Appearance
- Skin
- Hair
- Body decoration
- Personal space
- Pocket money
- Talent spotting
- Encouraging talent
- Networks
- Encouraging participation
- Risk assessment
- Making friendships through recreation
- Recognising achievement

HSC 38a Work with, and provide advice for, children and young people about their clothes, appearance, environment and pocket money

What children and young people wear

(KS 6)

At the most basic level, clothes keep us warm and provide the covering of our bodies which society, and the law, requires. However, at every stage in history, and particularly in today's world, clothes have far more significance than this. Clothes are an important statement about who we are. They increase in significance at different times in our lives – they are very important to many children and young people but they play a major role throughout life.

As a society, we have clothes to mark particular occasions. For example, Christians dress babies in special white robes and shawls for baptisms. For certain occasions, different cultures may require different clothing. Weddings are traditionally white with special dresses and a veil in the Christian, Jewish and Arab Muslim traditions, but Asian Muslim brides wear bright coloured saris. We even have special clothes when people die: for some cultures black clothes signify mourning; in others it is white.

At various periods in history, particular clothes have been restricted to certain people: for example, only Roman senators could wear clothes with a certain type of purple colouring, and only Native American chiefs were allowed to wear certain headdresses.

We recognise special occasions by dressing up, and have dress codes for some places: for example, there are restaurants and other places where men will not be admitted unless wearing a tie, and where no one is allowed to wear jeans or trainers. These kinds of restrictions are used to signal that this is a place where certain standards are observed.

Particular clothes have meaning in a certain culture or religion

Why clothes matter to children and young people

(KS 14, 25)

You may be in the position where some of the children you work with do not have the basic requirements of warm and suitable clothing – or they have been in such a situation in the past. However, the vast majority of children and young people who have any interest in the clothes they wear will be more concerned about what the clothes *look like* than the function they perform.

The interest children have in their appearance and the clothes they wear increases as they grow and develop. Some quite young children will want to choose particular types or makes of clothes. This interest in 'designer brands' has been brought about by the massive marketing industry and some very successful brand images, and these influences are a key part of the way children and young people relate to clothes.

Wearing 'uniforms'

Clothes can also be used to signify that everyone belongs to the same group; this can be anything from the boy scouts to the local gang – all of them have a uniform. Some uniforms are formal and compulsory and others are informal – but equally compulsory.

For example, if you are in the armed forces or are a nurse, you will have a uniform. The uniform will make you easily recognisable, both to others who are part of the same group and to the outside world. It also makes everyone equal, regardless of whether you are rich or poor or where you come from. A gang will also have a uniform. It may be the type of jeans, or the way they are worn, or a certain type of hat or shoes or even distinctive colours for tops or bandanas. Regardless of the nature of the distinctive clothes, there will be a way to identify members of the group to other members and to outsiders.

You can extend the idea of uniform to many areas of life – have you ever looked at a commuter train in the morning? Men in grey suits are everywhere. This has long been the standard business 'uniform' for men; there are a few changes creeping into some professions, where people dress more informally, but generally it still applies. Go into any legal firm or barristers' chambers and you will see women in the standard uniform of black suit and white blouse. Uniforms are also a major form of corporate identity: everywhere from banks and building societies to supermarkets, the uniform is part of the corporate

My story

Hi, I'm Chas. I'm 16, and belong to the Blues. No one messes with us or touches anyone who belongs. Everyone knows who we are, we wear a special sort of blue scarf type thing. You have to be OK to get in, not just anyone can be in the gang. You feel really proud and like you belong when you get the scarf. There's stuff you have to do first, to sort of prove yourself. Mostly we don't cause any bother, we seem to scare a few people just by being there – that's good, I like that feeling. Makes me feel safe too – I know that if I see a brother with the blue scarf then he's going to look out for me and I'm going to look out for him. You need that now; the way things are on the streets, it's not safe – you want to be careful.

My story

Hi, I'm Jason. I'm 16 and I'm in the Army Cadets. I want to join the army as soon as I can. I have been a cadet for a few years, I joined at school. We have to wear a uniform which is good and makes you feel really proud; my gran says I look dead smart. It's great, we get to do loads of good stuff and go away on camps and do training. We do marching and parades which is a bit boring, but it's worth it for the exercises when we go away – they are really good. You see another guy in the same uniform and you know that you're going to look out for each other.

brand and image and many are instantly recognisable. School uniform is almost completely confined to the UK. Most other countries do not have it at all! School uniform plays an important part in identifying which school a child attends and in building a spirit of belonging to and ownership of the school. Those who support uniforms also argue that it is a great equaliser and means that there are less obvious inequalities between rich and poor pupils.

First impressions

Clothes and appearance are one of the first things people notice about us, and our clothes will enable people to form a first impression of what sort of a person we are. Research shows that these impressions are made very quickly and are very hard to change. American researcher Albert Mehrabian (A Mehrabian, 1968) showed that we form first impressions within 90 seconds of meeting someone, and that 55 per cent of our first impression is based on appearance. From how people look, we believe that we can deduce a great deal of information about them.

Clothes and feelings

Some children and young people have very definite ideas about clothes; others care little for what they wear or what they look like. Sometimes this is simply due to different interests and personalities, but for some children it can indicate deeper feelings: children or young people with very low self-esteem (see page 154) may not consider that they 'deserve' nice clothes, or may not want to draw attention to themselves. Others will use clothes to make people take notice of them and will want to show off like a peacock!

Clothes can give messages about how you feel about yourself

Clothing and the fashion industry

The children's clothing market is huge in the UK – over 5 billion pounds according to Mintel, the retail research organisation. As a result, there is massive interest by manufacturers and promoters of fashion (and all the surrounding industry) in marketing children and young people's clothes. The impact of 'designer' labels is significant: many children and young people will want clothes or shoes with a particular 'label', and the style, price and suitability is often not considered as important. Fashions for girls and young women are heavily influenced by female pop stars and celebrities, while fashion for boys and young men is far more influenced by sport and the

Reflect

Think about your practice in relation to clothes and appearance for children and young people. Have you ever really thought about the importance of clothes and how much appearance can matter? How much do you know about the significance of clothes? Are clothes important to you, or are you one of those people who don't really care about what they wear?

Think through the times you have had to deal with an issue relating to clothes over the last few months. How satisfied were you with your practice? Can you think about areas where you need to do more work – do you need more knowledge? Or do you tend to impose your views about what is appropriate? What happened about choosing clothes when you were growing up?

If you feel that you need to improve your practice in this area, speak to your supervisor and find out what development opportunities may be available.

Active knowledge

Look at the pictures below for a short time – what do you think you know about each of the people? Note down quick impressions: don't spend time thinking, just put what first comes into your head – how old they are, how much money they have, what job they do, what sort of house they live in, what their family circumstances are.

Now that you have made the notes, sit back and think about the reasons for your views. What was it about each of the pictures that made you think the way you did? Of course it has to be about appearance, because you have no other clues, no real body language and no opportunity to listen to anything. See if you can identify what it was about the appearance that helped you to decide as you did.

associated brands and logos (*New Consumers? Children, fashion and consumption*, J Pilcher, C Pole and S Bowden, 2004). You are likely to find that you will have to respond to requests to select clothes reflecting the current favourite logo for a team or sports personality, or the type of clothing worn by the latest girl band to hit the music charts.

All of this is the normal identification process that many young people go through. Wearing the same clothes as all their friends is about feeling part of the group (see Wearing 'uniforms' on page 174).

Your role with clothes

(KS 2, 3, 4, 5, 16, 23)

Your role will very much depend on the ages and circumstances of the children you work with. If you are working with children who live at home, you may not have much to do with choosing or buying clothes. If you are working with the family as a whole,

your role may include supporting children and young people and their parents or carers to choose and buy clothes. However, as you are working on this unit, it is likely that you are working with children in a residential setting where you could be quite involved in both the choosing and buying processes.

Clothing for disabled children and young people

Some disabled children and young people will need accessible clothing, or clothing which is 'wheelchair-friendly': clothing which is cut a bit longer to allow for the fact that the wearer is always sitting. Accessible clothing will make full use of easy on-and-off features such as elastic rather than buttons, and Velcro fastenings wherever possible.

Accessibility is important because this maximises the level of independence when getting dressed and undressed. The more children and young people can do for themselves, the better it is for their overall well-being and development.

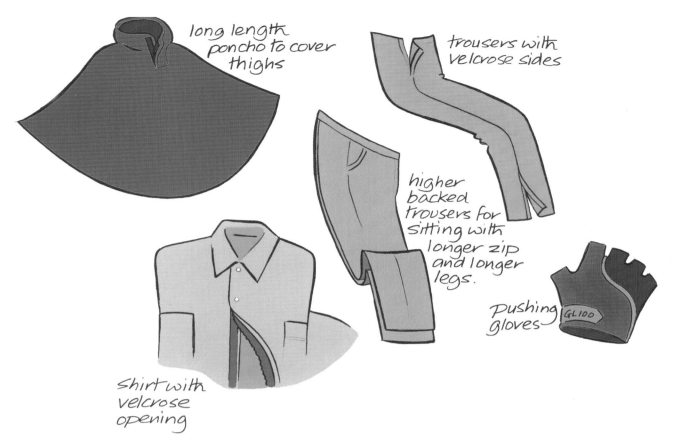

long length poncho to cover thighs

trousers with velcrose sides

higher backed trousers for sitting with longer zip and longer legs.

Pushing gloves GL100

Shirt with velcrose opening

A wide range of accessible, attractive clothing is available

However, you will need to work closely with the child or young person to balance accessibility and fashion. It may be important for many young people to have the latest brand fashions, and they may prefer to have extra help to manage the clothing, rather than have to wear clothes which are not trendy, or do not fit with the 'uniform' worn by friends.

Younger children

Every local authority provides a clothing allowance for each child it looks after. Currently, there is no nationally agreed figure so it varies between local authorities, but there are suggestions that a national figure may be laid down in the near future. There is a strong view among children who are looked after that there should be an increase in the amount of money allocated for items like clothing and pocket money. If you are working with younger children, you may be very involved in choosing and buying their clothing.

Meeting the standards

All of the standards for residential children's homes, regardless of the country you work in, state that children must have their own clothes, which they have had a say in choosing. In the past, it was not unusual for children in residential homes to just wear clothes from a central 'pool' which was shared among all the children. This was viewed as making economic sense, as clothes would not be 'grown out of' and could be used for younger children. The loss of individual identity and lack of choice for the child was not considered.

These examples of children being looked after in a way which met the needs of the organisation, not the needs of the child, are not horror stories from a Victorian past, but practices which were still commonplace less than 25 years ago.

There are several issues to consider when choosing clothes. First and foremost are the views of the child, if they are old enough. Even quite young children may have opinions about the colour of clothes. It is important that children are asked their views: children need to know that their opinions count, and that you want to know what they are. This is part of making sure children are front and centre of all your practice. Once you know if the child has any preferences, you need to check that the clothes are:

- suitable for the season of the year
- suitable for the purpose they are needed for
- made of materials which will wash and dry easily.

You will also need to consider any particular needs the child may have in relation to the type of material or clothing, as some children may have allergies to particular types of materials. For example, wool or feathers can cause an allergic reaction in an asthmatic child, while nylon and other man-made fibres can cause rashes and excessive sweating in some children.

Helping to choose clothes

You may hear concerns that some quite young children, particularly girls, may be wearing clothes that are inappropriately adult in style: this can be seen as the over-sexualisation of young girls. As part of the safeguarding process, you will need to be aware of the type of clothes children are asking for, and work with the child to make judgements about how suitable they are.

There is always a balance to be found between giving children freedom of choice and setting reasonable boundaries so that children are wearing clothes that are appropriate for their age and for the purpose.

Taking a child or young person to choose clothes is not always easy, and you may have to deal with some conflicts and arguments. You should use the techniques agreed in the care plan for managing the child or young person's behaviour, but bear in mind how important clothes can be and recognise that, although it may seem trivial to you, these issues can be very important to children and young people.

Active knowledge

Explain the role you play in supporting children to choose and buy clothes. Check out what the policies are in your workplace for how much money children and young people have to spend on clothes and how it is spent. Find out how much freedom children and young people have in relation to the clothes they wear.

Appearance

(KS 16)

The way children and young people look is linked to the way they dress, but overall appearance is about more than just clothes: there is hair, body decoration and adornment, jewellery and make-up. The interest in appearance, like clothes, varies with age. Many people who have brought up boys will remember the period when the bathroom was almost permanently occupied by a child who, just a few weeks previously, had to be dragged, cajoled and bribed to put himself, soap and water in the same space. Around the time of

My story

Hi, I'm Jemma and I'm 9 years old. I live with my foster carers, Jo and Stuart. They get a clothing allowance for me, so I said I wanted this great top and jeans from Top Shop. The top was lovely: it had really thin straps and was dead short; you could see all my tummy. It was bright pink and had like sequin stars all over it. The jeans were cut dead low, and they had bright pink embroidery which exactly matched the top. After we'd seen them, Jo said we could go and get an ice-cream and think about it before we decided. When we got the ice-cream, we sat by the window and me and Jo had a real laugh looking at the people walking past and talking about the clothes they were wearing. I was showing Jo which people looked like mingers and which ones looked cool – I don't think she knew really because she asked me to explain why some people looked better than others. I saw Louise, a girl from my class, and she had the same top I wanted. She didn't look very good – it didn't look right, not like on the model in the shop. Jo asked if I thought it might be because she was a bit skinny and didn't have no boobs. I think it was: the top looks better on someone with boobs. I wish I had boobs – Jo says I will soon enough. We did have a laugh though. I'm really glad I didn't let Jo buy me the pink top. I don't want to look as sad as Louise – and I got this gorgeous purple blouse. It's satin and it's got sparkly buttons. I did get the jeans with the pink embroidery, I think they go lovely with the blouse – Stuart says he's putting on his sunglasses!

puberty, both boys and girls tend to begin to take a far greater interest in appearance. They are also likely to become more interested in personal hygiene and will be concerned that they smell attractive.

Keeping clean and maintaining personal hygiene is important for children and young people of all ages. If you work with younger children, you will have a role in helping them to bathe and keep clean, but as children grow and mature, it is important and appropriate that they undertake this type of personal care themselves. Personal cleanliness is also important because it improves how children and young people feel about themselves, and is an essential part of maintaining a pleasant appearance.

Skin

(KS 7, 18)

Why being clean matters

The skin is the largest organ of the body. It provides a complete covering and protection for the body, and it is the skin that is the main area to be cleaned. The skin consists of two layers: the outer layer (the epidermis) and the inner layer (the dermis).

The epidermis is constantly being renewed, as it sheds its cells and the body grows new cells to replace them.

You will have noticed how the skin cells are shed when you undress or change bed sheets. The skin also contains some glands producing sweat and others producing sebum, an oily substance that maintains the waterproofing of the skin.

As we age, skin loses its elasticity and begins to show wrinkles, creases and lines. Keeping skin moisturised will help, but unfortunately not avoid, these signs of aging.

Skin becomes dirty because of exposure to the environment, but it also collects dried sweat, dead skin cells and oily sebum from the sebaceous glands. All of these factors combine to provide a breeding ground for an assortment of bacteria. These bacteria can cause offensive odours and can even lead to infections, so skin needs to be washed regularly and the bacteria removed from the skin.

Some form of cleaning should be undertaken every day. Children and young people should have a daily bath or shower to remove accumulated dirt and waste products.

Skin problems

Most young people experience some degree of skin problems when they go through adolescence. Excess oil clogs the pores of the skin and causes spots, and often boils in young men and, for some, the torment of acne.

 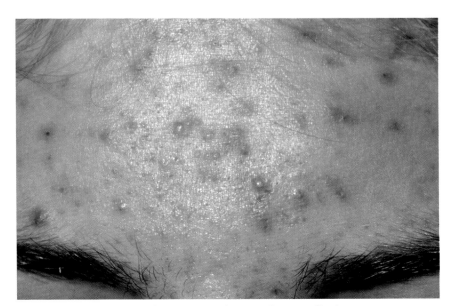

Most teenagers can deal with ordinary spots themselves (left), but acne (right) requires medical treatment

If a young person simply has teenage spots caused by an oily skin, they should be advised to keep their skin clean and to try to keep their hands away from their face as much as possible. However, for those how have more serious conditions, such as acne, medical help is essential. There are medical treatments that can greatly improve and almost completely eradicate acne over a period of about 6 months. The young person's GP is the right starting point for any young person with a serious skin problem.

Hair

(KS 2, 4, 5, 23)

Younger children need to have clean hair that is brushed, tidy and regularly cut into an appropriate style for the child. Your first and foremost consideration must always be the wishes of the child (if they are of an age to be concerned). A child should be encouraged to think about his or her lifestyle and interests when choosing a hairstyle. Some young girls will want long hair and will be happy to go through the daily 'torture' of brushing and tidying which is inevitably involved; others may recognise that, because of active involvements in sport, a shorter style may be easier to manage. Hair length is also related to the type of hair a child has: long hair which is thick and curly presents a very different prospect for management than hair which is straight and fairly thin.

Reflect

How do you feel about your own appearance? Is it important to you, or are you the sort of person who has a quick shower, flicks a brush through your hair and forgets it for the rest of the day? Have you thought about why you feel the way you do about how you look? Were you encouraged to look good when you were young? Or were you told that your appearance didn't matter? Do you feel more confident when you have taken time over your appearance and are wearing nice clothes? Why do you think this might be? If you can spend some time reflecting on how you feel about your own appearance, it will help you to understand better how young people feel.

Black hair

Black hair requires additional and different care from the hair of **Caucasian** children. The hair is thicker and curlier; it is also drier and prone to breaking and splitting. There are many specialist products available for black hair and they should always be used. If black hair is cared for using the same products as Caucasian hair, it will become very dry and brittle. Make sure you get specialist advice.

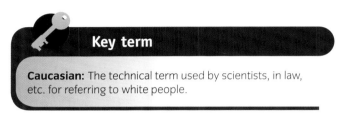

Key term

Caucasian: The technical term used by scientists, in law, etc. for referring to white people.

Structure of hair

Hair is made up of the following parts:

Cuticle: Outer layer of the hair. It is made up of layers of scales that interlock with the cells of the hair's inner root-sheath to anchor it firmly in the follicle. This is a thin and colourless layer. Black hair cuticle layers can be twice the thickness of those of Caucasian hair.

Cortex: The middle layer. It is composed of cells that are tightly bound around one another. These bands provide the hair with elasticity and strength and are very receptive to chemicals. As a result, they can easily be influenced (and/or damaged) by dyes, perming or the relaxers often used on black hair.

Melanin: This is contained in the cortex and is the substance that determines the colour of our hair and skin. The more melanin there is, the darker the hair or skin.

Follicle: This is the name for hair before it emerges from the skin. Follicles are composed of many elements, including carbon, hydrogen and oxygen. Healthy amounts of these elements can improve the hair's condition and appearance once it emerges.

Sebaceous/Sudoriferous glands: Attached to the hair follicle are the sebaceous (oil) and the sudoriferous (sweat) glands. The sebaceous glands open and close continuously to release waxy sebum oil into the hair

The Caucasion hair shaft can be straight, wavy or curly and is oval shaped

The African-Caribbean hair shaft can be tightly or loosely curled and is kidney shaped

The Asian hair shaft can be straight and/or coarse and is round in shape

Different types of hair have very different qualities

follicle and on to the scalp. The sudoriferous glands contain many small structures with porous openings leading to the skin. They produce substances that dry on the skin including salts, acids, water and bacteria. If not completely dissolved and effectively removed from the scalp, these substances can cause itching and dandruff.

Older children's and young people's hair

All of the same needs for hair to be clean and properly looked after apply as children get older too.

However, as children mature, the appearance of hair and hairstyles become more important. Many hours can be spent agonising over a new style or colour. You will need to work with older children and young people to support choices around hair and styling.

Choosing a 'look'

There are now computer programmes which allow young people to upload a photo of themselves and try various hairstyles 'digitally' before making a final choice. However, only a hairdresser is likely to be able to give advice about whether a certain style will work with particular types of hair.

Encourage children and young people to look through magazines to find a style they like, then check with a hairdresser if this will work for them.

For many boys and young men, hair is minimal or even shaved; others like the longer look. Some schools will have regulations about hair length; some do not allow hair to be too short or too long. Other schools do not impose restrictions on appearance or hair length. You must make sure that children are complying with the requirements of their school.

Body decoration

(KS 1, 2, 3, 8, 16, 18, 23)

Tattoos and piercings

A key part of appearance for many young people is decorating their bodies with tattoos or piercings.

Keys to good practice: The importance of clothes and appearance

✓ Remember that clothes and appearance are very important to children and young people.

✓ Support children and young people to choose and wear clothes that are appropriate, but also a personal choice.

✓ Recognise when particular clothes are important for being part of a group.

✓ Make sure children and young people know why keeping clean is important.

✓ Use methods for skin and hair care that are correct for the individual child or young person.

Tattoos are only for those aged 18 years old or more; piercings are legal at any age

Young people under the age of 18 years old cannot have tattoos; a tattooist can be prosecuted for tattooing anyone under that age. There is no minimum age in England and Wales for any sort of body piercing, but in Scotland, young people under 16 years old must be accompanied by a parent or guardian, who must give permission.

Tattoos are unlikely to present you with an issue because the vast majority of children you work with will not be old enough to have a tattoo, but piercings can be a different matter. A majority of young women, and a considerable number of young men, are likely to have their ears pierced – at least once! You may have to have discussions about other facial piercings such as lips, eyebrows and so on. It is unlikely that most schools will be keen on the idea of facial piercings from a health and safety perspective, and many employers do not welcome this type of decoration.

You will need to take the child's or young person's views about piercing into account and discuss the risks with them. There are definite risks involved in any sort of body piercing: the main risk is of a blood-borne virus such as hepatitis or even HIV, although

hepatitis is more likely. In order to reduce the risks as far as possible you should make sure that the young person only uses a reputable, licensed company where:

- only single-use equipment is used for piercings. This is the safest way to reduce the risk of blood-borne viruses or other infections (some premises will use an autoclave to sterilise; this is reasonably effective, but not as safe as single-use equipment. Equipment left soaking in disinfectant is not sterile.)
- used equipment is disposed of in a sharps container.

Healing

After the piercing, the pierced site must be kept clean whilst it is healing. It is also important that young people are fully aware of the risks of piercing procedures and that they know the potential healing time. Of course, some young people will heal more quickly than this, but the following table shows the time it could take:

Piercing site	Maximum time to heal
Ear cartilage	up to 12 months
Ear lobe	up to 2 months
Eyebrow	up to 3 months
Lip	up to 2 months
Navel	up to 12 months
Nostril	up to 6 months
Septum	up to 2 months
Tongue	up to 6 months

As part of the decision-making process for the young person, it may be useful to have a discussion around the issues of healing, the potential risks and the level of pain and discomfort that will be caused by the piercing. Unlike tattoos, body piercing is largely reversible: simply removing the ornament will enable the holes to heal, although scars may be left.

Genital piercing should not be encouraged in young people; decisions to undergo genital piercing may be made as adults.

Make-up

For girls and young women, and for some young men, applying make-up to their face is important and increases confidence in looks and appearance. The purchasing of make-up, discussions about colours and styles and learning the art of applying make-up are a very important part of growing up. Depending on your own level of skill with make-up, you may be involved in planning and choosing suitable cosmetics and then in providing lessons in application. One of the most important aspects of wearing make-up is ensuring that it is removed each night before bed, and that the skin is left clean before applying lotion to moisturise. Even young skin should be moisturised – it's too late if you leave it to middle age.

Personal space

(KS 2, 4, 23, 24, 25, 26, 27)

In an ideal world, a child or young person needs to be able to have some space to make his or her own. This could be a bedroom, or even just an area of wall and floor surrounding a bed, or the corner of a living room. The location of the space is not important; what matters is that it is personal and the child or young person can do what they like with it. The personal environment in which looked-after children live is very important to them. Many of the children who are looked after have very low self-esteem and have experienced emotional or physical trauma that can make them very vulnerable. You may find that you need to support and encourage the development of personal space. Children and young people may not have the confidence or any idea of what to do with a space of their own. The previous living situations of many of the children and young people whom you are supporting may have meant that personal space was not an option and this may be the first opportunity to do anything at all.

If you are living in a situation with several other children and young people, personal space becomes even more precious. Children can put an identity on to a personal space. Children and young people should be encouraged to decorate personal space as they wish and to put up pictures and posters, and use material and colours as they wish, in a way that expresses their own personality.

Pictures and posters

These are a relatively cheap and effective way to personalise space. Some children and young people may want photographs of family, friends and others who are important to them. Photographs like these are often very precious and framing and displaying them attractively will help with security and self-esteem. Children and young people will often insist that you admire their photos and tell you about the people in them in great detail. Make sure that photos are framed in non-breakable frames such as Perspex or plastic rather than glass. This is partly from a safety point of view to reduce the risk of injury from broken glass and partly to protect precious photographs from harm.

Posters are a cheap and cheerful way of brightening up and personalising a space. They may be of a favourite pop group or celebrity or they could be of animals, people or places, according to individual taste. Posters do not have to be framed, although they can look quite good in proper frames. There are often arguments about how posters get fixed on to walls: the damage done by adhesive tape has generally made it unacceptable for poster fixing; drawing pins tend to fall out and then get trodden on, causing injuries; so Blu-tack should be the material of choice.

If a child or young person has his or her own room, personalising it is going to be relatively straightforward. The options are there, within budgets, to add colour and finishing touches such as cushions, rugs and decorative pieces.

Personalising space in a shared room is much more of a challenge. Personal effects, photos, favourite colours and posters can still be introduced, but if the space is just part of a wall, or a bedside table or chest of drawers, a little more creativity is needed. Encourage the child or young person to put a personal stamp on the space, by moving furniture (if possible) to create a personal area, or using cushions, rugs, pictures and lamps if appropriate. If physical space proves a considerable challenge, think about the personal space created by personal music and a

Pictures are a good way of personalising space

set of headphones. Even in a busy space, lying on your bed listening to music through headphones can help to create some 'time out' where children and young people can feel that they have some time for themselves.

They should always, of course, make sure that this does not infringe the rights and personal space of someone else.

Pocket money

(KS 2, 3, 5, 7, 8, 10, 15, 16, 21, 23, 24, 25, 26)

The amount of pocket money local authorities provide to children and young people whom they look after varies considerably. There is no set figure, and there can be several pounds' difference between authorities. Amounts can also differ depending on the setting in which children and young people are placed. If you are working with children living at home, they may or may not get pocket money depending on the home circumstances.

Pocket money is important because it enables children and young people to start to manage their own money. The principles of good money management are the same regardless of the amounts involved. The more money there is, the more complex it becomes, but you are unlikely to be working with children or young people who need to understand how to manage large amounts of money.

Reflect

Can you remember your first pocket money? How much was it and what did you do with it? Can you remember how it felt to buy something you had saved for? Did your early experiences influence how you handle money now? Are you a saver or a spender – what influences that? Recalling your own experiences with money can help you to understand the impact of early experiences.

Getting money

In some families, and in local authority care, children and young people can be given pocket money regardless of anything they may or may not do. In other families, pocket money is only earned in return for household chores or general help.

As children grow older, they may decide to find work in order to earn some extra money. There are laws relating to employment of 'compulsory school age' children. Children are of compulsory school age up to the last Friday in June in the academic year of their 16th birthday. Once this date has passed, the young person is viewed as having reached the Mandatory School Leaving Age (MSLA), and they can apply for their National Insurance Number and may work full-time. When young people begin work, they must be paid at least the current national minimum wage at the 'development rate' until they are over 21 years old, when they receive the full rate.

Part-time working

The youngest age at which a child can work part-time is 13, with the exception of children involved in television, theatre, modelling or similar activities. Children doing this type of work need a performance licence from the local authority, who will liaise with the child's head teacher to make sure that the child's education will not suffer. There are regulations governing the employment of children, with which employers must comply. For example, children cannot be employed:

- in any industrial setting, e.g. a factory, industrial site, etc.
- during school hours

As children grow older, they can work to earn extra money

- before 7.00 am or after 7.00 pm
- for more than 4 hours without taking a break of at least 1 hour
- in any occupations prohibited by local by-laws or other legislation, e.g. in pubs or betting shops
- in any work that may be harmful to their health, well-being or education
- without having a two-week break from any work during the school holidays in each calendar year.

Different regulations apply for work in school holidays and in term time. For example:

During term time, children may work a maximum of 12 hours per week, including:

- a maximum of 2 hours only on school days and Sundays
- a maximum of 5 hours on Saturdays for 13- to 14-year-olds, or 8 hours for 15- to 16-year-olds.

During school holidays, 13- to 14-year-olds may work a maximum of 25 hours per week, including:

- no more than 5 hours on weekdays and Saturdays
- no more than 2 hours on Sundays.

During school holidays, 15- to 16-year-olds may work a maximum of 35 hours per week, including:

- no more than 8 hours on weekdays and Saturdays
- no more than 2 hours on Sundays.

If you work in a residential setting, the children and young people you work with will not be employed, but if you work in the community, many children may have part-time jobs after school and at weekends. You need to be sure that they are working within the regulations and not being exploited by employers, either deliberately or because of lack of knowledge of the law.

Remember

Early advice and guidance on managing money can have a lifelong effect, so it is important that children and young people begin to take responsibility for looking after personal money. Pocket money belongs to the child or young person: you can only advise – not instruct.

Managing money

Increasingly, we hear about the amount of debt people in the UK are carrying. Many adults have serious difficulties in managing money and seem to have no idea how to construct and stick to a budget. If you work with children and young people, it is important to help instil good habits at an early age; it is more likely that they will carry on managing money well when they become adults with much larger sums to manage.

It is not always easy to get children interested in budgets and saving, but if you relate it to an interest or hobby, you are more likely to capture the child's imagination. If there is a potential reward at the end of the saving – like a particular toy, computer game, concert tickets, holiday or new shoes, depending on the age of the child or young person – you are much more likely to gain co-operation and involvement.

Budgets can be drawn up in many ways, but a simple one may look like this:

Budget for Sam

Income	Spending	Savings
£10.00 – pocket money	Music downloads £5.00	For clothes £4.00
£5.00 – washing Gran's windows	Sweets, drinks, etc. £3.00	For presents £2.00
£15.00 paper round	Movies, bowling, swimming, etc. £8.00	Holiday spending money £3.00
	Bus fares £2.50	
	Extras £2.50	
Total £30.00	Total £21.00	Total £9.00

From a budget like this, Sam can still plan to have a good time downloading music and going out with his friends, while seeing how he can save for new clothes, to have holiday money to spend and to have money for presents for birthdays of friends and family.

Setting saving goals

Like all goals and targets, it is important that saving goals are achievable, and that the timescale is realistic.

It is pointless Sam setting a goal of saving £750 for a laptop computer: if he saved all his clothes money, it would take him almost 4 years. Such long-term goals are not easy for children and young people to attain. It is far better to talk with Sam about what he wants. Perhaps he wants a new pair of trainers which are £50; this will take him just over 3 months from his clothing savings – or less if he decides to allocate his holiday money too. A goal that seems attainable is far more likely to result in success, and more likely to encourage children and young people to make other plans in the future.

Using monetary sanctions

If you work with children and young people who are looked after by a local authority, you may have control over how and when pocket money is received. This also means that you may choose to use the delaying of pocket money, supervised spending or the requirement to pay compensation as a sanction for unacceptable behaviour. Your workplace will have guidelines governing the use of sanctions and what is considered acceptable practice within your organisation. In general, guidelines are likely to include the following principles.

- Pocket money can be delayed, but not withdrawn. There is likely to be a time limit on the reinstatement of withheld pocket money, usually of no longer than a month.
- As with any sanction, it is vital that children and young people can demonstrate acceptable behaviour and have the sanction withdrawn. If a child or young person cannot see that a change in behaviour brings about a changed response, he or she will not see the point in changing behaviour.

My story

Hi, I'm Ayesha and I'm 13. I wasn't very good with my pocket money, it never seemed to last. By the time I had bought some CDs, and magazines and sweets and stuff, it just went. I hate it when there's birthdays and holidays because I never seem to have any money. Now I've just started doing this money plan thing with Kerry, my key worker. We drew up this budget on a chart and I can see how much money I've got and what I need to spend. I've got a bank account so I can keep money in there for stuff like birthdays. I stuck to the budget for a whole month and had enough to buy a new top, and I've got some towards my sister's birthday, but that isn't for another 6 weeks, so I should have enough by then. It's quite easy to make it work – you just have to stop buying rubbish!

- Most guidelines would suggest that not all pocket money is delayed. Amounts will vary between organisations, but it is unlikely that any child or young person would be left with less than a third of their pocket money.
- It is also important that sanctions involving the delay of pocket money are appropriate for the age and level of understanding of the child; the temporary withholding of pocket money is likely to have minimal effect on a 5-year-old, but could have a significant effect for a 12- or 14-year-old.

Compensation

Sometimes, financial compensation is necessary where a child or young person has caused damage or loss to the property of others: for example, if they damaged a computer game belonging to another young person during a violent episode; or if one of the girls helped herself to someone else's new top, went out, got drunk, vomited down the top, then ripped it on a fence on the way home.

If you are intending to use compensation as a sanction, you should not use it to obtain the full replacement value of the item in question. It is more important that the deduction of payment is linked to the income and understanding level of the child or young person concerned, and that the time period over which payment is made is appropriate, and not excessive.

All guidelines will specify that it is not acceptable to use monetary fines as sanctions. It is simply not right to withhold money permanently that belongs to a child or young person.

Ethical issue

You suspect that Brendan, who is 16 years old, is spending all of his pocket money in the gaming arcade. You think that there may be a real addiction developing. After your challenge, he absolutely denies that this is what he is doing. You decide to put Brendan on supervised spending. However, when Brendan makes a formal complaint and takes the issue to the Independent Reviewer, your manager feels that you do not have any evidence and tells you that you must remove the sanction. The only way you could find the evidence is to follow Brendan and see what he does – effectively spying on him. If you do this, and he finds out, he will feel betrayed and your relationship with him will be damaged. If you fail to do it and he really does have a gambling problem, have you missed an opportunity to intervene?

Test yourself

1. Think of five different ways in which we use different clothes for specific occasions.
2. What should you take into account when working with a child or young person to select clothes?
3. Why are 'uniforms' important?
4. How do young people try to decorate their bodies?
5. What sort of sanctions may be imposed concerning pocket money?

HSC 38b Support children and young people to identify and develop their talents, interests and abilities

Everyone is good at something. All the children and young people you work with will have a talent for something. Everyone likes to feel that they are good at things, and most children and young people will thrive on praise and celebration of their achievements.

If someone has a talent or an ability that is nurtured and encouraged, it will grow and develop and may result in a career, or simply in a hobby or pastime, which brings pleasure and enjoyment.

Talent spotting

(KS 12, 14, 22, 25, 26, 27)

Some children and young people have obvious talents that everyone can see. A promising young footballer, an accomplished guitar player or someone who can produce a stunning drawing all have obvious talents, which should be encouraged from an early age. Many of those people who have 'made it' as adults will say that it was their parents who encouraged and supported them to make the most of the talent. Some parents go beyond encouragement and become 'pushy' parents who will drive young people forwards. There are some well-reported cases among prominent tennis and golf stars where a parent has been the primary driving force, pushing the child to make the best use of his or her talent and ability.

Active knowledge
HSC 38b pc 2–4

Explain how your organisation promotes and supports young people who show talent or ability in a particular area. Check if there is any financial support, or if any special arrangements are made to promote and develop talent.

Children who are assessed as 'gifted and talented' will also largely be identified through the education process. The government definition of 'gifted and talented' says that gifted pupils have abilities in one or more subjects in the statutory school curriculum other than art and design, music and PE; talented pupils, on the other hand, are those who have abilities in art and design, music or in sports or performing arts.

Additional challenges and learning opportunities will be provided for these children so that they are able to reach their full potential. Not all gifted and talented children are identified through the school system; some are identified as presenting challenging behaviour and others are labelled as a 'nuisance' or even excluded from school as a result of their behaviour.

The National Academy for Gifted and Talented Youth has identified that the children and young people who are referred there (over 37,000) are overwhelmingly from white, affluent backgrounds. One report (*The social origins of students identified as gifted and talented*, J Campbell et al, 2005) showed that children from wealthy backgrounds were significantly overrepresented, whereas children from socio-economic groups identified as being of 'moderate means' or 'hard pressed' were far less likely to be recognised. It is clear from the research that, although families of 'moderate means' or 'hard pressed' make up 40 per cent of the population, only 17 per cent of children recognised as gifted and talented are from these groups.

Typical characteristics

The UK does not have specific tests to identify gifted and talented children as some countries do, but there are some general features that may lead you to consider the possibility. No child or young person

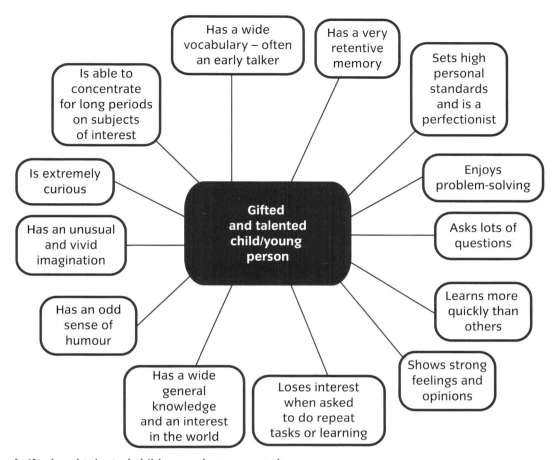

Indicators of gifted and talented children and young people

will show all of these, but those in the diagram above are useful indicators.

It is likely that you will come across children and young people who have been excluded from the system, and have not been recognised as being gifted and talented. It is important that you work with the child, the family and other professionals to gain recognition for the child's or young person's particular gifts or talent.

However, not all children who have an interest or an ability in a particular area will be gifted or have an outstanding talent; some will simply be good at something, or be interested in it. For example, a child or young person may have an interest in photography or gardening and may be good at it because they enjoy it.

Active knowledge

Think about all the children you work with. Note down the interests and abilities each one has. Some may be very obvious because of a particular interest or hobby, but others may need more thought. A child or young person whose only interests are watching TV, chatting on MSN and hanging about with mates may present you with a bit more of a challenge. Do they have a particular social ability like good communication? Do they have a real interest in fashion and always manage to put together really good-looking outfits? You can always find something – though sometimes you may have to look very hard.

Talents and abilities are relative to the overall ability of the child, so disabled children or children who have a learning disability or a sensory impairment are no less talented, you just have to see it in the overall context of the child.

When you have identified at least one ability or interest for each child or young person, think about what you are doing to nurture and develop it, and make notes on what you could do. Talk to the child and your manager about the results of the exercise.

Encouraging talent

(KS 2, 4, 5, 12, 13, 22, 24, 25, 26, 27)

Children and young people will have their own views about what is important to them, and your key role is to encourage and nurture the interests they have by providing opportunities for individuals to recognise and discuss their own interests. Sometimes it can be hard for children to admit to their interests because these would not be seen as acceptable among the peer group they belong to. For example, a young man who is part of an inner-city gang may find it difficult to share his ability to write poetry. Part of your job is to provide these young people with the confidence and self-belief to make the best use of such talents and abilities. Writing poetry does not mean that someone has to plan to make a living from it, but there are many people who write poetry throughout their lives and gain great pleasure and enjoyment from doing so.

The classic example of how talent and ability can be incorporated and channelled into a young person's culture can be seen in the graffiti art on the streets of many large cities – most spectacularly in places like New York. The artistic ability of the young people who do this is obvious, but rather than being seen in a more conventional form, this ability has been expressed in a way that is acceptable and provides recognition and status to the artist. However, graffiti is not always seen as 'public art', and there is a huge difference between the intricate pictures and lettering of some real artists and the spraying of obscenities on the local motorway bridge.

It's clear which one of these shows talent!

My story

Hi, I'm Jason. I'm 16 and I live with my mum. I met my support worker, Imran, about a year ago when I got sent on this project about cars. It was good though: we got to fix cars and do stuff with them. Before I only nicked them – now I can fix them too. I'd been nicking cars since I started hanging about with my mates when I was about 13. We also got to drive on this track which was really good. I was a really good driver anyway but it was OK doing it there – we'd have races and that and have a laugh. Anyway, I really like Imran. We just got on right from the start. I can't even remember how it happened now, but I ended up telling him about how I really like making cakes. Don't laugh – I know it sounds weird, but I think it came from when I was a kid and I used to bake cakes with my gran. I really loved it and there is just something about the smell of cake batter and baking and the warmth of the kitchen. It reminds me of my gran; she's dead now, she got cancer and died about three years ago. Anyway, I still make cakes, but I made Imran promise not to tell anyone – not something you'd want to go on about, is it?

Anyway, he got me to make a cake for him and he thought it was really good: he went on about it and kept saying about I had a real talent and all that, said I was like Jamie Oliver – I don't think so, but I wouldn't mind his money! He wanted me to go to the college about a catering course. He went on that much that I said I'd go to shut him up. He made me take a cake with me and the guy running the course tasted it and was dead impressed. I'm doing the course now – everything's different, all the people make cakes and no one thinks it's funny or weird.

Hi, I'm Imran. I have worked with Jason for just over a year. He was one of those kids that you just know shouldn't be here. Apparently, he was very close to his gran because his mother worked full-time and she looked after him and virtually brought him up. Even though he had lived on the estate all his life, he had never been in trouble until his gran got sick – then he just seemed to get in with one of the gangs and into the whole car scene. Fortunately he got one final chance to come to us rather than going down from his last court appearance. He's a great kid; he's bright and he's funny – he was also a very angry and hurt young man when he arrived with us. We spent a lot of time talking and this is how I found out about the cake-making. I thought this might be his route out if he could be persuaded to use the ability. I have to say, his cakes were fantastic – almost as good as my mum's! Finally, after a lot of work, he agreed to go to college to do his course – hopefully the rest will be history!

Making it OK

Children and young people need to feel that you believe in them and their talents and abilities, and they need to feel that they are in an environment where they are encouraged to think and talk about what interests them. Sometimes, you may find out about interests and abilities that families may not have even known about. You have learned about the importance of self-esteem in Unit 34b (page 130). It is about the way we value ourselves, and there is no doubt that knowing that other people recognise and value our gifts and abilities is a huge boost for our self-esteem and overall well-being.

A key part of what you do is creating the right environment in which children and young people can identify what their interests are. This will vary depending on where you work. If you work with children who are living with their families, you will need to encourage parents or carers to be supportive of the children and the interests they have.

It is not always easy for parents to feel that they can support their children in their interest. Consider the following two responses to a child who tells a lone parent struggling on benefit that they love horses and have a dream to learn to ride.

1

'Well, there's no point you being interested in horses – we don't have money for riding lessons, so you may as well forget it.'

2

'Well, that's great. I bet you'd be really good with horses too. We'll have to see what we can find out about how you can get to do more with horses – there must be some way of you getting involved even though we don't have the money for lessons. We'll make a start in the morning.'

The first response is very understandable for a parent struggling to make ends meet. However, such a response can be crushing for a child who has a passionate interest: it will only take one or two responses like that before the child decides that there is little point in talking about having an interest in anything because what they want clearly isn't important; it just makes everyone cross.

Imagine how a child would feel with a response like the second one. The difference in the two responses is obvious and the impact on the child is immediately different. The first response writes the idea off and excludes the child from an interest, with an argument based on affordability. The child's dreams are dismissed as if they are unimportant and the child is made to feel foolish to have even considered such a thing. The second response makes everything seem possible: it acknowledges exactly the same hard facts as the first, but also offers the hope of getting close to the dream and developing the child's interest in a different way.

You may need to work hard with parents to support them in recognising the importance of the interests and dreams of their children and the best ways to nurture and encourage aspirations and interests, rather than dismissing them.

Making it happen

If you are working with children who are looked after by the local authority, you may be the person who does the encouraging and developing of talents and interests. This could involve you in:

- supporting the child or young person to find information about activities related to their interest
- helping make links with others who have the same interest
- liaising with schools, coaches or tutors
- sourcing funding for equipment or clothing
- sourcing funding for activities
- providing encouragement and enthusiasm and making sure that you are familiar with the child's area of interest
- wherever possible, encouraging the involvement of the child's parents and family.

Remember

Children and young people with gifts and talents will need support and encouragement. Do not assume that just because he or she is talented, the child or young person will have the confidence to do anything with it. There are sources other than the local authority for supporting talented youngsters.

Obtaining resources

Finding resources for children and young people can be just as difficult for those who are looked after as for those who are living at home. You may have to persuade the budget-holder that additional money should be spent in order for a child to be able to take part in activities. Some activities may be quite cheap to organise: joining a local football team is not without cost – there will have to be money for a strip and time spent taking the child to matches and training – but it is a far smaller cost than a child wanting to learn hot air ballooning!

If there is simply nothing left in the budget for any additional expenditure, or you are supporting a parent who does not have any additional money, you may have to look at other ways to find funding. First of all check if there are any 'no cost' options: for example, the child in the previous 'horse riding' example may be able to help out at a local stable in return for free riding lessons; or with football, local sports teams may have strips that others have outgrown which can be made available, and so on.

If you draw a blank with all these options, you may have to try charitable foundations, which will often give small grants to individuals. Your local library will have a copy of *The Charities Digest* which will give you details of local charities and their criteria, or you can get the information online. Many local radio stations also have features where you can appeal for funds or equipment. The important thing is that the child or young person does not end up feeling that what they want to do is out of reach, or is being ignored. Most things can be achieved with determination – and some clever planning!

Celebrating success

Children all have talents and abilities, and it is very important that they are recognised for what they achieve. This is how they will build confidence and improve self-esteem, and if they know that they can do something and do it well, they are going to feel more positive about having another go and trying new and different things. Work in Scotland to identify ways to improve the lives of looked-after children (*Looked after children and young people: We can and must do better*, Scottish Executive January 2007) noted that:

'Many looked-after children and young people will have had experience of separation, loss and/or trauma and many lack self-esteem, confidence, resilience and self-worth.'

It is therefore doubly important that any progress or success, however small, is recognised and celebrated, and that the child or young person is left in no doubt of the importance and significance of what they have achieved. Progress and achievement will vary

Progress or success should be recognised and celebrated

depending on the child and where they started from. For example, someone who was already playing football for the county team will still have achieved fantastic success if they are picked for a national youth team. However, the celebration should be just as great for the child with a learning disability, whose speech and language impairment meant that no one could understand her three years ago, but who has just got a part in the school play!

Ethical issue

There is a child in your residential home who is a very talented artist. She has had her work exhibited locally and is on the final shortlist for a national young artist award. She has an opportunity to take her work to an exhibition in Florence; very few young artists from the UK are ever invited to this exhibition and it is a wonderful opportunity for her work to be noticed in an international arena. There are also three other young people who enjoy making music: one plays the piano and the other two play guitar. All of them have done well in music lessons at school, but they have each asked if they can have extra tuition. The available budget you have will either pay for music lessons for three young people for a year or pay for the young woman's trip to Florence. How do you decide?

HSC 38c Support children and young people to participate in recreational activities

Recreation and having fun are important parts of all our lives. Sometimes it is good to relax by doing very little apart from talking to friends and enjoying good company, but an equally important way to relax and enjoy ourselves is to take part in activities around something we enjoy doing.

Networks

(KS 2, 3, 14, 17, 18, 22, 24, 27)

Social networks are of real value to children and young people and will often be an important outcome from involvement in a recreational activity. Many of you will be connected to a computer network at work; all of our public transport is usually described as a network – a network of railway lines, or a network of roads; most of us communicate through a mobile telephone network; and so on. Essentially networks are about the routes by which things link together. Social networks are about how people link together.

Formal networks

If knowing about networks is useful for big business, it is most certainly useful for you in terms of supporting children and young people to extend the ways in which they relate to others. Some networks are formal ones and are advertised as such. For example, 'Diabetes network', 'Patient network', 'Mums and tots network', 'Musicians network' and 'Women in business network' are all formal networks.

Q. *What do you notice about most of the networks you hear about or see advertised?*

A. They are based around a common factor that brings people together.

In 2005, Valdis Krebs, a researcher into social networks, said that there are two basic, powerful drivers that bring people together to form networks, summed up by these two phrases:

- 'Birds of a feather flock together'
- 'Those close by form a tie'.

This is why so many networks are based around a shared interest, which could be a hobby, a job-role or even a local neighbourhood activity (for example, 'Crimewatch' groups are a type of network). Formal networks are usually organised by an individual or a committee, and will have a structure; it may not be a very formal structure, but there is likely to be some basic format. Such a network will have:

- a purpose or common interest
- an identifiable membership that may or may not be recorded
- an agreed means of communication – e.g. meetings or via the internet
- a means of sharing information about itself and attracting new members.

One of the increasingly common ways of being involved in a network is through the internet. The internet can provide an excellent way for people to make contact with others across the world and to share views, interests and issues. However, there are always precautions to be taken when children and young people are making contact with others on the internet, especially through chat rooms or networking sites. There will be guidelines to follow for your setting, and you should always advise parents to give their children the following guidance about being online.

- Don't take other people at face value – they may not be what they seem. Remember, people can pretend online – no one can see them.
- Don't give out personal details like your name, password, photographs or any other personal information that could be used to identify you, such as information about your family, where you live or the school you go to.
- Never arrange to meet someone you've only ever previously been in contact with on the internet without first telling your parents and getting their permission. Even then, you should take a responsible adult with you, and the first meeting should always be in a public place.
- Always stay in the public areas of chat rooms where there are other people around.

- Don't open an attachment or downloaded file unless you know and trust the person who has sent it.
- Never respond directly to anything you find disturbing or really rude – save or print it, log off and tell an adult.
- If you get someone bothering you online, it's not your fault – tell an adult.

Informal networks

These are networks that can grow and develop without there necessarily being a shared interest, but there will always be something in common: it may be friendship, or family, or where the child or young person lives or goes to school. These networks will not be advertised or have a formal structure or set means of communication, and they will often not have a set membership. For example, some schools have a place where people hang out after school and at weekends; nothing is arranged, it just happens. This is an informal network. In networks like this, there is often a core of young people who are always there, and others who drop in and out. Communication and arrangements are likely to be by word of mouth. Many families form strong networks: individual members of the family may have particular close links, but they still have an overall involvement in the wider family network.

An informal network will have:

- a flexible membership
- various means of communication, depending on the need at the time
- no definite purpose or goal
- no public advertising of its existence.

Active knowledge   HSC 38c pc 3, 4

Think about how many informal networks you are involved in. List three benefits you gain from each of them, then three things you contribute to each of them. Do the same for formal networks. You may find this a useful exercise for thinking about the sorts of areas to discuss with a child or young person who is looking to get involved in recreational activities through a network.

A formal and informal network

For children and young people, the opportunities to take part in a whole range of recreational activities are huge. It may help here to look at the different types of recreational activity that exist. Not all involve physical activity; some will be completely intellectual pursuits. Recreational activity can be grouped into physical activities, intellectual activities, cultural/creative activities and social activities. Some examples are given in the table at the bottom of the page.

The table below just begins to give you an idea of the number of options available to children and young people for recreational activity. Some of the activities shown below are likely to make a significant contribution to the overall well-being and

development of the child or young person; others may have less obvious benefits. However, you can see that there is absolutely no reason for the complaint of 'I'm bored'.

Encouraging participation

(KS 2, 4, 22, 24, 25, 26)

If children and young people show an interest in a particular type of activity, you have a role in helping them to find out as much as they can about how to get involved in the way they want. How much you do will depend on the child or young person, and his or

Physical activities	Intellectual activities	Cultural/creative activities	Social activities
athletics	board games	gardening	charity volunteering
football	bridge	knitting, sewing and other craft activities	clubs
golf	chess	listening to music	going out with friends
horse riding	computer gaming	looking at art and sculpture	going to parties
ice skating	discussion/debating groups	painting	shopping with friends
mountain climbing	IQ tests (Mensa)	playing a musical instrument	
rugby	quizzes	reading	
sailing		sculpting	
skiing		writing	
tennis			
walking			

her age and level of ability. For some children, you may only have to suggest the sort of places they might find out information; others will need you to sit with them whilst searching to find out. The sort of information the child or young person will need will vary depending on what they want to do, but is likely to include:

- where the activity takes place
- when the activity takes place
- if there are any special requirements to participate in the activity – such as age, height, previous experience, etc.
- whether any special equipment or clothing is needed
- whether there is a cost, and how much it is
- whether any transport is needed to get to the activity and back
- whether permission is needed from someone with parental responsibility.

Once all the information about the activity is collated, you can support the child or young person in planning how he or she will take part and how you will make sure that anything he or she needs is available.

Risk assessment

(KS 7, 8, 9, 18)

Some activities will carry risks. This is an inevitable part of joining in with life, and children cannot be protected from every risk. However, you will need to undertake a risk assessment if the child is looked after, and you may be able to assist parents in considering any risks for a child who lives at home.

There are three main factors that can affect the levels of risk to a child or young person participating in a recreational activity.

1 **The nature of the activity.** A child is far more likely to be injured playing rugby than painting in an art class.

2 **The location of the activity.** Rugby is always played on a rugby pitch, but an art class may be set up on the edge of a steep drop halfway up a mountain in order to catch a particular view. The balance of risk then changes considerably.

3 **The child or young person himself or herself.** Wheelchair rugby is pretty brutal (it used to be

Risks vary greatly from one activity to another

called 'murderball'), but if you insist on taking your wheelchair halfway up a mountain to paint a view, then that gets fairly risky too!

A risk assessment is not designed to stop children and young people taking part in activities; it is there so that you can identify the risks and look at ways of reducing them. Risks do not have to disappear; they just have to be reduced as far as possible. A child at the bottom of a rugby scrum can still get a paralysing neck injury, but professionally trained coaches and referees, proper training and an understanding of how to scrum properly all help to reduce the risk of injury.

Remember

Risks go along with some activities, but other risks result from inactivity such as isolation, lack of stimulation, obesity and medical problems associated with inactivity.

Making friendships through recreation

(KS 14, 19, 22, 26, 27)

The importance of friendships

Friends become increasingly significant as children grow. For very young children, pre-school individual friendships with other children, whilst important for their social development, are relatively insignificant as influences on their lives; their relationships with other members of their family or their main carer are far more important. As children progress through school and into adolescence, their friendships become more important and have a huge influence on their behaviour. The ability to form friendships with others is an important skill and is a need that most human beings have. For a child or young person, being unable to make friends or being in a situation in which they feel they do not have friends, or being bullied or excluded by others with whom they had hoped to be friends, can be extremely distressing and have a serious effect on the child's self-image and

self-confidence. Adults too find it difficult to cope with being excluded and being unable to relate to others as friends. Most people, regardless of circumstances, need to have a close relationship with another person, through which they can share confidences, worries and joys.

Making friends through recreational activity

Children and young people will undertake some recreational activities with existing friendship groups, but activities can also provide the opportunity to meet new friends or to develop relationships in a different context.

You have an important role in encouraging any new friendships that children may develop through an activity. However, your safeguarding role is your main priority, so it is important that you ensure that there are no risks relating to any new friends that a child or young person has made at a recreational activity. This is particularly important if the new friend is an adult; this may be quite common where older young people are involved in a recreational activity with people over 18 years old. You will need to be aware of the issues around protection, both for the young person themselves and for any other children or young people in the establishment.

Recognising achievement

(KS 22)

The previous element looked at ways to make sure that children and young people get recognition of achievements and that success is celebrated. Similar considerations apply to recreational activity – there needs to be as much excitement over the winning of a chess game, a third place in a swimming tournament or simply having framed a first picture or played their first recognisable tune!

We all like recognition and congratulation for what we have achieved, but it is especially precious for children who may not be convinced that they are worth making a fuss about.

My story

Hi, I'm Julie and I'm 10. It was very scary when I came to live with Mike and Heather; my mum went to prison and my nan couldn't look after me. It's only till Mum comes out, she'll be sorted then and I can go home. Anyway I didn't know anyone and everyone at the school already had friends. I didn't really mind, I just stayed in and talked to Heather, she's dead nice.

I love horses, I've got lots of pictures of horses in my room, I watch all the riding competitions on the telly and I've got a lovely book that Heather got me from the library. Anyway, Heather said I could do riding lessons – it's fab, I ride Nutmeg, he's not very big, just 12.2hh, and he's a chestnut. I love him. Going to the stables is dead good and I've met Anne Marie who's in my class, I didn't know she went riding. She's really nice and I've been to her house for tea and Heather says she can come to ours, and now I hang round with Anne Marie and a few other friends at school. It's all much better now.

Test yourself

1   What are the main categories of recreational activities?

2   List three types of information you need about recreational activities.

3   What factors affect a risk assessment?

4   Identify two key benefits from participating in recreational activities.

HSC 38 UNIT TEST

1   How important are clothes, make-up and hair to a teenage girl?

2   How important are they to a teenage boy?

3   Can pocket money provide effective sanctions for unacceptable behaviour?

4   What are the accepted guidelines about use of pocket money for sanctions?

5   What are the issues around appropriate clothing for young girls?

6   Why are risk assessments important for recreational activities?

7   What would you do if you thought a child was gifted or talented?

8   What would you do if a child wanted to take part in a recreational activity?

9   What benefits does a child gain from outside recognition of his or her achievements?

10   How can you involve parents and families in celebrating achievements?

Don't forget to refer to the evidence opportunities grid (see pages 357–375) for more ideas for suitable evidence for your NVQ.

Support children and young people to achieve their educational potential

All children and young people should be able to benefit from an all-round education that will enable them to develop into happy, confident adults who are doing something which is satisfying and fulfilling.

Most of us have experienced the frustration of working with a child or young person who is simply not fulfilling their potential. A child or young person who has limited ability but who is achieving as much as they can is likely to be happier than one who is functioning at a level far below their capability.

This unit is about your role in supporting children and young people to achieve as much as they possibly can. Your work may involve you in supporting families to see the potential that their children have, or you may work directly with children who are looked after by the local authority. You will need to work closely with professional colleagues working in schools to make sure that you focus on the child or young person and are all working towards the same goals.

In this unit you will find 'Active knowledge' features containing activities that will contribute to assessment for your NVQ. Remember that these features only offer the opportunity for partial assessment; you can also refer to the evidence opportunities grid (see pages 357–375) for more ideas to provide suitable evidence for your NVQ.

What you need to learn

- Aspirations
- Starting places
- Team work
- Know what the children learn
- Know your colleagues
- Changing goals
- Disabled young people
- Nurturing talents and interests
- Planning a future
- Theories about how children learn
- Learning through play
- Not all plain sailing
- Learning styles
- Ways to support and encourage
- Out of school activities
- Family learning
- Learning outcomes
- Being involved
- Learning how to learn

HSC 39a Support children and young people to identify and develop their educational aspirations

For many children and young people, the question 'What do you want to do with your life?' presents a real difficulty. Apart from a wish to become a famous pop star or a footballer, many children and young people have no real idea about what they want to do or what goals to aim for, much less any idea about how to get there.

Regardless of the role you have – whether it is working in a residential setting, providing support in the community or working in a day setting offering education and learning – you will need to be able to engage children and young people in planning the direction of their lives, and how they will get there.

Aspirations

(KS 2, 3, 4, 5)

Most children and young people will have hopes and dreams. Many of these are doomed to disappointment, but it is important that children and young people are able to have something to aim for. Although the aspirations of children should be nurtured and encouraged, one of the factors known to demotivate children and young people from learning is a history of failure. You will need to work to support children so that they have positive experiences of learning, and encourage their hopes and dreams whilst introducing some realism and achievable goals.

Starting places

(KS 1, 2, 4, 5, 7, 8, 9, 10, 15, 23, 27)

Whatever work you do with children and young people to help them to identify and shape their plans for life, you need to 'start where the child is'. You need to be sure that you have enough information to understand the child or young person and the factors that have influenced their lives. In the example below, Jody has understood that Sarah is completely

My story

Hi, I'm Sarah. I'm 12 years old and I am going to be a famous pop star. I might be in a girl band, but I think I'd really like to be a solo artist. I know that this is what I will do; I think I've always known. I'll probably just get discovered I think, or I might win something like the X Factor. You have to be 16 to go in for any of those shows, so I can't do it just yet. They go on about school, but it really doesn't matter because I don't think that I will need any exams or nothing. No one famous has any qualifications: they are just not important. I think I would like to be managed by Simon Cowell or Louis Walsh, because they are really good and get you great record deals, but I might consider someone else if they were any good. I'm going to have a great big house and loads of nice clothes – so many clothes that I can give them away to charity auctions to raise money. I'm going to buy a nice house for my Mum and my Nan too and then Mum won't have to keep going into hospital and she won't have to do all that stuff to herself because everything will be better. Jody, my support worker, says I'm really talented and she went on about doing performing arts stuff in school and music lessons and that. I thought it was going to be a waste of time, but I went and it's dead good. I'm learning the guitar and I didn't know that you could 'read' music – it's just like a book when you know how. The auditions for the school show are next week – and I just want to get picked for one of the big parts.

Jody's really on the ball. Until we talked about it, I just hadn't thought about how much goes into being a pop star. I thought you just did it, but you might be a 'one hit wonder' like that. If you want to be famous for years, then you have to know a lot of stuff. It's not just the learning music and performing, you need to know loads of other things, like about all the countries you might tour in so that you understand what kind of performance to do, and about money and how to work it all out, otherwise agents and managers and people just rob you – it's happened to lots of stars. You also have to understand design and art so that you know about clothes and image and sets and everything – there's a lot more involved than you'd think.

convinced that she will be a famous pop star. Telling Sarah about the odds against achieving this and trying to persuade her to focus on schoolwork so that she has an alternative career are very unlikely to succeed. It is more likely to simply convince Sarah that Jody is yet one more adult who doesn't understand her and doesn't understand anything about life as a pop star, and so can safely be dismissed and ignored. What Jody did was to encourage Sarah's dreams and give her concrete steps to reach achievable goals, like getting a part in the school concert. She also was able to help Sarah to see the relevance of other areas of learning and how they could be important to her future whilst, at the same time, not dismissing Sarah's dreams. Jody's approach is more likely to result in Sarah being increasingly motivated to learn as she sees the relevance to her life.

In Unit HSC 36, you learned about the different needs we all have and the importance of needs being met before any of us can achieve our full potential. You also learned about the importance of assessing children and young people, so that you have as full a picture as possible before starting work.

Active knowledge
HSC 39 pc 4, 5, 6

Think about the children you work with. Has the assessment process given you all the information you need to understand about the educational aspirations any of them may have? Would you know where to start work with any of them? If not, find out about what information is missing and how this could be incorporated into the assessment information.

What is education?

Education is about more than school; it is about learning in the broadest sense of the word. Children and young people learn from their experiences and the activities they undertake outside school; they learn from many different sources, not just teachers. There are many arguments about the definition and purpose of education but, essentially, it is about giving people the motivation to *want* to learn and

also providing the right tools so that people know *how* to learn. The word 'people' rather than children and young people is deliberate because education and learning does not stop after school; learning is lifelong.

Reflect

Think about your own experiences of school – did you enjoy it? Was it a good time because you had plenty of friends and had good fun? What about the learning? How easy was that for you? Were you motivated or did you find it hard to raise interest and enthusiasm? Did your attitude change at any point? When? Can you work out why? Are you doing an NVQ because you learn better this way than on an academic course? What were you interested in at school? What were you good at? Can you see how any of the things you were good at in school have been useful in the work you do now?

Even though education is about much more than school, the time children and young people spend in school is what forms the foundation for any other learning. School is still the main place in which educational goals and aspirations will be identified, planned for and achieved, so it is essential that you work closely with colleagues in education.

Education for looked-after children

Looked-after children do not have good outcomes from the current education system. Only 11 per cent of children in care achieved 5 GCSEs compared with 55 per cent of all children and an even smaller percentage of children in care with a statement of special educational needs achieved GCSEs when compared to all children. The Government have produced a Green Paper, *Care Matters*, in which there are plans to improve the educational experience of looked-after children. For example: most children in care are in the lowest performing schools. The Green Paper proposed that schools will be required to admit looked-after children even if they are full. There is also a proposal to have a 'Virtual Headteacher' in each local authority so that the progress of all looked-after children can be monitored and outcomes measured.

Team work

(KS 1, 3, 4, 7, 8, 9, 13, 15)

Helping and supporting children and young people to achieve their maximum potential is a team effort. This is not a job for one worker; you have to work closely with all the other people who are involved with the child, from parents and relatives to play worker and GP (see below). The list can go on, and no child or young person will have all of these people involved, but it is important that you ensure that you are a part of a team where the focus is on the child and everyone is working to the same ends. The legal requirements are that integrated service provision is the way to achieve the best outcomes for children and young people, so there will need to be a team perspective for any work you undertake to support children and young people to reach their educational potential.

Legal basis

The Children Act 2004 is the legal basis in England, Northern Ireland and Wales for providing integrated services for children and young people. In Scotland, the Children (Scotland) Act 1995 and, more recently, the Education (additional support for learning) (Scotland) Act 2004 promote the integrated working of education, health and social work to ensure that all children and young people get the most possible benefit from education. Other guidelines such as *Working Together to Safeguard Children* also stress the importance of working with other colleagues and the child or young person along with parents or carers.

All education in England and Wales is based in the Education Act 1944, but the Education Reform Act 1988 made some of the most significant changes, introducing the National Curriculum, the option for schools to become self-governing and the introduction of Ofsted to inspect schools. There have been other

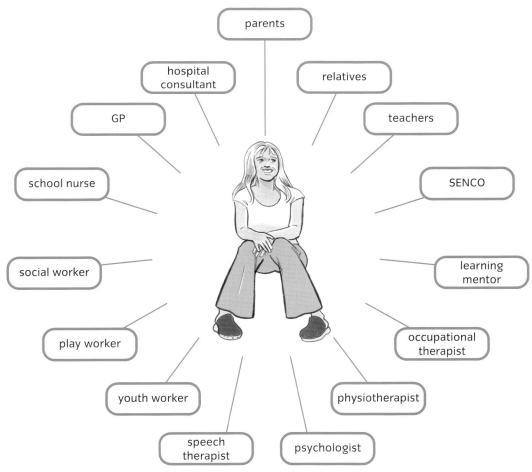

The team involved with a child

Acts of Parliament that have developed specific aspects, such as the Special Educational Needs and Disability Act 2001, which identifies the ways in which educational establishments must meet needs and be accessible for all children. The Education Act 2002 introduced the Foundation stage of the curriculum, the concept of City Academies and the requirement that schools share a legal responsibility to safeguard and protect children and young people.

The Scottish education system is different from the rest of the UK. A major review of the Scottish curriculum has been undertaken and a national curriculum for children from 3 to 18 years old is due to be introduced in 2008/9. Similar proposals have been made for Wales, where it is proposed that there will be a single, coherent curriculum framework for all children from 3 to 19 years old. In Northern Ireland, the Education (Curriculum Minimum Content) Order 2007 set out the requirements for a revised curriculum for children aged from 3 to 18 years old.

Know what they learn

(KS 8, 9)

It is important that you know what the children you work with are learning at school, and what

assessments they will need to undertake at what stage. The National Curriculum, regardless of the country you work in, is set out in Key Stages, covering the areas laid out in the table at the bottom of the page.

The National Curriculum sets out:

- the subjects taught
- the knowledge, skills and understanding required in each subject
- standards or attainment targets in each subject – teachers can use these to measure a child's progress and plan the next steps in their learning
- how a child's progress is assessed and reported.

The subjects that must be taught are:
- Art and design
- Citizenship
- Design and technology
- English
- Geography
- History
- Information and communication technology (ICT)
- Modern foreign languages (MFL)
- Music
- PE
- Science.

Age	Stage	Year	Tests
3–4	Foundation		
4–5		Reception	
5–6	Key Stage 1	Year 1	
6–7		Year 2	National tests and tasks in English and maths
7–8	Key Stage 2	Year 3	
8–9		Year 4	
9–10		Year 5	
10–11		Year 6	National tests in English, maths and science
11–12	Key Stage 3	Year 7	
12–13		Year 8	
13–14		Year 9	National tests in English, maths and science
14–15	Key Stage 4	Year 10	Some children take GCSEs
15–16		Year 11	Most children take GCSEs or other national qualifications

The Key Stages of the National Curriculum

The National Curriculum also includes: religious education, careers education, work-related studies and personal, social and health education (PSHE).

Starting in September 2008, young people between 14 and 19 will have the opportunity to study for a Specialised Diploma. These new diplomas will enable students to learn the skills for a particular area of specialism alongside general areas of learning. They will work for young people who learn best in a practical and focused way.

They will provide important opportunities for young people who want to be able to apply learning, make early links into industry-based skills and to prepare for careers and progression into further and higher education. There are 14 areas of learning where Specialised Diplomas will be available. They are being rolled out from 2008 to 2010.

Start date	Area of learning
September 2008	Information technology
	Society health and development
	Engineering
	Creative and media
	Construction and built environment
September 2009	Land based and environmental
	Hair and beauty
	Manufacturing
	Hospitality and catering
	Business administration and finance
September 2010	Public services
	Sport and leisure
	Retail
	Travel and tourism

Diplomas will be available at three levels, so that young people will be able to take the level best suited to the outcomes they want to achieve.

Level 1 will compare with taking four or five GCSEs, so will involve a similar amount of study and a similar level of demand.

Level 2 will be comparable to taking five or six GCSEs.

Level 3 will involve about the same amount of work as taking 3 A levels.

All schools will begin to offer the Specialised Diplomas from 2008.

Early years foundation stage

Babies and young children have a framework that supports their development. There is not a specific curriculum, but it is based around four key principles and there is extensive guidance about how the principles should be put into practice. The principles are:

A unique child

Every child is a competent learner from birth who can be resilient, capable, confident and self-assured.

Positive relationships

Children learn to be strong and independent from a base of loving and secure relationships with parents and/or a key person.

Enabling environments

The environment plays a key role in supporting and extending children's development and learning.

Learning and development

Children develop and learn in different ways and at different rates and all areas of learning and development are equally important and inter-connected.

Know your colleagues

(KS 4, 12, 15, 18, 22, 24, 26)

In order to work effectively to support children and young people's educational goals, you must know the other key people whom you need to work alongside. Sometimes, this will depend on the age of the child, or it could relate to any particular additional needs a child may have. Where services are available to all, such as schools, these are called *universal services* and where they are in response to particular needs, they are called *targeted services*. This section looks at the colleagues you will need to work with in both universal and targeted services.

Parents and family

A child's family is one of the greatest influences on them

First and foremost you need to work alongside parents and family or other carers. They are providing care and support for their child and they are the child's first and most important educators. A child's family is a key influence in how likely they are to achieve their full potential. Families where learning is seen as being important and the parents or carers are involved with, and co-operate with, school are much more likely to produce children who will achieve and progress through educational milestones. Families in which parents have had poor education experiences themselves, and therefore do not view it as important, or who feel actively antagonistic towards schools and teachers, are far more likely to have children and young people who are not engaged with education and do not view it as having any relevance for them.

Any plans or projects to support educational goals, need to be discussed and agreed with parents. Later in this unit we will look at the concept of *family learning* and how it can enable adults and children to learn and develop together.

Babies and young children

Nursery workers are a key contact where children under school age are concerned

Children under school age will have an early years worker: this could be a nursery nurse, a playgroup worker, a child minder or a nanny. They will also have a health visitor and, depending on needs, other professionals such as speech therapists, physiotherapists, etc. It is essential that you work along with the early years staff who are providing care for the child and draw on their expertise in the early years sector.

Primary school children

Universal services

Aside from parents, the key person you need to work with is the child's teacher. You may also be able to include a teaching assistant if there is one working with the child's class.

Targeted services

Depending on any additional needs, an educational psychologist or speech and language therapist, portage worker, physiotherapist or others may be involved.

Secondary school children and young people

Universal services

Every child or young person will have a form teacher/personal tutor who takes overall responsibility for the child or young person's welfare and progress. If you are interested in working on a particular curriculum area, there will be a relevant subject teacher to contact. As the school days extend to incorporate other provision before and after school, more and more children and young people also have important and influential relationships with play workers who run the pre- and after-school activities. The Youth Service provides for all young people in a local community through youth clubs, outreach work and activities focused on an area of interest. Youth workers are significant for many children and young people.

Targeted services

If the child or young person receives additional support, then the Special Educational Needs Co-ordinator (SENCO), learning mentor, educational psychologist, School Counsellor, Children and Adolescent Mental Health Services (CAMHS) or other professional therapists may also be involved. If a young person has been, or is at risk of being, an offender, then there may also be a social worker from the Youth Offending Team (YOT).

Children needing additional support may have more key people in their lives

Young people over 16 years

Universal services

Just because some young people leave school, it does not mean that their educational goals and aspirations no longer exist. For many, this is the period where they begin to work out what they really want to do and the direction they want to take. Sixth-form colleges and further education colleges provide a learning environment that may suit some young people, especially those who find school very restricting. A great many young people are also more motivated by the vocational programmes offered at this age than by the more academic curriculum at school. At an FE college, it may be more difficult to find one person to relate to, but many colleges have a system of personal or pastoral tutors, who will take individual responsibility for a student's well-being. The Youth Service continues to work with young people up to the age of 25 years old, and Connexions works with young people to support them in planning a route through qualifications and career choices. The Connexions Advisor is a key person to involve for this age group.

Targeted services

FE colleges will have learning support services that provide assessment, help and support with young people's learning needs. If counselling support is needed, this will be provided through the student counselling service. The Probation Service may also be involved if young people of this age are offending, while the CAMHS service will still continue to provide support for young people with mental health needs.

Changing goals

(KS 2, 5, 6, 14, 26, 27)

As children grow and develop, so their educational and life goals will change. There are very few of us who go on to achieve the goals and ambitions we had as 5-year-olds; not many fulfil the dreams they had at 12 years old; but many more achieve the goals they set as 16-year-olds.

There are some obvious reasons for this. The way we grow and develop means that young children have limited life experience and do not have the capacity to see events separately from themselves. A five-year-old can only respond to the idea of a future in which they will 'be' or 'do' something by thinking of something they have seen or heard. So, 'I want to be a bus driver' or 'I want to be a doctor' or 'I want to work on the checkout in Tesco' makes sense to a five-year-old, because they know what bus drivers, doctors and people who work on the checkout do. They will have no concept of what people who manage Tesco do; nor will they understand what Stockbrokers or City dealers or lawyers do – unless they are in direct contact with them.

By the time children are 12 years old, they can see the world as being separate from themselves and are likely to have a broader experience on which to base goals and aspirations about their own future. At this age, goals may be influenced by heroes and by images and icons from popular culture. Many will have dreams of pop music or film careers or of becoming sporting heroes; some may have more general views like 'I want to be a scientist' or 'I want to work in engineering' or 'I want to do something in medicine'. At this age, ideas may not be clear, or even realistic; children may not have ideas about how they will achieve their goals or what may be involved. It is unlikely that most will have a clear plan.

By the age of 16, young people are usually clear about what they need to do in order to achieve their goals. Some may know what they want to do with their lives and have an understanding of how they will get there; others will have general aims to work in technology or commerce or health or education, but be less clear about how this may happen; and some will still have no aims, plans or ambitions, and will not be in any type of training or employment, but simply drifting without any clear direction.

This last group of young people has been identified as needing a great deal of help and support. They are referred to as NEET – Not in Employment, Education or Training. According to the office of National Statistics, at the time of writing, there are 220,000 young people in this group in England, whereas there are 1.5 million young people in education, training or employment. Government figures show that those in the NEET group are 20 per cent more likely to commit a crime than similar young people who are in work or training and girls in this group are 22 per cent more likely to become pregnant whilst still in their teens.

Ethical issue

The 2007 government Green Paper *Raising Expectations* proposes that school leaving age will be raised to 18. There are proposals that young people who refuse to stay at school, undertake training or have a full-time job with at least one day each week for training will be fined, with the potential for imprisonment if they fail to pay. Do you think that this is a good way of raising the school leaving age and improving the staying-on rate? Currently, Britain is 20th out of 30 western countries for staying-on rates, and large numbers of young people are still leaving school at 16 without qualifications or training. This move will ensure that young people are able to develop knowledge and skills whether for further academic study or to be able to move into the workplace. Or do you think that proposals to criminalise the most vulnerable young people are not a positive way to achieve the aim? If young people are remaining in school or entering training because they are forced to do so or face prosecution, how receptive will they be to learning? Consider your response to this proposal – discuss it with your colleagues, especially colleagues from different organisations and see if there is a consensus of opinion.

Disabled young people

(KS 11, 19, 26, 27)

One study (Burchardt, *The Education and Employment of Disabled Young People*: Joseph Rowntree Foundation, 2005) that compared the aspirations of disabled and non-disabled young people found that, at 16 years old, the aspirations were similar; 60 per cent wanted to stay on at school, and between 25 and 33 per cent were aiming for a professional qualification. Both groups had the same expectations of earnings from a full-time job.

Goals change as children grow

The differences emerged when the aspirations translated into reality.

- Only half of the disabled young people reported that they had received the training or education they had wanted, compared to 60 per cent of non-disabled young people.
- By the age of 18 or 19, almost half (48 per cent) of the disabled young people had a qualification equivalent to NVQ L1 (GCSE D–G) in comparison to only 28 per cent of non-disabled young people.
- At age 26, disabled people were nearly four times as likely to be unemployed or involuntarily out of work than non-disabled people. Among those who were in employment, earnings were 11 per cent lower than for their non-disabled counterparts with the same level of educational qualifications.

The evidence is clear that disabled young people do not lack aspiration, but more support needs to go into translating the aspirations into reality.

Nurturing talent and interests

(KS 2, 4, 17, 22, 25)

A few children and young people have truly exceptional talent. This is true in every generation and in every field; there will always be sports people, musicians and artists who are gifted and have real talent. This should be recognised, nurtured and encouraged by everyone involved with the child.

However, such talent is unusual: you are more likely to be working with children and young people who are good at art, music, writing, science, etc. and have a real interest.

A key part of your work should be to encourage children and young people to recognise what they are good at. Involving parents and carers, if appropriate, is an important part of helping children and young people to value their own abilities and interests, because praise and encouragement from the adults in their lives matters a great deal.

Recognising talent

No one is asking you to become a talent scout or hold auditions! However, as you develop relationships with the children and young people you work with, you will inevitably see where their abilities lie. Children and young people will talk to you about their interests and may well want to share with you the things that they are proud of.

Use your communication skills to listen to what children and young people are telling you, show that you are interested and encourage them to talk more about what interests them. Talent and ability often go hand in hand with an interest in a particular area. In Unit 38, we looked at recreational activities and how important they are for children and young people to relax and enjoy, but it may be that you are able to see ability and talent in other areas too. Some of the things in which children and young people may be interested are not obviously part of education, but it may be possible to encourage them to see where the links are. The table on the next page gives some examples.

Active knowledge
HSC 39b pc 6 (part), HSC 39 KS 22, 23

Find out the educational milestones for each of the children and young people you work with. Make sure you know which assessments are relevant to them and when and how they are carried out. Check if there are tests, exams or assessments undertaken by teachers or early years professionals. Find out if any preparation is needed and how you should support the child and contribute.

Of course, these ideas will not work for everyone, but it is encouraging to find that something you are good at and enjoy can also help you to pass exams and achieve educational goals and milestones.

Personalised learning

Schools are now required to make sure that they are providing learning that meets the needs of each individual pupil. In order to do this, pupils' learning needs are assessed and any barriers to learning

A young person interested in:	Could be encouraged to see links with:
Sport	Physiology/biology
Pop music	Music/design/creative art
Fashion	Design/design history/art
Cars	Physics/design
Celebrity magazines	English language/writing/design
Video games	Graphics/computer science/ICT/art
Graffiti	Art/design/graphics

Some links between interests and school subjects

identified and addressed. A range of approaches have been used – for example:

- sharing learning objectives with students at the start of each lesson, then using a plenary to evaluate progress
- helping students to know and recognise the standards they are aiming for – using 'pupil-speak' version of mark schemes and/or levels statements for coursework and exam questions, giving examples of answers or solutions to problems, making displays of ongoing and finished work and using the previous year's work to illustrate different levels of achievement
- involving students in peer and self-assessment – regular marking of own work and other students' work, students use examiners' mark schemes to give a mark and then justify it when challenged to do so
- involving both teacher and students in reviewing and reflecting on assessment information – to set personal targets for next set of exams/tests that teachers use when writing reports to parents
- using ICT to create a 'virtual school' where pupils can access lesson notes and homework tasks online from home
- vertical tutor groups – mixed age groups for pupils with a particular interest, enabling pupils to mix and learn from older and younger pupils
- workshops for parents to enable closer 'home–school' partnerships
- 'buddy' and mentoring schemes to enable pupils to feel safe and secure.

This personalised approach, especially when linked to the proposal in *Care Matters* is very important for looked-after children. There are often barriers that can make learning difficult. Many looked-after children have had to overcome disruption, moves, changes in carers as well as personal trauma, so making sure that you work closely with an education team to look at what each individual child or young person needs is a key task.

Planning a future

(KS 2, 4, 9, 17, 22, 25)

Once you have worked with a young person to identify aspirations and goals, you need to support them in making a plan for how the goals are to be achieved. Many aspirations and dreams are never achieved because nothing concrete was ever done to set about making them into a reality. Remember the study about disabled young people? Their aspirations were no different from those of non-disabled young people, but it was much harder to overcome the obstacles necessary to turn them into reality.

Making it all happen

How to work out a Personal Development Plan depends on the age of the child or young person. The discussions you have with a 10-year-old will be different from the detailed planning you may do with a 14- or 15-year-old. Assuming that you are dealing with a young person at an age when important decisions need to be made and opportunities need to be seized, you need to encourage them, with their families, to set out some goals with achievable targets on the way.

- Goals are where you eventually want to get to.
- Targets are the steps to be climbed on the way.
- Remember – targets must always be SMART:

SPECIFIC
they say exactly what you mean

MEASURABLE
you can prove that you've reached them

ACHIEVABLE
you can reach them in the next few weeks

REALISTIC
they are about action you can take

TIME-RELATED
they have deadlines.

Use the following checklist to make sure that you have covered all the important stages of planning.

- Set some educational and career goals that say what is to be achieved and by when.
- Set SMART targets to help reach educational goals.
- Identify tasks to help reach targets.
- Have a plan to improve learning that is being actively worked on.
- Have a plan to reach career goals that is being actively worked on.
- Keep a development log updated so that progress can be seen.

One sort of action plan to help a young person achieve a long-term goal of getting to university to study computer graphics could look like this:

Goal: Get the grades I need in assignments, practical tests and exams.		
Target: Do a revision schedule this week (March 15th) and use it to prepare for the exams in June.		
Date to be done	**Task**	**Date done**
This week	1. Sort out my subject files and fill in the gaps	
	2. Talk to my form tutor – how do I do a revision schedule that will work?	
	3. Draw up a revision schedule (leave time for my part-time job).	
Next week, and until the exams	1. Get help from teachers/tutor/library.	
	2. Review what I know and concentrate my revision on what I don't know.	
	3. Work through old exam questions or practical tasks.	

Example of a young person's action plan

This action plan identifies a target, which is:

Specific: do work out a revision schedule and use it.

Measurable: you know if a revision schedule has been done and if it is being used.

Achievable: developing a revision schedule can be done without too much difficulty.

Realistic: there is nothing unreasonable about someone putting together a revision schedule in the time identified.

Time-related: there are clear time boundaries set – the schedule is to be developed in a week and used until the exams.

Another key part of planning is to identify any particular areas for improvement and make sure you have thought about how the improvements are to be made. For an example, see the table on the next page.

Target: Learn how cell structures work by the end of this half term.

Tasks	By when	Date done
Get some information from the library on basic cell structure to give me a better idea of what the subject involves.	10th April	
See if I can get some more help from my science teacher.	23rd April	
Work through some exercises and try applying what I've learnt.	May	
Review how far I've improved and what else I need to do.	End May	

Example of an action plan for an area for improvement

This target and area for improvement are part of the overall goal of achieving the grades needed in all assignments and exams: understanding cells is essential for getting the necessary grade in science. The tasks to help achieve the target are clear and have dates so it is evident if progress is on track.

The plans can be adapted to suit individual young people and their own circumstances. Some may not want anything so structured and may prefer to just talk about a general direction and get some ideas about what they need to do next, but some young people like a clear plan which they can follow and can use to see how well they are doing. It is important that you recognise, praise and value the progress the young person makes with the plan, as this is one of the best ways to motivate and encourage.

Test yourself

1   Who are the key people you need to work with when supporting educational aspirations?

2   What are the areas of the National Curriculum?

3   What is the curriculum programme for pre-school children?

4   Disabled young people have lower expectations of training and careers than non-disabled young people. True or false? Give reasons why.

5   What would you do differently when discussing educational goals with a 9-year-old and a 14-year-old?

HSC 39b Help children and young people to identify, plan and access educational opportunities and activities

Theories about how children learn

(KS 14, 26)

The psychological theories of how children's learning develops form the basis for the way education is delivered in nurseries and schools. It is important that you understand the outlines of the various learning and educational theories and approaches in order to better understand the educational opportunities and activities available to the children and young people you work with.

There are three key theoretical models of children's learning, as well as other theories and approaches that have developed from each of them. You need to know the basic models and how they influence educational practice.

The transmission model sees a child as a blank board to be filled in

Transmission model

The transmission model of learning came from the thinking of the philosopher John Locke (1632–1704), who thought of the child as a blank clay tablet (in Latin this is called a *tabula rasa*: you may well hear this expression used) or an 'empty vessel' capable of being moulded and shaped by adults. People who work using this sort of approach are referred to as **behaviourists**: they are concerned with the way individuals behave, rather than how they feel or how they interact with others.

This model sees children as basically passive: in other words, they react to what goes on around them and absorb information from their experiences and will react in a way which can be predicted. It also recognises that human behaviour can be modified by consequences (called 'reinforcement' in such models). For example, if a child puts a hand on a hot

iron, the child will get burned and will not be likely to repeat the act.

Transmission models are concerned with the child's environment and the effect that experiences have on the way the child learns. These models are based on the idea that children are entirely influenced by the environment around them and not at all by any genetic, inherited factors: in other words, nurture rather than nature.

There are two main aspects of transmission theory: learning theory and social learning theory.

Learning theory (learning from experience)

Classical conditioning

Pavlov's work on the behaviour of dogs is a well-known example of how learning theory developed during the 20th century. Pavlov fed his dog when the church bells rang, or a light was flashed before feeding, and at the sight of the food the dog salivated. After some time, the dog would salivate at the sound of the bell or when the light was flashed even when no food was in sight; it associated the bell ringing or light flashing with the arrival of food. Salivation at the sound of the bell or flash of light indicated a 'conditioned' response.

Active knowledge
Links to HSC 326

Think about how many times you react automatically to a particular stimulus. For example; if you hear a phone with the same ring tone as the phone at work, your instinct is to respond – even though it is not your phone. Anyone who has ever breastfed a baby will know that you respond to a baby's cry by producing milk – it can be any baby, not just your own. Make a few notes about other occasions on which you react automatically to particular stimuli.

How we learn from practical experience

In Unit HSC 33 you looked at the Lewin/Kolb experiential learning cycle in relation to your own professional development. The learning cycle works in exactly the same way for young people when learning from experience. So for example, in a laboratory science experiment, a young person heats sodium iodide and sulphuric acid in a test tube – this produces hydrogen sulphide and that unmistakeable smell of 'rotten eggs'.

The learning cycle works like this:

Concrete experience: making the gas as part of a science lesson, discovering it has an awful smell.

Reflective observation: thinking about how easy it was, what it could be used for, how it works.

Abstract conceptualisation: understanding where this new knowledge fits and making sense of it; realising that this could be very useful as a disruptive tool if it was used to make 'stink bombs' – why has no one thought of this before?!

Active experimentation: making the gas again and capturing it in a container, then opening the

container during a maths lesson – using new found experience in a different way!

Operant conditioning

Operant conditioning was a further development of Pavlov's work by the psychologist B.F. Skinner. It is concerned mainly with shaping and modifying behaviour. Like Pavlov, Skinner also worked with animals, but only rewarded them with food if they did as he required: the food reward acted as a positive reinforcement – a good consequence. When animals did not do as Skinner required, he subjected them to unpleasant stimuli such as electric shocks: the unpleasant stimuli acted as negative reinforcers – bad consequences – and these gradually stopped the behaviour.

Learning theory has had a great effect on how adults shape or modify children's behaviour. This is the theory that underlies the reward-based 'positive behaviour' schemes which operate in many schools. By rewarding (reinforcing) behaviour that is wanted by providing good consequences, adults can change the way children behave. This is called 'behaviour modification' and is based on the view that children learn ways of behaving as they learn anything else, and can be made to 'un-learn' or modify it in the same way.

Active knowledge
Links to HSC 326

Star charts are a very widely used way of managing the behaviour of young children. If they behave in the way that is required by the adult, they get a star on the chart. Note down the different ways in which you use operant conditioning at work and in your own life.

Social learning theory (learning through example)

Social learning theory accepts the basics of learning theory but also emphasises that children learn behaviours by observing and imitating adults – especially those adults who are important to them. Albert Bandura is a well-known social learning theorist and he found that a wide range of behaviours were learned by observation, including aggression, sharing, sex roles and altruism (willingness to do things which benefit other people, even if it results in disadvantage for yourself). Social learning theory emphasises the need for adults to model socially acceptable behaviour to children. For example, if staff within a nursery or primary school regularly become angry and shout, children will learn that this is an acceptable way to behave and will copy the behaviour. If a child is brought up in a household where disagreements are resolved using aggression and violence, this is what they learn as being the way to deal with an argument.

Active knowledge

Try to think of aspects of your behaviour that you can trace back to behaviour you saw in the adults around you as you grew up. These could be anything from being polite and showing good manners to always doing things in a particular order. Then consider the children and young people you work with. What learned behaviours can you see when you look at their families?

The beautiful poem by Dorothy Law Nolte, 'Children learn what they live', summarises the ways in which the behaviour of adults affects children. Everyone who works with, or is a parent or carer of, children should think about what it says.

Laissez-faire model

This model is based on the work of the French philosopher Rousseau (1712–78). Rousseau taught that children learned naturally, like the opening of a flower bud, and were programmed to learn certain things at certain times. Rousseau's thinking was that children's development would proceed anyway, whether or not there was a significant influence from adults or the environment. Developmental scales were first developed as a result of the laissez-faire approach. These were used to measure children's development: they assumed that there is a 'normal' stage of development and that most children will have reached certain stages by a given age.

In the following years, many people built on Rousseau's thinking. If you think about how children develop complex concepts such as number, space, music, time, cause and effect, you begin to realise how difficult these ideas are. Some psychologists such as Fordor believe that the development of mental concepts is 'wired in' to internal structures in a child's brain and that the role of the adult in the child's development is limited.

Noam Chomsky's work on language development is similar. Chomsky believed that children learned the complex grammatical structures of language just by hearing it spoken. He taught that children are born with structures within their brain that allow them to

Children learn what they live

If children live with criticism, they learn to condemn.

If children live with hostility, they learn to fight.

If children live with fear, they learn to be apprehensive.

If children live with pity, they learn to feel sorry for themselves.

If children live with ridicule, they learn to feel shy.

If children live with jealousy, they learn to feel envy.

If children live with shame, they learn to feel guilty.

If children live with encouragement, they learn confidence.

If children live with tolerance, they learn patience.

If children live with praise, they learn appreciation.

If children live with acceptance, they learn to love.

If children live with approval, they learn to like themselves.

If children live with recognition, they learn it is good to have a goal.

If children live with sharing, they learn generosity.

If children live with honesty, they learn truthfulness.

If children live with fairness, they learn justice.

If children live with kindness and consideration, they learn respect.

If children live with security, they learn to have faith in themselves and in those about them.

If children live with friendliness, they learn the world is a nice place in which to live.

Copyright © 1972 by Dorothy Law Nolte

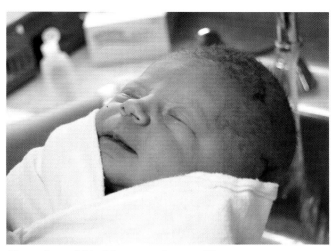
Chomsky said babies were born with grammar 'wired in'

develop language, and that children develop new sentences and apply rules of grammar to their speech rather than just copy sentences they have heard. You can see how this works when you listen to children making errors by applying speech rules to new situations, e.g. 'mouses' instead of 'mice' because they expect to add an 's' to make it plural. If children only copied what they heard, they would never use 'mouses'.

Social constructivist model

This model is based on the work of Piaget (1896–1980), Bruner (b. 1915) and Vygotsky (1896–1934). It is the most influential model in current children's learning provision. The social constructivist model views children as partly 'empty vessels' (see the transmission model on page 214) and partly as pre-programmed (see the laissez-faire model on page 216) with links between the two. The social constructivist model stresses the importance of environmental, biological and cultural factors and sees the child as an active participant in his or her own learning and development.

Piaget

Jean Piaget was a constructivist whose work has been a major influence both on developmental psychology and on learning and education. Piaget's influence cannot be underestimated as he changed the way in which young children's learning was viewed and

opened the door to further research and development. Piaget's view was that, from birth, a child actively chooses and makes sense of information from its environment and has the ability to adapt and learn. Piaget believed that children constructed higher and more complex levels of knowledge for themselves because they have the ability to interpret the information from the environment surrounding them.

For example, you will often see young children looking very purposeful, obviously doing something very important – this could be picking objects up and moving them, or going backwards and forwards with a pram or other push toy. Piaget would say that this is children actively organising their own learning, and that they are doing this activity in order to find out information and to learn and understand.

Piaget believed that children pass through a series of stages of cognitive or mental development always in the same order, but that different children go through the stages at different rates. Although he recognised the social world of the people around the child as having a role in the child's development and learning, Piaget did not emphasise this and his work focused on the role of the individual child in actively being involved in its own development.

Piaget believed that children learn through processes of adapting and understanding known as:

- **Assimilation:** taking in new information from the environment through doing everyday actions: crying, feeding, rolling, crawling, etc.
- **Accommodation:** modifying and changing existing patterns of actions to accommodate new information and knowledge: e.g. avoid crawling into table leg, it hurts! Can you see the link here with learning theory (see pages 214–216)? The difference is that Piaget does not think that the child is passive and just responding to external events and consequences; he believes that the child actively looks for new learning and seeks to find ways to confirm and understand what it sees.
- **Equilibration:** balancing what they already know with new experience to make sense of the world: 'I can crawl on this but it is hard and cold, I can

crawl over there too – but it is soft and warm. Whatever it is that makes them different does not stop me crawling on both surfaces.'

Piaget's stages

Sensori-motor (birth to about 2 years): The child progresses from basic reflexes, by learning through its senses, to more complex activities such as grasping and hitting.

Pre-operational (2 to about 7 years): Child begins to think and can represent actions with other symbols such as words. Children can use the word 'Mummy' and understand it represents their real Mummy. Children begin to understand that words mean particular objects. Children think very differently from adults at this stage: they do not separate themselves from the actions going on in the world around them; neither do they have a sense of time or of the sequence of events in relation to each other.

Concrete operational (7 to about 12 years): Children are able to think in a more systematic way and begin to grasp the idea that abstract concepts can exist, but they can still only think about concrete objects and activities.

Formal operational (12 years onwards): Children are now capable of abstract thought: they can grasp abstract concepts like justice and truth; they can also develop ideas and test them out.

Bruner and Vygotsky

Bruner and Vygotsky use Piaget's work as a base but put more emphasis on the role of play and interacting with adults and other children. Piaget's view of the child as a solitary learner is replaced by that of the child as a social being. The child uses what it has come to know and understand from adults to develop ideas and learning that it could not do alone.

Like Piaget, Vygotsky thought that children were active in their own lives and learning, but unlike Piaget, he believed that social relationships and interaction were essential for intellectual development. Vygotsky emphasised the important role of adults in helping children learn. Bruner

Bruner and Vygotsky saw children as social learners

believed that children learn through 'doing', and by thinking about what they have been doing and then talking, writing and drawing about it. Bruner views the ordinary everyday interactions between adults and children as important tools that children use to help them make sense of the world.

The social constructivist model is the most widely used in early years provision. It emphasises that children have distinct and different ways of thinking, behaving and feeling at different stages of development and that children's thinking is different from that of adults. This is most likely to be the model that you will come across when working with early years colleagues, and is most likely to have been the model used for the early education of the children you work with.

Learning through play

(KS 14)

Children's play is one of the most important aspects of their lives and how they play has a huge influence on their development and learning. Bruce (1996) says that play offers children the opportunity to do several things:

- Learn through first-hand experiences – children cannot learn by proxy. Second-hand experiences such as watching television or playing computer games are not likely to bring about quality learning experiences. However, if these build on the child's real experiences, this is more likely to deepen the learning. Listening to stories is not active play but has other benefits for the child.

- Take part in games with rules – this allows the child to learn the rules of the game and of their own culture. They learn how rules are negotiated, who has authority, and how to belong and be part of a community, e.g. the rule is to take turns or to count to 100 during hide-and-seek.
- Represent – children represent their experiences through language, dance and movement, drama, creative expression. They need to represent their own experiences, e.g. drawing from close observation of real things.

Not all plain sailing

(KS 16, 17, 20, 21, 26, 27)

For many of the children you work with, school and education in general may be a struggle. The whole process of learning and understanding may have been unable to engage and interest them. This can come about for many reasons – it could be to do with: the experiences of parents who may not value education if they have had poor experiences themselves; the ability of teachers to engage the child, as not all teachers have the same level of skill and ability; or the influences of peer groups – at various points it may not be 'cool' to show an interest in schoolwork.

It can also be as a result of genetic factors and their effect on ability, as the education system may be unable to meet the needs of particular children. In large classes in big schools, sometimes children who are just not able to learn in a particular way may find the system hard to reach. You will look more at children with particular learning needs in Unit 316, but here you will look at the more general ways in which you may need to support children to make sure that they are able to make the most of the learning opportunities they have.

In Unit 33 you learned about the different ways we learn as adults. Children and young people also have preferred learning styles and not all are able to take in information directly from a teacher standing in front of a classroom – often called 'talk and chalk'.

Not every child responds well to 'talk and chalk'

My story

'Hi, I'm Jenny and I'm 7. I hate school. I don't like Mrs Roberts. She shouts and she's got a hairy chin and she smells funny. If I don't do my reading right she makes me stand at the back and I can't go out. I can't do reading. My Mum says school is no good, she hated it too. I like drawing pictures. I drew Mrs Roberts with a big broomstick and a witch's hat – she made me stand at the back.

Hi again – I'm 12 now. I still hate school, except for seeing my mates, that's good. We have a good time and hang out. There's some real swots and nerdy people who do lots of work. Sometimes we beat them up just to teach them a lesson for being so nerdy – 'teach them a lesson'… hey, that's quite funny! I mean school really is so stupid. What use is all this stuff ever going to be? Why do I need to know any of it? I can't remember it anyway. It's all stupid.

Hi again – I'm 16 now and I've started this health and social care course, and it is dead interesting. We had to find out about what health and medical places were in our town. We had to go and ask people questions about how often they went to the doctor's, or the dentist or the optician, or the chiropodist and if they were OK to get there or if it was really difficult. We had to write out a questionnaire and then go and ask people, then write up the results. Did you know that there is only one optician in our town that has disabled parking anywhere near? And lots of people really like the new health centre because you can get treatment for small things there instead of having to wait ages for a hospital appointment. They've been able to do that because of the new way that money is going into the health centres, not that people were interested in that bit, but I think it's very interesting and very important. Our tutor, Sue, is great. She's dead helpful and gives us lots of ideas about where to find stuff out – I wish all my teachers had been like her: I would have learned a lot more. I remember this one when I was in primary school, her name was Mrs Roberts and she was horrible…'

There is a Chinese proverb that applies to learning:

'Tell me and I may forget.

Show me and I may remember.

Involve me and I will understand'.

This is about the importance of active learning: all learners will remember something they have discovered far better than something they have been taught.

In the My story box above, you can see how Jenny blossomed when given the opportunity to take a vocational course where active learning – learning by doing – is the main approach. There are many young people who respond well to this way of learning. Can you see the links back to Piaget and being an active participant in organising your own learning?

Additional support

It may not be just the approach to learning that means that a child or young person is struggling: he or she simply may not have the ability to take in and process the learning in the timeframe of a school lesson. Sometimes some extra one-to-one help can be useful. If a child has been assessed as needing additional support, the school or children's services can provide some additional one-to-one help in the classroom. In a primary school, this may be a learning assistant who will be able to sit with the child and explain the work; in a secondary school, it may be a learning mentor who will be able to spend time with the child or young person looking at any barriers and how they can be overcome.

Regardless of the support which is finally decided on, you will need to work closely with the child or young person's teacher, as they will have the professional expertise to identify the most appropriate response and should be able to contribute constructive ideas.

You need to agree what your role will be to back up the support provided through the school. You may need to support parents to work with the child or young person; if an adult has little confidence in their own ability, it can be a very big step to agree to listen to their child reading or to agree to help out with homework. Without support and encouragement, many parents will simply be unable to maintain the effort necessary to do it.

If it is not possible for parents or family to support, you may need to support the child or young person directly by carrying out activities agreed with the school. For example, if a young child needs support with numeracy, you may agree that you will spend a certain amount of time playing games which require number skills; or if you have a young person who is struggling with English, you may agree to read a magazine each and then share content, or read the same newspaper and comment on current stories. There are so many ways in which you can work with the child or young person to support the work of education professionals in making sure that they can take full advantage of every opportunity that arises.

Learning styles

(KS 14, 17)

Most of us fall broadly into one of three types of learner:

- Auditory – hearing the learning
- Visual – seeing the learning
- Kinaesthetic-tactile – touching and participating.

The main characteristics of each are:

Auditory learners:
- enjoy oral discussion
- remember by talking out loud
- need to have things explained orally
- have trouble with written instructions
- talk to themselves while learning something new
- repeat a telephone number in order to remember it.

Visual learners:
- remember visual details
- prefer to see what they are learning
- like to have paper and pens handy
- doodle while listening
- have trouble following lectures
- like to write down instructions or telephone numbers.

Kinaesthetic-tactile learners:
- prefer activities
- want to actually do whatever is being talked about or learned
- like to move around while listening or talking
- often 'talk' with their hands
- like to touch things in order to learn about them
- remember things by recalling who did what rather than who said what.

Of course, children can learn in other ways than their preferred style, but they are likely to learn best in one of these ways. Some children are highly attuned to one particular learning style; others have a more moderate preference, but can learn in all ways.

Beware of the biggest 'elephant trap' – you attempt to support children and young people to learn using *your* preferred learning style, not theirs!

Knowing and understanding how different children and young people learn makes a huge difference to the ways you support them. For example, you may be an auditory learner, setting out to work with Sam, who is a visual learner, on his project which is about Greek history. After ten minutes talking to Sam and carefully explaining in detail how Greek temples were constructed, he still looks blank and bored. However, go online and find pictures of Greek temples, or draw a few diagrams, and you have his interest and attention.

Having learned (think about Lewin/Kolb) from your experience with Sam, you sit down with Neela to help with her citizenship homework about local government. You draw diagrams of how power is delegated from central to local government, go online and find articles about local voting and how your local council works. Neela wanders off with vague excuses and you find her on MSN. Neela is a kinaesthetic-tactile (k-t) leaner, so off you go with her to the town hall and sit in the gallery for the local council meeting. She is fascinated by the debates and arguments and wants to know all about how people get to be on the council and starts to make a list of all the different departments and what they do.

Getting children and young people to focus on learning is not always easy – learning in their preferred style goes a long way to making it better.

You looked at learning styles in Unit HSC 33 in relation to your own development. These styles apply just as much to children and young people. The theories of Honey and Mumford about the different styles of learning and the cycle of learning from experience can be helpful in working out the preferred learning style of a particular child or young person and, therefore, being able to design the best ways to support their learning.

Some young people learn best in a group

Ways to support and encourage

(KS 2, 4, 17, 18, 20)

Your role is to use your communication skills to help children and young people feel that they can share worries, issues and concerns with you, and that they can trust you to find ways to help and support them. You will also need to make sure that you involve parents or carers in any plans to help children and young people make the most of education. If children or young people live at home, then the rest of the family must be involved and committed to any plans.

This is not always easy because many parents do not see education as being important: it is hard for them to see the value of it if they have never been part of a world where people need qualifications to get jobs and to feel fulfilled. They may not have had good educational experiences themselves and cannot encourage their own children because they have no positive concept of education. Spending time and encouraging them to talk about their own views about education can be useful; sharing information about the potential opportunities for their child can help them to take a more positive attitude or, ideally, you may try to involve them in their own child's learning. Involvement can take several forms, from simply helping with homework or listening to a child read to direct involvement through helping at school or being part of a family learning activity.

For example, imagine that a young person cannot complete homework because there is no quiet space

at home. First, you may want to involve the family in discussions and help the young person to explain the problem, then see if there is any way that the family can make some space available – even if it just for a specific period. If this is not possible, or the family are not able to view this as a priority, then consider some options:

- an after school club or homework group
- going to a relative or friend's house where there is quiet
- using the local library on the way home from school.

What matters is that the young person sees that you are responding and knows that their concerns are being taken seriously. It is often not easy for children to say that they want to do something positive about education, and it may seem easier for them to just abandon the idea if they find that they have no support and it all looks just too difficult.

Out of school activities

(KS 2, 17, 23)

Education is about much more than just what happens in school. If you think back to the theories about how children learn, you will remember that all of the theories recognise that children take in and process information from the whole world around them, not just from formal education. Just as very young children learn through play, so older children learn through activity.

Learning doesn't stop when children grow older, or even when they become adults. Many of the activities which children and young people are involved in will involve learning, even though they may not realise it, and the old saying of 'you learn something new every day' is absolutely true.

Most schools will organise some out of school activities, which can include sports, chess, drama, photography, music, debating and quizzes. The list is huge, and although they may not directly relate to the curriculum, the skills, knowledge and self-esteem that children and young people gain from taking part can be very significant and have a direct impact on their formal education.

Wherever possible, you should encourage children and young people to take advantage of any out of school activities available. It may take some initial persuasion for a young person to see that it is not just for 'dorks' and 'nerds', and that a computer or a music group after school can be a place where they can try out new ideas and get lots of extra information, to help them learn new and interesting stuff. Similarly, those who already have an interest in performing arts could be encouraged to join the drama group and get involved in school productions. Getting a school concert onto a stage involves learning important new skills such as team work and problem solving, not to mention the boost to self-esteem from taking part.

Family learning

(KS 17, 18)

Many schools are involved in family learning. This is inter-generational learning when at least two generations of a family learn together. The effects of this can be very encouraging: parents who may have had poor experiences of education can come along with their children and work together to learn new skills. There are many different sorts of family learning projects such as:

- Art projects: parents and children work together to produce pieces of art using a whole range of techniques and materials. All the materials and the expertise are provided by the school.
- Language projects: parents and children work together to learn a new language, which could be English or another language.
- Science projects: families work together to understand science and produce experimental results, such as a working light bulb or a moving cotton reel.
- Sports projects: such as joint football or swimming or a whole range of sporting activities.

Family learning can have a range of positive outcomes. It can:

- improve relationships between parents and children because they learn more about each other when they spend time together, and when they work as a team to produce a result
- provide new learning, not just for the children but for the adults who may have missed out on learning opportunities as they grew up
- improve relationships between parents and school: if the school has not been able to engage parents as a result of past poor experience, then doing something positive in the school and with school staff may help to change some of the attitudes.

My story

Hi, I'm Liz. I'm on my own bringing up Jack. He's 8 and goes to the local primary school, They've just become one of those new things – some fancy name I can't remember – anyway they seem to be doing lots of things at all hours of the day and evening now. Jack comes home the other week and he's going on about this class after school: it's about science – he loves all that stuff – but you have to take a parent. He went on and on about it, I said I wouldn't go – I hated science, well I hated it all because I'm really stupid and just never got the hang of any of it. Eventually he went on that much that I said I'd go just to shut him up, but I said I couldn't join in because I wasn't clever enough but I'd watch.

When we got there they'd got all kinds of wires and batteries and little Christmas trees and stuff out on tables and you had to sit with your kids. The teacher talked a bit and explained about circuits. It must have been the really simple stuff because it all made sense even to me, and I'm thick! Then they said we had to make a light on the top of the Christmas tree light up – you'll never believe it, but me and Jack did it! I was so excited when ours lit up that I shouted and cheered and jumped up and down. Can't wait for next week now.

Test yourself

1. What are the main theories about how children learn?

2. What are the main differences between these theories?

3. Which model is the most influential in educating young children?

4. Identify at least two key professionals who would be involved with a child or young person at each of the four stages of education (early years, primary, secondary and further education).

5. How would you encourage a parent who does not think education is important?

HSC 39c Encourage and support children and young people to carry out educational activities

This part of the unit is about more than just making sure that children do their homework! (Although making sure that tasks are done is an important part of what you do.)

One of your most important roles is to make sense of it all for the child or young person, and to make sure that they have all of the tools they need to be able to learn effectively. This is not about resources; this is about information and understanding about what they have to do. Research has shown that people learn best when they:

- understand clearly what they are trying to learn and what is expected of them
- are given feedback about the quality of their work and what they can do to make it better
- are given advice on how to go about making improvements
- are fully involved in deciding what needs to be done next and who can give them help if they need it.

You need to be on hand to make sure that all these key components for learning success are available, or to support the parents in making sure that they are.

Learning outcomes

(KS 3, 17)

It is important for children and young people to know what it is they have to learn and how much they are expected to know. Think about the different levels and depth of learning. If all you were told was that you had to know about the structure of English grammar, you would have no idea if that meant know enough to be able to:

- *produce a page of text which is correctly structured and punctuated using sentences and paragraphs*

or

- *understand inflectional and derivational morphology, parsing, syntax, generative notation, semantics and other linguistic areas of knowledge*

or

- *know that English is a complex language with a grammatical structure which has many exceptions and anomalies.*

These examples are about very different levels of knowledge and understanding – don't worry if you don't understand the middle one! What enables us to know what we need to learn is having a **learning outcome**: in other words, what is going to be the end result of our learning. For our example, that would mean a learning outcome like this:

> *Know the rules that structure the written English language and the main word classifications.*

In order for people to be able to assess whether or not you have achieved the outcome, there need to be criteria that can be used to make that judgement. The criteria provide a way to say, 'If you can do these things, then you have achieved the outcome.' So, for the outcome above, you may have criteria such as:

> *You will be able to:*
>
> - *identify the eight word classes*
> - *correctly construct a piece of prose of at least 500 words.*

Being clear

Children and young people need to be clear about what and how much they need to do, and what is expected of them. If there is information that is not clear, you can offer help and support by encouraging the child or young person to clarify exactly what is required. Learning outcomes are available for all examinations, so you can obtain the information about GCSE subjects. If the child or young person is not yet at the stage of public examinations, you can look at the National Curriculum, which will give you information about what children are expected to know about and how much they are expected to know.

Active knowledge

For each of the children and young people you work with, find out about the work they have to do for each subject area. See if you have information about outcomes. If not, try to find out exactly what outcomes are expected and how they will be assessed.

Feedback and guidance

This is identified as another vital part of learning. We all need to know how we are doing and if we are making progress. In the past, teachers' marking did not tell students very much: 'could do better' or 'a reasonable effort' is not a lot of help if you want to plan how to improve. It is important for children and young people to have some feedback that tells them:

- Are they doing it right?
- Can it be improved – if so, how?
- Is it nearly right – what else needs to be done?
- Are there things wrong – if so, what?

The level of this feedback will depend on their age and ability. For young children a simple 'That's very good – I like the way you've done the sky' is fine as a comment on a painting. However, such a comment is not much use to a student preparing a portfolio for GCSE Art; much more detailed, specific feedback would be needed in that case, so that the young

Encouragement and recognition are vital parts of feedback

person could make any changes to improve and develop their work.

Encouragement and recognition are also vital parts of feedback – praise is so important. You need to make sure that you pick up on achievements such as when someone has had a good result in school, or has been praised for good work or making progress or effort. Try to make sure that the praise and recognition are reinforced at home and that all the people who are important to the child or young person are able to celebrate the achievement.

Being involved

(KS 2, 4, 14, 15, 17, 20)

Children and young people should be active in their own learning (remember Piaget!). They need to be a part of planning what they do and planning how they are going to reach the learning outcomes they have to achieve. All learners are much more likely to learn well if they feel that they are part of the process, rather than just having learning 'done' to them. You can support children and young people by keeping them involved in all plans and discussions about their education. Earlier in this unit, you looked at how to draw up various action plans and development plans. These need to be constantly under review to make sure that they are still meeting the child or young person's needs and that they are still fit for purpose.

Reviewing plans

Like any review, you need to make sure that all the key people are involved and that educational, career and life plans are regularly reviewed and kept up to date. You have already looked at the ways in which children and young people's educational goals change over time, so the regular updating of any plans is essential. There may have been a change in career direction; or a different qualification may be on the horizon; or a child's circumstances may have changed and they may be living in a different setting. Each of these factors can have an influence on whether or not the tasks that have been planned are still the right ones and if the goals and targets still apply.

Working with school or college

If there are changes to be made to the plans for a child or young person's education, you need to work closely with the educational establishment involved. There may be matters that need their agreement, such as the changing of timetables or exam entries, or others which need their professional expertise, such as learning problems in one subject area. Regardless of the needs, the co-operation and input of educational establishments are vital.

When it all goes wrong

Sometimes, despite all the efforts and all the planning, nothing seems to work. The most frustrating part is when the child or young person is simply not able to engage with the whole plan and is not able to deliver their part. This is always difficult to handle, because the last thing you want to do is to make the child or young person feel that everything is their fault and that they have failed. Many of the children you work with will have a history of failing and will have an expectation that they will do so again.

If you have set out goals and targets, you need to make sure that targets are small and achievable – there is nothing like a 'quick win' and an early achievement to motivate children to carry on. If even this strategy does not prove successful, you may need to work with the child or young person by getting them to look at what it is that is preventing them from achieving the targets. They may be behaving in ways that make it difficult: if they spend every evening hanging out by the shops or talking on MSN, they will not have time to do the extra work which may be in the plan; if they are behaving aggressively, getting involved in fights and spending considerable time excluded from school, they are not going to be able to keep up with the learning they agreed to.

Try using techniques like exposure to role models, so that children and young people gain an understanding that they can make a difference to their own life chances by using educational opportunities.

You may want to consider using some of the approaches outlined in the unit on challenging behaviour (Unit HSC 326), particularly if behavioural issues are preventing a child or young person from making the most of their educational opportunities.

Learning how to learn

(KS 2, 16, 17, 21, 25)

Children and young people who have missed out on many of the positive early learning experiences or those who have missed a great deal of school time may need support in understanding how best to study. The development plans earlier in this unit (pages 212 and 213) can be adapted to be used in many different ways and can be a useful aid in helping to plan learning.

Study skills are particularly important for young people approaching exams. You can help them by encouraging them to make use of the school homework timetable to plan how long they need to spend studying each day, making sure that there is plenty of time for other activities and socialising; otherwise the plan will not be realistic and it won't be used.

Another very important skill is learning how to access the information needed for completing assignments and projects. If young people have missed out on periods of school, they may not know the best ways to find information or what to do with it once they have collected it.

Encourage young people to plan any assignments or projects, so they know what they are going to do and what information they need to get. (You can see an example of a plan at the bottom of the page).

In the unit about your own practice (Unit HSC 33), you have learned about ways to learn and how to understand the information you read; this is also applicable to young people carrying out assignments. Make sure that they understand how to tell when information is from a reliable source and the potential risks of getting information from the internet.

Your support and encouragement can make a major difference as to whether or not a child or young person is able to make the best possible use of the opportunities they have. Sometimes your support and encouragement of a whole family can change a vicious circle of failure to an engagement with education and learning – what an achievement when that happens!

What do I need?	By when?	Where from?
Info on start of Welfare State	Friday 22nd	Course text book, library and Gran
Info on NHS changes	Friday 29th	Internet – NHS site and gov.uk
Case study from a patient	Wednesday 3rd	Aunty Sue about her hysterectomy

Planning work can really help young people

	12.00	13.00	14.00	15.00	16.00	17.00	18.00	19.00	20.00	21.00	22.00
Monday								History		History	Maths
								History	History	Maths	
Tuesday							Geography	Geography			English
							Geography	Geography			English
Wednesday								Science	Science	Science	
								Science	Science	Science	
Thursday									ICT	Spanish	
								ICT	ICT	Spanish	Maths
Friday							Maths		DT	DT	
							English		DT	DT	
Saturday	English	English	English			Music			Maths	Maths	
	English	English	English			Music		Maths	Maths		
Sunday			ICT	ICT		Maths	Maths		English	English	English
			ICT		Maths	Maths			English	English	

✔

	12.00	13.00	14.00	15.00	16.00	17.00	18.00	19.00	20.00	21.00	22.00
Monday								History			
								English			
Tuesday							Geography				
							Science				
Wednesday											
Thursday									Maths		
									ICT		
Friday							DT				
Saturday											
Sunday					Music						

Look at the two timetables. Are they both suitable?
Remember, the plan should be realistic or the goals
won't be achieved.

Keys to good practice

✓ Work alongside families and make sure children are involved.

✓ Work closely with other professional colleagues.

✓ Help children and young people to set clear goals and targets.

✓ Make sure you know what children and young people have to learn and achieve and check that they know.

✓ Plan the learning process and monitor progress.

✓ Give praise, recognition and encouragement.

✓ Look out for any opportunities that can contribute to educational achievement.

Test yourself

1 What are the important aspects of effective learning?

2 Why are learning outcomes important?

3 How would you approach behaviour that was preventing a young person from learning?

4 Why is feedback important?

5 What is the key to making the best use of education?

HSC 39 UNIT TEST

1 How good do outcomes tend to be for looked after children from the current education system? Why do you think this is? Which Government Green Paper discusses plans to improve the educational experience for these children?

2 Give four examples of how schools can personalise learning for a student. What are the benefits of personalised learning?

3 What are the main three types of learner? What are their main characteristics?

4 What are the benefits of out of school activities?

5 What are the benefits of family learning?

6 What skills do young people need to improve their chances of success? What help could you offer to help them develop these skills?

Don't forget to refer to the evidence opportunities grid (see pages 357–375) for more ideas for suitable evidence for your NVQ.

Work with children and young people to prepare them for adulthood, citizenship and independence

You could take the view that everything you do is about preparing children and young people to become happy and resilient adults able to make a positive contribution to society. You would be right – but this unit looks particularly at work that aims at preparation for adult life.

Citizenship and independence are not exclusive to being an adult – children and young people are citizens too; they can make significant contributions to society and should be able to take advantage of the benefits of citizenship as soon as they are able. As young people grow and develop, there are always tensions and balances between independence and protection and so, although legally adulthood may arrive with an 18th birthday, many of the rights and responsibilities that go along with living in society can be taken up much earlier.

Children and young people who are looked after by a local authority, whether at home or in foster or residential care, have a particular need to be ready to take their place in society. Many have had traumatic and difficult pasts and the present, supported environment is the opportunity to prepare for a fulfilled and happy future.

In this unit you will find 'Active knowledge' features containing activities that will contribute to assessment for your NVQ. Remember that these features only offer the opportunity for partial assessment; you can also refer to the evidence opportunities grid (see pages 357–375) for more ideas to provide suitable evidence for your NVQ.

What you need to learn

- Becoming an adult
- Learning to become an independent adult
- Leaving care
- Your role
- Identifying skills and behaviour
- Being an effective citizen
- Taking responsibility
- Behaviour
- Transitions
- Preparation

HSC 310a Support children and young people to access support, advice and information about adulthood, citizenship and independence

Becoming an adult

(KS 1)

Becoming an adult is not a clear-cut process. There are no specific physical or developmental changes that can identify the point at which anyone passes from being a child to being an adult. The law, however is clear: in the UK a young person becomes an adult at the age of 18 years. At this age people are able to vote, take financial responsibility, drink alcohol on licensed premises and provide legally binding signatures to documents. However, other rights, responsibilities and powers are conferred at different ages. The following table gives some examples:

Active knowledge

Find out the ages at which children and young people can assume responsibility for: driving a car, driving a heavy goods vehicle, driving a public service vehicle, owning a shotgun, firing a shotgun, being left (unpaid) in charge of young children, doing paid work caring for children, being an astronaut, being a commercial pilot, standing for election as an MP, becoming an MP.

Age	A young person can:
At 13	• have a part-time job
At 14	• enter a pub, but not buy or drink alcohol there • a boy can be convicted of rape, assault with the intent to commit rape and unlawful sex with a girl if she is under 16
At 16	• have a full-time job after leaving school. • live independently, subject to certain conditions being met • get married with parents' or guardians' consent • buy cigarettes and tobacco • ride a moped of up to 50ccs • pilot a glider • a girl can legally have sex with a boy – it is illegal for a boy or man to have sex with a girl under 16, even if she has agreed • a male may consent to a homosexual act if he and his partner are both over 16 • have an abortion without parental consent • a boy can join the armed forces with his parents' or carers' consent • apply for a passport • have beer or cider whilst eating a meal in a restaurant or an eating area of a pub, but not in the bar

Age	A young person can:
At 17	• hold a licence to drive most vehicles • pilot a plane • emigrate • no longer be the subject of a care order
At 18	• be seen as an adult in the eyes of the law • vote in general and local elections • get married • open a bank account in his or her name without a parent's or carer's signature • buy and drink alcohol in a bar • see birth certificate (applies to adopted children) • change his or her name • be called to serve on a jury • sue or be sued • make a will • place a bet • have a tattoo

Learning to be an independent adult

(KS 13, 17, 20, 21, 25, 26, 28)

The physical and developmental changes take place gradually during puberty and adolescence, so it is difficult to identify a specific point at which someone becomes an adult. It may be easier to think of it in terms of growing independence and assuming greater responsibilities. On reaching adulthood, a young person may gradually become more independent and take on responsibilities for:

- accommodation
- personal health care
- food provision
- managing own finances
- managing difficult relationships
- career and training.

These responsibilities are not something that all young people are able to take on without support and guidance. Many of the young people you work with will be extremely vulnerable and will need to have ongoing access to guidance and support.

Being an adult and being independent are not necessarily the same thing: some adults also struggle with independence and find it hard to survive without ongoing support. As children grow, we prepare them for adulthood. Children learn a lot about how to be adults by watching their parents, but many of the children who are looked after have parents who have not been able to model adult behaviour because of their own poor experiences. Children and young people need to be able to understand the differences between adult and child behaviour, to find out what is expected of them as they mature and to be able to work out how to deal with new responsibilities.

Reflect

Can you think back to the first time you felt like an adult? Was it your first pay cheque? Your first home of your own? Becoming a parent? Losing a parent? For everyone, there is a different time or event that makes you feel as if you have grown up. Try to think about how you knew what was expected of you as an adult. If you can understand when you felt that way, and what it was that happened to make you feel that way, it will be easier for you to understand what you need to do to support the young people you work with.

Growing up means gradually becoming independent and taking on responsibilities

Leaving care

(KS 1, 3, 5, 7, 8, 9, 13, 14, 16, 18, 22)

Many of the children and young people you work with will be currently looked after by a local authority. If you are to work alongside a young person and any family or other professionals, you must be clear about the rights young people have on leaving care and how your role will fit with the work of others in ensuring a smooth transition from care to independence.

You need to understand exactly what young people can expect from you and from the care system in general as they move towards independence. This is crucial if you are going to be able to make sure that they get the information and support they need when they move away from the care you have been providing and into a more independent way of life.

Historically, outcomes have not been good for children growing up in the care system. Research has shown that outcomes in education, health, careers and personal relationships are not good in comparison to children and young people who have not been in care (see Broad B, 1998, *Young People Leaving Care: Life After the Children Act 1989*, Jessica Kingsley, DfEE/DoH Department of Health, 2001, *Children Looked After by Local Authorities Year Ending 31 March 2001*, England, Department of Health. Clayden J and Stein M, 1996, 'Self care skills and becoming adult', in Jackson S and Kilroe S (eds.), *Looking After Children: Good Parenting, Good Outcomes*, HMSO).

The sort of information you will need about the system and how it works will depend on your job role. If you are working with a young person who is living with their family, you may not have such a formal role as if you were responsible for a young person looked after by the local authority. If you work with disabled young people, you will need to be aware of an even wider range of important information about living independently and to make sure that the young people you work with both access the system and understand the implications of it for their own circumstances.

The Green Paper *Care Matters* which covers England, contains a proposal that young people should be able to veto being made to leave care before the age of 18 years and should be able to continue to live with foster carers until they are 21. The consultation on the Green Paper received widespread support for this proposal.

Legal basis

In England and Wales, the support available for young people leaving care is laid down in the Children (Leaving Care) Act 2000.

The Leaving Care Act has two main aims:

- to ensure that young people do not leave care until they are ready
- to ensure that they receive effective support once they have left.

Active knowledge

HSC 310a pc 1 (part)

Find out the way your organisation provides information for young people on the verge of becoming adults. How do you find out about what information young people need? How is the information maintained? Is there a clear policy about what information is given to whom or can anyone have anything? How does your organisation ensure that the information is current and up to date?

Ethical issue

Imagine that the proposal to allow young people to veto leaving care until they feel ready and the ability to remain until they are 21 has become law. You are in charge of a children's home run by a voluntary organisation. In the last three months you have had to turn away numerous requests for placements for young people under 15 years because you have four young people who wish to remain: two are 17, one 18 and one 20. They have all been with you since they were in their early teens. You know that social workers have been desperate to place some of the young people you have turned down. Two have been placed on the Child Protection Register, but have had to be left at home even though this represents a risk because there are no available places; one other has had to be placed over 300 miles away from her family; and one has ended up in a young offenders institution. You understand that there is a similar situation with foster care placements. What are the issues?

There are some minor differences in the provisions in Scotland and Northern Ireland under the 2004 Regulations and Guidance for young people ceasing to be looked after and the Children (Leaving Care) (NI) Act 2002 respectively. Broadly all the legislation requires local authorities to put a plan in place for each young person, called a Pathway Plan, and to provide each young person with someone to support and guide them through the transition from care.

Who is covered by the Act/s?

The Local Authority has a duty towards *eligible* and *relevant* and *former relevant* children:

Eligible:

Young people still in care aged 16 and 17 who have been looked after for (a total of) at least 13 weeks from the age of 14.

Relevant:

Young people aged 16 or 17 who have already left care, and who were looked after for (a total of) at least 13 weeks from the age of 14 *and* have been looked after at some time while 16 or 17.

Former relevant:

Young people aged 18–21 who have been **eligible** and/or **relevant** children in care - young people who are looked after by a local authority, either through a compulsory care order or remanded or accommodated by voluntary agreement, including accommodation under section 20 of the Children Act.

Essentially, this means that the vast majority of the children and young people being looked after by a local authority will be eligible or relevant under the Act.

What duties are required under the Act?

Aged 16–18:

- Duty to ensure Pathway Plan is in place by 16th birthday
- Duty to make assessment and meet needs
- Duty to provide financial support
- Duty to provide a Personal Adviser (Pathway Co-ordinator in Scotland)
- Duty to ensure accommodation.

Aged 18–21

- Duty to maintain contact and to provide support through a Personal Adviser (Pathway Co-ordinator in Scotland)
- Duty to assist with costs of education, employment and training.

Aged 21 and over:

- Duty to 18- to 21-year-olds continues if still in education or training
- Duty to ensure vacation accommodation for higher education.

How does it happen?

Firstly, an assessment of the outcomes a young person wishes to achieve must be undertaken in close partnership with the young person him- or herself and any family or friends he or she wishes to be involved. It is important that all assessments and plans must be person-centred: in other words, must focus on the strengths and abilities of the young person and plan to achieve outcomes.

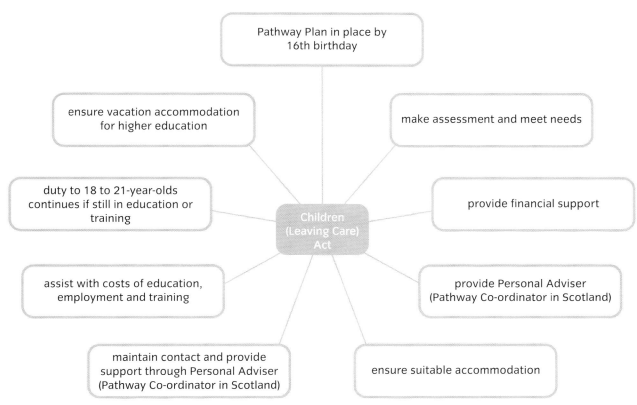

Duties under The Children (Leaving Care) Act

Pathway Plan

The result of the assessment is a Pathway Plan. This must be in place by the young person's 16th birthday, so work on it will need to start well beforehand.

The plan looks at the support and assistance requirements in order to achieve the outcomes identified in the assessment, and identifies timescales and how the outcomes will be achieved until the age of 21 (or longer when the young person is in education or training).

The Pathway Plan needs to include:

- accommodation
- details of how the young person will be supported to develop the necessary practical life skills to live independently
- detailed plan for education and training
- how the authority is to assist and equip the young person to find and sustain employment
- financial support

- specific support needs to enable the young person to develop and maintain social and family relationships
- health needs, including mental health needs and how they will be met
- contingency plans for support if independent living breaks down

Both the assessment and pathway plan must be recorded and be reviewed every six months or earlier if the young person or the Personal Adviser requests it.

Person-centred

Pathway planning is not about professionals or local authorities, it is done so that young people can achieve what they want to achieve, work out their goals, aspirations and expectations. It is also about giving them the confidence and resilience to take risks, get it wrong and be successful in achieving their hopes and dreams. A well-developed plan should enable them to identify the support they will need to reach their personal goals. The Act requires that young people are actively involved and their ownership of the Pathway Plan is paramount.

The principles of person-centred planning (*Valuing People: Towards Person Centred Approaches. Planning with People – Guidance for Implementation Groups*) should be part of the process.

- The young person is at the centre.
- Family members and friends are full partners.
- Person-centred planning reflects the young person's capacities, what is important to them (now and for their future) and specifies the support needed to enable the individual to make a valued contribution to the community.
- Person-centred planning builds a shared commitment to action that will uphold the young person's rights
- Person-centred planning leads to continual listening, learning and action, and helps the young person to get what they want out of life.

Personal Adviser

Each young person covered by the act will have a Personal Adviser or Pathway Co-ordinator in Scotland.

The Personal Adviser/Pathway Co-ordinator:

- does not have to be a social worker.
- does not hold a budget.

Personal Advisers play a key role in creating Pathway Plans

The role is to:

- provide advice and support
- draw up the Pathway Plan and ensure it addresses any changes
- keep in touch with the young person
- co-ordinate services and link with other agencies.

The young person's wishes as to who will be his/her Personal Adviser should be respected as far as possible and issues such as ethnic origin, gender and race should be borne in mind. There are no specific qualifications required for the role, but people need to be highly skilled in engaging with young people.

Personal Advisers can come from a range of professional backgrounds and from the statutory or voluntary sector. It may also be that the young person will express a preference for a particular individual,

My story

Hi, I'm Kevin and I'm 17. I've been in care since I was about 12. I don't think my Mum could cope with me as well as all her own problems. She was always in and out of hospital and I have been too, once or twice. I've lived in a few places. Foster homes never seemed to work out: it was probably my fault, it usually is. None of the foster places could cope with the stuff I did to myself. I don't do it so much now, but it still helps sometimes when people get to me or when I get really worried about something. I have had this CPN – Martin – from CAMHS for years. He's great and he's helped me through a lot of really bad scenes. I live in a small children's home. It's part of a special project for kids like me with mental health problems: they don't freak out if you do stuff or have a bad day, the staff are great and they really understand what's happening in your head. I am worried about what's going to happen. We did this Pathway Plan and Martin organises it all. I want to make art. I have been doing a lot of work with a local artist – there's some sort of a scheme where you can work along with them. He's been really helpful and says my work is coming on really well. I want to go to art college, so Martin has put it all into the plan. I've got an interview next week, and I'm working hard on keeping it all together. I was getting in a state thinking about all the really scary things like going somewhere new, and not knowing what I had to do, but Martin says just to think about getting the place, then think about everything else. He says that if I get a place, the council will help with money and a place to stay in the holidays and all kinds of stuff, for quite a few years – but I'm not thinking about that just yet. If I get famous and have an exhibition, the staff at the home say they'll organise a trip to come and see it!

in much the same way as can happen with a Lead Professional (see Unit 33). In fact, for some young people, it may be that the Lead Professional is the right person to become the Personal Adviser or vice versa.

Personal Advisers working with disabled young people will need particular skills and experience. In some local authorities, staff skilled in working with young disabled people may work as part of the leaving care service. In others, Personal Advisers may be located in specialist transition teams, or even in adult teams. Arrangements need to be as flexible as possible so as to be responsive to the needs and wishes of individual young people.

Connexions

A Personal Adviser for a young person leaving care is not the same as a Personal Adviser from Connexions, although there is likely to be a Connexions Adviser involved as part of the team developing the Pathway Plan for the young person.

Complaints

In situations where a young person is not happy with the way the Pathway Plan is being delivered or feels that there are unmet needs, then the Act introduces an informal resolution stage for all complaints. A fortnight is allowed for the young person and the local authority to reach a satisfactory conclusion before starting the formal complaints procedure under section 26 of the Children Act 1989.

What has to be in the Pathway Plan?

Accommodation for care leavers

The Children (Leaving Care) Act requires that 16/17-year-old young people are provided with suitable accommodation by the local authority. This is most likely to be in a supported setting, or could be with a family member or friend. However, the local authority must be sure that the accommodation is appropriate and, in the unlikely event that accommodation is provided by a private landlord, that the landlord is suitable. Many young people move on from care into bedsits or small flats in

supported accommodation provided by housing associations. Guidance suggests that it is not appropriate for 16/17-year-olds to be expected to undertake a tenancy on their own without support.

Most 16- and 17-year-olds, especially those who have been in care, will continue to need an element of support as they gradually develop the skills they need to live independently. Many housing associations have young people's housing schemes. These provide bedsits or flats, but with a support worker on the premises or close by so that the young people have access to advice and assistance when they need it. This type of accommodation makes a good place to start; the accommodation is of a good standard with well maintained facilities and the opportunity to have adult intervention where necessary. Young people have the opportunity to make somewhere 'home' and to have their own space that can be decorated and furnished as they wish; this is an important part of establishing themselves on the road to being an adult.

Reflect

Think about the young people you work with and the type of accommodation they have moved on to. How appropriate was it? Did they get the sort of support they needed? If not, why not? How many ended up in accommodation that was not ideal? How hard have you worked to find the right accommodation? How often have you just been relieved to have found something, even if it wasn't completely right? Reflect on the processes your organisation has in place for finding the most suitable accommodation – how effective are they? What needs to improve?

Housing is a key part of the Pathway Plan and is one of the issues which should be addressed before a young person leaves care. Finding accommodation is only one part of meeting a young person's housing needs; furniture and essentials are also needed and young people will need to be supported to obtain these. Support will need to come from housing as well as children's services and you will need to work with the young person's Personal Adviser to liaise and co-ordinate.

It is important that furniture and all of the other necessary household items are not simply purchased by a central procurement unit and presented as a 'leaving care' package. Choosing furniture and planning a first home are important ways of ensuring that young people are able to put their individual stamp on the place they will live in.

The young person's circumstances will dictate the most appropriate type of accommodation. If the young person is a lone parent or is disabled or has any additional needs, the accommodation must reflect this. For example, a teenage lone parent with a young baby may choose to be with a specialist foster carer, who will be there to support her in developing parenting skills at the same time as she learns to live independently. Alternatively, specialist housing schemes, again usually with a housing association, will offer 'mother and baby' accommodation and support staff on hand to offer assistance when needed.

Disabled young people can often face a difficult task to find purpose-built accommodation especially designed to meet specific needs. There are some superb developments offering technologically advanced accommodation for disabled people, but it is not always easy to access this for young people of 16 or 17 years, and they are in very short supply. The rapid development of assistive technology has meant that there is potential for disabled young people to live with increasing independence, as technology is able to perform many practical and communication tasks.

There is no question of a local authority being able to offer just a 'roof': accommodation must meet needs and be part of the agreed plan. Bed and breakfast accommodation is not appropriate except as an emergency measure and even then it must only be used for a very short period of time.

There is no duty for social services to provide accommodation to a care leaver once he or she reaches 18, unless the young person is in full-time higher or residential further education. In this case, social services must provide accommodation during the college/university holidays or pay the young person an allowance sufficient to make it possible to find accommodation for the holidays if the term-time accommodation is not available.

This duty remains until the care leaver's 24th birthday.

Health

Young people leaving care must have a holistic health assessment of all aspects of their physical and emotional health and detailed health records must be kept. The importance of a holistic health assessment is that the whole of a young person's life must be considered, not just a quick physical examination – the assessment needs to assess overall well-being. Pathway Plans have to support the young person to maintain a healthy life style, understand how and when to use primary health care services and plan access to specialist health and therapeutic services if necessary. Accessible information on healthy living, sexual health, sexuality and mental health is important for all young people leaving care, and this will also form part of the Pathway Plan. The plan is vital for disabled young people to ensure that they can obtain access to mainstream health care services (GP, dentist, optician, etc.) as well as to any specialist service related to their impairment. Access to free or reduced-cost prescriptions should also be considered and the young person supported to complete any necessary forms.

Financial support

Most young people are encouraged to have their own bank accounts and to take responsibility, with support, so that they can develop financial management skills. The degree to which young people can manage their finances will obviously vary with each individual, so it is important that flexible arrangements are in place to meet the levels of support required for different young people. For some, a weekly or monthly allocation paid into their account from which they then meet their accommodation and other expenses may be appropriate. Others may need to have all significant outgoings taken care of on their behalf. The aim for all young people is to achieve the level of financial independence that is right for them. The extent of financial independence has to be agreed between the young person and their Personal Adviser and a package of support, effective until the young person is at least 21 years old, must be put in place.

It will be important to ensure that the young person has sufficient to cover basic requirements and to have money left over to enjoy themselves. How much direct responsibility individual young people want to take for key expenses such as rent will have to be discussed and agreed – what matters is getting the balance right between giving increasing independence and responsibility and assessing the risks of how likely an individual young person is to be able to cope with everything at once.

Key basics are:

- rent
- fuel bills (if not included)
- food (requirements are discussed later)
- transport fares
- clothes
- social life
- savings – short-term (holidays, presents, major new items)
- savings – long-term (pension, investment).

Claiming benefits

Most 16- or 17-year-old care leavers will not be able to claim benefits. This means that, under the Act, the responsible local authority must be the primary source of income.

Financial support provided includes the cost of:

- accommodation
- food and domestic bills
- pocket money
- transport costs for education and training
- clothing
- childcare.

The Personal Adviser/Pathway Co-ordinator is responsible for making sure that the young person receives the financial support they will need in order to establish an independent life.

Most 16- and 17-year-olds, especially those who have been in care, will continue to need an element of support as they gradually develop the skills they need to live independently

Weekly allowances will be calculated by each local authority according to the young person's individual needs. There are no set rates, but the allowances must be at least as much as the amount the young person would receive if they claimed benefits. Lone parents or those unable to work because of illness or disability can still claim Income Support or Job Seeker's Allowance but not Housing Benefit (this applies whether they are still in care or have left care).

Those who leave care at 18 are likely to be entitled to claim benefits and it is the role of the Personal Adviser/Pathway Co-ordinator to make sure that they receive their full entitlement.

Financial support for disabled young people

In addition to the financial support available to all young people leaving care, there are particular ways in which disabled young people can access financial support.

Direct payments and individual budgets

Pathway Plans should take account of the opportunity provided by the Community Care (Direct Payments) Act 1996 that gave disabled people more choice and control by enabling the purchase of services through direct payments. This has recently been extended to 16- and 17-year-olds and so the offer of direct payments should be made to young disabled people as part of the Pathway Planning process. Individual budgets are also currently being piloted and will be available for young disabled people leaving care.

There are some key difference between direct payments and individual budgets:

- With direct payments, the responsibility of recruiting and employing support service rests with the young person.
- Individual budgets involve an assessment and an agreement of a total available budget. The way this is spent is entirely in the control of the disabled person, but the responsibility for administering the process remains with the local authority.

Both of these schemes are important to young disabled people wanting to live independently, but support and training on how to use them effectively will be essential. This must be a part of the Pathway Plan. The use of direct payments and individual budgets are discussed in more detail in Unit 316.

The Independent Living Fund

The Independent Living Fund (ILF) is a useful source of funding for young disabled people who need higher levels of support in order to live independently. ILF can be paid whether or not a person is receiving income support and may be used if the young person is away at college but needs support during college/university holidays.

Keeping in touch

A local authority is required by the Act to keep in touch with care leavers. If it loses touch with a care leaver it must immediately take reasonable steps to re-establish contact and continue to do so until it succeeds.

The Personal Adviser is the person responsible for maintaining contact with a young person. The contact is important, in the same way as most people maintain contact with their parents even after they have become independent adults, so the local authority has to fulfil its role as a 'corporate parent' and keep in touch with young people in the period immediately after leaving care.

Education training and employment

The Act makes it clear that very close liaison is needed between the local authority and the young person's school. This will be supported by Connexions or a similar young person's service and the Personal Adviser will need to ensure that all of the relevant people are involved in making key decisions.

Local authorities also now have a duty to assist young people leaving care with the expenses associated with education and training. This duty runs until the young person has completed the programme of education and training agreed with the responsible local authority and set out in the Pathway Plan. This could include travel, books, special equipment and the accommodation discussed earlier.

In your role as a residential worker, you were key worker to a young man, Jason, for about five years. During that period, you developed a good relationship with him and you were able to support him in moving forward on many of his issues around behaviour and managing his anger. When Jason moved out of care, about 18 months ago, he was supported, through the Pathway Plan, to move to a bedsit and begin an apprenticeship in motor vehicle maintenance. You have been aware of a deteriorating relationship with his Personal Adviser for some time as you see the Adviser regularly at other meetings. You meet the Adviser who tells you that Jason has now lost touch and will not return calls, he is no longer living in the bedsit and has given up the apprenticeship. You are not very surprised as you have never felt that the Adviser appreciated Jason's potential and did not make much effort to understand him. Jason phones you out of the blue and asks you not to tell the local authority where he is as he does not want to have anything more to do with the Adviser. He is not convinced by you telling him about complaints, reviews and changing his Adviser. Jason is almost 18, and is vague about his living arrangements. You are concerned that he is in a squat or sleeping rough. He asks to meet you because he says you are the only person he trusts and he needs some help. He will not meet with you unless you promise that you will do this without telling anyone. What do you do?

Councils also have a duty to provide assistance to young people leaving care with the expenses associated with employment. This could include travel, clothing, tools and equipment and also contributions towards the cost of accommodation, which enables the young person to live near the place where he/she is employed or seeking employment.

Your role

(KS 16, 17)

As a key worker for a young person, you will need to work closely with the Personal Adviser and to be involved in the process of developing the Pathway Plan, provided that the young person concerned is happy for you to do so. You may also have specific roles agreed as part of implementing the plan. For example, you may be asked to contribute to providing the practical life skills needed or to liaise with the school or to work out a way for the young person to live with a family member. There are many potential ways to support young people during this important stage of preparation for leaving care.

Test yourself

1 Which Act of Parliament introduces the concept of Pathway Plans?

2 What are the areas covered in a Pathway Plan?

3 At what age does a Pathway Plan have to be in place?

4 What does a Personal Adviser do?

5 Once someone who has been in care reaches 21, there is no more help available. True or false?

HSC 310b Identify, with children and young people, the skills and abilities to become adults and effective citizens

If you were asked to list the skills you use as an adult and a citizen you may have to think for a moment about just what they are. You need to think what it is you do as an adult and the abilities it takes to do it well. Look at the table below for some examples.

Activity	Skills	In practical terms
Have a place to live	Planning and organising skills	• Search for a place • Find one you can afford • Pay the rent/mortgage • Arrange connections of services • Find furniture • Find appliances and equipment
Get on with others	Communication and social skills	• Engage others in conversation • Make new friends • Recognise signals about space and distance • Pick up on moods and tones of conversation • Recognise non-verbal communication; facial expressions, body language
Find and keep a job	Educational skills, reliability	• Achieve the qualifications needed for the job • Perform well at interview • Work conscientiously • Be punctual and reliable
Feed yourself	Planning, shopping, cooking	• Plan balanced menus • Check out best value when shopping for ingredients • Shop at right times – before you run out but so food not out of date and wasted. • Cook balanced, nutritious meals
Develop your potential	Study skills	• How to find information • How to understand research • How to complete assessments • Using different information sources
Manage your money	Basic numeracy and planning	• Know how much you have and how much you spend • Add up to make sure you spend less than you have • Plan to save some money • Work out how much you can afford to spend and how much to save

These are just a few of the life skills adults need, but it is not only skills that everyone needs in order to function in society; it is also important to behave in an acceptable way. Adults can be highly skilled, but if they behave badly it will be difficult to gain acceptance and participate effectively in many situations. Children and young people need preparation for these skills as they grow and develop.

There is no need for children to learn about adult responsibilities too early – many of the children you work with have already had more adult experiences than any child should have. However, it is important for children to be able to learn about adult behaviour by seeing it and by living alongside people who model the skills of adult life on a day-to-day basis. You may do this as a support worker, a residential worker or a foster carer, but you should not underestimate the importance of your behaviour: you can have a positive influence in giving children and young people a way to learn about what they need to do to function effectively as adults and citizens.

Identifying skills and behaviour

(KS 2, 4, 10, 16, 18, 24, 25, 28)

You have a vitally important role to play in preparing children and young people to think about, and commit to, their Pathway Plan. In preparation, young people need to think about where their strengths and abilities lie, and about parts of their lives where they will need support to strengthen or develop new abilities or look at and change behaviour. Skills and behaviours for functioning as an adult citizen in society fall broadly into four categories:

- personal and social
- life skills
- practical skills
- development and participation.

Personal and social
- communication
- listening
- considering others

- compromising
- negotiating
- being reliable
- being honest

Life skills
- numeracy
- literacy
- basic financial planning
- knowing rights
- knowing how to get advice and help
- understanding consequences of actions

Practical skills
- cooking
- shopping
- hygiene and cleaning
- basic health and safety
- basic household maintenance (changing light bulbs, etc.)
- dealing with emergencies

Development and participation
- study skills
- career planning
- knowing broadly how government works
- taking an interest in local community/ environment
- recognising the needs of others and offering help
- recognising responsibility to community/ environment

Active knowledge

Add at least two more skills in each category. Think about the young people you work with and plan how you could use this list of skills and behaviours with individuals and groups of young people preparing to leave care. You could think of ways it could be used as a skills matrix – to work out what individuals still need to work on, perhaps as the basis for discussions about what is most important or games using skills on cards, where people pick them up if they think they have the skill or give them to others if not. The possibilities are endless – think of at least two other ways you could make use of the basic list of necessary skills for life.

You can use groups or talk one to one

Not all of the items in the list will be relevant for all young people, and there are many other skills that are needed as young people mature, but this list can form the basis for doing some work with young people around identifying what areas they need to look at working on. For example, a young person may identify that she has good life skills and most practical skills are quite strong, but she knows that she needs to work on personal and communication skills.

One to one or in a group

You can do this work with individual young people by using the list as a starting point to talk around how they see their own skills and behaviours. It is not always easy to get young people to look at their own behaviour, but this degree of insight is an important part of maturity and adult behaviour.

This work can be done in a group, as long as you are experienced and confident in facilitating groups and you understand group dynamics. Groups will work best where young people are comfortable with each other, such as a school group or a residential group or a group that has been involved in a specific programme together. The key to making this a valuable exercise is to keep it positive – whether you are in a group or one to one, have a ground rule that no one can say anything negative about themselves or anyone else! That way everyone talks about the strong points and the areas that need work are identified by default.

It can be helpful to use a skills matrix or chart to help young people see where their strengths lie. As long as you are careful that it doesn't become a 'box ticking' exercise, it can provide a useful visual picture of what they know they can do and what they still have to learn. A simple matrix might look like the one at the bottom of the page.

When you have worked through the process of identifying skills and behaviours, the next task is to look at drawing up a plan, similar to the ones in Unit 39 on pages 212–213. This can help to identify what the young person needs to do in order to develop new skills and modify behaviours that will help in taking on the responsibilities of adulthood.

Skills for Jade	communication	listening	consideration	compromising	negotiating	being honest	being reliable	numeracy	literacy	financial planning	rights	advice and help	consequences	cooking	shopping	health/hygiene	emergencies	maintainance	study skills	career plans	government	community	others' needs	responsibility
Very strong									●	●		●									●	●		
Good – OK						●		●							●		●							
Not bad											●			●		●			●					
Could be worse	●	●											●					●		●				●
Needs work			●	●	●		●																●	

A skills chart like this can help young people identify their strengths

My story

Hi, I'm Jade and I'm 15. I've been in care for the past couple of years. I got expelled and excluded from school so many times I lost count, went to a PRU and they said they couldn't manage me! I've been here now for about 18 months. School is here so there's only a few of us and the teachers. They aren't stupid like the others, they don't disrespect you and so you don't disrespect them – stands to reason. Anyway, we sat down in our house with a couple of the staff and they started talking about when we leave care. I thought it was a bit scary really. I didn't want to think about it 'cos it feels like I've just settled here and now they're talking about throwing me out – so I went off on one. But Katya, my key worker, talked to me and explained about Pathway Plans and all that and it didn't sound so bad. We had such a laugh – she did this chart thing and we all had to say what we was good at and we could say what everyone else was good at too. It was good. I didn't know that other people thought I was good at stuff, but people said I was clever and that. The next week I talked with Katya about what was on it and about some of the stuff I'm not very good at and she's going to help me make some plans to do something about changing some of the things I'm not good at. You can see my chart – I think it tells you quite a bit about me!

Being an effective citizen

(KS 1, 15, 20, 24))

Citizenship is about taking a responsible part in the society you live in, Children can learn about responsibility to others in their own environment and community from quite early on. Most children relish the responsibility of being monitors and doing tasks from the start of primary school. What we encourage in young people and adults is the same in principle, just on a different scale.

At its simplest, being a citizen means taking part in choosing a government for your country, and your locality. This is about voting and exercising a right which people, if you are female, have died to give you. However, over two thirds of young people in Britain have little or no interest in voting (*Young People in Britain: Attitudes and experiences of 9–12-year-olds*, A Park et al, NCSR 2004).

Citizenship is more complex than putting a cross on a piece of paper every few years. It is about using the opportunities that society offers and making the most of chances to develop so that you can then make a contribution to society; in other words, 'taking something out then putting something back'.

For many of the children and young people you work with, the idea of making a positive contribution to society will be something new and not something they would ever have considered. Most will take the view that society has not given them a very good deal to date, so why should they be interested in making a contribution.

Making a contribution to society can take many forms

Only a very small percentage of young people undertake any voluntary work or have any 'civic' involvement. The National Council for Social Research found that only 16 per cent of young people had been involved in any voluntary or charitable activity. It is likely that the proportion among young people in the care system is significantly lower.

However, contributions to society are not only about volunteering and helping others directly. Not all contributions are so obvious, and you should encourage young people to think about the range of ways in which they can prepare to be effective citizens. The table opposite gives some examples:

Activity	Effect
Learning and training	Economic contribution through preparing for work
	Developing important skills which society needs
	Improving and adding to society's knowledge
Having a job	Economic contribution
	Direct skills contribution
Being polite and friendly	Contributes to society's social networks
Shopping	Economic contribution
Maintaining own home	Contribution to the fabric and infrastructure of society
Putting out the rubbish/recycling	Contribution to public health and to the environment

These are just some of the examples that you could use as a start for a discussion around ways that each individual can contribute effectively as a citizen. Many young people are interested in the environment and it may be a useful area to use as an example so that they can see how even small acts make a major contribution if enough people do them.

Young people will have learned about the basics of citizenship in school, so you should be able to draw on the knowledge they already have. However, that pre-supposes that a) they attended the lessons and b) they remember what they were taught.

Active knowledge

Add at least another four activities to the table, then plan how you will use these with the young people you work with. You could use it for discussions, for a quiz or for specific projects. Consider the young people and the most effective way of stimulating them to think around the issue of effective citizenship.

How society is governed

The United Kingdom is a parliamentary democracy, based on universal suffrage (one person one vote). It is also a constitutional monarchy in which ministers of the Crown govern in the name of the Sovereign, who is both Head of State and Head of the Government. The UK Parliament is the sovereign law-making body, but many powers and law making have been devolved to the Scottish Parliament and some to the Welsh and Northern Ireland Assemblies.

Government of the UK is based on a set of rules known as the British Constitution. The rules set out procedures such as how often elections must be held and specify what the government can and cannot do.

Unlike most other countries, such as the United States of America or India, which have a constitution document where everything is written down, the UK has an unwritten constitution. This means that the rights and responsibilities we have as individuals and as a society are formed from a number of different places. Much of the constitution is based on unwritten customs and rules called conventions. However, some laws are written down: these are the ones created and agreed by Parliament – known as **statute law.** Laws are also made by judges when they make rulings in court – these are called **common law.** Because the UK is a member of the European Community, there are also laws made in Europe that apply here – these are called **EC law.**

The country is run on a day-to-day basis by **the executive,** which comprises the Government (members of the Cabinet and other ministers responsible for policies), government departments and agencies (civil servants), local authorities, public corporations, independent regulatory bodies and certain other organisations subject to ministerial control. Judges make common law and interpret statute law.

In her role as monarch, the Queen is head of the executive and plays an important part in governing. She heads the judiciary and is both the commander-in-chief of all the armed forces of the Crown and supreme governor of the established Church of England. However, conventions limit the power of the monarchy.

Local authorities are made up of elected members (councillors) who are elected locally, are responsible for managing local services such as schools, waste disposal, roads, social services, cemeteries, parks and leisure facilities and can raise local taxes (Council Tax) to pay for them.

Other services such as health, fire, police and ambulance are run by relevant authorities appointed by the Government.

You are not expected to become a teacher and re-run the National Curriculum in citizenship, but you do need to check that young people have a basic understanding of the rights and responsibilities of being a citizen and how society works. Just in case you need to 'brush up', the basics are summarized in the box at the bottom of page 247.

Rights and responsibilities

There are a wide range of rights within the UK, covering all aspects of life from human rights, such as freedom of speech and freedom from torture (these are included in the Human Rights Act) to more specific rights such as the rights to education and healthcare, and protection from discrimination.

Rights also carry responsibilities such as loyalty to the country, which means not plotting against the state, abiding by the law as a responsible citizen and certain civic duties such as voting, jury service and giving evidence in court.

Citizens all have a responsibility for protecting the environment whether on a local, national, international or global level. Contributions to protecting the environment are important and will make a major difference if enough people take a share of the responsibility.

It is important that you get across the basic message of being an effective citizen: 'it's your world and you have a responsibility to it'.

Taking responsibility

(KS 5, 18, 19, 20, 26, 27)

Taking responsibility is difficult for many of the children and young people you work with. Many find it difficult enough to cope with the day-to-day demands of life without wanting to take on responsibility for anything else. It is also important that children and young people do not take responsibility for actions that are not theirs – for example, the actions of an abuser. It is not easy to manage the tensions between not allowing children and young people to take the blame for abusive and damaging parts of their lives and letting them slide into a 'victim' approach to life, where everything is someone else's fault.

You will be familiar with these common responses:

'It wasn't me', 'It's not my fault'

'They should have…'

'They never…'

The key is in getting young people to look positively at accepting responsibility and to recognise ways in which they can take actions which make a difference, without making them feel that they must take responsibility for everything.

Taking the blame

Being an effective citizen is about accepting responsibility, not taking blame. Do not underestimate how hard this is for young people who have been through difficult and traumatic situations. So many children and young people feel that everything is their fault; they struggle to work out what they did to deserve the abuse they suffered or how their behaviour caused the problems of the adults in the family. They spend their lives with low self-esteem and minimal confidence, often confused and angry.

Be careful then, that looking at being an effective citizen is kept practical, light and focused on the positive ways young people can contribute.

Reflect

How good are you at taking responsibility for your own actions? Do you always acknowledge when something is down to you? Or is your life full of issues which are the responsibility of other people? Are you sure that all of them are someone else's fault? How far do you accept responsibility for the society you live in? Or do you believe that 'they' should do something? You need to understand how your own behaviour is modelled to the children and young people you work with and thinking about your own attitudes to responsibility will make this easier to see.

Behaviour

(KS 2, 4, 5, 18, 19, 20, 21, 23)

Many of the young people you work with will behave in challenging ways, which may be a useful and valuable means of communication in a care setting but is not acceptable in society in general. Earlier, in the skills and behaviour matrix, you looked at some of the behaviours that underpin adulthood and independence. It is also important to try to work with young people to identify some of the behaviours that could mean that they will struggle to function in society.

It is sometimes hard to take the step back to think about what the issues are likely to be. It is easy to get used to the behaviours that are tolerated and part of day-to-day life when working with children and young people. You need to reflect and plan how you will encourage young people to identify and change those behaviours that are likely to make it difficult for them to make the transition to independent adulthood. You could work one to one or in a group, and try using **OK lists**.

OK lists

In making an OK list, you discuss behaviour that is acceptable and behaviour that is not. There are two lists: an OK list and a Not OK list. Some entries are obvious:

Not OK

- ✗ Hitting or kicking people who disagree with you
- ✗ Being verbally abusive to people who don't give you what you want
- ✗ Swearing at people
- ✗ Not turning up for work or training because you fancy a lie-in or because you want to go shopping with your mates
- ✗ Not paying your rent because you spent the money on a night out
- ✗ Wearing dirty clothes because you couldn't be bothered to go to the launderette
- ✗ Grunting at people while you continue to listen to music through earphones

OK

- ✓ Being friendly and sociable
- ✓ Being pleasant and polite to colleagues at work or training
- ✓ Being reliable and turning up on time
- ✓ Keeping your home reasonably clean and tidy
- ✓ Paying your bills

These sorts of lists can form the focus for a discussion and help young people to recognise some of the behaviours that could become barriers to them making the most of the opportunities that they will encounter.

You should also make the most of situations you encounter in everyday activities such as being out in town with a young person. For example, if you experience a rude shop assistant, take the opportunity to look at the effect the rudeness had and how it made the young person feel.

Interestingly, one of the actions that often makes young people very angry is unreliability in adults. For many this will stem from a childhood of uncertainty and lack of security, so the reliability of the adults around them becomes very important. Students at school and colleges get really fed up and outraged when teachers and lecturers are not available for whatever reason. Use these incidents as opportunities to talk about the importance of being reliable and how fed up people become if you are not.

If you work in a residential setting, use the debrief sessions following incidents to help young people identify the behaviours which are unacceptable and how things could have gone differently. If you support young people living with family, then use the feedback they give you on situations at home to draw out similar examples about how things could have been different with different behaviour.

Active knowledge

Add at least three items to the OK and Not OK lists. Find out how your organisation addresses unacceptable behaviour. Does the process allow for you to identify the potential impact on a young person's transition to independent living? If not, speak to your line manager about how this could be included.

Helping young people to work out what they need to do in order to make an effective plan for their future is an essential part of your work with this age group. The prospect of independence is both an exciting and a terrifying prospect for all young people, but it can be a huge challenge for the very vulnerable young people you work with, so good preparation gives the best chance of success.

Test yourself

1 Why is it important to identify skills young people will need as adults?

2 What are the potential issues if unacceptable behaviours are not addressed?

3 How is the UK governed?

4 What rights do UK citizens have?

5 What responsibilities do UK citizens have?

HSC 310c Prepare children and young people to move on and become independent

There are many reasons for the differences in outcomes for young people who have been in care and young people who have not. However, all of the research indicates that one of the major barriers is the transition into adult, independent living, which is not handled adequately – young people are not well prepared and do not have good access to ongoing support.

Reflect

How old were you when you stopped looking for support and guidance from your parents? Do you still do it? Most adults do. It is rare that at the age of 16 or even 18 a young person would leave home and have no further contact with his or her parents. However, that is what young people who grow up in care have to do. If you consider the amount of support you had, and are maybe still having from your parents, it may help you to realise how abandoned young people moving out from care must feel.

Comparisons

The facts are alarming:

- 28 per cent of young people still leave care aged only 16 years old. The average age for the rest of the population to leave home is 24 years old, but even after that most will remain in close contact with their parents.
- Children who leave care at 17 or 18 years old are 50 per cent more likely to be unemployed or not in training than those who stayed in care until 20 or 21 years old. Similar results apply around the dependence and abuse of alcohol and drugs.
- Only 58 per cent of care leavers are in education or training at 18–19 years old in comparison to 87 per cent of the general population.
- 60 per cent of young offenders and 27 per cent of the adult prison population have been in care.
- 33 per cent of rough sleepers have been in care.

There are new proposals that young people should be able to remain in care for longer, possibly up to 21 years old, and that more control about when they feel ready to move on should be in the hands of the young people themselves. Moving into an independent life is a transition and should be a gradual process, not a sudden leap in the dark.

In February 2006 the Children's Rights Director produced a report of children's views on leaving care. Young people stated clearly that they did not want to be made to move on from care until they were ready to do so, and that they should be allowed to leave gradually and to return if they need to. Some of the comments were:

'When social services put something in your plan they should follow it through.'

'The ideal way to leave care would be when they wanted to leave.'

'The amount given (i.e. leaving care grant) should be the same wherever you live.'

'Social services should provide you with what you need as your parents normally would. They take you away, they should look after you.'

And the most important quote of all from the report. A comment that should be on the notice board – preferably on the front door – of every establishment where people work with children and young people:

'If you cannot ensure that I will leave your care in better conditions and circumstances than I arrived, then don't bother.'

Transitions

(KS 7, 11, 22)

There are huge differences between priorities in adult and children's services. Disabled young people may well have a planned transition into adult service provision, but for other young people there may not be an available service.

For example:

- a young person who has been in care because of his or her parents' inability to care for him or her would not be offered support by adult services
- a young person who has been in care because of behaviour issues would not be offered a service

from adult services unless a clear mental health need was identified

- a young person who has been in care because of offending behaviour would not have support from adult services unless he or she re-offended, and then probation may be involved.

It is easy to see why so many young people feel that they have been pushed out into the world and that no one cares about what happens to them.

Preparation

(KS 18, 19, 20, 28)

Apart from the comments about leaving care too soon, young people also said that they needed to be prepared to carry out basic, everyday tasks. Concerns about health and safety may result in many young people never having the opportunity to learn to cook or to carry out basic household tasks, like changing a light bulb or a plug or painting a ceiling.

You may find that an important role for you is to ensure that young people who want to do so are able to carry out these basic tasks.

Cooking and healthy eating

Although some young people will have done some cooking in school, they may not have sufficient skills to feed themselves adequately, nor may they understand the importance of a balanced diet for maintaining health.

You will need to explain the principles behind a balanced diet:

- There are five main food groups. Eating a variety of foods from these five groups in the recommended proportions will provide a nutritionally balanced diet, i.e. one that contains all the nutrients we need to stay healthy.
- While water isn't a nutrient, our bodies need it for a number of reasons: for example, to prevent dehydration, to produce sweat which helps control body temperature, to get rid of waste material (in urine and faeces) and in the production of blood

and other body fluids. Everyone should aim to drink around two litres of water a day.

Using a balanced diet as a guide, young people can be shown how to cook simple, easy dishes that will not require a great deal of time or preparation, are not expensive and do not need too many utensils.

TV chefs have made healthy eating a popular pastime and people are much more aware of the importance of maintaining a healthy diet and ensuring that there is not too much fat, sugar or salt in the food they buy. The Food Standards Agency recommends 'traffic light labelling' for food products. This is not a legal

Food group	Proportion of daily diet	Examples of foods
Bread, other cereals & potatoes	We should aim for this food group to make up about 1/3 of what we eat every day.	Bread, chapattis, rice, pasta, breakfast cereals, maize, millet, green bananas, potatoes, beans, lentils
Fruit & vegetables	We should aim for this food group to make up about 1/3 of what we eat every day. We should try to eat 5 portions of fruit and vegetables every day.	Fresh, frozen and canned fruit and vegetables
Meat, fish & alternatives	We should aim for this food group to make up about 1/6 of what we eat every day.	All types of meat (preferably low fat) and fish, eggs, beans, nuts, soya
Milk & dairy foods	We should aim for this food group to make up about 1/6 of what we eat every day.	Milk, cheese, yoghurt (preferably low fat)
Foods containing fat & foods containing sugar	These foods should be eaten only occasionally and in small amounts.	Butter, margarine, mayonnaise, oily salad dressings, crisps, sweetened drinks, ketchup, sweets, biscuits, cakes, puddings

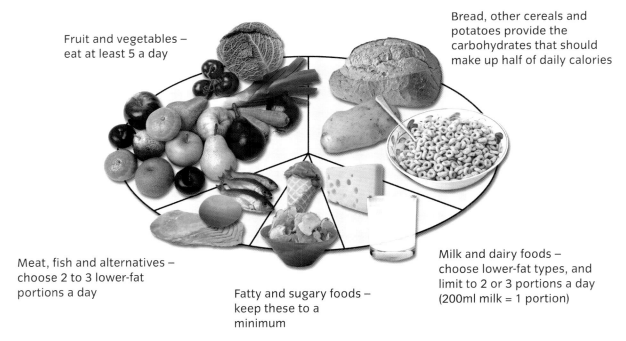

Fruit and vegetables – eat at least 5 a day

Bread, other cereals and potatoes provide the carbohydrates that should make up half of daily calories

Meat, fish and alternatives – choose 2 to 3 lower-fat portions a day

Fatty and sugary foods – keep these to a minimum

Milk and dairy foods – choose lower-fat types, and limit to 2 or 3 portions a day (200ml milk = 1 portion)

Healthy eating is vital for young people leaving care

requirement and, although some supermarket chains provide this, not all do so yet. There are advantages to this straightforward approach for young people who are buying their own food for the first time as it helps them to see the foods they should be choosing for a healthy diet.

With traffic light colours, you can see at a glance if the food you're looking at has high, medium or low amounts of fat, saturated fat, sugars and salt in 100g of the food. In addition to the traffic light colours, you can also see the amount of these nutrients that are present in a portion or serving of the food.

- Red = High
- Amber = Medium
- Green = Low

You will also see the number of grams of fat, saturated fat, salt and sugars in what the manufacturer or retailer suggests as a 'serving' of the food.

So, if you see a red light on the front of the pack, you know the food is high in something we should be trying to cut down on. It's fine to have the food occasionally, or as a treat, but try to keep an eye on how often you choose these foods and try eating them in smaller amounts.

If you see amber, you know the food isn't high or low in the nutrient, so this is an OK choice most of the time, but you might want to go for green for that nutrient some of the time.

Green means the food is low in that nutrient. The more green lights, the healthier the choice. (Information from The Food Standards Agency.)

Shopping

Most young people are really good at shopping! However, shopping for food is not nearly as exciting as shopping for clothes or music. Learning about how to buy fresh ingredients can be a new experience for many young people, so a few shopping trips in order to purchase the ingredients for the recipes will be valuable. Shopping is also a good opportunity to encourage young people to think about budgets and how they will manage their finances.

Budgeting

Finances were another area of concern for young people leaving care, and some lessons in making and managing a simple household budget are very important. A budget can be drawn up on a piece of paper, or there are many computer programmes now that will allow people to budget and manage all their money very effectively. If the young person is confident with IT, then using a computer programme may be the best solution. Regardless of the approach, the principles are the same: making sure that the amount of money in is greater than the amount of money out.

How to draw up a simple budget

Step 1: List income from whatever source. This can include allowances, earnings, benefits and any regular gifts from family or friends.

Step 2: List all expenditure. Most types are listed in the chart on the following page, but just add in any that are missing. Not every young person will have all the expenses listed. There are advantages in completing the weekly, monthly and yearly columns: this means that you are less likely to miss any payments which occur less frequently and it also gives an overview of the young person's complete financial position.

Step 3: The completed chart allows you to see the financial position by looking at the total yearly income and taking away the total yearly expenditure. This will show you whether the young person is able to live within the income they currently receive. If they are not and the expenditure is greater than their income, you need to look at ways of either increasing their income or reducing expenditure.

How to make payments

Part of learning financial independence is about knowing how to pay the bills – not how to have the money to pay the bills, but actually *how* to pay the bills. Most young people moving to independence will never have paid an electricity bill, paid rent, made sure they have a TV licence, or any of the day-

Step 1 – Income	Weekly	Monthly	Yearly
Salary/wage			
Other income			
Leaving care allowance			
Jobseeker's allowance			
Income support			
Housing benefit			
Other benefits			
Interest on savings			
Total			
Step 2 – Expenditure			
Mortgage or rent			
Council tax			
Water rates			
Ground rent			
Repairs & maintenance charges			
Buildings insurance			
Contents insurance			
Gas			
Electricity			
Telephone			
Food			
Clothing			
TV rental and licence			
Prescriptions			
Public transport			
Holidays			
Credit cards and loans			
Contribution to pension			
Reserve for emergencies			
Regular savings			
Total			
Step 3 – Financial position			
Total income			
Total expenditure			
Financial position			

Income and expenditure budget

to-day tasks which are necessary in order to survive. Spending some time with young people so that they can understand how to manage banking and bill payments is important. Many young people will now choose to bank online, but the advantages and disadvantages of the various ways to make payments should be discussed.

Method	Advantages	Disadvantages
Cash	• Easy for those who receive wages or benefits in cash. • Easily understood. • Allows people to see exactly their financial position.	• Safety – keeping cash represents a serious burglary risk. • Loss – cash is easy to lose. • Inconvenience – cash cannot be sent in the post, so cash payments have to be made directly, or through a bank and this can mean having to make special arrangements to go out to visit the offices or the bank of the payee.
Cheque	• Convenient, can be sent by post. • Is more secure than cash. • Is accepted in most places (with a cheque guarantee card).	• Can incur considerable bank charges. • Becoming less accepted with the advent of electronic bank cards. • Cheque book can be lost or stolen. • Cheques can be misused.
Electronic bank card, e.g. Switch or Delta	• Convenient, generally accepted. • Easy to carry and convenient. • Easy to stop if stolen. • More secure since chip and pin.	• Can be stolen and misused. • May be a minimum amount for acceptance.
Standing Order – set up by young person	• Regular payments made by bank. • No action needed by young person after set up • Makes payments direct.	• Young person needs to remember to alter if payments change. • can incur bank charges.
Direct Debit – set up by payee	• Regular payments made by bank. • No action needed by young person. • Makes payments direct.	• Can incur bank charges.
Credit card	• Makes payments even if temporarily short of money. • Convenient. • More secure since chip and pin	• Can accumulate large amounts of debt. • Has high interest charges. • Is easily stolen and misused. • Not accepted for all types of payment.
Armchair/online banking	• Can be used by young people who have bank accounts with access via telephone/internet/satellite TV. • Can be used without leaving the house. • Does not require any permanent set up arrangement. • Is reasonably safe and secure.	• Only available to those with the necessary hardware and IT skills.

Different methods of making payments

Basic maintenance

Many residential establishments would be horrified at the idea that a young person should be allowed to practise changing light bulbs or plugs, but these sort of practical lessons are really important. There won't always be someone around when the light bulb in the loo goes at half past midnight! No one is suggesting a construction and building course, but the skills to do some simple every tasks make the prospect of independence a little less daunting. At the same time, making sure that young people have information about how to contact the utility services in case of emergencies is useful. Even if they are moving into a supported living environment initially, they won't be there for ever and knowing where to find the phone numbers for emergency help is a comfort.

It's all a bit scary out there

One of the most valuable things you can give young people as part of their preparation for adulthood and independence is time and the opportunity to share with you, and with others if they wish, their worries and concerns about moving on. Some will say that they can't wait to leave and be on their own, but even some of the ones who claim to be keen to leave will admit to some anxiety about how they will manage. This group are often among the most vulnerable, particularly because it will be very hard for them to come back looking for help and support if things do not go well. Always make sure that every young person knows that they can ask for support, advice and help whenever they need to.

Reflect

Think about the time you first took responsibility for yourself? Was it when you got married? Went away to college? Got your first flat? Can you recall how you felt – were you frightened or excited or both? Think about the emotions of a young person who may have found security in care for the first time in their lives now being told they have to leave and fend for themselves. How has your practice been influenced by your own experiences? If you were excited by the prospect of independence do you consider how different it could be for these young people – and why? Consider how you can improve your practice in preparing young people for leaving care.

For those who are unhappy and frightened at the prospect of independence, you should make sure that they have every opportunity to talk about their fears and worries, as well as offering all the practical skills to help with the areas of concern. Do not ever dismiss their fears; they are real and very justified when you consider the statistics quoted earlier about the outcomes for children from the care system. Offer advice, support and practical help and, above all, offer a safety net for young people who don't make it first time.

Test yourself

1 What are the main risks for children leaving care?

2 What are the main food groups?

3 What practical help do young people need?

4 Why is it important to budget?

5 How would you recommend that young people should pay bills?

1   Some young people say they are concerned about having to leave care too early – is this concern justified?

2   What additional support do you think needs be given to young people moving on from care?

3   How can a key worker support a young person to leave care?

4   What is the impact of the Children (Leaving Care) Act 2000?

5   On balance, what is the key advantage for young people who have not been in care?

6   Can you identify any positives for young people coming from the care system?

7   Who needs to be part of preparing a Pathway Plan?

8   Why is the review of Pathway Plans important?

Don't forget to refer to the evidence opportunities grid (see pages 357–375) for more ideas for suitable evidence for your NVQ.

Support the needs of children and young people with additional requirements

Article 23 of the UN Convention on the Rights of the Child states that disabled children should: *enjoy a full and decent life, in conditions which ensure dignity, promote self-reliance and facilitate the child's active participation in the community.*

There are around 770,000 disabled children in the UK. This is about 7 per cent of all children.

Children and young people can need additional support in particular areas of their lives for many different reasons. It is not only a physical, sensory or learning disability that means a child or young person will achieve improved outcomes best if they have some additional support. It can also be that universal services are not enough to compensate for the trauma a particular child or young person has experienced. Your role may be a specialised one, and you will have developed particular skills to provide expert support in specific areas.

Alternatively, you may have a more general role, such as working in residential care or as a foster carer, but you will need to be aware of additional support you may need to provide for particular children and young people.

Regardless of your job, the key to giving children and young people the best possible opportunity to become fulfilled and happy adults is to focus on the strengths of each individual, and recognise that an accessible environment means more independence and less support.

In this unit you will find 'Active knowledge' features containing activities that will contribute to assessment for your NVQ. Remember that these features only offer the opportunity for partial assessment; you can also refer to the evidence opportunities grid (see pages 357–375) for more ideas to provide suitable evidence for your NVQ.

What you need to learn

- Children's health promotion
- Assessment and measuring
- Observation
- Putting people in control of assessments
- Support activities
- Child-centred planning
- Planning process
- Setting the criteria for success
- Preparation for activities
- Ways to give feedback and encouragement
- Risk assessment
- Resources
- How to evaluate progress towards outcomes
- How to share the information with the care team

HSC 316a Contribute to the assessment of children and young people's specific developmental levels and support needs

The disabled children's standard from the National Service framework for child and maternity services states:

Children and young people who are disabled or who have complex health needs receive coordinated, high-quality and family-centred services which are based on assessed needs, which promote social inclusion and, where possible, which enable them and their families to live ordinary lives.

All children and young people are assessed at the point of referral to a children's service, to ensure that any support offered is appropriate and will meet their needs. This will most likely be done under the Common Assessment Framework (CAF). This assessment identifies children and young people who have requirements for additional support and where specialist diagnostic assessments have to be carried out by appropriate professionals in order to be able to offer the right support for children or young people with physical, sensory or learning disabilities or mental health problems.

However, the early identification of children who have additional requirements does not generally happen through social care agencies, but through universal services such as health and education.

Children's health promotion

(KS 7, 8, 9, 10, 15)

Historically, children's development was universally checked at specific intervals on the basis that this would identify any issues or failure to reach specific developmental milestones. Developmental checks, carried out by health visitors, were designed to identify developmental problems. Thinking has changed over the last decade and there is now a more holistic approach that is based on child health **promotion** rather than child health **surveillance** as previously.

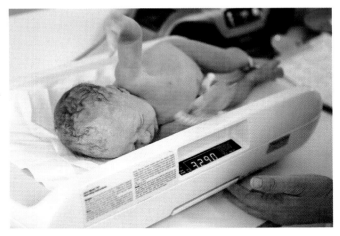

Developmental checks are designed to identify developmental problems

There is universal provision for every child in the country at particular stages where a child health promotion programme is offered. Programmes are offered at the following ages and are likely to include:

Newborn and eight week tests

All newborn babies have an examination and some specific tests to identify particular problems. A newborn examination takes place any time between 4 and 48 hours after birth and will check for any physical indications of problems. The baby's head, mouth, spine, skin, hips, reflexes, hands and feet will all be checked. Tests are also carried out on all newborn babies. The Guthrie test, where a prick of blood is taken from the baby's heel, tests for an enzyme deficiency (phenylketonuria), cystic fibrosis and thyroid deficiency. Sensory impairments are tested for through the Newborn Hearing Screening Programme (NHSP) using the otacoustic emissions test (OAE), and any early indications of visual impairment are checked by shining a light into the baby's eyes and checking for pupil movement and a red reflection. At eight weeks, similar checks are made, but at this stage observations of attention and communication are also made.

8 month check

- Descent of testes – a referral is made if not descended at this stage
- Further check of hips and heart
- General review of developmental progress
- Should be able to distinguish parents from other adults: ask about vocalisations
- Vocalising – 'babbling' by this age and trying to join in 'talking' with parents

- Can play 'peep-bo', likely to be demanding attention using voice
- Will reach for a toy offered by parent
- Gross motor development – in prone position should be able to roll over, may be able to push arms up enough to lift pelvis clear of floor. May sit up on its own or with very little support
- Should brace legs with feet plantigrade (soles downwards) when lowered in standing position to floor
- Around 95 per cent of babies at this age can localise a sound source accurately, except directly behind their head
- Right or left handedness may be becoming evident at this age
- Primitive reflexes that all babies have at birth should be being replaced by other reflexes as they grow this is checked at this stage

18 month check

Gross motor ability – should be able to:
- achieve sitting position (usually at 6–11 months)
- pull to standing position (usually at 6–10 months)
- walk supported by furniture (usually at 7–13 months)
- walk unsupported (usually at 10–15 months)

May be able to:
- climb stairs (usually at 14–22 months)
- walk backwards (usually at 12–22 months)

Fine motor ability – should be able to:
- point with index finger (usually at 9–15 months)
- use careful pincer grip (usually at 10–18 months)
- bang two bricks together (usually at 7–13 months)

May be able to:
- scribble (usually at 12–24 months)
- put 3–4 bricks on top of each other (usually at 16–24 months)

Hearing and talking – should be able to:
- turn towards sound of own name
- jabber constantly

May be able to:
- say 'Mama' and 'Dada' (usually at 11–20 months)

- say three words other than 'Mama' and 'Dada' (usually at 10–21 months)
- point to named facial features (usually at 14–23 months)
- follow simple instructions (usually at 15–30 months)

Behaviour – may be able to:
- hold spoon and take food to mouth (usually at 14–30 months)
- explore surroundings (usually at 13–20 months)
- remove shoes and socks (usually at 13–20 months)

Pre-school check

General information, advice and support
- Management of minor illnesses, using community pharmacists where appropriate
- Access to appropriate services when necessary
- Participation in own care planning and delivery
- Behavioural difficulties: including advice for mild to moderate behavioural disorders, such as tantrums, feeding difficulties and sleep difficulties
- Information about specific health issues, e.g. safety, dental hygiene, diet

Information gathering and assessment
- Immunisations are up to date
- Child has access to primary and dental care

- Any physical, developmental or emotional problems that had previously been missed or not addressed
- Picture of child's general development through listening, talking and observation, which can be more valuable than a formal assessment tool

Gross motor development:
- by 4, stands on one leg, jumps up and down
- by 5, skips, broad jumps

Fine motor development:
- by 4, draws a circle and a cross
- by 5, dresses without significant help, copies a square and a triangle

Social development:
- separates from mother easily
- uses knife and fork
- bladder and bowel control

Language development:
- talks clearly
- uses adult speech sounds
- has mastered basic grammar

Physical development:
- checks including weight and standing height
- heart sounds
- descent of testicles
- sweep test of hearing

Follow-up

If a potential developmental issue is identified, there will be a follow-up referral to the appropriate specialist practitioner for further assessment. Following specialist assessment, the team of professionals around a particular child or young person, the parents and the child or young person, as appropriate, will take decisions about the best ways to meet any additional requirements identified by the assessment process. The lead professional responsible for the individual child or young person will take the role of co-ordinating the work of the various specialists involved.

Active knowledge

Find out from the records of the children or young people you work with how many had all their developmental checks. See if any of the checks resulted in referrals for further specialist help. Of those who had few or no developmental checks, think about the possible benefits if they had. Could it have made a difference to any of them? Could issues that became problems have been picked up earlier? If parents had been able to make use of advice and support, what differences could it have made?

The purpose of this type of universal programme is to highlight any specific developmental issues for individual children that can then be assessed in more detail using specific scales and tests. Many developmental issues are identified by earlier, similar programmes or by Early Years practitioners. Nursery staff, childminders and pre-school playgroup staff have extensive training in child development and are often the first to pick up on developmental issues as they constantly monitor and review children's progress. The Early Years Foundation Stage programme also identifies children needing additional support at an early stage through the constant monitoring, recording and review of children's progress.

Early Support is a government programme that works to provide materials, information, tools and training to develop and improve the quality of services for disabled children and their families. Most of the resources and materials developed are aimed at professional practitioners, but several are for families. The 'family file' provides a resource that families of disabled children can use alongside their national health record book to record information about their child. The family file is useful for passing on information to the professionals who work with the child and family.

The people who are most likely to identify issues, and who are usually right, are parents. One of the key principles for Early Years practitioners is 'always listen to parents who tell you that there is something wrong with their child; there probably is.'

Diagnostic assessment and measuring

(KS 4, 9, 12, 17, 18, 22)

Diagnostic assessment of children's specific needs will be undertaken at the point where the issue is identified. This may be at birth, or later through parental concerns, or picked up in a developmental check by a health visitor or identified in nursery or school. Regardless of how concerns are identified, the process is the same: the child or young person is referred for a specialist assessment in order first to identify if the concern is justified and then to find out how it is to be addressed and the extent of additional support that may be required.

Ethical issue

Imagine that you are working with parents who have just been told that their newborn baby girl has Down's Syndrome. This was not picked up by scans because their chaotic lifestyle meant that ante-natal appointments were not always kept. You feel responsible as you should have made sure the mother kept appointments for scans. This baby will need a lot of care and it will be a big undertaking. The parents want to take the baby home. They say that this has made them realise that they have to change their lives and that they want to look after her. Doctors are convinced that the parents will cope and that they are genuine in their wish to care for this baby.

You have known these parents for a considerable time and you are less convinced; you are working to support them with their other two children and improvements have happened. Your relationship with them is good and you have been able to improve outcomes considerably for the other children. You know that the assessment meeting will take a lot of notice of your opinion. The parents have assumed that you will support them in their decision to take the baby home, and if you oppose this in the meeting you risk losing the relationship and the work you have been doing with the other children. You are worried that they will not cope and will be unable to meet the needs of this child. The assessment meeting is tomorrow – what will you do?

Types of diagnostic assessments

There are many different types of diagnostic assessment depending on the area of concern, but essentially they are all about measuring against an agreed set of measures and then interpreting them using a standard system.

Day-to-day records are important because they can indicate developments, progress or issues of concern. Regardless of the particular needs of the child or young person you are working with, it is important to measure and record development progress as this makes a vital contribution to any formal assessment and identification of needs.

Measuring is different from finding out about needs, or how much support a child or family needs. Measurements provide valuable information to feed into an assessment. In order to measure anything, there must be something to measure against – an objective measurement. The most obvious example is measuring length or height, which cannot be done without some form of measuring instrument. The instrument can be as simple as a ruler or tape measure or as complex as a laser electronic measuring device used by engineers. If measurements are not accurate, all kinds of problems can develop.

Active knowledge

HSC 316a pc 1

There are many different assessments which are used in health and social care. Identify those which may be used with the children and young people in your setting and explain their purpose and how they may lead to a possible intervention.

What needs to be measured

What is being measured will vary depending on the individual child. The specialist services carrying out the diagnostic assessments may want to measure a range of abilities, depending on the circumstances and the outcomes identified. For example, it may be important to measure the degree of sensory impairment a child has in order to make a decision about the type of development activities that are going to be of most benefit.

If measurements are not accurate, all kinds of problems can develop

Many specific assessment programmes and tests have been devised to measure specific conditions; health professionals and psychologists, for example, use a wide range of tests to measure conditions ranging from cerebral palsy to autistic spectrum disorders and from dyslexia to sensory impairment. These are called 'standardised tests' because that is what they are. They measure against an agreed standard, so that the results are comparable for all those being assessed. Formal assessments are usually administered by the relevant professional for the condition being assessed and will provide a clear set of measures and a system for making judgements – often using a scoring system. Well-known everyday examples of formal assessment are:

- *an IQ test*, which asks a series of questions or gives problems to solve, the results being measured against a scale and an IQ score being given. IQ tests are usually administered and scored by psychologists or, occasionally, teachers. This means that if you know your IQ, you can compare it with other people's IQ scores and have a picture of how they compare.
- *an eye test*, which involves reading letters that gradually decrease in size This provides an optician, or a doctor, with some basic information about your sight from which they can go on to find out more by using a series of other tests. An eye test means that you can compare your vision with the vision of others and make comparisons such as:

'You are more short sighted than me.'

'My distance vision is better than yours – I don't have to hold the menu at arm's length to read it.'

You may also know about other, more specialist, diagnostic tests and assessments, for example:

- Portage workers undertake an assessment of a child, along with the parents, using a checklist. This checklist is used to measure a child's abilities in six areas: infant stimulation, social development, communication, speech and language, self-help, cognitive development and motor development.
- Health visitors can do a preliminary test called CHAT (Checklist for Autism in Toddlers) which

Standard snellen eyechart

can identify the potential for the development of autistic spectrum disorder in toddlers as young as 18 months old. This is a questionnaire which the health visitor will ask parents, followed by observations which the health visitor, or other primary care worker (such as the GP), needs to make. Both sections of the test are scored and the results give an indication that the child may be at risk of developing a social-communication disorder.

Sometimes diagnostic assessments will need specialised equipment to carry them out, for example testing someone's fine motor skills may involve them in being asked to pick up and move small objects, or to draw or fill in outlined objects. Standardised psychological tests will have scoring charts and documentation to interpret the results. Tests designed to measure sensory impairment may use computer technology and specialised equipment, as will many of the tests designed to measure physical levels of functioning.

You will need to be familiar with the types of assessment tools used as you may need to be a participant in some of them, or to gather information or take measurements. It may also be important for you to support the child, young person and the family, as waiting for assessments can be stressful and worrying. You can make a major contribution by providing clear and accurate information. A few examples of tests used to measure sensory

impairment that you may regularly come across are outlined in the table below.

The table below gives just a few examples of the wide range of standardised tests that measure what a child or young person can do without additional support. Some of the tests will be able to give a clear result or diagnosis; others will give an indication so further tests can be conducted; others may be a measure to establish the extent of what a child or young person can do. For example, it may be known that a genetic condition means that a child's hearing is impaired; what may still need to be established is how much the child can hear.

Testing is not the same thing as assessing needs and the level and type of support that will be necessary for the child or young person to achieve all the outcomes they are aiming for; that comes later. All the tests will establish is the existence of a particular condition or the extent of the condition. Diagnostic

Name of assessment tool	Area of additional requirement	Used to assess
NFER-Nelson detailed profile	Hearing/speech and language	Screening/intervention programme
Pre-school language scale (PLS)	Hearing/speech and language	Pre-school language
British picture vocabulary scale (BPVS)	Hearing/speech and language	Understanding of vocabulary
Test of reception and grammar (TROG)	Hearing/speech and language	Understanding grammatical contrasts
Renfrew action picture test	Hearing/speech and language	Expressive language – information
Pure tone audiometry	Hearing	Extent of hearing loss
Tympanometry	Hearing	Test for 'glue ear'
Snellen chart/reduced Snellen	Vision	Visual acuity distance/near
Maclure reading type	Vision	Reading text size
Ishihara test	Vision	Colour blindness
Diagnostic interview for social and communication disorders (DISCO)	Social and communication disorders	Diagnoses ASD
Checklist for autism in toddlers (CHAT)	Social and communication disorders	Indicates possible ASD

Tests to measure what a child can do

tests are not designed to determine what needs to be done next and you may well find yourself being asked these sorts of question:

The doctor said the test showed he's got a hearing impairment. Does that mean he's deaf?

What happens next?

Was it because I didn't eat properly when I was pregnant?

The psychologist said he's dyslexic – he won't be able to read and write now, will he?

What help can we get?

How will he cope?

Answers to these questions may, or may not, be clear. If you know the information because you have had it from the person conducting the test – then you should go ahead and explain it again to the parents. It is surprising how much information people forget.

On the other hand, if you do not know the answers for certain, do not guess. Explain that you do not have all the answers, but that you will find out and come back. Tell the parents exactly when you will speak with them and make sure that you do.

Many of the answers to parents' concerns will be answered through the CAF process as they are able to identify the needs of their child and their own needs, and agree plans to make sure the needs are met.

Monitoring and measuring

A helpful example of monitoring and measuring is the Monitoring Protocol from Early Support (see page 262). The Monitoring Protocol provides parents of deaf babies and children with a tool to record their child's progress and development. The protocol also provides resources for activities and information to support and guide parents over four main areas: Communication; Attending; Listening and Vocalisation; and Play. The Protocol is designed to be used by parents in partership with a relevant professional, or by a professional in partership with parents.

You will need to make sure that you are familiar with any specific tests being undertaken for children or young people you work with. If you are not sure about the test, ask the professional who is carrying it out and follow up any information with further research.

Asking questions

Parents, carers, families and young people do not always find it easy to ask questions during assessments. You can usefully support people by helping them to plan out questions in advance, reminding them of the questions they want to ask and going over the information they have been given.

 Keys to good practice

✓ Find out about the diagnostic assessments being carried out.

✓ Find out the results if you can, and the parents agree to it.

✓ Answer parents' questions clearly and openly.

✓ Only give information and explanations you actually know about – never guess or make assumptions.

✓ If you need to find out more information, do so promptly.

✓ Give clear information about the CAF process.

✓ Reassure parents that the needs of the child and parents are considered in the CAF process.

✓ If you promise to recontact people with more information, do so as quickly as possible.

For example, before a diagnostic test, you might help a family to draw up a list of questions such as:

- What is this test designed to diagnose?
- How accurate is it?
- Is this the only test or will you need to follow up with more?
- What exactly are you going to do?
- Is this a standard test?
- When will we know the results?
- Does anyone else get the results?

After the test, they may need to ask the following type of questions:

- What do the results mean?
- What causes this?
- Can anything be done about this condition?
- If so, what?
- Please can you write down the medical terms for the condition?
- What happens next?
- Where can we go for help?

Encourage families to ask questions and to take the time to write down the answers, otherwise they may forget what they have been told.

Observation

(KS 17, 30)

Observation is an important skill, and can form a key part of assessing what is appropriate to meet the needs of a particular child or young person. Observation is about much more than simply looking at someone or something. In order to observe, you will need to know the importance of what you see, watch carefully and note down details of the relevant observations you make.

For example, you may have observed that a particular young person with a learning disability has a noticeable improvement in motor control when he is working on a computer keyboard. This could be valuable information if you are thinking about the types of activities that could improve his motor skills.

Good observation is a key part of assessment. Although observation can be a specific, planned assessment tool, it can also be spontaneous and part of your everyday work. Remember: good observations involve the following:

- Be unobtrusive – do not sit and stare!
- Always be alert to what is happening around you.
- Observe details such as children's and young people's body language and non-verbal communication.

 My story

Hi, I'm Jeanette, I'm 21 and I live with my son Rory, who is almost 4 years old. Rory has finally been diagnosed with ASD. I have always known that there was something wrong with Rory: his behaviour was so strange, it was like he didn't care if I was there or not. He never wanted a hug, he had terrible tantrums – I thought he hated me. I ended up going to Children's Services because I couldn't cope with him. I live on my own with Rory. My mum's very good and helps when she can, but it's mainly me and him. I really thought that I must be doing something terribly wrong because of the way he was behaving. I didn't know why he seemed as if he didn't love me and he was just so naughty. Just the slightest thing seemed to send him into a tantrum and it didn't matter where we were. It got so I didn't want to go out with him. I really couldn't manage and so I went to ask them to take him into care; I didn't want him to go away, but I was desperate. The social worker was really good and she arranged for Debbie to start coming in to help me. It was Debbie who got the referral for the tests. She said she thought there may be something the matter with Rory and that he ought to be tested.

Debbie was brilliant. She explained it all to me and went through all the leaflets and stuff they give you. We thought about the questions we wanted to ask and when we went for the tests with the doctor, she explained to me what was going to happen and what to expect. It was all just like she said and they were really nice. They told me loads, but I couldn't really take it all in – Debbie was there and she said she'll go through it all with me tomorrow. I don't know how I would have managed without her.

Observing well is an art you need to practice

- Look at children and young people's reaction to their environment and others around them.
- Make notes about what you observe – you will not remember the detail.

Putting people in control of assessments

(KS 3, 4, 7, 9, 10, 16, 23, 24)

Remember this is the child or young person's assessment. It is about them, and they are the most important person in the process. So it is essential that they feel that they are involved and not that the assessment is something which is being 'done to' them. Parents are also central to the assessment and should feel that they are involved, are able to contribute and will be listened to and valued.

This is not always easy, particularly if the assessment is a standardised test or a formal diagnostic process. These are often not designed in a way that encourages people to feel they are gaining something from the process or making a meaningful contribution. It is easy for people to feel that their children are being tested or experimented on, a bit like a laboratory animal. So, a key role for you is to make sure that children, young people and families you are working with are clear about:

- what is going to happen
- why it is happening
- how it will be carried out
- what they need to do
- how to stop it if they are unhappy
- what the results mean
- the next steps.

Needless to say, make sure that children, young people and families are able to be involved and that there are no barriers such as:

- language
- communications
- access to locations for assessment
- transport difficulties
- literacy difficulties.

If you do a check like this, you can make sure that the information you and other professionals are sharing is relevant and can be understood.

Obtaining agreement

Only by carefully explaining the purpose and process of the assessment and any subsequent recommendations for development activities can you ensure that the parents agree with the assessment and activities you have identified. Parents and young people must be able to make an informed decision, and to do that they need to know all the details and implications.

Your workplace will have a protocol relating to parental consent for assessments and diagnostic tests. It may or may not involve the signing of a written consent form, as these are not usually invasive or risky procedures; however, you will have to comply with the procedure in your workplace for obtaining consent.

Active knowledge

Find out your workplace's protocol for parental consent for diagnostic assessments. See if it varies depending on the type of activity, or if it is always verbal or always written. Check how this relates to the overall policy regarding parental consent for other procedures. Is there a difference? Try to find out the reason and justification for the difference.

Informal assessment

(KS 2, 9, 12, 24, 30)

Informal assessment does not use a formal system of scoring results against a set of agreed measures in the same way as standardised tests. However, you may need to make judgements based on what you have learned from observations, simply talking to the child or young person or using a checklist. For example, you may have a view about the extent to which a young person with Down's Syndrome is likely to benefit from an activity you are planning around using ICT as an aid to daily living, or whether a group of young people you support, who have limited concentration as a result of learning disability, will benefit from a memory game designed to improve concentration. You should share your views with the young people you are working with, if they ask for an input from you, particularly if you feel that they may wish to embark on an activity that may not provide much benefit for them. You should also be clear about suggesting alternatives that may be more appropriate.

Identifying and agreeing

In your workplace, you could use a checklist of factors you will encourage children, young people and families to take into account before decisions are taken as to whether or not they will benefit from an activity. Your checklist will, of course, be specific to your workplace and the particular children or young people you work with.

An example checklist for a technology activity is likely to include the following areas for consideration.

- familiarity with technology
- ability to follow instructions
- ability to retain information and repeat actions
- likelihood of direct benefit from using technology
- problem-solving skills
- interest in technology.

However, if you are working with someone who is very keen to be involved in working with technology, then you would have to give a great deal of weight to the last factor on the list, as this may well prove to outweigh any other concerns. Discussions around possible activities and the likely benefits are very important and also give you the chance to deal with any questions or concerns that may arise. If the young person is someone you work with regularly, you will also have other valuable insights to support the identification of suitable activities. For example, you will know whether or not there are family members or friends who are likely to be supportive and interested in activities based around technology, and you will know the young person's previous responses in situations where they have been involved in something new.

Recording information

(KS 7, 11, 30)

Recording both the process and the results of diagnostic assessments is important. If there is a formal assessment method, the assessment process is likely to include a scoring or record sheet. This will need to be completed in order to obtain the results of the assessment, and is then usually kept in the child or young person's records for future reference. If you have carried out observations or measurements to contribute to the assessment process, you will need to make sure that you have recorded the results in the way required by the test, or as agreed with the professional responsible for the test. This will provide useful information for other members of the child or young person's team, and will mean that future plans will be able to make use of the assessment results you have obtained and recorded.

All recordings which are not on a formal record sheet accompanying the assessment should be clear and readily usable by others. In order for assessment records to be of the maximum possible use, they need to include the following.

- the date, length and place of the assessment
- the purpose of the assessment
- who was present
- the methods used for the assessment
- the child or young person's view of the assessment
- the results
- the implications of the results
- the activities that are planned as a result of the assessment.

They also need to be readily accessible and be understood by colleagues, in order to be of most use.

The records of assessments carried out under the CAF will be maintained by the lead professional (see Unit 33) for the child or young person. The lead professional may be you or another of the team, but the outcome of any diagnostic tests and assessments will be considered in the overall needs assessment.

HSC 316b Support the implementation of programmes and support activities to meet the needs of children and young people with additional needs

Support activities

(KS 2, 30)

Activities carried out for the specific purpose of promoting a child's or young person's development, health or well-being can be classed as support activities. It is the purpose, not the type of activity, which decides whether it qualifies as a developmental support activity. For example, a commercial artist painting a picture because they have been commissioned to do so is doing something with a different purpose to the young person who has mental health issues and is using the medium of art as a therapeutic means of expressing many complex emotions and feelings.

Again, a group of children playing a hopscotch game in the playground is different from a child doing hopping and jumping as exercises under the supervision of a physiotherapist in order to develop improved muscle tone and strength. The activity is the same, but the purpose is different.

Reflect

Think about activities which you undertake in your own life which may be repeated, but have a different purpose. For example, reading a magazine to look at the latest bathrooms or hairstyles or cars and reading a magazine because there is an article in it that your NVQ assessor has told you to read – by tomorrow! Then think about activities you carry out in your workplace. When does talking to a child or young person stop being just chatting or communicating and start being a development or therapeutic activity? Discuss this with your line manager or assessor.

A wide range of activities can be carried out with the purpose of promoting the development of an individual child or young person. Some of these may be undertaken by a specialist professional such as a physiotherapist, occupational therapist, speech and language therapist or play therapist. Other activities may be carried out by the child or young person with support from parents or from professionals in a child care setting. You could be involved in planning and preparing for many different activities depending on the group of children or young people you work with and their identified needs. The sorts of activities which you may be involved in planning and carrying out could include these:

Type of activity	Possible development objective
Word recognition games	Developing language and reading skills
Team and taking turns activities	Social and communication skills
Physical activity games	Physical strength and fitness and/or gross motor development
Creative activities	Cognitive skills, fine motor skills
Sound recognition games	Language skills

Child-centred planning

(KS 2, 3, 19, 22, 23, 24, 25, 31)

The examples in the table on page 271 show some of the activities which may be implemented in your workplace, with some general suggestions about the developmental value they may have. However, the value is only realised for each individual child or young person if the activities are planned in response to their identified and assessed needs. A fun, fast, physical game of water-balloon relay would provide a positive and enjoyable way of improving general fitness and gross motor skills for a young person with spina bifida using a wheelchair, or be an absolutely confusing and frightening experience for a young person with ASD! An extreme example perhaps, but it makes the point that any activities must be related to the child or young person's assessed needs and must be within their capability.

In the first part of this unit, you looked at the ways in which assessments are undertaken and needs identified. The planning of activities is the next step and this is always based on the results of the identification and assessment process.

Depending on the type of activity, the planning may be undertaken by the relevant professional – for example, a programme of muscular exercises for a child with muscular dystrophy will be planned by a physiotherapist, or a programme of activities to support speech and language development will be planned by a speech and language therapist.

As a professional child care worker supporting an individual child or young person, you may need to develop a programme of activities designed to promote and meet social, intellectual or emotional needs. This could include:

- outings
- games
- exercises
- relaxation
- work experience.

Activities must meet a child's needs and be within their capability

Clear directions

All plans must be moving towards a clearly identified goal or goals. Without this, a plan is just a list of a series of actions which are not focused and are without direction. Imagine a football team that took to the field without a game plan – everyone would be running everywhere without any clear idea of what they were doing. Something similar can happen to a child's team that works without planning clear goals!

Goals can take all kinds of forms depending on the needs of the child or young person. An overall aim will have been identified and agreed by the child or young person and the family, along with all the professionals involved.

Planning process

(KS 2, 3, 24, 30)

In order for planning to be effective in promoting development goals, it needs to be about far more than just making sure that the timetable works or that you don't forget a vital piece of equipment! Of course, these things are important, but good planning is as much a part of the final benefit as the activity itself. Planning is part of a process which begins with assessment and identifying needs, and the two are closely linked. The assessment will have helped the child, young person and parents to identify needs and to make a judgment about participation in any developmental activity. An assessment will also have identified the likely activities which are appropriate and beneficial for the child or young person. It is important that any planning takes all of this into account. The plan is a means of meeting the identified needs.

Planning as a shared process

Making sure that children and families are a part of the planning process is one of your vital roles. Children and young people have a right to decide what they want to achieve and how they want to go about it to the best of their ability. They and their parents should be taking control of the planning process to whatever extent they wish. The methods you use to encourage participation will vary depending on the setting in which you work and the wishes of the children and families concerned.

Any of the following methods could be helpful in encouraging participation:

- one-to-one planning
- involvement in the review process
- discussions with children and young people and parents
- preparing written plans for comments following discussions
- taking the child, young person or parents to see activities to provide examples and ideas
- asking a young person or parents to prepare their own plans.

Each of these approaches may be valuable for different people – getting it right can result in this kind of feedback:

'We really felt as if we were able to control what was happening and that our views were listened to as much as everyone else's in the planning meetings.'
(Parents of 3-year-old girl with Down's Syndrome)

'Being able to write my own plans was just so much better than before when I had to do what other people thought. Not only did I write my own plans, but they got agreed at the review meeting – I feel great.'
(15-year-old boy with cerebral palsy)

'I was much happier letting Jane take the plans to the meeting, but she was really good about making sure that I was happy with everything before she went. I'm glad I didn't have to go with all those people there.'
(Mother of a 4-year-old boy with a hearing impairment)

'We weren't really sure about the therapy, but after Chris took us to the centre to see how it worked it all made much more sense. It was so good to see the other children and to talk to other parents like us.'
(Parents of a 2-year-old boy with acquired brain injury)

Teamwork

Any plans for activities for children and young people must link to the overall plan for the child and will need to be co-ordinated with the activities of others working with the child or young person. Pulling everything together and making sure that everything happens will be done by the lead professional for the individual child. Any plans you make for activities should be agreed as part of the overall planning process. The detail of the activities will be your responsibility, but the type of support activity is likely to be included in the overall plan.

For example, it may be agreed that work with a particular child with a learning disability will focus on using shape and colour over the next couple of months.

You could work together on a colour shape game on the computer that involves clicking on shapes and matching them with their twin. This will also help to develop memory and fine motor skills.

You could do a similar 'snap' card game using cut-out coloured shapes. If you work with the child or young person to make the cards, this also helps fine motor skills.

You could play a game where designated areas of a room or outdoor space have a large coloured flag. Children have to move to the space when you shout out the colour, or as a variation, each child is given a coloured card and has to match themselves with the area. A further variation is to pin cards on each child's back and they have to ask another child to tell them which colour they are – this also supports the development of social and communication skills.

Any of these examples would support the plan to work around colour and shape recognition. And remember, your feedback on the activities and their effectiveness will be an important part of monitoring the child or young person's progress.

Setting the criteria for success

(KS 2, 4, 5, 16, 19, 21, 24, 25, 27, 29, 32, 33)

There is no point in setting goals and targets unless you are going to know when you have achieved them. You know when footballers score because there is an accepted criterion that the ball has to go into the net – if it misses, it's not a goal. Everybody is clear about that.

So, with a development activity programme:

- you know what the overall aim is
- you know what the goals are along the way
- so you now have to agree what the criteria are going to be so you will know if the goals have been achieved.

Think about goals as the steps on the way to achieving the overall aim for the child or young person. You have looked at setting goals and targets in Unit 39, and the principles are the same here. However, setting goals is all very well, but achieving them is essential. In order for children and young people to be able to achieve the agreed goals, the goals must be realistic and achievable. There is no quicker way to demoralise and demotivate a child, young person and their family than to set unrealistic expectations which they constantly fail to meet. Goals are better when they are small and achievable rather than large and out of reach. Goals must be related to an assessment of both need and ability.

Each goal is a step along the way to the trophy – success!

For example, a child with a significant learning disability is unlikely to achieve a goal of writing a short story. However, a goal of being able to manipulate a computer mouse and see the relationship between touching the mouse and making something happen on the screen may be achievable for the particular child.

Reflect

Think about an occasion when you have failed to achieve something you had planned to do. Remember the feelings of disappointment? Did it make you more determined, or did it make you give up? Try to recall your feelings. Think about the way you work – are you always careful to set achievable targets? Are you sometimes so keen to see the children or young people make progress that you can push too hard?

Expectations

All of your communication skills may be needed to walk the fine line between aiming too low and not challenging a child or young person to develop and increase skills and abilities, and aiming too high and so contributing to a feeling of frustration and disappointment by setting someone up to fail.

Expecting too much

For some parents it is hard to accept that goals and targets must be achievable; it does happen that parents have unrealistic expectations of what their child can achieve. This can result in children and young people losing motivation and contribute to poor self-esteem if they feel that they have 'failed' their parents.

It will take time to help parents to see even small steps as major achievements. One of the most effective ways is to use 'modelling' techniques. This involves you in displaying the behaviour that you want others to adopt, so, in this case you make sure that you praise the child's achievements and make a big fuss about every small achievement. Through this process, some parents can be supported to value the achievements of their children, and to see the effects of achievement, recognition and praise.

Expecting too little

Far more common, though, are parents who want to protect disabled children from risk and challenge and have low expectations of what their children can achieve. In this situation, you will need to work alongside parents to help them to develop confidence in their own child, and to realise that they are capable of more than expected. This is a gradual process. Sometimes it can be useful to involve parents in writing the risk assessment for an activity; this way they have a chance to examine and consider risk and to look at ways it can be managed.

You: 'There is a risk that Tom will fall from the horse.'

Mum: 'Well, he can't go if he's going to fall.'

You: 'It's not the falling that matters – the risk is that he will get hurt. How can we reduce the risk of him being hurt?'

Mum: 'Wear a riding helmet.'

You: 'Yes – what else could we do?'

Mum: 'Ride inside where they've got that special surface.'

You: 'That's a good idea, especially to start with – so if he wore a helmet and only rode inside to see how he gets on – what do you think?'

Mum: 'He would love it – as long as you promise to keep a very close eye on him.'

You: 'I promise, I'll stay right beside him.'

Setting the pace

The timescales and pace of activities are also an important part of planning. As with the setting of goals, the speed at which goals need to be achieved is also a key as to how realistic it is for the individual child or young person. As always, the child, young person and parents should be the ones setting the timescale for the achievement of their goals. You may find that you need to encourage and support children and families in thinking about what is realistic for their own circumstances and history. For example, a young person with a long history of stress-related illness may decide that they want to be off medication and back in school in six weeks. However, a more realistic timescale may be six months. Asking anyone to work towards something so far away is unlikely to meet with success – smaller goals that can be achieved over relatively short periods of time are more likely to be achieved. So a plan to reduce medication by half, and to go out with a friend at least once a week for the next four weeks is far more likely to be achieved and provide the motivation to carry on with the plan.

Remember, nothing succeeds like success – achievement and praise make children grow in confidence and therefore more likely to go on achieving.

Active knowledge

In your own workplace, find out the method for agreeing and recording goals for children and young people. Check who makes decisions about activities and the extent to which children, young people and families have control of the process. Discuss the basis for the procedures with your line manager or assessor.

Preparation for activities

(KS 2, 6, 16, 24, 29, 30)

Preparing for your role

You could be supporting, organising or participating in a wide range of activities, and your role will be different depending on the child or young person involved and the identification of their needs and abilities. The extent to which you are directly involved or participate in the activity is also likely to vary, partly because of the activity, but also because of the child or young person's needs. In some activities you may be taking part alongside the child or young person; in others you may need to demonstrate what needs to be done; and sometimes you may only be needed in order to set up the activity and give any advice and support.

Preparing equipment

Depending on the activity, you may need to have equipment or materials ready. Nothing is more guaranteed to make children and young people lose enthusiasm and interest and start thinking of other interesting things to do than equipment being

Type of activity	Likely role
Swimming for all ages, but particularly for children and young people with a physical disability	Participation/demonstration
Assertiveness group for young people with mental health problems	Participation
Relaxation for all children and young people	Advice and instruction
Outings and visits for all children and young people	Participation
Creative activities – art, music, writing, drama, etc.	Demonstration if you have the skills and talent/participation/observation
Outdoor sports/activities	Demonstration if you have the skills and qualifications/participation/observation

Activities and roles

missing or you having to constantly disappear to get the missing items!

As part of the planning process, it is useful to make a list of any materials or equipment you will need and to make sure that it is ready, working and available. For example, if you are planning to run a relaxation session, you will need relaxing sounds, a music CD or an MP3 player. Your checklist may look something like the following.

Checklist of items for activity

- ✓ Numbers participating
- ✓ Music CD and laptop
- ✓ MP3 player
- ✓ Check where power socket is
- ✓ If no power socket – use batteries
- ✓ Check battery levels – bring spare batteries
- ✓ Check room is warm
- ✓ Individual mats or towels
- ✓ Soft and warm floor covering
- ✓ Check lighting – use lamps if too harsh
- ✓ Privacy – curtains/blinds

You can add tick boxes like those above to your checklist and tick off the items as you collect them together.

Your list for a visit to a zoo or adventure park, designed to promote social and cognitive development, will look very different, and will include items such as tickets, guidebooks or programmes and transport arrangements.

If the activity is a creative session designed to develop motor and cognitive skills, such as making a collage, you may have prepared some materials in advance. You could have already cut up pieces of material and torn out magazine pages. Your list of materials in this case may be lengthy and will need to include items such as glue, scissors and paper. Access to water for cleaning up afterwards will be important, as will good lighting and sufficient tables and chairs – all of these things will need to form part of your checklist.

If you are preparing for a board games session with a group, in order to improve concentration, cognitive and social and communication development, you may need to think about the games you are going to use and check that they are all available and are complete – Scrabble with half the letters missing or Monopoly without the dice or the Park Lane card is not much fun!

As with all the planning and preparation processes, the needs of the children and young people you are supporting must take priority. There is little point in planning a relaxation session that involves lying on the floor with a group of children who will have difficulty getting up and down. Wheelchair relaxation is fun and just as good. Similarly, the materials and equipment you are planning to use for your activities will need to be useable by the group or individual child or young person for whom the activity is designed. For example:

- If you are going to plan a craft session using glue, can the handles of the brushes you have selected be gripped by the children or young people who will be participating?
- If you are planning a games session, can everyone in the group see/read the cards and dice?
- If you are planning a speaking game, does anyone in the group need support in hearing what is going on?

Ways to give feedback and encouragement

(KS 18, 24)

Few things are worse than doing something and getting no information about how you are doing, especially something new or something you are unsure about. For example, you may have taken a driving test. One of the most difficult aspects of the test is that you have no feedback while it is going on: you only know at the end how well you have done. Throughout the activities you should make sure that you provide feedback and encouragement.

Feedback should always be constructive. Negative feedback is very destructive and demotivating. If you need to offer criticism, it should always be positive and offer alternatives. For example:

'Lucy, you are relaxing much better now. If you keep going on the breathing pattern, you'll find it will work even better.'

'Jack, that spreadsheet is so good – I think we could use it in the office if there was a date column added.'

'Jo, the way you have made contributions in the group recently has been fantastic. I'd love to see how well you can use your listening skills to help others to join in.'

These are all really positive alternative ways of saying:

'Lucy, you won't ever relax properly unless you get your breathing right.'

'Jack, you've missed out the date column.'

'Jo, you need to not talk so much and give others a chance to get a word in edgeways.'

Reflect

Think of occasions when you have been put down by negative criticism. Try to remember how you felt. Make a list with two columns: one for negative and one for positive feedback. Use the examples above and add to them. For each one give the positive and negative versions. Over a period of about a week, make a note each time you make a criticism of how you could have done it more positively.

Risk assessment

(KS 17, 19, 22, 25)

Some development activities will have health and safety implications. You must carry out a risk assessment before undertaking most development activities. Those which involve physical activity, or going off site will definitely need a risk assessment. Games and activities such as board games may not – but an exercise group or a dancing class may. It is always useful to check with your line manager about the activities that will require risk assessments.

Risk assessments for activities

Risk assessments for development activities are the same as for anything else. They are not intended to eliminate risks, but to identify and reduce them as far as possible. The process of assessing risk gives you the opportunity to decide if the risks are too great to go ahead, or to make a judgement that the potential benefits outweigh the risks.

My story

Hi, I'm Janine. I am 8 years old and I have cerebral palsy. I live with my Mum and Dad and older brother Michael. I go to school at Foxwood; the bus comes every day and my wheelchair goes on the lift into the bus. We do lots of great things at school; my favourite is swimming. Sue, the physio, comes in the pool with us and gives us exercises to do. My key worker Jane comes in too and she helps me in and out of the pool and with the exercises. Jane helps when we do other stuff too, like cutting out and making things with glue – I always get in a mess but Jane helps me to clean it off. Sometimes we go on days out. We went to the Technology museum last week. There were lots of things to do and you could touch things and press buttons. Jane helped with the buttons I couldn't press, but most of them were quite easy. There was a bit where you could do photographs like they had in the olden days. That was fun. They took one of me and Jane. I really like Jane, she's my best friend – well next to Vicky Johnson who's my best, best friend!

Some development activities will have health and safety implications

Assessing risks in activities for children and young people is different from assessing risks for adults. Adults are able to make judgements about risks for themselves, provided they are given the information to do so. For example, wheelchair mountaineering is a risky activity, but an adult can make the decision to do it (and many do!) having considered all the risks and possible consequences. On the other hand, it is difficult to imagine any organisation with responsibility for the care of disabled children agreeing to take a group wheelchair mountaineering!

Resources

(KS 1, 8, 13, 29, 30)

Having sufficient resources to meet the needs of all the children is always a balancing act for organisations. Priorities can change and new initiatives or guidelines can change the way resources are allocated. Resources for activities need to be found on several levels.

- Macro or strategic level: it is the role of senior managers in the organisation to ensure that funding is allocated, and services commissioned, in such a way as to meet the needs of local populations.
- Operational level: it is the role of the managers of individual programmes or establishments to make sure that budget allocations are used in the most effective way to enable the maximum benefit for the children and young people. (You may be working at this level.)
- Individual or micro level: you may also be working at this level, where you are responsible for ensuring that resources are available to meet the needs of the individual child or young person you are working with.

Resources is about more than just money, it also means staff, equipment, buildings and time.

Putting parents in control

The Health and Social Care Act 2001 laid down a requirement that all parents of disabled children who are assessed as needing, and being eligible for, a service must be offered 'direct payments'. This means that parents of disabled children can decide upon and commission staff and services for their child if they wish to. Over 10 per cent of parents of disabled children have chosen to do this already, and the number is rising. Parents cannot use the money to buy local authority services, but if you work for the private, voluntary or independent sector, you may find that parents are purchasing your service directly, using their child's direct payments. You may also be employed directly by the parents of a disabled child to provide some or all of the services identified in the assessment. This is truly changing the traditional balance of power and puts the parents in direct control of how their child's needs are met and the way in which this is done.

Test yourself

1   List the three key things to remember when planning activities.

2   Why is it important to gain agreement from the child or family?

3   List three development activities you might undertake with the children or young people you work with.

4   Do any of them require a risk assessment? Give reasons for your answer.

HSC 316c Contribute to evaluating children and young people's participation in programmes and support activities

The vital part of support activities and programmes is to evaluate how effective they have been in reaching the planned outcomes, and what changes, if any, need to be made. There is no point in continuing activities that have not been beneficial or in stopping those that have contributed to improved outcomes.

How to evaluate progress towards outcomes

(KS 9, 15, 30, 34)

The outcomes set during the planning process are the basis for evaluation; there will be goals that identify progress towards the overall outcome. You will need to measure progress towards these goals.

Some goals are easier to measure than others. For example, the planned outcome for a young person recovering from a spinal injury was to recover sufficient mobility to resume all activities prior to the injury. A goal such as walking unaided to the end of the hospital corridor could be one of the ways of evaluating progress towards the outcome. The achievement of this goal, or progress toward it, can be measured and recorded. This sort of information is 'quantitative', which means it can be measured against known criteria. The criteria will have been set in advance, when you were planning the activity. You will have jointly agreed what the criteria for success would be – in this case, the criteria are about:

- distance, i.e. 'to the end of the corridor' and
- amount of support needed, i.e. 'unaided'.

You may also consider including additional 'targets' to measure progress such as walking part of the way, or walking all the way but with some assistance.

You could decide to have a progress chart or map to show how well a child or young person is doing. This can be very helpful in keeping a young person motivated. In doing this, it can be useful to 'convert' your criteria into a scoring system; for example:

- achievement of goal is 100 points
- walking unaided past the first to doorways on the corridor is 25 points
- walking the full length of the corridor with help is 50 points.

Another example might be a child who has been sexually abused, who may have a very low self-esteem. A planned outcome for the child to develop improved self-esteem and to value herself is more difficult to measure because it is about how the child or young person feels, which is not easy for children to put into words. However, changes in behaviour will indicate progress and the areas of expected change can be identified at the start of the programme and form the criteria for making judgements as in Example 2.

> **Example 1:**
>
> Sam walked two-thirds of the way along the corridor unaided. He feels that this is excellent progress towards his goal and is keen that the exercise programme should continue.

> **Example 2:**
>
> Ayisha has voluntarily joined in three activities in the past three weeks at the group. She makes eye contact with most children now, but not with adults. She has asked to be included in the trip to the park tomorrow for the first time.

Decisions about the extent to which goals have been met will be made by the child or young person and their family along with all of those involved at the regular reviews of the initial assessment planning.

Identifying the questions

A list of questions can be useful when you are preparing an evaluation and thinking through what has been achieved and the next steps. Depending on the age and ability of the child or young person, they should be involved in the evaluation along with parents. It is not easy to just ask children, young people and their families to make evaluations without a framework to start the process. Each child or young person will be different, and everyone will need their own list. However, something like the list below may help.

> ### List of questions on achieving goals
>
> 1. What did we want to achieve?
> 2. Did we achieve it fully, partly, or not at all?
> 3. How do you feel about progress?
> 4. Has the goal changed?
> 5. If so, what is the goal now?
> 6. Do you think the way you set about achieving the goal worked?
> 7. If not, why not?
> 8. What do you want to do next?
> 9. How will this help towards your goal?

Depending on their circumstances and personal choice, families may prefer to think about this independently, or may wish to work it through with their key worker or other trusted professional.

You will also need to share your own evaluation of the progress towards the agreed goals and the effectiveness of the activities and approaches chosen.

Ethical issue

You are working with a teenaged young man who has an inoperable brain tumour. He has limited vision and now his mobility is being affected. The prognosis is very poor and he is deteriorating rapidly. However, he has been working very hard on his physiotherapy programme to try to improve his mobility. He is highly motivated and is convinced that he is improving. However, it is clear from the evaluation that there is no improvement and his condition is getting worse. He is determined to participate in the review and his mother begs you to change the evaluation and tell the review that he is doing well. She fears that if he hears the facts he will lose all his motivation and will give up the fight. What do you do?

How to share the information with the care team

(KS 4, 12, 16, 20, 24, 26, 33, 34)

Other members of the team will participate in the evaluation process, either because they may have their own contribution to make, or because they have an interest in the progress of the individual. Progress reports and evaluations are generally shared at a regular review meeting. The process will involve all the professionals involved with the child or young person, and the family. If the child or young person is looked after by the local authority, the review will be undertaken by the Independent Reviewer.

Review meetings give the opportunity for everyone to make a contribution and develop the next stage of activity or programme.

Who decides

You should make sure that the child or young person and their family are aware and able to attend. Everyone should have the opportunity to contribute, using advocates if necessary, and should be able to reach agreement on the next steps. However, ultimately, it is the families who must direct what the next steps should be; your role is to ensure that there is sufficient information to make a clear decision.

Regardless of the method, it is important that all progress and evaluations are recorded and any changes are clearly made in the child or young person's plans.

The people with parental responsibility have the power to make decisions about what happens to the child; in most cases this will be the parents. However, if there is sufficient evidence that they are not acting in the best interests of the child, steps can be taken by the local authority to safeguard and protect the child. This would be a very unusual circumstance as most parents want to do the best for their child and will work alongside professionals to achieve this. Parents whose children are in receipt of direct payments will have more control over reviewing and planning provision for their child but, again, the vast majority will still want to work closely with professionals to achieve agreed outcomes.

Prepare a report of a review concerning an individual child's progress towards an agreed goal, or set of goals. The report can be based on a child you work with, or have done previously, or it can be entirely imaginary, or a combination of the two. If you do use a child you work with, make sure that the parents agree to you using information about them and that child cannot be identified.

Your report should include:

- information about the child's circumstances and background
- the goals or targets and the reasons for them
- the development activities and why they were chosen
- the criteria agreed to measure success
- the results of the development activities
- the results of measuring against the criteria
- a judgement as to how successful the activity has been
- a proposal for the next steps.

HSC 316 UNIT TEST

1. Why are development activities important?
2. List at least three purposes of development activities.
3. What types of activities can be useful for improving development?
4. What are the important aspects of planning?
5. Why is careful preparation important?
6. How can you support clients during activities?
7. What are the most effective ways of giving feedback?
8. Why is evaluation important?
9. How can you share information with the rest of the team?

Don't forget to refer to the evidence opportunities grid (see pages 357–375) for more ideas for suitable evidence for your NVQ.

Support families in their own home

Families are the place where the vast majority of children grow up. Families consist of people from at least two different generations, and often more than that. There is at least one adult and any number of children and other relations. Families vary enormously in structure, size, how members relate to each other and in attitudes, expectations and culture.

Families provide all children with their earliest experiences of relating to other human beings; the nature of those early experiences will impact forever on the personality and behaviour of the child. The influence can be positive or negative: children can be made to feel safe, strong, resilient and confident or they can be made to feel worthless, frightened, insecure and angry. Much of the way adults relate to others can be traced to early experiences with their family.

Most children remain within their families throughout childhood and adolescence, and increasingly into adulthood; currently 58 per cent of men and 39 per cent of women aged between 20 and 24 live at home with parents (Office of National Statistics, Spring 2006).

Your role in supporting families includes working with both the adults and the children – but never forget that the purpose of supporting the family is to improve the outcomes for the children. The children are at the centre of everything you do.

In this unit you will find 'Active knowledge' features containing activities that will contribute to assessment for your NVQ. Remember that these features only offer the opportunity for partial assessment; you can also refer to the evidence opportunities grid (see pages 357–375) for more ideas to provide suitable evidence for your NVQ.

What you need to learn

- Changing families
- Family relationships
- Gathering information
- Sharing information
- Cultural backgrounds
- Knowing the purpose
- Assessments
- What families need
- Planning the outcomes
- Putting it into practice
- Making changes
- Supporting parents

HSC 319a Prepare to visit families in their own home

Changing families

(KS 16, 17, 24, 26, 27, 33)

Ask someone what they think of as a 'traditional family' and the answer is likely to be different depending on the culture in which the person has been brought up. For some people, a traditional family is a father, a mother and two or three children, but for others it is a multi-generational family with grandparents and other relatives as a part of the family unit.

In 2004, eight out of ten people in the UK lived in a 'traditional family' household, but this type of household is becoming less common. Since the 1950s and 1960s, there has been a huge change in the way people look at marriage and children. Far fewer marriages are taking place now and many more children are born outside marriage. This, coupled with a divorce rate of almost one in two marriages, means that far more children are being brought up by a lone parent. The increasing divorce rate also means that some children are more likely to experience family disruption than would have been the case in the past.

The figures (ESRC 2004) over the 136 years from 1870 to 2006 show dramatic changes:

In 1870 – women had, on average, between 4 and 5 children.

In 2006 – women had, on average, between 1 and 2 children.

The number of babies women have has more than halved.

In 1870 – the average life expectancy was about 42 years for a woman and about 40 for a man.

In 2006 – the average life expectancy for a woman was 81 years and for a man between 76 and 77 years.

Life expectancy has doubled.

Projections for the next 20 years show that households with just one person are set to rise, married couples are set to fall and cohabiting couples will rise.

This is an obvious result of the increase in divorce rates, so more people will live alone. Also, women's increasing life expectancy means that older women are more likely to be widowed and living alone.

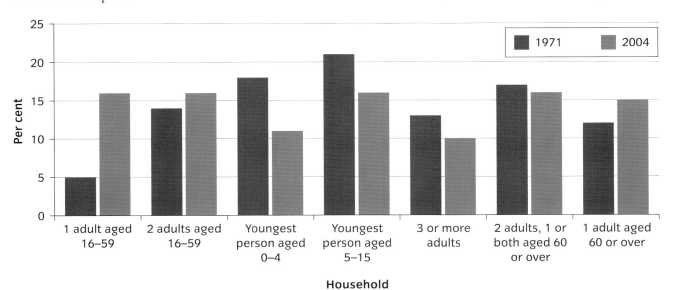

How household types have changed in Great Britain between 1971 and 2004 (source: ESRC statistics)

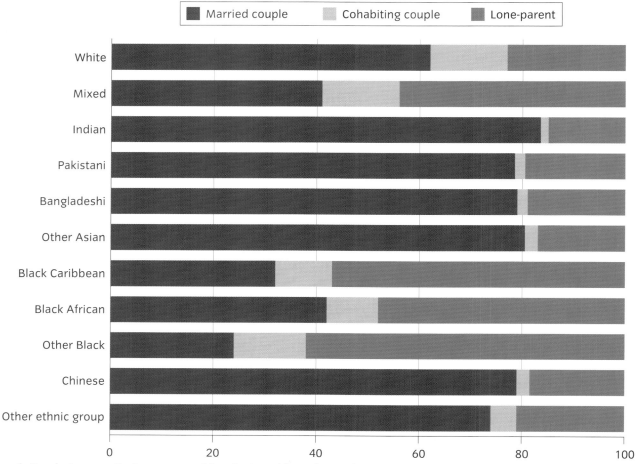

The relation between ethnic group and family type (data drawn from the 2001 Census)

Look at the graph on the previous page. Essentially, what you can see is that families have become smaller, and more people are living alone; there are fewer children in families; and there is a greater likelihood of children being brought up by a lone parent. This does vary in different cultures, as the table above shows.

The table above, prepared by ESRC, shows a much smaller number of Asian lone parents, and a very small number of Asian cohabiting couples when compared with white or black Caribbean families. Cultural influences in favour of marriage are clearly evidenced in these statistics.

Different types of family structure

Not all families are structured in the same way, and the very significant changes that have taken place over the last century have resulted in a wide range of different family types. It is less easy now to describe a 'normal family' as there are so many possible ways that people live together as a unit, so 'normal' has to mean whatever is normal for a particular child or young person. As recently as the early part of the last century, family structures were very different from how they are now. Less than 100 years ago, the most common family structure was an **extended family**, with mother, father, grandparents, aunts and uncles living close to one another, if not in the same house. Children would move between different members of the family regularly and would be equally at home being cared for by a range of relations. Fifty years ago, for a UK family, the most common family structure was a **nuclear family**, with mother, father and children living in the same house but not necessarily living close to other members of their family. While both nuclear and extended families are still quite common, there is now a much wider range of family structures and, as a result, a wider range of relationships and patterns of communication within families.

The following are examples of family structures:

These are the basic types of family	Features
Extended family	Parents, grandparents, aunts, uncles, sisters, brothers, children, nieces, nephews living together or in close proximity. All family members take part in bringing up children.
Nuclear family	Two parents and children living together. May or may not have close contact with other members of the family but less likely than in an extended family. Other family members do not have a significant role in bringing up the children.
Lone parent family	One parent bringing up children without a partner.

Within the main types, families can be:

Reconstituted family	Parents both with children from previous relationships. These can be either an extended or a nuclear family, but are more likely to be a nuclear family.
Step-parent family	Families where one parent has children from a previous relationship and the other takes a step-parenting role – again, these are most likely to be a nuclear family.
Cohabiting family	Unmarried partners who may also come into any of the categories above.
Same sex family	Same sex partners with or without children.
Communal family	Children may live with their parents in communes where other members of the commune, not family members, are also involved in the childcare.
Nomadic family	No permanent place of residence and move frequently, such as travellers or Romany families.

There are many ways to be a family

Effects of different family structures

There is limited research about the difference in outcomes for children living in extended families and those in nuclear families. Research carried out with Korean families by the Thomas Coram Foundation in 1998 found that there was a lower score for challenging behaviour among children from extended families than children from nuclear families. Research from Columbia University and University College London in 2004 found that children in Bangladesh had better educational outcomes when they lived in a family with a resident grandmother. Extended families (in the sense used in the table on page 287) are not the same as extended family networks, where families may not live together, but they have close and regular contact. Many nuclear and lone parent families have very close links into extended family networks. Such links can be a vital means of both practical and emotional support for many families.

Research does, however, show that lone parent families result in negative effects on outcomes for children, although this is affected by other factors such as poverty, conflict before separation and continuing conflict. Research conducted by the Joseph Rowntree Foundation concluded that children from lone parent families:

- tend to grow up in households with lower incomes, poorer housing and greater financial hardship than intact families (especially those headed by lone mothers)
- tend to achieve less in socio-economic terms when they become adults than children from intact families

- are at increased risk of behavioural problems, including bed wetting, withdrawn behaviour, aggression, delinquency and other antisocial behaviour
- tend to perform less well in school and gain fewer educational qualifications;
- are more likely to be admitted to hospital following accidents, to have more reported health problems and to visit their family doctor
- are more likely to leave school and home when young and more likely at an early age to: become sexually active; form a cohabiting partnership; become pregnant; become a parent; give birth outside marriage
- tend to report more depressive symptoms and higher levels of smoking, drinking and other drug use during adolescence and adulthood.

Source: 'Divorce and separation: the outcomes for children', Joseph Rowntree Foundation, 1998

Legal basis

(KS 1, 2, 4, 9, 10)

The Human Rights Act 1998 contains two articles relating to families: Article 8 gives people the right to have respect for private and family life; and Article 12 gives everyone the right to marry and found a family. Although these are the basic human rights of everyone, there are other pieces of legislation that define how families work, how any split of families should be dealt with, and how families must behave in relation to children.

The Family Law Act 1996 relates to arrangements for marriage and divorce, and the concept of parental responsibility (rather than the previous parental rights) is introduced in the Children Act 1989. Parental responsibility (PR) describes the legal relationship between parents – and in certain circumstances other adults – and their child or children (PR normally lasts until the child is 18). It is not clearly defined in the Children Act, apart from a general duty to care and protect the child/children and contains no requirement to promote the child's welfare or to consult the child in decision making. It does give parents the ability to make decisions about the child's welfare such as: medical treatment, health care, where the child will live and education.

The way adults exercise their PR should reflect the developing capacities and age and maturity of the child, and they should increasingly consult and include the child in decision making. This is not always the case and can be the cause of tension and difficulties between parents and children. There is a range of laws that give children rights at different ages, as discussed in Unit 310. In practice, young people at 16 are relatively independent.

Parental responsibility is automatically given to both parents if they are married when a child is born. The situation is different where parents are unmarried. Parental responsibility is given to the mother but unmarried fathers can acquire parental responsibility for their children in several different ways, depending on when their children were born.

For children born before 1 December 2003, unmarried fathers can get parental responsibility by:

- marrying the mother of their child or by obtaining a parental responsibility order from the court
- registering a parental responsibility agreement with the court or by an application to court.

For children born after 1 December 2003, the situation is different. Unmarried fathers can get parental responsibility by:

- registering the child's birth jointly with the mother at the time of birth – this is now quite common and many parents choose to do this
- re-registering the birth if they are the natural father
- marrying the mother of their child or obtaining a parental responsibility order from the court
- registering with the court for parental responsibility.

Family relationships

(KS 18, 24, 30)

Family relationships are usually those that influence people most. For most children the type of relationships they have within the family where they grow up influences the rest of their lives and the kind of people they become. Primarily it is the relationship with their parents or main carers that is the most influential during childhood. For a growing child, relationships with parents and other extended family members, such as grandparents and siblings, provide the emotional security that is important in establishing a positive self-image and in developing confidence. As children grow through adolescence and into early adulthood, family relationships become less dominant as an influence; however, they remain significant for most people throughout their lives. It is notable that most major occasions in people's lives, such as weddings, christenings, and 'coming of age' birthdays, are regarded as 'family occasions', when members of the immediate and extended family are usually involved and invited to join the celebrations.

As family life has changed, so have the roles and relationships within families. As a result, the way in which people understand relationships and the way in which they view themselves has changed. Working patterns in families have changed considerably and the roles are now less clear-cut. At one time, the work force was largely male, and mainly undertaking physical labour, although not exclusively. Traditionally, women had the roles of caring for children and running a household. The decline of manufacturing and heavy industry meant the decline of manual work, once the traditional occupation of men. Technology and service industries have grown and there are now more women in employment, many of them in high-tech and service industries. This is true even in UK families from cultures where women, traditionally, do not work outside the home.

One of the consequences of increased career opportunities for women has been a change in the patterns of childcare, with many women choosing to start their families at a later stage in their lives and more children being cared for by professional carers rather than a parent. Children now are less likely to have regular contact with members of their extended family than children 50 or 100 years ago.

All of these factors contribute to how children learn to form relationships and the way in which they relate to others. For example, children who have only experienced relationships with their own parents, their parents' friends and other children may have no idea how to relate to older people. Children who have had the experience of growing up in a family where there is regular contact with family members of different generations will feel much more comfortable in relating to people across a wide age range.

Reflect

Think about a family you know well; it could be your own. Look at the family structure and list the relationships and work roles within it. Talk to family members about what sort of relationships and work roles were evident in the family 50 years ago. Go back even further if you can find someone to talk to. Compare the difference in relationships and work roles now and 50 years ago. Consider how the family structure and roles in your own family have influenced the way you practice. Do you have certain expectations of the roles people adopt? Do you have expectations about family values and how people are respected and treated within a family? Do you sometimes find this influencing your response to particular families? Be honest and consider what it is that influences you. It will make it easier to develop and improve your practice.

Gathering information

(KS 7)

In making preparation to visit a family, it is vital that you research and gather together all the information you may need. This will include:

- the initial and core assessments that have been undertaken with the family or the children

- health information
- criminal justice system information
- information about substance or alcohol abuse.

Two very useful documents that may have been completed during the assessment process are a **genogram** and an **ecomap**. The genogram identifies the relationships in the family over three generations and an ecomap identifies the networks and contacts that are important.

Key terms

Genogram: A diagram that uses symbols and lines to show the relationships in a family over three generations, giving a visual overview of the family as a whole.

Ecomap: A diagram that uses lines to show what the different relationships in a family are like: weak, strong, stressful, etc.

A genogram uses symbols and lines to identify individuals and relationships. The resulting diagram gives a visual view of the family and the current and previous relationships within it.

The ecomap gives a different focus by showing the nature of each of the important relationships. Different types of lines show relationships that are strong, weak or stressful. If either or both of these tools are included in an assessment, they will give you a very useful insight into how the family works.

These charts are useful tools, but not all assessments will have them. You may find that there is other information that is incomplete, or does not give you as much background as you would like before visiting a family. It is important to check through any records, assessments and information that are available so that you are well prepared for a visit.

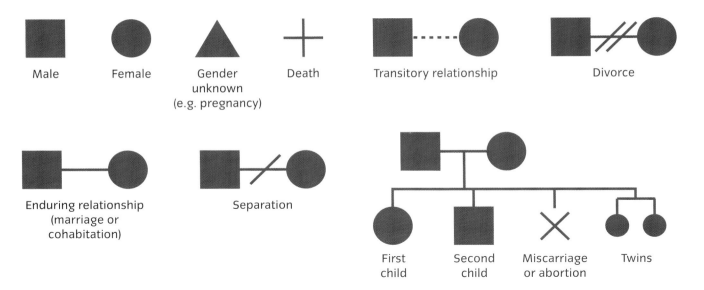

Some of the main symbols used in a genogram

Here is a checklist of the information that is useful.

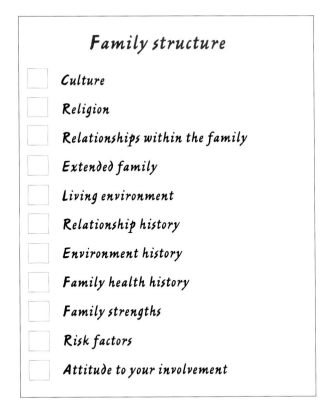

Family structure

- [ ] *Culture*
- [ ] *Religion*
- [ ] *Relationships within the family*
- [ ] *Extended family*
- [ ] *Living environment*
- [ ] *Relationship history*
- [ ] *Environment history*
- [ ] *Family health history*
- [ ] *Family strengths*
- [ ] *Risk factors*
- [ ] *Attitude to your involvement*

It is unlikely that you will be able to find out all of this information in advance, but try to gather as much of it as you can.

Sharing information

(KS 1, 2, 3, 4, 5, 8, 10, 11, 12, 15, 16, 20, 22, 31)

Colleagues and other professionals working with the family are an invaluable source of information, provided that the family have agreed for them to share information with you. Sharing information is one of the Common Core of skills and competences that all those who work with children should develop. The guidelines about sharing information are clear, but many people are still concerned about exactly what information they can, or should, share. There are two main areas of concern for professionals:

- professional confidentiality
- data protection.

Professional confidentiality

Information that:

- is of a sensitive nature,
- is not already in the public domain,
- is not readily available should people choose to look for it
- has been shared in a situation where it was clear that it would remain confidential

can be regarded as 'confidential information'.

- Place child or couple or family in central circle.
- Identify important people or organisations and draw circles as needed.
- Draw lines between circles where connections exist.
- Use different types of lines to indicate the nature of the link or relationship.

——————— = strong   – – – – – – = weak   · · · · · · · = stressful

An ecomap shows the nature of different relationships within a family

For example, you may have been told by Jamie that his dad is in prison for burglary, but this was reported in the local press so is not considered confidential.

Even where information is confidential, you can still share it if the person concerned agrees, or if they gave it to you knowing that it would be shared with a specified group of people. For example, you may be given information when you are talking to someone to find out information for a review meeting; they know that the information is to be used for a review meeting, so their consent to sharing it with the meeting can be assumed.

Gaining agreement to share information is always the best option, but you can still break a confidence even after consent is refused if it is in the interests of the public to do so. Judging public interest is always difficult and there are no absolutes, but the following may be the sort of factors that would influence a decision to break confidence:

- there is evidence that a child is suffering, or is at risk of serious harm
- there is reasonable cause to believe that a child is suffering, or is at risk of suffering significant harm
- to prevent significant or serious harm to children, young people or adults
- to assist in the prevention, detection or prosecution of serious crime.

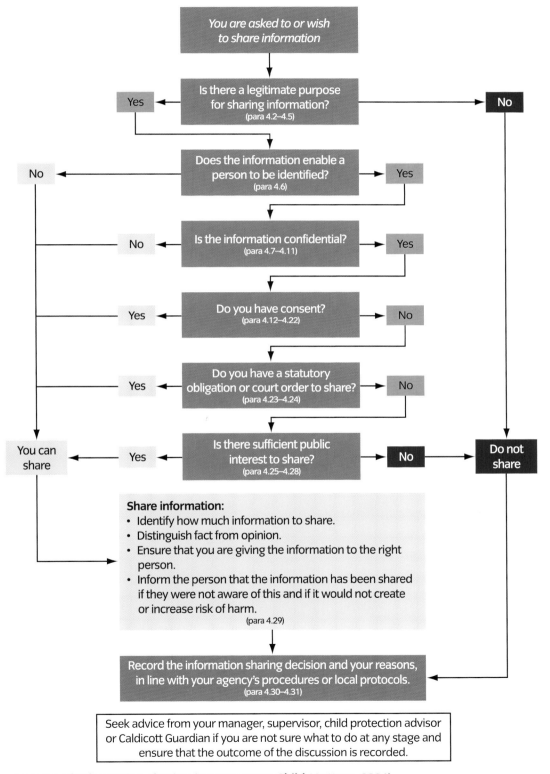

The principles of information sharing (source: Every Child Matters, 2006)

Nothing can ever be prescriptive in situations like these and, ultimately, it will come down to making a professional judgement by weighing the impact of sharing the information against the consequences of not sharing it.

Data protection

The Data Protection Act 1998 is often given as a reason why information cannot be shared. However, the Act does identify what can and cannot be shared and under what circumstances. There are basic requirements under the Act (see page 42) about processing and handling information. The key concerns likely to arise when you are looking to share information about a family are as follows.

- *Does the information enable an individual to be identified?* If so, then Schedule 2 of the Act means that you can only share it if: consent has been given; it is necessary to protect the interests of the person concerned; it is in response to a court order, or a legal or statutory function; or it is in the legitimate interests of the organisation holding the data or the third party with whom it is being shared.
- *Is the information sensitive?* If so, Schedule 3 of the Act sets out similar grounds to those in Schedule 2 about giving consent, but adds that consent

cannot be unreasonably withheld. It also allows sharing if seeking consent would preclude the prevention of a crime or it is necessary for medical purposes and is undertaken by a health professional.

The flow chart on the next page is a useful guide to applying the Data Protection Act.

Active knowledge

Explain your organisation's interpretation of the Data Protection Act and the extent to which you can share information with colleagues. It might be interesting to compare this with other organisations and try to draw some conclusions about how consistent the approach is in your local area.

Remember

Health warning! There is a balance to be maintained between finding out as much background as possible so that you are well prepared, and going into a family with your judgements already made. You may need to have some initial expectations, but do not make premature decisions or judgements before you have tested out the information for yourself.

My story

Hi, I'm Jackie and I'm a family support worker. I work for a project called Crisis Call, and we provide a sort of 'flying squad' to go in to families in crisis to try to support them through the crisis and avoid children having to come into care. We got a call one evening to go a family with three children under 10 years old where Mum, Hayley, had been taken into hospital with suspected Hepatitis C. We checked the records and there were some initial assessments, mainly referrals from the police where they had arrested Hayley for prostitution. The children were usually looked after by a neighbour's 15-year-old daughter when Hayley was out, but this was not appropriate if Hayley was to be in hospital for some time. Previous assessments had expressed concern about Hayley's lifestyle, but the school had not had any worries about the children.

I expected to go into a chaotic household and was surprised when I arrived to find this neat, clean house. A neighbour answered the door and two of the children were still up, although in spotless pyjamas, and were a bit shy, but chatted away once I had been there for a while.

I got to know Hayley and the children over the next few weeks and realised that she was doing a great job of being a parent: the children were well fed and cared for, they were also polite and well behaved. I don't think I have ever seen such a warm and loving relationship between a mum and her children. Hayley was quite honest: she works as a prostitute because of the money she can earn. The downsides are the risks she has taken, like contracting Hep C, and so the long-term prospects for her health and the care of the children are not good. However, it was my lesson in making judgements before I've seen something for myself.

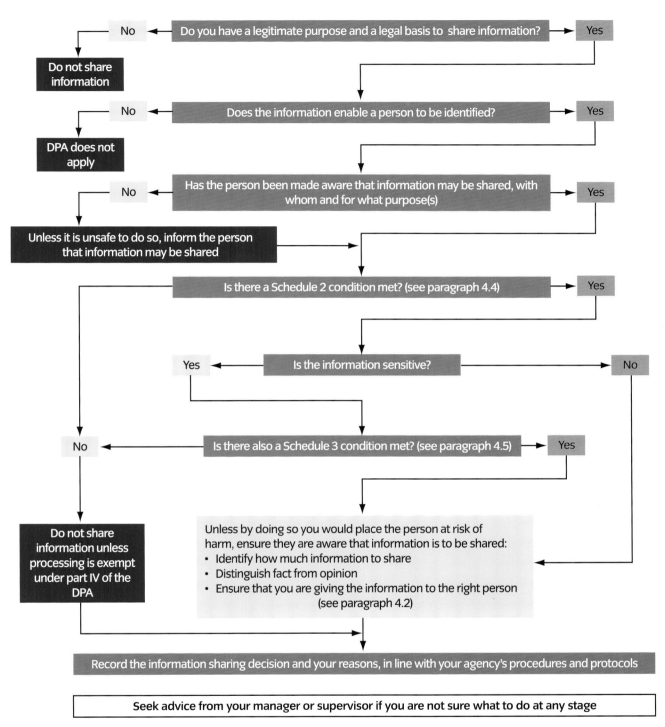

No ← **Do you have a legitimate purpose and a legal basis to share information?** → Yes

Do not share information

No ← **Does the information enable a person to be identified?** → Yes

DPA does not apply

No ← **Has the person been made aware that information may be shared, with whom and for what purpose(s)** → Yes

Unless it is unsafe to do so, inform the person that information may be shared

Is there a Schedule 2 condition met? (see paragraph 4.4) → Yes

Yes ← **Is the information sensitive?** → No

No ← **Is there also a Schedule 3 condition met? (see paragraph 4.5)** → Yes

Do not share information unless processing is exempt under part IV of the DPA

Unless by doing so you would place the person at risk of harm, ensure they are aware that information is to be shared:
- Identify how much information to share
- Distinguish fact from opinion
- Ensure that you are giving the information to the right person (see paragraph 4.2)

Record the information sharing decision and your reasons, in line with your agency's procedures and protocols

Seek advice from your manager or supervisor if you are not sure what to do at any stage

A guide to applying the Data Protection Act 1998

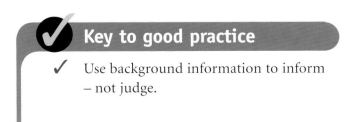

Key to good practice

✓ Use background information to inform – not judge.

Cultural backgrounds

(KS 7)

The way that families work can be strongly influenced by culture and religion. The relationships and loyalties can be very powerful and there may be clear views about the friendships and social activities for some family members, and expectations about when family members will be at home, acceptable forms of dress and behaviour. Preparation and serving of food can also be of major importance in some cultures. Children and young people may be expected to conform to certain ways of behaving and some social activities may not be acceptable. A key factor in good practice is that you become familiar with the cultural norms of the family you are going to work with. This supports your understanding of issues within the family and should help to ensure that you do not alienate the family or propose courses of action that would be considered inappropriate.

However well your organisation plans its work, you may still find yourself working to support a family from a culture and background you know nothing about. If so, it is your job to find out. The responsibility is yours, and it is a key part of preparation.

Knowing the purpose

(KS 3, 4, 7, 8, 23, 25, 29, 31, 36)

A key part of preparation is knowing what you are being asked to do in supporting a family. You could be going in to support the family in practical ways to help them develop a more ordered lifestyle; you may be going in to support parenting or to work with the family towards agreed outcomes for relationship or behaviour issues; or your input could be part of a wider plan, perhaps to safeguard a child at risk or support a young carer or family carers for a disabled child.

Regardless of the reasons, you need to be very clear about the purpose of your involvement and what you are trying to achieve; otherwise, you will not be able to plan your work effectively nor will you be able to review whether or not you have achieved what you set out to do. This is not to say that you will simply steamroller ahead with your own plans regardless of the wishes of the family! You may find that plans and outcomes will change once you discuss them with the family, but as part of your initial preparation you need to be clear about what you are going to do.

Letting the family know

Sometimes your involvement may be as the result of an emergency or a crisis and so you will not have time to contact the family in advance to let them know about your visit. Most of the time your intervention will be planned and is likely to be expected by the family. You need to make sure that you let the family know:

- who you are – your name, job role/title and organisation
- when you will be there – the day and time
- who you will need to see
- any information you would like them to have available – such as care plans, school records, etc.
- a brief outline of what your visit is for: if this is for general support with parenting and family management, you may want to make it clear that everything will be done in partnership with the family; if it has already been agreed, then a quick recap is helpful.

The way you communicate this should be the way the family have told you they prefer. Ensure that the means of communication is right for the family's level of language and literacy, if you are writing. Some people will prefer the telephone to written communication or text or e-mail. You should comply with these choices as far as possible.

Your communication could be like this one.

Support worker

Address & Telephone

Date

Dear Mrs Johnson,

My name is Chris Jones. I am a support worker and this is just to let you know that I will be starting to work with you and the family next week. My first visit will be on Wednesday 22nd. I will arrive at 9.30am and will be there for about two hours on this first visit. I would like to be able to talk to you and your husband on this visit, and to see Shane's school record file.

During this visit we can talk about exactly what we need to do, and then I will start working with you the following day.

If you need to get in touch with me, my phone number is at the top of the letter. You can always leave a message if I am not in.

Or you could have a phone conversation, like this one.

'Hello, Mrs Morrison?

Kathy Williams, family support worker. You remember it was arranged at the review last week?

OK, I'd like to come round next Wednesday – that's the 22nd – if that's OK. Everything will start exactly as we planned at the review. I will start work on the exercise programme with Jenny and we will do a two-hour session, then I'll show you how to play those games with her on the new computer. I need you to have her care plan there so I can look at what happened before.

If you want your Mum there, because I know she helps a lot with Jenny, that's fine. If you need to get hold of me before then, I'm on 734 6287. Any questions?

Great. See you Wednesday.'

If you need help to communicate effectively with the family through an interpreter or using specialist equipment, follow your organisation's procedures for arranging this.

Test yourself

1 Identify at least three different types of family structure.

2 How does the structure of a family affect the relationships?

3 What are your likely sources of information about a family?

4 Under what circumstances can you share information you have been given in confidence?

5 What are the key questions you need to ask about information you hold to ensure that you comply with the Data Protection Act?

HSC 319b Liaise with families and others to identify and support the families' needs

The most important people to tell you about a family are the family members themselves. No matter what information you have had from other sources, you need to talk to the family to find out just what support is needed and how they have worked that out.

Assessments

(KS 3, 8, 13, 14, 19, 21, 23, 25, 34, 35)

Assessments may have been carried out and you may have been involved in them. There are a range of tools and assessment methods for assessing families and identifying needs; your organisation will have an approach to assessment that you will use. If you work for a private, voluntary or independent sector organisation, you may be starting to work with a family who have already had their needs assessed as part of the process of assessing a child in need.

Some of the most commonly used assessment tools are:

- *Family pack of scales and questionnaires.* This contains a whole series of questionnaires and marking scales. It enables parents to participate in identifying the needs of the family as well as the needs of the child or young person. The questionnaires cover aspects such as: Family Activity, Parenting Daily Hassles, Recent Life Events, Home Conditions, and several others. Most of the questionnaires are designed to be completed by parents and are a useful way of gathering evidence about what families' needs are. They work because the process of completing a questionnaire, and subsequent discussion with a childcare professional trained to use them, helps to identify the existence and extent of issues and areas of difficulty for both the family and the professional.
- The *HOME (Home Observation for Measurement of the Environment) Inventory.* This is essentially about observation and an interview, and looks at the whole of the family environment. The inventory has a number of scales, and it scores different aspects of the environment, family activity and parenting.
- The *Family Assessment* uses a model of family functioning to look at the strengths of a family as well as the areas of difficulty. A wide range of aspects of a family is included in the model such as:
  - how the family adapt to problems and stress
  - how they resolve conflicts
  - how decisions are made
  - how parents promote development
  - the strength and nature of the bonds and attachments
  - how effectively children are guided and managed
  - how the family connects across generations
  - how the family communicates.

There are other models that assess the resilience of families by looking at how they respond to stresses and problems. These define resilient families as those who are able to continue to function through stressful and difficult events and emerge stronger from the experience.

Active knowledge

Look at the models of family assessment used in your organisation. Are assessments carried out using tools and models, or are they done using professional judgement? Are assessments only carried out by professionals who have been given special training to use the tools, or can anyone do it? Research other models of assessment and see how they compare to the approach used in your organisation.

Evidence-based assessment

The move to using assessment models and tools, rather than the professional judgement used in the past, is to ensure that assessments are evidence-based, in other words, a judgement is backed up by the facts. You should encourage and support families to do this for themselves. Often families will feel that they have failed and will have little confidence in their own ability; working alongside them to identify positive aspects of parenting and family life and backing those up with evidence and clear examples will provide a positive base to work with the family.

It is the difference between:

'I just don't know what to do with him. He just seems to do what he likes and never listens to me. I'm hopeless at getting him to do anything. I just end up shouting at him.'

'Yes, I can see how difficult that is for you, but we will be able to work with you to try to improve how you manage Darren's behaviour.'

and

'I just don't know what to do with him. He just seems to do what he likes and never listens to me. I'm hopeless at getting him to do anything. I just end up shouting at him.'

'I don't know. I heard you two laughing away in here yesterday – what was that about?'

'Oh, that was just over something daft on the telly. Most people wouldn't think it was funny – we've just got a twisted sense of humour.'

'I think that's really important. If you and Darren can laugh together, then that means that you share a way of looking at the world. That's a huge connection that lots of parents and children don't have.'

'Don't they? So there's some worse parents than me then? I'd never thought about that. I suppose we do see the same things as funny. Maybe I should try to get him to laugh more – we might fight less.'

'Absolutely. It's difficult to fight while you're laughing. You could try switching on the funny programmes when he's in, or saving up funny things that have happened in the day and tell him about them.'

The second response recognises a strength and positive aspect of the relationship with her son and

---

Ethical issue

You are visiting a family with three children. The living environment is chaotic, dirty and untidy. It is certainly unhygienic, and is probably dangerous: there are broken and boarded up windows, the floors and chairs are dirty, the stair carpet is lethal and the lino is ripped. There are cupboard doors hanging off in the kitchen and rubbish spilling out of the bin most of the time. The bedrooms do have beds and bedding, but this only gets changed very infrequently. The children are grubby, have dirty hair and rarely wear clean clothes. You are concerned that the children are at risk of injury or illness because of the poor conditions. However, regardless of the state of the house, the evidence is that the children are happy, well adjusted and healthy: they always greet you excitedly and happily when you visit, they show you the things they have made with Mum; they have had all their immunisations and are never ill. School has no concerns apart from the fact that the children are grubby and often smelly; their behaviour and educational achievements are fine. Mum is adamant that this is how she lives. She says she would rather spend time with the children than cleaning the floor. She will not agree to change her lifestyle and is quite amused by your offers of support and help in managing her house: she has politely refused to even consider it. You are worried about the welfare of the children and believe that they will be at risk in that house. What should you do?

---

looks for ways to build on it; it identifies a concrete example that the mum can look at and recognise. The message is: 'You're a good mum – you've got strong links with your son. Go for more of the same!' The first response, on the other hand, although professionally reassuring, takes away all the power and control and gives the message: 'Yes – you are right, you have messed this up. But it's OK – we'll fix it.'

What families need

(KS 3, 23, 31)

Families should have been a part of any assessment process and may have had the opportunity to decide the sort of support they need. If an assessment has been effectively carried out it should have helped the family to think through how they can make the best use of any available help. It is not always the case that families have had this opportunity and you may need to spend some time working with the family to agree the sort of support they need.

Planning the outcomes

(KS 3, 6, 8, 19, 21, 25, 28)

Outcomes are what the family wants to achieve – the end result – but are also the 'big picture'. Thinking about ways to identify and achieve outcomes is a very positive way to look at how to support a family. Think of it like creating a painting – you decide what the painting is to be about, but you have to assemble all the paints, brushes, canvas and any other resources necessary to complete the painting, then carry out the actual painting – and all the way through the process you will know the picture you are aiming to produce.

Looking at needs is about looking at what is missing. This is known as a deficit model: in other words, looking at what the family does *not* have. Deficits can be in physical or material requirements or they can be in personal or emotional capacity.

My story

Hi, I am Alanya and I came to the UK as an asylum seeker five years ago. My two children were very young then. My husband had been killed in the fighting and some friends got me out. We have done OK here, but Gregor, my eldest son, has been having problems at school. There has been a lot of bullying with other children saying that we are scum and we are illegal immigrants and telling him he smells and that they can't understand what he says. This is rubbish because he sounds exactly the same as them: I have an accent but the children don't. I know how cruel children can be – I was a teacher back home, but of course, all that stopped when the war came. Anyway, he got beaten up a couple of times and then refused to go to school. He started kicking and screaming every morning if I tried to get him to go. I could teach him at home of course, but it couldn't go on, I knew that something had to be done. I went along to the assessment meeting at the school; there were a lot of people there – about five or six of them, just to try to help us. It made me feel as though I was not alone and I felt stronger. I was asked to say what I wanted to happen. I thought that they would have all decided and I was just there to listen, but they wanted to know what I thought and what I wanted. I asked for help to get Gregor to school and for something to be done about the bullies. Now Mike comes every morning and he works with Gregor. At first he went to school with him, but now he just goes to the gate. He has these older children called 'buddies' now at school and they look out for him. He said that the school have been doing lots of stuff in lessons and assembly about all sorts of different people from all over the world. Gregor said that one of the ones who had been bullying him had to do a project on our country and came to him to ask him stuff and said to him that it was really interesting. They seem to be quite friendly now.

It is always disheartening to look at what is wrong and much more comfortable to look at what is right. Concentrating on the outcome is the positive way to get families to look at how you can support them. Look at what they want to achieve, look at what resources, personal or practical, they already have, then look at what has to be provided to fill the gaps.

Think of the outcomes for children that you work towards for all children; they are 'big' outcomes: 'Be healthy', 'Stay safe' and so on. So the aim of a family may be:

'Be a happy family' or

'All get on together' or

'All achieve as much as we can'.

The overall outcome they want is the dream or vision – it is the 'big picture' – but in order to achieve it, there will be outcomes or goals along the way. Working out how to reach the outcome the family wants is the important planning part, because outcomes do not get achieved by wishing for them. They require planning and determination. For example:

All achieve as much as we can

This could be the overall outcome for a family with a disabled child or a child who is terminally ill. The outcome involves all members of the family, not just the disabled child, in achieving their maximum potential. You could plan to achieve this through a series of goals or outcomes along the way. Of course, plans will depend on circumstances, but a plan for 10-year-old Annie's family may look like the table below. Annie has Down's Syndrome.

Overall Outcome: To all achieve the best we can	Annie	Margaret	Brian
Outcome 1	Be able to know more	Feel that Annie has a future	Feel more confident to help Annie
Goals	Learn how to use the internet (and MSN)	Support Annie on the computer and see her make progress	Go into school with Annie and learn from the staff

Plan for Annie and her family

The key to making this work is that the family have sat down together and worked out what they want. You know that Annie and her parents have decided that they want to promote Annie's achievement in the first instance through building on her interest in computers. This may need additional resources for a tutor or even some support towards a computer for Annie to have at home. You will need to support the family by finding ways to access the resources necessary for this. Annie's parents could look at asking for direct payments of Annie's assessed budget, then they can choose how they spend the money. Alternatively you may be able to find a local project providing recycled computers, or offering computer tuition at reduced rates. You need to make the best possible use of whatever resources you can find to support Annie and her family.

Different resources

Sometimes the resources may not be as simple as a computer. A family may be looking for expensive equipment, or another service may provide what they need. For example, if one of the issues the family has is with one of the children who is on the edge of criminal activity, you may need to discuss and explore the possibility of getting him or her into a programme run by a specialist team. You will need to liaise with colleagues and possibly your manager or the budget-holding lead professional in order to secure the resources the family needs.

It would be wonderful if you were always able to get all the resources for everyone you work with. However, this is not reality and there will be times when you will need to negotiate with both the family and other colleagues to reach an agreement on exactly what can be provided. Even if it is not perfect and compromises have been made, you should have been able to move the process forward and improved outcomes to some extent.

Test yourself

1 What are some of the different ways families can be assessed?

2 Why are outcomes important?

3 How does looking at outcomes differ from looking at needs?

4 How may families consider getting the resources they need?

HSC 319c Support individuals and the family to function more effectively as a family unit

How families function is of massive significance to the outcomes and life chances of children and young people.

Ideally, a family should:

- provide a child with a safe, secure and nurturing place in which to grow and develop
- make sure that children like themselves
- provide children with models of acceptable behaviour and how to relate to others
- provide children with confidence and belief in their own abilities
- provide children with a desire to explore and learn about the world around them
- provide children with love and a caring environment
- be able to overcome difficulties and problems by working together
- be able to use support networks in times of stress
- be able to offer support and help to others.

That may look like a long list, and you can probably add to it, but families need to be able to provide almost everything a child needs as the foundation to grow into a happy and fulfilled adult.

These are some of the outcomes that families you work with may want to achieve. In order to do all of this, families need to have the strong relationships you looked at in the first element. When relationships within families are not so strong or circumstances are very difficult and stressful, the impact can be seen in the development of the children.

Putting it into practice

(KS 26)

This is where all the assessment and planning begins to deliver support towards the outcomes. Depending on the circumstances of the family, you will have worked out what needs to be done to build on their current strengths and achieve the outcomes they want.

You will be involved because there is a child in need, but it could be for a wide range of reasons:

- there is a child on the edge of care
- there is a disabled child and the family needs support
- there is a young person caring for a disabled relative
- there is a child at risk of harm
- there is a history of abusive behaviour in the family
- the family is chaotic and struggling to cope on a practical level
- there is a child on the edge of or involved in criminal or anti-social activity
- there are relationship difficulties within the family.

Making changes

(KS 8, 13, 21, 23, 25, 35, 38)

As part of your planning to achieve agreed outcomes you will have worked with the family to identify any areas where changes need to be made if the family is to be able to move forward on reaching their goals.

Making changes is never easy but if, for example, one of the outcomes for a particular family was to improve relationships – 'to all get on better'– one of the first steps may be to get people to share with each other where the problems lie. You will need to use all your communication skills to make sure that family members are able to share feelings in an open and honest way. Before this can happen, there have to be 'ground rules' so that everyone knows what is happening. The rules can be very simple, but they are important. You may have something like: no one can interrupt anyone else – you must wait until they have finished; no one can become aggressive or abusive; no physical violence; people must say what they feel honestly; no one is allowed to storm off – if you are upset and angry, there is no problem with crying but you have to stay put.

During this type of discussion session you could find this sort of exchange.

'Do you want to start, Liz? Tell us why you were so angry yesterday.'

'I just feel so put down when Mick speaks to me in that way as if I'm stupid, and just never listens like I have anything worth saying.'

'Are you surprised Liz felt that way, Mick?'

'Stupid she is, always dramatic – I didn't put her down; she just doesn't know anything about football, so what's the point in making a comment?'

'See what I mean? I told you there was no point in this. I'm not even allowed to have feelings without being told I'm dramatic.'

'Mick – can you see why Liz is angry?'

'Suppose so – a bit – but why's it always my fault? I'm always the bad guy.'

Is that how you feel – that you always get the blame?

'Always – she tells the kids everything's my fault and then they turn against me. Paul wouldn't come to the football with me on Saturday because she told him I'd shouted at her and then he was p***** off with me. That really upset me.'

'Liz, how do you feel hearing Mick say that?'

'A bit shocked really. I suppose I do that a bit – but I didn't think he was bothered anyway.'

You can see the possibility of some progress emerging over a period of time when you look over this extract. These kinds of sessions can involve children and young people and can prove very useful. You should only undertake this kind of work if it has been agreed with the rest of the team working with the child or young person, or with your line manager. You also need to be confident that you have had the necessary training to facilitate this sort of family exchange.

A family may need you to work with them to improve practical skills such as domestic management, budgets, cooking and shopping. This is a large task and may need people to make big changes in the way they live. All members of the family will need to participate; the children and young people should all take a share in any new routines and new responsibilities. Household budgeting of the sort you looked at in Unit 310 is an important skill. Very often, families struggle financially because they are living in poverty and because they are not able to organise what little money they do have. Some support in showing parents how to do a household budget and supporting them to stick to it for a while can make a big difference.

Learning about how to prepare and eat healthy meals can involve the whole family in making changes. The balanced diet discussed in Unit 310 is equally applicable here, and making changes in shopping habits to buy fresh ingredients may need your support for some time.

Although the main focus of your work here is practical, there will inevitably be emotional issues raised by these kind of changes, and these will need to be talked through as a family. It is important that the family works together to deal with practical challenges because each experience of dealing with something difficult, or even just surviving it, makes the family stronger.

Many families who need support have only ever experienced failures: situations that went wrong, relationships that failed, plans that never came to anything and a history of giving up when things get difficult or challenging. Hardly surprising then that when things get tough, the answer is to walk away, thus adding to the vicious downward spiral that means they do not have any positive experiences to call on to help them through difficult times.

It is for this reason that reinforcing and celebrating every achievement, even the little ones, is essential because it builds the 'bank' of positive experience for the family to draw on. Being able to say 'Come on, we got through worse than this when…' gives people encouragement and confidence to make more changes and face more difficult challenges.

Reflect

Think about how you have dealt with difficult challenges in your life. Have you drawn on the resources of close family and friends? How well do you cope in adversity – do you fall apart or are you a 'coper'? Try to think about how you have built confidence in dealing with difficult issues from having done it before. How do you think your own ability to meet challenges impacts on the way you practise? Do you bring that to your work in that you believe that you can work with even the most challenging of families, or do you find that you sometimes lack confidence in your own ability? Understanding how you deal with challenge will help you to understand how to help others face theirs.

Supporting parents

(KS 3, 20, 23, 24, 27, 32, 33, 37, 39)

You may be involved with a family because there is a need for support with parenting. Some families need assistance to find out how to be an effective parent; this may be because they have not been effectively parented themselves and so have no model to base anything on. Being a parent is not easy, and putting a child's needs ahead of your own may not be possible for parents whose own needs are overwhelming. Adults who did not have their own needs met when they were children will have to work very hard at parenting. Many do a fantastic job, but some find it very hard to move on from seeing themselves as the centre of the world. Remember Piaget? Children move on from the stage where they are at the centre of everything before they reach adolescence, but their needs in earlier stages of development must be met to enable them to do so. See Unit 39, page 217 for a reminder.

If a parent feels that everything is about them, they will find it almost impossible to cope with the demands of a young baby. If you assume that when your baby cries it is to annoy you, or if it is sick or dirties a nappy just as you are about to go out, that it is deliberate, then very quickly you will resent the baby because it seems to be making your life difficult on purpose. This is a very high-risk situation and will need very close and careful monitoring. However, with support and working with someone who models the sort of behaviour expected of a parent, progress can be achieved and changes made.

Parent Education is now recognised as being an important provision and it is widely available from specialist practitioners. Getting agreement to and setting up support from a specialist practitioner may be an important task alongside practical support work. Teenage pregnancy is still a huge issue, and those young people who have not had the opportunity to experience or even see effective parenting in action need extensive support to see them through the very challenging early stages of parenthood. Support to teenage mothers is provided through a multi-agency team involving midwife, school, Connexions, housing and social worker if there are care concerns. Key areas of support are maintaining the health and well-being of the young woman and her baby, supporting her through the process of reaching a decision about the future for herself and her baby, maintaining her in education and/or training and ensuring that she has accommodation and the necessary financial support in place throughout her pregnancy and after the baby is born. Following the birth, contraceptive and sexual health advice is vitally important in avoiding further pregnancies.

My story

Hi, I'm Janice. I'm 18 now and I live with my daughter Cherise; she's three. I was in care when I got pregnant. I've been in care since I was 12 and my mum's boyfriend was sexually abusing me. She didn't care; she knew what was going on but she never bothered. She was either drunk or off her head most of the time. Haven't seen her for years.

It was really hard when Cherise was born. I was so chuffed to be pregnant: I thought that I'd have someone to love me at last. That's not how it was though. It was OK for the first few days in hospital: everyone was making a fuss and it was great. Then I came back to the unit and it was awful. I was so disappointed because she didn't love me; she cried and screamed if I didn't get her bottle the second she wanted it. I got really angry because she was so horrible to me. My key worker, Hannah, was really good. She talked me through lots of stuff and explained loads about babies and what they need and that and about how they don't love you at first – they just need you to love them. Then they love you later, but they don't understand when they're just babies. I'm really glad I had Hannah, because I really think I could have hurt Cherise, or at least just walked off and left her. I hate to say it now because she's so gorgeous and I just love her to pieces and she says, 'I love you Mummy' – it's just the best feeling ever.

HSC 319 UNIT TEST

1   What are genograms and ecomaps? How do they differ?

2   What sort of information is useful when preparing to visit a family? Try to suggest at least 6 areas of information.

3   If you need to visit a family as the result of an emergency or a crisis, what information do you need to supply the family with before the visit?

4   What is evidence-based assessment? Why is it important to use this style rather than the professional judgement used in the past and how does it help the family you are working with?

5) What reasons might there be for a child or young person being in need?

Don't forget to refer to the evidence opportunities grid (see pages 357–375) for more ideas for suitable evidence for your NVQ.

Contribute to childcare practice in group living

This unit is primarily for those practitioners who live, as well as work, with children and young people. Working with children in a residential setting is a different experience to working with them in a school or hospital or project setting where children attend, but then return home.

Providing a home for children in addition to working to support them to address issues and challenges brings a new dimension to the work and the skills you will need. By definition, the children and young people you are working and living with are vulnerable: they may have a limited concept of 'home' and what it means, and the experiences they have had to date may not have been positive.

You will need to understand how groups of children and young people function. The dynamics are not the same as a family, nor are they the same as some other sorts of groups. A residential care situation is different in the demands it makes and the tensions, checks and balances that exist when numbers of children and young people live together.

There is an assumption that group care is the least beneficial situation for children and young people, and that a placement in a family is always preferable; that is not always the case, and there are some young people for whom the dynamics of group living work well. Do not ever assume that your role in residential care is a 'damage limitation' exercise. Group living can be a very positive and beneficial experience for children and you can have the hugely privileged role of supporting and guiding children and young people as they grow and develop into happy and productive citizens.

In this unit you will find 'Active knowledge' features containing activities that will contribute to assessment for your NVQ. Remember that these features only offer the opportunity for partial assessment; you can also refer to the evidence opportunities grid (see pages 357–375) for more ideas to provide suitable evidence for your NVQ.

What you need to learn

- Changes
- The unique job
- The Lifespace approach
- The three Rs
- Positive choices
- Making plans
- Assessing risk
- Participation and power sharing
- Making order
- The culture of a group
- Resilience
- Little groups have smaller groups…
- Monitoring and evaluating development
- How groups work

HSC 323a Contribute to planning, implementing and reviewing daily living programmes for children and young people

Children in care in the UK are less likely to achieve good outcomes than children who are not in care.

Let's take a look at the fact file of prospects for looked-after children:

FACT: 11 per cent of looked after children achieved 5 GCSEs at C or above in 2005 compared with 56 per cent of all children.

Being looked after by a local authority 'corporate parent' means that a child is less likely to achieve educational qualifications.

FACT: around a third of the UK's homeless people have been in care.

Being looked after by a local authority 'corporate parent' means that a child is more likely to face a future on the streets.

FACT: over half of young people in care over the age of 16 years are neither in training nor employment(compared to less than a quarter in other European countries).

Being looked after by a local authority 'corporate parent' means that a child is likely to face a future without a job.

FACT: half the girls who have been in care become lone mothers within two years of leaving.

Being looked after by a local authority 'corporate parent' means that a young woman is very likely to become a lone parent.

FACT: 60 per cent of those in young offenders establishments have been in care – 27 per cent of the adults in prison have been in care, despite only just over 0.5 per cent of all children being looked after.

Being looked after by a local authority 'corporate parent' means that a child is more likely to end up in prison.

Changes

(KS 13)

There is concern across the UK at the prospects currently on offer to children in care: all governments are looking at what is wrong with the current system and ways to address the issues. New legislation and initiatives are planned or in place. For example, in England, the Green Paper *Care Matters* has outlined plans to change many aspects of the care system, including giving young people more control over when they leave care and improving educational opportunities for children and young people in care. The *Changing Lives* programmes in Scotland will also have a major impact on the way residential care is provided.

As a residential social worker, you are not going to change the system and suddenly make everything right, but you can make an incredible difference to the lives of the children you work with. Sometimes you may not even know it until years later when they come back to visit; sometimes you know at the time, either because you can see a different child slowly emerging or because the child will tell you so!

The unique job

(KS 7, 16)

The residential social worker is in a unique position; you have the chance to live alongside the children you work with. Even if the residential establishment is not actually your home, you will still spend large amounts of time living in the same space as the children and young people. It is this time that is so important and it is this time that makes this job so different from other work with children.

There is a wonderful comment, made by Professor Urie Bronfonbrenner in 1977:

> 'Every kid needs at least one adult who's crazy about him.'

What you have in this unique job is the opportunity to 'be crazy' about the children and young people you work with – at least some of them!

More than any other role in children's social care, the role of a residential worker requires the involvement of the whole of you. The tools of your trade are your personal qualities and your relationship with the individual children and young people and with the group. Although there is a need to observe, communicate and maintain professional boundaries, do not confuse boundaries with distance and formality – they are not the same thing. Being warm and caring and responding to children and young people with thoughtfulness and respect as well as

Living alongside the young people you work with puts you in a special and important position

with laughter, fun and spontaneity is in no way in conflict with professional boundaries.

Professional boundaries matter, and they must be observed, but they are not about any of these things. They are about:

- avoiding abuse and exploitation
- avoiding inappropriate behaviour
- maintaining confidentiality
- personal behaviour, morals and ethics
- avoiding emotional involvement – as opposed to emotional commitment which is an essential part of the work
- taking responsibility
- not colluding with criminal, anti-social or harmful behaviour.

It is the relationship between the child and the worker through the fact of living in the same space that is the key to the child or young person developing and moving forward with some new views of the world and some tools for tackling life. The very fact of meeting with an adult who is offering such a relationship helps the child to develop a sense of belonging and being connected.

The Lifespace approach

(KS 21, 24)

The most important part of what you do is in the very ordinariness of it, the fact that it is about day-to-day living. This is where you have the opportunity to make the real difference for children. It does not have to be in planned 'sessions' and interviews. Important as they are, the place you will make the difference for children is in the mundane, everyday activities that we all have to do.

The concept of Lifespace is one of the most useful approaches to residential childcare. It recognises the importance of the special relationship between children and those workers who share their lives and their living space, and that it is the day-to-day living together that offers the opportunity to provide the child with the development opportunities that he or she needs.

Traditionally the 'care' of children and young people was seen as something different from the 'treatment', 'therapy' or 'work' that was being undertaken with the children. These were carried out by specialists, while the care was seen as the substitute parenting role and was provided by residential workers who were not specialists.

The Lifespace approach describes the overall environment of a home as the 'milieu'. Basically it means everything about the place: the physical environment, the atmosphere, the way the staff relate to the children and to each other and the sense of how the place feels.

Environment is only partly about the physical space, although it is a very important part: a home must feel warm and welcoming but there must be room for those who live there to have personal time and space as well as having public, open space to meet and share being with others, meals and conversations.

The other aspects of environment that make a difference are organisation, attitudes, ethos and approach – and above all the three Rs.

Reflect

Think about a children's home you have gone into – not the one you work in unless you count your first visit – where you immediately felt comfortable, where you knew that the atmosphere was calm and ordered and where you could feel the warmth. Think about another children's home where you went in for the first time and felt none of those things, where the atmosphere was cold, the physical environment unattractive and there was no sense of order and comfort. Reflect on what it was that made you feel that way about each of the homes. It may take a while for you to think through all of the details, some of them quite tiny, that contributed to those different feelings.

The three Rs

(KS 2, 4, 15, 17, 23)

The three important Rs in residential care are:

- rhythms
- rituals
- routines.

Rhythms

These are partly about the pace and feel of the place. The rhythm is about a sense of order, certainty and security about what happens next. This is not the same thing as a procedural, rigid, imposed order. Rhythms in residential childcare are about the feeling that everything is working in tandem and at the same pace and going in the same direction, and that everyone is comfortable and content with it. A rhythm can be flexible and can alter, but only in a co-ordinated way with everyone moving at the same pace and in the same direction. Henry Maier (in, *Core of Care*, 1979) wrote that rhythm is what happens when a relationship between a child and a residential worker begins to 'gel' and the rhythm of the child's care needs is understood and the needs are being met. Maier believed that the development of children was all-important and that, although all children have the same developmental milestones, it is essential to recognise that each individual child has their own rhythm of needs around all aspects of daily living such as eating, sleeping, needing space, moods, habits, cold, warmth and safety.

Rituals

These are not about ancient practices or religion! In this context, rituals are the features and symbolic acts that grow and develop among a group of people who share the same living space. Rituals can be as simple as always doing a silly hop or a daft face when you pass in the corridor, or the fact that there is always ice-cream for pudding on a Saturday but Julie always pretends that there is none left, or that we always sing that same song when going on a trip – but never any other time. Rituals can also be important for individual children. It may be something as simple as James always has to get ready for bed in the same order – drink, teeth, pyjamas – and once his key worker is tuned in and responds to this, observing the ritual provides James with the knowledge that someone knows and cares about his needs; or that Katie always kisses everyone in the room before going to bed. Rituals are comfortable: they foster a sense of belonging to the group and they provide reassurance and security for children who have probably found both of those in short supply.

Routines

Children need to have routines. They need the safety of knowing that there is an order to daily living. Many children will have led chaotic lives where they had no idea of bedtimes, mealtimes, if and when adults would be at home or regular attendance at school. From birth babies and children benefit from a regular routine to provide security and a sense of order, time and place. However, comfortable and comforting routines are one thing; regimented and rigid timetables are something completely different. Establishments attempting to impose inflexible times and activities on children and young people are doomed to have children who are rebellious, unhappy and completely disengaged and, therefore, these establishments are unable to realise the potential of using the shared living to make the relationships with the children. In this kind of establishment, staff are 'policing' or 'monitoring' the children rather than building relationships over the washing up or tidying the lounge before going to bed.

My story

Hi, I'm Vicky. I'm 13 and I've been in care for about four years. It all happened because Mum's boyfriend was abusing me and then they made him leave and then Mum couldn't cope with us – there's my little sister as well. I had been in six placements in a year until I came here, all of them in foster homes – they were awful. They always like wanted you to be part of the family – well, I've got a family, I've got Mum and Jenny, and just because we're not together at the moment doesn't mean we won't ever be. I know we will. Foster homes just want you to fit in with them and it felt like they were saying 'Oh you poor little thing, you've got no family, come and share in ours.' Well, I don't need their family thank you very much. When I came here it was different: there's space here. If you want to be with people, that's OK; if you don't, that's OK too. I've been here three years now and my social worker keeps on about me going back to foster care – no way. When I first came here, I thought they were all weird. Stuff like mealtimes when everyone sat at the table – I'd never done that before – well except at the foster homes. There was no pressure, no-one made you go, but after a few days it sounded like everyone was talking and laughing and it seemed like more fun than eating on my own in front of the telly. It's good having the staff join in everything – some of them are a real laugh. Like Simon – he's off his head. He always sings these stupid loud songs when he's doing breakfast on the early and if he sees you round the home, or even in the street, he always says: 'Yo Victoria – my queen – what can your humble servant do for you?' He's a nut. I have to tell him to shut up. Kirsty, my key worker, is really great. Some nights she'll say: 'Come on, girly night' and we chuck the lads out of the lounge and her and Julie and some of the others like Jade and Marisa and me all sit around painting our nails and watching a chick flick. When I go to bed, last thing she always says is 'Night night, sleep tight, don't …' and then I say ' …let the bed bugs bite' and we both laugh and say goodnight. Things will work out with Mum, she'll get better one day, but till then I'm OK here.

'Come on, girly night'

Positive choices

(KS 8, 14, 17, 21, 22, 23, 24)

Vicky's story is not uncommon. During the 1980s the UK revolutionised childcare by closing large children's homes and moving wholesale into fostering and some small group children's homes, most with six or eight beds. In the 1970s, on any given day there were around 20,000 children in residential children's homes, compared to about 6,000 today (Department of Health 2002). The placement of children in residential care over the last 25 or 30 years has always been a last resort when foster care had broken down or children were considered 'not fosterable' because of challenging, violent or aggressive behaviour. The same does not apply in other countries: in places like Germany and Scandinavia, children's residential care is the first choice, homes are somewhat larger – usually with 16–20 places – and staff are trained and qualified in a very different way. Foster care in these countries is the last resort if group living breaks down.

Zvi Levy (in 'Negotiating positive identity in a group care community', 1993) wrote that:

> 'What a homeless child needs is something that behaves and feels – to the child – like a family, not simply something that looks like a family from the outside.'

Active knowledge
HSC 323 KS 1

Find out the policy on placements in your local authority. Find out which placements are regarded as the first option. See if you can find any comments in any policies about residential care and the criteria for its use rather than foster care. Find out how many of the children you work with are placed with you because fostering broke down and how many are with you as a positive choice placement.

There are, undoubtedly, some children for whom residential care is a preferred option: to them, it can offer an environment where they can flourish and develop without feeling split loyalties and where there is a recognised personal space just for them.

Daily living

The whole concept of daily living sounds ordinary and mundane, and largely that is exactly what it is. Ordinary, normal, everyday tasks include cooking, shopping, washing, bathing, doing homework – except that for many of the children you work with 'normal' and 'ordinary' are not as easy to achieve as they may seem. 'Abnormal' and 'extraordinary' are the terms that describe their lives to date, so never assume that anything is simple for children who have experienced trauma, loss and deprivation. Daily living in a group setting will always have a different feel to living in a small, nuclear family – not better or worse – just different. Group living has its own difficulties and there are tensions, stresses and irritations about living with others in close proximity.

Group living is additionally hard for children and young people who may have limited emotional resources as a result of their early life; so tolerance, consideration and being reasonable are often simply not on the agenda. Living with other people can be difficult, even when people do not have the issues that many children and young people in care have. Have you ever shared a flat with friends? Or even gone on holiday with friends? Such situations can be quite trying and not as easy as you thought!

However, the mundane tasks can often provide a useful way of connecting to hurt and angry children and young people and the simple fact of the presence of a caring, consistent adult can offer a sense of security and comfort.

Remember

Just because it is ordinary doesn't mean it is easy.

Most organisations require the completion of a daily living file for each child or young person. Everything the child does needs to be recorded. There will be guidance from your own organisation about the level of detail necessary for the records but it will certainly include records about:

- sleeping – or lack of it
- going out
- visiting friends
- eating meals
- disputes or arguments with other children or staff
- any visitors
- any leisure activities.

Reflect

Of course, you must comply with the requirements of your organisation, but it is important that you consider why you are keeping such detailed records. Can you truly say that this is for the benefit of the child? Do you, or does anyone else, actually look at this very detailed record in order to see the child or young person's progress or to identify any emerging issues? Or do you do it to safeguard the children? Studies (New York Commission on Quality of Care 1992) have shown that there is a higher rate of reported abuse perpetrated by staff during evenings or free time when there are no planned activities. Is the record's primary purpose a defensive one? Are you protecting yourself and your organisation from the possibility of future claims and allegations made by children and young people in future years? Not a difficult position to understand, given what has happened in the past – but you must be honest with yourself and the children about why you do it.

Making plans

(KS 4, 20)

Making plans for daily living 'programmes' or 'activities' can sound very formal. In reality it does not really need to be, however, some organisations use charts or timetables to outline the activities of the day and the week. These can include the basic living tasks like:

- get up
- shower
- get dressed
- breakfast
- school
- after school activity
- homework
- help with dinner
- dinner
- leisure or social time.

At various points plans may diverge depending on the interests and commitments of an individual child or young person. Some may have activities they are involved in after school; others may have places to go in the evenings or sports practices; some may be having friends or family to visit – all of these activities constitute part of a plan for daily living.

Some parts of a plan will be communal like mealtimes and house meetings (it is important that children and young people are given the responsibility to make contributions to plans and decisions about their home). Other daily living activities such as organised visits or evening activities like a 'pizza night' or an outdoor activity may be open to general discussion and agreement.

Assessing risk

(KS 16)

You may need to carry out a risk assessment for activities you plan. Sometimes it may be a group activity such as a visit to the cinema or a football match where you will need to judge the risks of someone getting lost or injured, or you may have to do it in respect of an individual child or young person. For example, a young person with a history of substance abuse says that she wants her pocket money so that she can go shopping for clothes on Saturday afternoon. You will have to assess the risk that she will use the money to buy drugs rather than clothes.

Participation and power sharing

(KS 2, 4, 20)

Involving children in the day-to-day running of their home is essential. Giving responsibility and having expectations of children and young people is an important part of giving them a sense of control and an understanding that they have the ability to make decisions. Many children will have grown up with no sense of being able to control and influence events in their lives; enabling and expecting them to do so begins to change everything for them. Once you are no longer a victim of circumstances, you can start down the road of believing that you can determine the shape of your life.

Children and young people can participate through formal groups, reviews and house meetings but also through just sharing the Lifespace. Often it is in doing simple things like clearing up the dishes or folding the clean washing or giving someone a hand to tidy their room that you get some of the most spontaneous and most useful contributions. Children and young people are more relaxed in an informal setting and having something practical to do, rather than the 'talking' being the focus of the activity; it can often make it easier for them to say what they really think and to articulate their own needs.

This is the kind of conversation that you could get from sorting the clean washing from the dryer:

'Can you pass me the other pink pillowcase please? Ta.'

'I'm looking forward to the beach trip on Saturday. Are you?'

'Yeah – it'll be a laugh.'

'You were quite quiet in the meeting – are you sure you're OK with it?'

'Yeah, I said, didn't I? That's Jackie's shirt, not Leah's.'

'Mmm – I wish someone had come up with a bright idea for Sunday though.'

'Well, I know what I think'd be good – but it's probably stupid.'

'Whatever it is, it won't be stupid – you don't say stupid things.'

'Don't I? That's 'cos you don't know me.'

'Well – try me out. I'm willing to listen to anything at the moment.'

'I don't know what it's like – I've never had one – but people down the road used to have them when it was hot, and I always really wanted us to have one, but Dad said it was stupid. Just the whole idea of it was like magical somehow – sitting out with one of those umbrellas like they have in Asda. I know we couldn't have done it in our garden 'cos of the dog s* and those old washing machines and our Garry's old car. But could we have one – could we have a barbecue?'**

'What a great idea!'

'It's stupid, it'll probably rain – you can't have one in the rain.'

'It won't rain – and anyway a bit of rain doesn't stop a barbecue. You wouldn't believe the number of times I've grilled burgers under a big brolly! Just get the other end of this sheet.'

'Really – can you? So can we have one even if it rains?'

'Sweetheart – you will have a barbecue on Sunday if it snows!'

This is a perfect example of how the Lifespace shared between the worker and the young person meant that the connection was made with the child and she was able to use the occasion to talk about what she really wanted to happen and to ask for something for herself.

Making order

(KS 2, 20)

Planning is important and it contributes significantly to developing a sense of order and predictability. For those children with a chaotic history it is impossible to overestimate the importance of developing a belief in the fact that some things are always there and some things will always happen and there actually are some things in life that can be relied on. It is this experience that gives children and young people the basis for developing trust in the reliability of others and gives them the opportunity to begin to lose some of the suspicion and mistrust that fuels much of the behaviour we find challenging.

All the children you work with have plans for their care; all will have a lead professional and regular reviews. The planning for internal activity within their own home must fit within the agreed direction of the child or young person's plan and with any therapeutic or clinical activities being undertaken as part of the plan. However, it is not necessary that this level of daily living activity is referred for agreement at a review, only that other members of the team are kept informed of any significant events, achievements, concerns or developing issues.

Although there is no need to refer the ins and outs of daily living to a review meeting for agreement, you do need to keep reviewing the activities you plan and undertake. It is essential to review the work and activities you undertake with children and young people because:

- the activity may no longer be achieving its original aim
- the child or young person may no longer enjoy or be interested in the activity
- the child or young person may have progressed and need to move on
- the child or young person may have other ideas and interests they want to try out
- circumstances may have changed.

Reviews matter because they keep you constantly thinking about what you are doing and why – reviews make you reflect and consider if you are doing everything you possibly can to improve outcomes for this child or young person. When you review what you are doing, you must involve the child or young person. However, we are not necessarily looking at a formal process here; reviews can involve a very simple conversation. For example:

'Jay – do you want to carry on doing the punchbag session every evening, or do you feel as though you've got a grip on the anger enough to back off a bit?'

'Na – let's carry on – it really helps.'

'OK then – fine.'

Or

'Katie – your last two maths tests were so good. Do you want to carry on with the number games?'

'No, I'm fine with it now. Can I do one of those make up sessions instead?'

'Sure – I'll speak to Nicky and see when she's in.'

Test yourself

1   What is the most important tool for working in group care?

2   What are the three Rs of residential care?

3   Explain each of the terms of the three Rs.

4   What is the Lifespace?

5   Why does planning matter?

HSC 323b Work with groups to promote individual growth and development

Each of the children you work with is an individual and has different needs. An obvious statement of course, but it reinforces the importance of addressing the needs of the individual child, although this must be achieved in a group living situation. You are inevitably in the position of managing the tensions that will sometimes exist between the benefit of the individual and the benefit of the group.

There are basic needs that all children and young people have and an effective group can meet those needs and support the development of individuals within the right environment.

The culture of a group

(KS 6, 9, 14, 17, 21, 23, 24)

The culture of a group will depend to some extent on its nature and its purpose. For example, a residential unit with eight young people who stay usually from early teens until leaving care will have a very different feel from a unit with 25 beds where young people come for a four- or six-week assessment before moving on. However, just because the units serve very different purposes and the individual children and young people will have very different needs, there is no reason why the fundamental ethos should not be the same. Listening to children, respecting children's opinions, giving them personal space, providing a warm and welcoming environment with order and predictability should still happen, regardless of the length of stay children and young people will have, or the nature of the issues they are working on.

In a community where children and young people are moving on, it is not as easy to provide the longer-term view of security, and the relationships formed between staff and children will be different because there is a known time period. Children will be less likely to commit to a relationship that they know will be short term. The key rhythms, rituals and routines should still be the underlying foundations of practice. However, what matters is whether you do enough to make a difference to the development of a child, even in a short period.

What makes the difference

A recent study in Canada (Professor James Anglin: *Pain, Normality and the Struggle for Congruence*, 2003) looked at what made the difference in

What you can do	The effect it can have
Listening and responding with respect	Develops feelings of self-worth and being valued and a sense of dignity
Building rapport and relationships	Gives a sense of belonging and being connected to others
Putting in place structure, routine and giving permission to expect something	Creates a sense of order and confidence about predictable events, develops trust in people
Providing emotional and developmental support	Develops a sense of caring and also mastery
Challenging young people's thinking and actions	Develops a sense of potential and a recognition of ability
Sharing power and decision making	Encourages a sense of personal power and effective decision-making processes
Respecting personal space and time	Develops a sense of independence

children's residential care. They were looking for 'congruence': in other words, something that had some of the aspects of 'normality' and a way of functioning for a residential unit that was harmonious and made sense. The study identified the significant ways in which residential workers can make a difference to children's lives by giving them some of the aspects of 'normality' that make it possible for them to tackle the challenges they will meet in the world around them. These are referred to as 'interactional dynamics': in other words, the exchanges between people (see the table on the previous page).

The table shows just some of the impacts of your decisions about how you work with the children and young people and the way that their development is affected by what you do.

James Algin also helpfully defined the difference between reacting and responding to children.

- **Reacting** is based on your own needs and feelings and can be impulsive.
- **Responding** is thought out and purposeful and based on the needs of the person you are responding to.

Reflect

Look at the table on page 315 and identify which things are part of your normal practice – be honest. Look at the things that aren't . Try to think about why – is it because they are difficult? Or because they can't be done with the children you have at the moment? Or are these weak areas of your own personality and practice?

Resilience

(KS 14, 16)

A great deal of research has been undertaken into the importance of resilience for children as they grow and develop. Occasionally, a particularly resilient child may come along, but the majority you will work with will be fragile and will have to be helped to develop the resilience they will need to achieve

positive outcomes as they mature. Resilience is about the ability to cope with adversity, the ability to 'bounce back' and keep going, sometimes called 'stickability'. Some elements of resilience are thought to be 'nature' rather than 'nurture'. Babies who are contented and those who have a high level of intelligence are more likely to be resilient than babies who are tearful and grizzly or are born prematurely.

Resilience helps children and young people protect themselves in the face of setbacks and problems

In terms of the factors that build resilience, most result from 'nurture' rather than 'nature'; educational achievement has been shown to have the most significant effect. Research has shown that 28 times more adults who have been in care but have achieved well at school are in employment than those who did not achieve. Less than 4 per cent of high achievers became single mothers as against almost 42 per cent of young people who did not achieve. Those who did well at school were also much less likely to be in prison or become homeless.

Studies have also shown that taking part in hobbies, interests and activities out of school also contributes to resilience.

In 1997 an international project looking at resilience across 30 countries developed a framework for assessing children's resilience. This can be very useful in finding out where a child's strengths lie and which areas need more development. (See the table below.)

Little groups have smaller groups...

(KS 3, 5, 12, 16, 17, 19, 23)

Inevitably in a residential setting, children will form their own, smaller groups based around friendship or common interests. These groups can be beneficial in enabling children to develop the relationships with their peers which are known to be important in developing resilience.

Sometimes, you know that you would rather that a particular child was not associating with another group simply because you are aware that the influence may not be positive. This is always a hard one to handle, particularly where you have a child who is vulnerable and who is likely to be influenced. The best action is always prevention and protection where possible:

- make sure the child maintains contact if possible with his or her own family
- make sure that any friendships with children not in care or others in the unit are encouraged
- reinforce, through your own work and using all opportunities, the positive aspects of the behaviour you want the child to model.

Active knowledge · HSC 323 pc 5

Think about a situation where you had a child in a friendship group you knew would not be a positive influence. How did you deal with it? Does your unit have any guidance about how to handle such situations? If not, discuss the issue with your line manager.

Sometimes children are keen to get involved in activities and a few of them get together. Provided that what they want to do is not dangerous or illegal, you may need to carry out a risk assessment, but where possible any positive activity should be encouraged.

I have...	I am...	I can...
trusting and loving relationships with others	loveable	communicate
structure at home	loving	solve problems
role models	proud of myself	manage my feelings
encouragement to be independent	responsible	understand my temperament
access to health, education and social care	hopeful and trustful	seek out trusting relationships

A framework for assessing children's resilience

Source, Grotburg 1997

My story

Hi, I'm Hassan, I'm 12 and I like playing the keyboard. I used to have music lessons when I was little, before my grandparents died and life changed a lot. I do some keyboard at school, but it's good to be able to use the one here. It's a big old house and there's a special room for music. We're forming a band: there's me and Sam, he plays guitar – well sort of – and Rob, he plays dead good and he can sing and I can sing too. Jade is playing the drums – she said she used to play on her brother's before he went inside; she's not too bad really. Everyone has been great about it and the staff keep coming to listen. Phil says he's dead impressed – and that's good 'cos he's not easily impressed. Chris says we're doing really well and Joanne even danced last night. Some of the others moan about us practising. Phil says he's going to see if there's enough in the budget for headphones – that'd be good. We've called ourselves the Lax – get it? Lax – Lacs – Looked after... Oh never mind!

Monitoring and evaluating development

(KS 7, 9, 10, 14, 15, 20)

Each child's plan will set out the developmental goals and the outcomes planned by the next review, so you will be able to continually monitor the child or young person as they grow and evaluate how well they are developing against the targets set. The positive and supportive environment of a well-functioning residential home is an effective place for vulnerable children to develop. The advantages of a residential unit are that it can be less pressured than other care environments, it can adapt to the child (not the other way around) and children know that there are staff available day and night if needs be. Your role in monitoring is essential as it is important to pick up any issues as early as possible.

Social pedagogy

In the first element, it was mentioned briefly that in some European countries, the approach to working with children in care is very different. If you work in the UK, you are unlikely to have come across many social pedagogues, unless you work for Rudolf Steiner where the approach has been used for many years. In the UK we associate the term pedagogy with education and teaching, but social pedagogy has a much broader focus on the child as a whole person, and support for the child's overall development.

Key terms

Pedagogue: A teacher or education specialist.

Social pedagogy: Education with a focus on the child as a whole person, aiming to support their overall development as well as their academic education.

- Pedagogues view their role as being part of a key relationship with the child.
- Children and staff are seen as inhabiting the same life space, as in the Lifespace approach.
- Pedagogues are encouraged to be constantly reflective practitioners, but there is a strong requirement to do this with self-knowledge, not just theoretical understanding.
- Pedagogues are also practical: their training prepares them to share in many aspects of children's daily lives, such as making art, playing music and preparing meals.
- When pedagogues work in group settings, they recognise that the way children interrelate with the rest of the group is very important and they will work to support a child in entering a particular group.
- Pedagogy has an understanding of children's rights in the broadest sense, not just rights conferred by legislation or policies and procedures.
- There is an emphasis on team work and on valuing the contributions of other people – families, community and other professionals.

The principles of pedagogy lie in the 'head, heart and hands' approach that could be described as:

- think it
- feel it
- do it.

All of these have to be in place for a pedagogue to function.

The personal, relational approach is emphasised in students' training and education where fostering

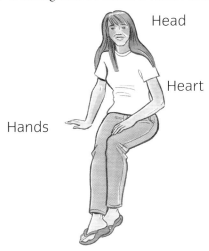

The 'head, heart and hands' approach is at the centre of social pedagogy

sound pedagogic values and attitudes is seen as at least as important as the acquisition of knowledge and skills. Governments in the UK are looking at pedagogy and discussing whether the approach has a relevance for practice here. It is completely in tune with the Lifespace approach, but would considerably change the tradition in the UK of splitting up 'care' and 'education' as two completely separate disciplines.

Keeping the balance

There can be issues about balancing the need of an individual child against the benefit of the wider group. These situations are always difficult to handle and you will need to consider carefully, in discussion with other team members, whether the potential importance to an individual outweighs some disadvantage to others. These judgements are not made in a vacuum, and not only by you. They should involve the child or young person if possible and their family. Decisions must also take into account the plans for the child and any impact that the decisions may have. There can never be a right or wrong answer to these kinds of dilemmas – but there are ways of approaching these difficult issues that can help to make the decisions clearer.

 Keys to good practice

✓ Never try to tackle these sort of dilemmas alone – get support from your line manager and senior colleagues.

✓ Involve the key people around the child or children concerned – this could be family or other carers, the lead professional or other members of the team.

✓ Make sure you have full information about the potential impact and consequences of all of the available options.

✓ Write down the potential 'fallout' for each of the possible options.

✓ Where possible, give the child or children concerned as much information as you can and take their views into account.

✓ Make sure that you have the views and opinions of the children, family and key professionals.

✓ Once you have all the information and have consulted as thoroughly as possible, ensure that a decision follows quickly.

✓ Act on any decision firmly, but in a planned and ordered way.

✓ Keep everyone informed of what is happening.

Ethical issue

You have been working hard on your relationship with Troy. His behaviour is very challenging. He becomes very aggressive over very small matters, although he has improved considerably since coming into the home six weeks ago. He is learning about managing his anger and still has a long way to go, but you know that he is beginning to trust you and he has an amazing amount of potential. He is bright, he is talented and can be funny and charming for short flashes of time.

However, there are serious concerns about Troy's behaviour. He frightens the other children and young people – even the self-styled 'hard men' give him a wide berth. Last night he lost his temper and smashed up part of the kitchen. Other staff are discussing how realistic it is for him to stay. Normally, smashing a few cupboards and crockery would not mean a move, but there are some very vulnerable children currently living at the home. There are two children who were badly beaten by a stepfather over a period of several years, and they are terrified of Troy's outbursts.

You believe that you are just on the edge of a breakthrough with him – you know that you can reach him and that he is one who will make it. Your worry is that, if he sees he is rejected from here, then he will lose heart and not be able to make any further progress. What should be done?

Test yourself

1 Identify the ways your actions can change how children develop

2 What is resilience?

3 What genetic factors influence resilience?

4 What environmental factors influence resilience?

5 What is a social pedagogue and how is the role different from what you currently do?

HSC 323c Contribute to promoting group care as a positive experience

Throughout this unit you have looked at the ways in which residential care is a positive experience for many children and young people. The risk has always been the question of whether children were safeguarded adequately whilst in residential care. We know from investigations that have been undertaken that children have not been adequately safeguarded in the past and appalling abuses have taken place, perpetrated by people in positions of trust. Ensuring that such abuses do not continue must be the aim of everyone working in group settings whatever the size.

A study carried out by the NSPCC in 2003 made the following list of recommendations to safeguard children in residential care:

- **Children's rights and participation:** involving and consulting with children on decisions alongside strategies for increasing workers' participation in the decision-making process

- **Contact:** regular contact between children and families (where appropriate), independent visitors, advocacy services and the local community
- **Better recruitment procedures:** including vetting of staff and participation of young people in the selection procedure
- **Training:** a nationally accredited qualification that is specific to the demands of residential childcare work
- **Supervision:** regular, open, supportive supervision by properly trained supervisors, which is systematically recorded and reviewed
- **Monitoring:** regular monitoring and assessments of staff and managers' working practices, spot checks by social services and statutory bodies
- **Safeguards:** protection for whistle blowers
- **Staffing patterns:** ensure senior staff are present at the most vulnerable shift times – early mornings and late at night – adequate staff/child ratios
- **Leadership style:** head of home's leadership style should be based on consultation and respect, where a clear vision of the establishment's aims is shared by managers and staff
- **Complaints:** complaints procedures should be independent, child friendly and well publicised
- **Organisational factors:** including:
  - the establishment of interdisciplinary working practices
  - the development of open, effective and participatory line management, including regular contact with young people
  - external professional input
  - placement policies should ensure that all children's needs can be fully met and that a 'good' residential mix can be achieved
- **Cultural:** the eradication of 'macho' and hierarchical peer cultures based on inequality.

All of these recommendations are about using and developing the system to safeguard and protect children. There are arguments that say that systems do not abuse children, people do; but it is the systems that allow the abuse to happen.

How groups work

(KS 14)

This unit is not about formal group therapy; it is about groups of children, young people and adults living together and how that can be an effective way of promoting the development of the children and young people. However, it is useful to understand the principles of some theories of group dynamics so that you will be able to recognise and explain behaviours.

One of the best-known theories of how groups perform was developed by an American, Bruce Tuckman. According to this theory, groups go through a range of stages during the lifetime of the group. This theory is about how adults perform in a group, so it is not completely relevant for younger children, but it works reasonably well for groups of young people.

The four stages are:

1 forming

2 storming

3 norming

4 performing.

Forming

The forming stage, as you might expect, is the early stages of the group. It occurs when a group has just begun to be together. You need to remember that when group members change it produces a new group, even though some members may have lived together before. A different member makes a different group. During the forming stage, young people are getting to know each other, getting to understand the way in which each other works and establishing what the group is about. It is during this stage that groups need to work out what they want to achieve and to make plans for the way in which they will work together. The forming stage is a stage at which young people assume particular roles within the group. The roles within a group are not allocated by anyone; they will be taken up depending on individual personalities:

- there may be somebody who is a **natural organiser**, who may take on a lead role in planning and organising the group
- there is likely to be another group member who will be a **peace maker**, who is always keen to settle disagreements and arrange for young people to compromise
- someone else may take on the role of being the **jester**, keeping everyone amused and always seeing the funny side
- somebody else may be the **finisher** who makes sure that tasks which the group has set out to complete are achieved
- the group may have a **bully**, somebody who is aggressive and challenges others constantly
- there may be someone who is an **innovator**, who always thinks up new plans and new ideas and makes sure that the group stays on its toes.

Active knowledge

Think about the group of young people you work with. Think about how the group is structured and how it operates. Make a list of the roles that young people have assumed within your group; you can call them any names you wish (try not to use rude ones!). The names should describe the way in which they behave in the group. When your list is complete, you should be able to see how each individual within the group assumes a particular role. A good way to do this is to do it immediately following a house meeting when you have had a chance to observe behaviour in the meeting.

Storming

This is the stage at which the group seems to do nothing but argue. It is a stage when, after the initial development, the group members are feeling more confident with each other and each individual is fighting to establish their position. This is the stage at which you may see particular individuals emerging in what may seem to be a power struggle, where one or two young people may be fighting to take control of the group. This can be a distressing and worrying stage for some young people in the group as they feel intimidated and you may need to intervene.

Storming is a natural part of the development of a group and in forming strong bonds and relationships between the members. However, it is important at the storming stage that debate, discussion and argument do not become destructive: while challenge and disagreement are a normal part of this stage, this should not degenerate into aggression, bullying or intimidation. If this begins to happen, then you will have to address the issues openly with the young people and, hopefully, any issues should disappear if addressed early.

Norming

Norming is where the group begins to settle down and young people firmly adopt the roles that you may have identified in the forming stage. The points at which these different stages occur will vary tremendously depending on the individuals in the group, the needs they have and the overall effectiveness of the home and how it is run. The transition from one stage to the next may almost be unnoticeable unless you are carefully charting the progress of your particular group. You are 'norming' as a group when you have stopped the storming stage and people have settled down and are living together, beginning to accept each other's roles, and becoming more tolerant of them. This can happen almost before you realise it and it may be only on reflection that you will recognise this stage of development.

This stage of group formation also involves establishing the rules for behaviour in the group and sees the general acceptance of the way people will behave towards each other. The sets of rules that were considered at forming stage and battled over at storming stage have begun to settle down by norming stage, and have been accepted as the 'normal' ways of behaving within that particular group. The young people should be able to share living space, ideas, constructive criticism and suggestions openly at house meetings. Any unacceptable behaviour should be openly challenged and be established within the norms of group behaviour as unacceptable.

Performing

If there are no changes to group members, then groups can reach the performing stage and remain there for a considerable period of time. There is no reason why a group which works well when it first begins to perform effectively should not continue to do so, provided all of the factors remain the same. But there are many things that influence a group's stability: for example, if there are changes of group members, significant behaviour changes in individual young people or changes in circumstances. It is important to be aware of the changes that can be brought about by any of these factors and the way in which they can influence the behaviour of the group.

Other theories concern the nature of leadership and how that can change the nature of groups. This is important for residential childcare because of the impact of the leadership of the home and the staff on the group. One theory identifies three different types of leader:

- democratic
- autocratic
- laissez faire.

It was found that groups of children performed much better under a democratic leadership where they were consulted and had a direct share in making decisions about the group. Children were enthusiastic and motivated with a democratic leader. The laissez faire type, where there was no recognisable leadership, left children confused, in chaos and unhappy; and the autocratic leadership style where participation was not permitted and instructions were simply issued made children demotivated, crushed and rebellious.

'T group' theory is borrowed from science. T groups have a facilitator rather than a leader. The facilitator is seen as a 'change agent' and they act as a catalyst to bring about changes in other members of the group. Incidentally, it was the T group theory again borrowing from science that first used the term 'feedback', now such a popular term.

You have already looked at the Lifespace approach in some detail, where all group members work together using the personal relationships between staff and children to establish an environment for growth and development.

Roles within groups

(KS 14)

There are generally accepted roles that are taken on within groups – these are not consciously assumed roles, but reflect the different personalities and how they react when with other people. The most commonly observed roles that you are likely to see in groups of children and young people are:

- innovator: always has the new ideas
- questioner: always asks questions
- opinion-seeker: wants to know what others think
- information-giver: provides the group with information
- know-it-all: states his or her beliefs about every group issue
- changer: shifts the direction of the group's discussion
- critic: negative about everything, demotivates the group
- energiser: stimulates the group to a higher level of activity
- worker: performs practical tasks for the group
- clown/jester: always joking, deflects anything serious
- encourager: praises the ideas of others
- peace maker: mediates differences between group members
- compromiser: moves group to another position that is favoured by all group members
- follower: goes along with the group and accepts the group's ideas
- aggressor: attacks other group members, deflates the status of others, and other aggressive behaviour
- blocker: resists movement by the group – appears disinterested
- show off: calls attention to himself or herself
- scaremonger: seeks to raise anxiety in the group
- dominator: asserts control over the group by manipulating the other group members
- help seeker: tries to gain the sympathy of the group

- special interest pleader: uses stereotypes to assert his or her own prejudices.

Of course, you are not going to see all of those roles in one group, but you will see some in all groups and some children and young people may assume more than one role.

You need to be aware of the roles and try to use them effectively. For example:

- if you know you have a 'show off' – give them a key task that puts them at the centre, but also keeps them busy, so others have a chance to shine
- make sure that your energiser and encourager are around when you need the group to get on with a demanding task
- keep an eye on aggressors and dominators so that they do not exert too great an influence on others.

Being aware of how different children and young people will behave in a group is the key to being able to predict how the group will respond, and to identify the most effective way to assist the group to reach its outcomes.

When you work and live with children on a day-to-day basis, you are constantly working with a group. It is easy to think that theories about how groups function are related to other, more formal situations where people sit around talking with a 'facilitator' or 'group worker'. Some groups are like this and these kinds of therapeutic groups can be very valuable for children and young people with specific issues and challenges. They are usually run by people with specific skills and training in group work.

What you do on a day-to-day basis is not formal group work, but it is 'working with groups' and the theories still apply. You need to be conscious of the ways in which groups are developed so that you can see what is happening and why children and young people are behaving in particular ways.

Test yourself

1   What are the key steps to safeguard children in residential care?

2   Why is it important to understand group dynamics?

3   What are the four stages of group development?

4   What sort of leadership has been found to be most effective with groups of children?

5   Which point of group development is the most potentially difficult?

1   All children or young people have better outcomes when living in a family situation. True or false?

2   What are the key differences in approach to the training of residential social workers in other parts of Europe?

3   How do the three aspects of the Lifespace approach impact on children and young people?

4   What is the difference between behaving professionally and keeping your distance from the children and young people you work with?

5   Why do you think 'every kid needs one adult who's crazy about him'?

6   If you were appointing staff to a new children's home, what is the most important thing you would be looking for in candidates?

7   Why is knowing about groups important in residential childcare?

8   Why would you consider residential placements particularly suitable for some children?

Don't forget to refer to the evidence opportunities grid (see pages 357–375) for more ideas for suitable evidence for your NVQ.

Contribute to the prevention and management of challenging behaviour in children and young people

Behaviour that presents challenges because it is aggressive, abusive, destructive or illegal is one of the most difficult areas of working with children and young people. In this unit you will look at ways to work with children and young people to discover and achieve acceptable behaviour.

The key to supporting some children and young people to address challenging behaviour is to use a child-centred approach, to build on the strengths of the children and to provide clear, consistent boundaries along with ways to deal with their own particular challenges. In order to do this effectively, you will need to understand the basis for children's behaviour and some of the triggers that can result in challenging behaviour. You will also need to be able to work with children and families to support them in changing behaviour and responses.

The key fact you need to keep at the forefront of your practice is that all behaviour is a means of communication. Everything a child or young person does is telling you something – your job is to find out what it is.

In this unit you will find 'Active knowledge' features containing activities that will contribute to assessment for your NVQ. Remember that these features only offer the opportunity for partial assessment; you can also refer to the evidence opportunities grid (see pages 357–375) for more ideas to provide suitable evidence for your NVQ.

What you need to learn

- How to define challenging behaviour
- Reasons for challenging behaviour
- Psychological theories to explain why children and young people exhibit challenging behaviour
- Socio-economic factors
- Genetic factors
- Controlling or empowering – a different perspective
- Parental involvement
- Boundaries
- Planning for change
- Understanding young children's behaviour
- Review and evaluation
- Different approaches
- Positive approaches
- Supporting parents
- Relaxing
- Causes
- How to support children and young people
- Facing up to consequences
- Other help
- Dealing with challenging behaviour
- Responding to challenging behaviour

HSC 326a Work with children and young people to identify goals and boundaries for acceptable behaviour

Regardless of the job you do, or the setting you work in, you may come across challenging behaviour from the children or young people you work with. This may be directed at you; it may be directed at their family or carers or other professionals; or it may be directed at other children and young people.

Before you can define the behaviour that is acceptable, you need to know what you mean by it: in other words, you need to know the behaviour that will not be accepted. Much of this will depend on the context. For example, if you are working with young people in, or on the edge of, the criminal justice system, acceptable behaviour is to stay within the law. Unacceptable behaviour is anything criminal. Alternatively if you are working with a six-year-old who is disruptive in a classroom, acceptable behaviour will be about joining in lessons and helping them to understand that shouting, hitting others and throwing things around the classroom is not OK.

Dealing with challenging behaviour

How to define challenging behaviour

(KS 3, 4, 14, 15, 20)

There are various definitions of challenging behaviour, most of which relate either to challenging behaviour resulting from profound learning disability or to challenging behaviour in the classroom. A broader definition of challenging behaviour could be:

Behaviour that places the individual or others in physical danger or a state of fear, results in damage to the immediate environment or causes a period of disruption.

This could mean:

- aggressive or violent behaviour
- verbal aggression
- racist or sexist behaviour
- bullying
- shouting and using foul or abusive language
- damaging property or the immediate surroundings
- being disruptive, either through being noisy or refusing to co-operate with others
- sexually unacceptable behaviour such as masturbating in front of others or showing pornography
- threats or intimidation.

Beware of stereotyping

When identifying challenging behaviour, you need to be clear that it is actually behaviour that is causing challenges, disruption and risk and not behaviour that arises from being excluded or discriminated against. Children and young people can be behaving as a response to discrimination, or because their behaviour is culturally appropriate and acceptable within the peer group and culture in which they live.

This has been identified particularly in schools where studies have noted that, for example, the behaviour of black young people can often be misinterpreted as challenging, when it is actually the result of the fact that the National Curriculum does not provide

culturally relevant teaching (Blair, M. (2001) *Why Pick On Me? School exclusion and Black Youth*, Stoke Trentham). This concern was noted by many other researchers, including Ofsted, the schools inspectorate.

When you are dealing with behaviour that presents a challenge, always check that it is not due to your own prejudices and beliefs and that you are not simply misinterpreting behaviour as challenging because it does not conform with your own views about how children and young people should behave.

Reasons for challenging behaviour

(KS 3, 11, 12)

The underlying reasons for challenging behaviour in a particular child or young person are complex and include: the social and emotional development levels of the individual child or young person; the physical and social environment in which they live; states of both physical and mental health; relationships; learning needs; and, of course, the social and emotional management skills of the parents or carers and other key adults, including professional carers, teachers and support staff.

Behaviour does not happen in a vacuum: there are always a range of interacting factors that bring about a reaction from a child or young person. The causes and triggers of behaviour are not simple; neither should your response be. You need to think about all the factors that influence and impact on the particular child or young person and make sure that you are considering all the aspects of the behaviour of a child or young person. Do not look for a formula that you can apply to all children – there isn't one.

Why challenging behaviour happens

All of us become angry and distressed at some time and the causes are varied and differ from individual to individual. What will distress one person will not concern another; a situation that can reduce someone to a sobbing temper tantrum will simply make another person a little disappointed and they can shrug it off without any serious concern. Be careful that you do not confuse causes for a child or young person's distress and anger with reasons. **Causes** can be a great many external factors but the **reasons** are due to a much deeper, psychological influence, which affects the way different children respond in different circumstances. All children have a broadly similar process of emotional development, but as each child is an individual who has grown and developed in different circumstances, then it is inevitable that the overall effects will have different results for each child. However, psychologists have established theories for some basic forms of behaviour which can be broadly applied and explain the reasons why children behave in the way that they do.

Over 30 years ago, Michael Rutter (*Helping Troubled Children*, Rutter, M. 1975) suggested two main ways in which a child's behaviour might be understood. He developed the terms *emotional disorders* and *conduct disorders*. He defined emotional disorders as 'those in which the main problem involves an abnormality of the emotions such as anxiety, fear, depression, obsessions, hypochondria and the like.' Conduct disorders he described as 'those in which the chief characteristic is abnormal behaviour which gives rise to social disapproval'.

These definitions have often since been used to justify labels such as: 'the mad' and 'the bad'; 'the troubled and the troublesome'; 'the deserving and the undeserving'; 'the disturbed and the disturbing'; 'can't and won't'; and other similar comments. There are some issues with this rather over-simplified explanation. It is clear that children behave as they do because of a combination of factors and not just the straightforward labels implied by Rutter. In just the last 15 years the number of children diagnosed as suffering from ADHD (Attention Deficit Hyperactivity Disorder) has increased significantly and the number of prescriptions for drugs such as Ritalin has increased by almost 50 times to over 413,000 in 2004 (National Institute for Health and Clinical Excellence, 2006). In many ways, such a diagnosis can, in itself, become a label and can mean that it is tempting not to look for the reasons behind a child's behaviour, but simply to put it down to the condition.

Remember

Bear in mind that what follows are theories about individual children: make sure that you are looking at behaviour which is related to the particular background of the child or young person concerned, and not the result of discrimination or stereotyping. If you are clear that this behaviour is definitely down to individual development, then the theories about some of the reasons can be very useful in providing you with an overview.

Psychological theories to explain why children and young people exhibit challenging behaviour

(KS 12)

There is a range of psychological theories about why children behave in unacceptable and challenging ways. There has always been much debate about whether our emotional responses are genetic – i.e. we are born with them – or if they are learnt from our environment. This is known as the 'nature – nurture' debate. The most likely and feasible explanation is that they are a mixture of the two.

Most psychologists agree that there is genetic response evidenced through work with very young babies where there is pain or loss of support. Although these areas appear to be those that stimulate a basic genetic response in us all, as we grow and develop we learn to respond to other different circumstances in different ways. It is important that you recognise that, although these may be the basic stimuli that children respond **to**, what you have to deal with when working with children and young people is what they respond **with**. In other words what children and young people **do** in response to anger and emotion.

Key to good practice

✓ Do not confuse causes with reasons. Causes are **what** trigger challenging behaviour; reasons are **why** challenging behaviour happens.

No one is expecting you to be a psychologist or any sort of therapist, but if you are to work effectively to support children and young people to address their challenging behaviour, you will need to have some understanding of the reasons for the behaviour. There are a great many theories about human behaviour, and you only need an overview of the broad categories under which most of the theories fall.

Behaviourism

The theories of psychologists like Pavlov and Skinner are based on the belief that human behaviour responds to the consequences that result from it. So, if you drive your car past the speed camera at 90mph, you will get a fine and points on your driving licence – so you won't do it again!

This theory would suggest that challenging behaviour develops because children have been 'rewarded' for this sort of behaviour in the past. For example, a child is always given what it wants if it kicks and screams, so the child grows up believing that such behaviour is the way to get results.

Behaviourist theory suggests that challenging behaviour develops because children have been 'rewarded' for it in the past

Cognitivism

Developed by people like Piaget and Bandura, this is about how children develop behaviour as a result of what they know and understand about the world. Therefore, all of their assumptions, attitudes and beliefs will have an effect on how they behave. A child who has grown up in circumstances where violent and aggressive behaviour are normal ways of behaving will have understood that this is the way adults relate to the world. In a family where people behave in this way during a disagreement, or following a disappointment, children very quickly assimilate this as normal behaviour, and it becomes part of their personality. Similarly, children who have been smacked when they are 'naughty' have been shown that the way to get people to do what you want, or to stop doing something you don't like – especially if you are bigger and more powerful than they are – is to hit them!

Humanism

Psychologists like Rogers and Maslow focus on feelings and emotions, and view challenging behaviour as the result of low self-esteem or difficulties in dealing with emotions. Humanists would argue that children who grow up not feeling valued, or having missed out on some of the basic building blocks of emotional relationships, or not having been able to develop a strong sense of who they are, will be unable to relate well to others when they are adults. This can result from parents who have not been able to parent adequately – usually because they have not been adequately parented themselves – being unable to put their child's needs ahead of their own and so not providing the basic security that children need.

Cognitivist theory believes that children will base their behaviour on what they see demonstrated by those around them

According to humanist theory, children who grow up not feeling valued will be unable to relate well to others when they are adults

The psychodynamic approach

Psychologists like Freud would argue that it is our unconscious and subconscious that control our behaviour, and that we would all like to behave in a challenging way, but there are psychological controls which mean that we conform to the norms and expectations of society. If children present challenging behaviour, this is seen as a failure of part of the control mechanism, caused by a failed key relationship, or a failure to properly progress through all the stages of development. Freudian psychologists would also identify that a traumatic event, such as abuse, may also have been the trigger for the behaviour controls not to be in place.

Systems theory

This approach views the family as a 'system' with rules and structures for how family members relate to each other, how everyone expresses views and how people behave, although, as we grow into adults, we learn other 'systems' and ways of behaving. This is particularly relevant when children are living in a community, such as residential care, which also operates as a 'system', and all the parts of the 'system' influence behaviour. So, this approach would look at all the aspects of the environment in which the child lives, and see the impact on behaviour.

The interactionist approach

Interactionists link the two sides of the nature-nurture debate and take the view that children develop particular types of personality, but that

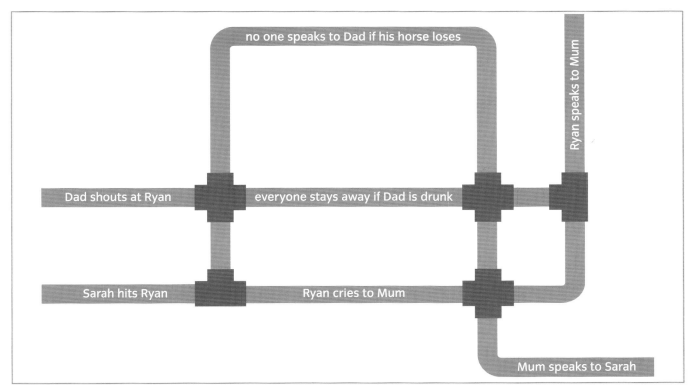

The systems theory views the family as a 'system' with rules and structures for how family members relate to each other

circumstances can make people with the same personality trait react in different ways. This theory identifies a range of personality types including:

- extrovert – introvert
- agreeable – disagreeable
- emotionally stable – emotionally unstable
- conscientious – careless
- open to experience – closed to experience.

Circumstances can change children and young people's usual personalities: for example, a young person who is normally agreeable may become quite aggressive if they feel that they are threatened.

Most of the psychological theories have one thing in common: they are about the experiences of early life. There is little doubt that much behaviour is influenced by upbringing – not only the emotional relationships with parents, but also the culture, environment and relationships children experience. It is these formative periods in children's lives that can have a major impact on how they react as adults when they are faced with difficulties, disappointments and setbacks. Being able to cope with adversity is

called **resilience,** and one of the key aims for those who work with young children is to support them to develop resilience. A child who is resilient will be better able to cope with uncertainty and difficult or traumatic experiences as they grow older. In order for children to develop resilience, they need to have experienced the three key 'building blocks':

- a secure base where a child feels a sense of security and belonging
- strong self-esteem
- a feeling of 'mastery' and control.

Active knowledge HSC 326 KS 16

Think about someone you could describe as resilient: choose someone who always seems to bounce back no matter what life throws at them. Try to think about what makes them like that. If it is someone you know well, you may already know about the sort of childhood they had. If you don't know, try to choose someone you could ask about their childhood. Note down the factors that have made them resilient.

Socio-economic factors

(KS 11, 17)

Poverty and poor housing and the associated health and development problems have long been linked to behaviour issues (Policy Action Team 12, 2000).

- Poorly achieving schools are concentrated in areas of economic deprivation (the proportion of young people in receipt of free school meals is usually the indicator of economic deprivation).
- Truancy is high amongst schools serving areas of low-quality housing estates that are difficult to let.
- School exclusions, teenage conceptions, youth offending and drug use are all highest in deprived areas.

Poverty, unemployment and crowded living conditions put additional stresses on families and can have a detrimental effect on parenting as well as directly on young people themselves.

Children and young people living with deprivation on a daily basis are more likely to behave in a way that is seen as challenging, particularly if other factors, such as inconsistent or ineffective parenting, family violence or abuse are also present.

Genetic factors within the child or young person

(KS 12)

The development and understanding of genetics has resulted in some work around the possibility that some children might be predisposed to experience learning and behavioural problems. This work is ongoing and there have been many discoveries about the impact of genetics on physical disease. Inevitably scientists have looked at the emotional impact of genetics and the extent to which children and young people can be predisposed towards particular behaviours. There is no general acceptance as yet that this work is conclusive but, if ultimately proven and accepted, it would have a major impact on the way we currently work with children, young people and their families.

Ethical issue

If current research confirms that behaviour is due to inherited, genetic factors as opposed to environmental and psychological factors, what should we do? Do we test all children, then separate out those with the 'bad behaviour' gene? Do we keep them segregated so that they do not represent a risk to society and we can eliminate crime and unpleasant behaviour? Or do we just keep an eye on them as they grow up and watch for any signs of problems developing? Or do we not use the knowledge we have on the grounds that it is unethical to discriminate in this way? Or is it unethical to have the knowledge to rid society of crime and anti-social behaviour and not use it?

Controlling or empowering – another perspective

(KS 2, 12, 16, 17, 21)

Your role is to support children and young people to find ways to make changes to their behaviour if they want to do so. You may have the knowledge and skill to show them how, but you cannot make them do things your way. The whole idea of 'managing' behaviour indicates some wish to control the way children and young people behave. Rather, we should look at ways to improve outcomes for children and young people, making changes in order to reduce the need for children to communicate hurt, fear, frustration and anger through challenging behaviour. All of the psychological theories have another thing in common: they are based on the individual. The focus of the learning for this unit is also around looking at how you change the behaviour of an individual child or young person through working with them to achieve change.

Social model and child-centred practice

However, there is another perspective. The social model looks at the barriers that are in the way of the achievement of the outcomes the child or young person has identified. These barriers need to be challenged and overcome to make it possible for the young person to achieve their goal. Barriers can be many different factors such as:

- education
- attitudes and parenting styles
- finance
- attitudes of teachers/employers
- expectations of others
- accessibility.

There may be many more depending on the circumstances of the individual child or young person. Whatever the barriers are, working to remove or overcome them can make it possible to achieve the identified goals. The difference is in not making the assumption that the problem lies with the child; the problems may lie in the environment and attitudes that surround the child.

Historically, explanations of challenging behaviour have tended to focus on the child or young person as being the problem. More recently, studies have also recognised that schools, and teachers in particular, can contribute to, or in some cases even cause, behaviour problems in pupils (*Pupil Behaviour and Teacher Culture*, Miller, A. 1996).

A range of factors can contribute to the effective management of a classroom and research findings that some teachers are simply not sufficiently skilled in some of these areas have been supported by Ofsted. The factors are:

- room layout
- classroom routines
- managing transitions
- maintaining momentum
- curriculum issues
- managing groups.

There is also a body of research that has indicated that the standard of pupil behaviour can be partly influenced by factors within a school's control.

Factors such as these identified by Ofsted can help in preventing behaviour problems in schools:

- common policies on behaviour
- clear rules
- consistent use of rewards

A range of factors can contribute to the effective management of a classroom

- a pleasant working environment
- young people feeling involved in the school
- attention paid to classroom management issues
- purposeful leadership
- good record keeping
- partnership with parents and other agencies.

Parental involvement

(KS 4, 5, 9, 13, 19, 20, 21)

Poor relationships between parents and social workers and/or parents and schools have also been shown to contribute to prolonging behaviour problems. A cycle can develop, with challenging behaviour by the young person resulting in either a defensive and aggressive parental response or parents becoming demoralised and 'giving up'; both result in the withdrawal of parents' support, followed by a breakdown of relationships. This can lead to a lack of co-ordination and support between school and home, which has further negative effects on the young person's behaviour.

The focus of professional practice is to place the child at the centre and child-centred practice is about building on the strengths of the child. Using psychological theories to help you to think about the underlying reasons for challenging behaviour can be useful. However, when you are working out a plan to deal with the issues around behaviour, be careful not to focus on what is 'wrong' with the child, or what his or her 'problem' is. Make sure that you look at the complex interaction of all the factors and do not just see the child or young person as the problem.

Reflect

Official terminology also has a tendency to place blame with the pupil, not the system. The formal definition of emotional and behavioural difficulties was provided about 20 years ago. It identifies 'children who set up barriers between themselves and their learning through inappropriate, aggressive, bizarre or withdrawn behaviour.' (Circular 23/89 Department for Education and Science, 1989.)

Think about how you respond to challenging behaviour. Do you sometimes make a difference between the children who 'can't' and the children who 'won't'? Do you believe that challenging behaviour results from issues in the physical, social and emotional history of the individual child? Or do you see that it is how the world around them responds that results in challenging behaviour from some children? Where do your boundaries for acceptable behaviour come from? Have they changed since you started doing this work? How often do you take time out to think about your own views on these sorts of issues? Take some time out now – think about it, talk to colleagues and your manager. The clearer you are, the better your practice will be.

Boundaries

(KS 30)

Boundaries are the limits of behaviour that is acceptable in any situation. For example, it might be acceptable to make a comment expressing disappointment and anger to a teacher who has just explained that a much-anticipated trip has had to be cancelled; it is beyond the limits to punch him because you are angry. It is acceptable to say that you don't like a particular meal that has been served and to ask for something else – you may even get away with being a bit rude about the meal; it is beyond the limits to throw the meal at the wall and shout that you are 'not eating this muck'.

Some children and young people who present challenging behaviour do so because they have problems knowing, or accepting, boundaries for their behaviour. Most of us learn and conform to boundaries early in life, and each time we move into

a new situation, we learn and conform to the boundaries there. Supporting children to recognise and conform to boundaries is a key part of enabling them to change their own behaviour. You can play a key role in helping children and young people to find out the difference between where they think the boundaries are and where everyone else thinks they are – and then to look at what happens because of the gap.

Planning for change

(KS 13, 18, 30)

As with any programme of change, it is important that children and young people set goals and targets and some means of checking when they reach them. One of your key roles is to support this process by working with children, young people and their families to identify the behaviours they want to change and the way they want to do it.

Workable goals

When planning a programme to work to change the behaviour of a child or young person, it is essential that the goals and targets developed and the boundaries proposed are within the ability of the child to achieve. If you are working with a child whose behaviour is a challenge because of a learning or sensory disability, you can work to bring about changes in behaviour that will make life better for the child or young person and their family, but do not set unrealistic expectations that can result in frustration and actually make behaviour even more challenging as a consequence.

Any work to improve behaviour should be part of the agreed overall plan for the child or young person, and you should ensure that, in addition to the family, all other professionals are aware of any work that you are doing. This is particularly important for people who have regular contact such teachers and learning support staff.

Hi, I'm Adam and I work in an independent living scheme for young people. I am the key worker for Jacob, who is now 17. I did ask him to write this, but he told me where to get off!

Hopefully, I can persuade him to talk to you later. He lives in a bedsit unit with four other young people, all of whom have been in care for fairly long periods – Jacob since he was 10. He has no contact with his family, apart from a very occasional visit to his grandmother, who is elderly and quite frail and confused. His father was never on the scene and his mother abandoned him and went to live in Spain with a new bloke when he was 10. Jacob is keen to find a permanent job, but has left every work experience he has tried because, as soon as someone tries to explain anything to him, or makes suggestions about what he can do to improve his work, he takes it as criticism and becomes abusive and storms out, blaming the employer. He is far less like this with us: he can be a bit quick to take offence, but not in any way that causes any serious difficulties in the hostel. When we were discussing work as part of his Pathway Plan, Jacob felt that it would be really hard to keep a job because they were all t******, and he couldn't understand why everyone was 'always picking on him'. We spent a long time working on this, and the other young people talked to him too, and he did begin to understand that it is his responses that have caused the problems, not anything done by any of the employers. Once he could admit that this may be a possible reason, although he was not fully convinced, we looked at ways to improve his responses to comments in the workplace. We began by getting Jacob to decide on his goal and his targets, then worked on a plan in order to reach each of the targets. The plan finally looks like this:

Goal: Find and keep a job				
	How	**With whom**	**When**	**What**
Target 1 **Make a plan**	Go through everything. Write everything down.	Work with Adam	By end of week	Plan on a spreadsheet
Target 2 **Work out the triggers that make me angry**	List all the incidents, check what happened.	Adam	End of June	List of triggers
Target 3 **Find boundaries of what is OK at work**	Look at people at work. Talk to mates who are working.	Mates in hostel Adam	End of July	Know what I have to avoid
Target 4 **Accept comments from mates**	Ask mates in hostel to suggest ways I can improve on everyday stuff.	Everyone in hostel	August	Am OK with people, don't get angry
Target 5 **Find job**	Jim at Connexions.	Jim	September	Am employed

This type of plan, that worked well for Jacob, helped him to see exactly what he needed to do and when. It also gave the opportunities for a review and evaluation at the end of each stage.

Plans like this would not be appropriate for younger children: they would be hard to follow and would not offer the sort of motivation needed by a younger child who may not see the need to change his or her behaviour. A young adult like Jacob is in the position of being able to see the advantages he can gain from changing the way he responds to situations; a much younger child will not be able to see this. Remember child development: young children only see the world from their own perspective; they are not able to look at anyone else's point of view.

Young children see how your behaviour affects them – and they will assume that they are responsible for any negative response to their behaviour. So, whilst they will say that they are sorry they have made you cross, sad, tired or whatever – and they will mean it – young children cannot have the insight to understand how they can change their behaviour. Young children will, however, respond to a change in environment, different attitudes and different responses to their behaviour. In the next element you will look at ways to work alongside children to achieve behaviour changes.

Understanding young children's behaviour

(KS 2, 5, 7, 26, 29)

Sometimes it can be helpful for you to have a checklist of questions to help you to work with the child and family to develop some realistic goals. As always, any checklist will not fit all circumstances, but will provide you with a basis to develop further.

- [ ] Does the child recognise that his/her behaviour is problematic?
- [ ] Does he/she care and want to find solutions?
- [ ] Does the child have a reason or explanation for his/her behaviour?
- [ ] Does the explanation make sense and does it present safeguarding/protection concerns?
- [ ] How does the child benefit from the behaviour?
- [ ] What seems to be motivating the child to behave in this way?
- [ ] Can this motivation be used for more positive behaviours?
- [ ] Are there any incentives and rewards that might help?
- [ ] How does the child demonstrate resilience in any aspect of his/her life?
- [ ] Can you build on this resource to help bring about change in his/her behaviour?
- [ ] How can you do it?
- [ ] What skills would he/she need to develop?
- [ ] Has the child had any previous success in coping with strong feelings and experiences in a positive way?
- [ ] How can you help him/her identify the skills and resources he/she used previously and apply them to current issues?
- [ ] Who are the role models for this child?
- [ ] Are they providing a positive influence?
- [ ] If not, how can a positive role model become part of the child's life?
- [ ] How are peer pressures influencing the behaviour?
- [ ] Can this be changed – if so, how?
- [ ] How do the significant adults for the child support him/her in developing resilience? (Parent, carer, teacher, teaching assistant, learning mentor, etc.)
- [ ] Do you need to develop this support further?
- [ ] Can you provide support for the adults?

✓ Using this sort of a checklist can be useful in helping to organise your thinking around a particular child and make it easier to see how an effective plan can be worked out. Think of it like a journey: You cannot think clearly about how you are going to get to Kent whilst you are lost around Trafalgar Square. You need to stop driving around in circles, look at a map and plan a route.

✓ Sometimes you are gathering information about a child, but it is not always easy to see its significance or meaning, and sometimes you will have more information than you think. It is only when you sit down and organise it and ask yourself a series of questions that you realise how much you actually know about the child. Taking time to work through some basic questions will pay dividends in the long term.

Review and evaluation

(KS 9, 13)

Getting feedback on progress is essential to keep children and young people motivated. Like any other programme included in a child or young person's plan, it is essential to review and evaluate progress. If there is an ongoing process of review built into the planning, then it is easier to pick up approaches to dealing with challenging behaviour that are working, and ones that are not, so that plans can be changed. There will be a regular review in any event, but it can be helpful to build in opportunities for you to give feedback on how the work is going. There two different types of review: de-brief evaluation and individual evaluation.

De-brief evaluation

This follows a major incident when it is important that everyone involved has a 'de-brief' and a chance to discuss and evaluate what happened. A de-brief review following a major incident of challenging behaviour should involve:

- the child or young person, if appropriate
- their family, carer or advocate
- the staff involved
- other members of the team working with the child
- management at the appropriate level.

The review should not be about blame or deciding who was at fault; it must be about looking at exactly what happened, how it affects those involved and strategies for preventing it from happening again. The result should provide recommendations for action by the organisation at a policy level and action with the individual child to develop new approaches to addressing the unwanted behaviour or with the young person in relation to managing his or her own behaviour with guidance and support.

Individual evaluation

The other type of evaluation is for individual young people or children and their families as part of the process of improving challenging behaviour. This is ongoing and may be part of a regular review or may occur at agreed review points in the plan.

The easiest way to review and evaluate progress is to:

- look at the plan
- identify the targets
- judge whether the targets have been met, then:
  - if not, try to work out why not and reschedule or develop different targets
  - if they have been met, move on to next stage.

Active knowledge
HSC 326a pc 8,
HSC 326c pc 10, 11

Outline the policies and procedures which you use in your setting to report and record incidents of unwanted behaviour.

HSC 326b Support children and young people to manage challenging behaviour

How many times have you behaved in a way that you are unhappy with and thought: 'Why did I do that?' You may have snapped or shouted at a child or a partner, or been totally unreasonable in your reaction to something quite minor. It happens to everyone sometimes. The key word there is 'sometimes'. For most people, behaving in an unpleasant or aggressive way is the exception: we don't like ourselves very much for having done it, but it is a rare occurrence. There are, however, some children and young people whose behaviour presents a challenge, both for themselves and for everyone else, on a regular basis.

The keys to working successfully to support children and young people in 'managing' behaviour are that you work **with** them and their families and not **instead of** them, and that you put the child and their strengths at the centre of the work. You will need to be careful that you are supporting young people and parents of younger children to reach decisions they are happy with about how to address the issues around behaviour, and not just imposing your own solutions.

In the previous section, you looked at an overview of some of the main areas of psychological theory in relation to the development of challenging behaviour. Each of the schools of thought takes a slightly different approach to managing challenging behaviour, and, although you are not going to work as a psychologist or a therapist, it is still important that you have an overview of the approaches taken by the main schools of thought.

Reflect

Think about a time when you know you behaved in a completely unacceptable way. Make some notes about what you did, how you felt at the time and how you felt afterwards. Particularly, try to remember whether you felt as if you were out of control. See if you can think about any reason why you might have behaved like that.

Different approaches

(KS 12)

Behavourist approach

The approach of behaviourist psychologists is to offer rewards for acceptable behaviour and sanctions for unacceptable behaviour. This is an approach that has been used with great success in schools, usually offering stars or stamps to accumulate points for a reward and public recognition of the acceptable behaviour. The 'positive discipline' models focus on rewarding acceptable or 'wanted' behaviour; the rewards motivate the children to change behaviour. For some children, this works because they are competitive and will work for any incentive; for others, it is the praise and recognition that is the motivating factor. There is plenty of evidence to show that these programmes work whilst the incentives are in place; you will need to make sure that any behaviour changes can be maintained and built on.

Active knowledge

Think of a time you have used the behaviourist approach in your own life. It may have been something like stopping smoking or dieting, or perhaps you used it with your children. Make notes about the circumstances, why you used it and whether or not it was effective.

Cognitivist approach

This theory focuses on the attitudes and beliefs behind behaviours: in other words, 'how you think affects what you do' and 'what you do affects how you think'. The approach to managing challenging behaviour is to provide children and young people with the tools they need to improve how they respond to the 'triggers'. This includes supporting them to develop problem-solving skills, self-control and showing ways to reduce and cope with stress.

Humanist approach

This approach believes that working on raising children and young people's self-esteem and abilities to deal with feelings and emotions will result in a reduction in challenging behaviour. The approach views the ability to form relationships as being of key importance for a child or young person in being able to manage their own behaviour.

Reflect

Think about a time when you have felt really down and low and did not like yourself very much. Then someone has been supportive and said or done something to make you feel better about yourself. How much did it help the way you were feeling when you felt better about yourself, and liked yourself a bit more?

Psychodynamic approach

The psychodynamic approach supports the use of therapy, family therapy, counselling and group work to support children and young people to resolve issues that are based on earlier experiences. This approach is often used to support children and young people who have had abusive experiences in their past. Your role is not to be a therapist or a counsellor, and these sorts of interventions require specialist training, but you do need to be aware that this may be appropriate for some of the children and young people you support, and that the assessment or review process will identify the need for a specialist referral.

Systems approach

Systems theory is based on the view that children and young people's responses to the world are based on the 'system' of their living environment. As a result, behaviour can become a 'vicious circle' because that is the only system children are able to function in. So, if a child is part of a system in which the response to what is seen as aggression from others is to be even more aggressive in return, the result is a vicious circle of aggression – leading to more aggression – leading to more aggression – and so on. The approach here is to try to break the circle of behaviour, by changing and replacing the negative responses with more positive alternatives – thus creating a 'virtuous circle'. For example, the child could be supported to view the behaviour of a teacher organising a class as 'making sure everyone got to take part' rather than 'making me stop talking to Stacy'. This shift in how behaviour is perceived will lead to a change in response – thus creating a different 'circle'.

Reflect

Think of an occasion when you have misinterpreted someone's behaviour. Perhaps you have thought they were being aggressive or confrontational, but when it was explained to you that they are actually very frightened, you feel very differently and this changes your response. This doesn't just apply to aggression – think of at least one other type of behaviour you have misinterpreted and how your response changed when you understood it differently.

Interactionist approach

Interactionist approaches work on the premise that there is a genetic predisposition towards certain behaviour – 'nature' – but that this is also influenced by the environment and circumstances people are in – 'nurture'. Managing challenging behaviour using this approach is about recognising and changing the circumstances, or the response to the circumstances, thus reducing the factors which can trigger challenging behaviour, and allowing the positive personality traits to be more in evidence. This means looking at what is stopping the child or young person behaving in an acceptable way; this could be the effect of limited parenting skills or it could be the school lessons that do not fire the child's imagination or hold his or her attention. Addressing these issues, rather than seeing the child as the problem, can bring about changes in behaviour.

Restorative approach

There are some basic principles that underpin restorative approaches.

1   Positive relationships are at the heart of success.

2   Those who have caused harm should have the opportunity to face those they have harmed.

3   Those who have been harmed should have a chance to be heard and have a say in how the harm should be repaired.

4   Those who have done harm should have the chance to make amends.

The restorative approach manages challenging behaviour by: working to restore damaged relationships; viewing the victim's needs as central to the process; looking for ways to make amends; and, most importantly, taking account of the needs, views and feelings of all those affected by the behaviour. This is often used in bullying situations, and is also used by the criminal justice system where those convicted may have to make amends with the victim.

Positive approaches

(KS 23, 24, 25, 27, 28, 29, 30)

Using your checklist should have helped you to work out the best ways to plan to work with a specific child or young person. Find areas of strength and build on them. There are no hard and fast rules here – different children have different strengths – but you could have an exchange like the following.

'Gemma, you know I was only thinking yesterday about how good you are at recognising how other people feel.'

'What? You sure you're talking about me? Remember I'm aggressive and unpleasant and not fit to be in the school, so Mrs posh Henshaw says.'

'Yes, I know that's what she said and that's what got me thinking about you.'

'Yeah – and?'

'I was thinking about how kind you were to Rose when she first arrived and she was so scared and kept wetting the bed and wouldn't speak to anyone.'

'What you on about? It was obvious what was up with her. I knew about the bed

wetting because that's what my sister did for years. I used to have to wash her sheets 'cos Mum was usually in no fit state – and she probably wouldn't have done it anyway. I just wanted her to stop 'cos she was in my room – that's all.'

'I don't believe you.'

'You calling me a liar?'

'You bet I am – you were really kind to her, you kept the others off her and didn't let anyone start anything. You talked to her all the time. I know you didn't go out with your mates some evenings because Rose was upset and you stayed in to talk to her.'

'Maybe once or twice – anyway, what's that got to do with Miss posh face and me being excluded for calling her 'a stuck up f**** cow?'**

'Well, because I was surprised that you hadn't picked up some of the same feelings from her as you did from Rose.'

'You having a laugh? She was so lah-di-dah from the first day. She just thought she could boss us around.'

'I'm sure she was – but this is her first teaching job, and you lot are not the easiest prospect. She was really nervous so came over dead strict so she could show her authority.'

'Do you reckon? I dunno – but you could be right.'

'I heard from Jamie that she came up against Maria yesterday and Maria threatened that she'd be waiting for her.'

'She did? She's only doing that because she thinks she's something while I'm excluded. She wouldn't be half so brave if I was there.'

'Well, I don't know about that, but she did anyway – Jamie said Mrs Henshaw seemed really upset afterwards when he went back in the classroom to get his bag.'

'Well, she would be, wouldn't she – having that b****** threatening her. Well, I'm back next Monday and madam Maria will get put back in her place. I mean – it's her first teaching job, they need to give her a break...'

Acceptable is good

Whatever approach you adopt, it is important that the child or young person can see what they have to gain from behaving in ways that are considered acceptable. This is not just about stars on a chart for cinema tickets or a mention in assembly, important as those motivators are, but also about what will happen in their lives. If you are working with a young person who is at an age where they can look at the benefits of behaviour change, then getting them to list, or just to talk about, the changes that could happen can be very useful. Using scenarios and 'what if …' can be a useful way to start. Here's how the conversation could go.

'What if you didn't fight with your mum every day. What would your life be like?'

'But I do fight with her every day because she is just such a pain.'

'Yes, I know you do – but I want you to tell me what would happen if you didn't. Just imagine it, how it could be – you come in from school – your mum's there – what happens?'

'What happens if we don't fight?'

'Yes – what do you say?'

'Hiya Mum – y'alright?'

'And what does she say?'

'Hello son – you had a good day?'

'Then what happens?'

'I make her a cup of tea, and we sit down and talk about what she's done and what I've done, then we decide what we're having to eat and she goes off to cook it. I get on the computer and MSN people. Then we eat, then we watch telly.'

'Sounds nice.'

'Yeah, but it's not real is it?'

'Could be.'

'Couldn't – not with her.'

'What about you? Isn't some of it about you?'

'Suppose.'

'If you did a bit about the things you say, maybe she would too, then you could have an evening like you just described.'

'Do you think?'

'I think so. Why don't we go and talk to her?'

'OK – worth a try.'

The two scenarios described and any other ways in which you decide to approach challenging behaviour must be carefully planned, and everyone involved must understand the rules and exactly what behaviour is acceptable and what is not. Children and young people need to know where boundaries are and they need the security that comes from having boundaries firmly implemented.

For example: if you have an agreed programme with six-year-old Katie that if she kicks or hits or hurts another child or adult, she goes to 'time out', then you must ensure that happens every time without fail; equally, you cannot send her to 'time out' because she has sworn at someone or thrown something because that was not in the rules. Only look at one unwanted behaviour at a time; it is too much to try to work on hitting and kicking at the same time as swearing or spitting!

Children and young people need behavioural boundaries

The single most important part of making this work is that you praise Katie to the hilt every time she is in a situation where she is angry and she would previously have hit someone, but she doesn't. She must get the praise and recognition she deserves for her efforts, and whatever stars or points she gets if there is a reward system.

Being positive

The attitudes of all the people in children and young people's lives are important in making this approach work. The National Programme for Leaders in Behaviour and Attendance (Department for Education and Skills 2005) developed a useful tool for encouraging teachers to look positively at children and young people displaying challenging behaviour. Here we use the tool for Gemma, whose conversation you heard a little earlier. We look at the difference when her teachers made comments about her for her report, and when they were asked to complete the same form but could only include positive comments and positive areas for further development.

Gemma D End of term report

SUBJECT	TEACHER	COMMENTS
Science	Mr Mason	Gemma is able to do more, but chooses to clown around.
Mathematics	Mrs Thomas	Appears incapable of listening to instructions, almost no homework completed.
English	Dr Stevenson	Gemma may always wants to be the star of the show but is not prepared to work at it.

SUBJECT	TEACHER	COMMENTS
German	Mr Jones	Gemma has poor concentration and can be disruptive. She is capable of doing much better.
Humanities	Mr Morrison	Often leaves work unfinished. Concentration poor. Wanders around the classroom.
Design Technology	Miss Johnson	Gemma has no interest in this subject. She is a very distracting influence on the class.
Art	Ms Howes	Gemma takes far too much of my attention and often interferes with the work of others. Her behaviour is poor.
Music	Mr Bell	Gemma is a very capable student who works hard and is enthusiastic.
PE	Mrs Vickery	Gemma is more interested in entertaining others than in PE.
PSHE	Mrs Henshaw	Gemma makes a positive contribution to class discussions, showing sensitivity and maturity when discussing the feelings of others.
FORM TUTOR	Ms Henshaw	It was pleasing to read about Gemma's progress in music, however, I was sad to read many of the other comments. I feel that Gemma has the potential to do well if she would only give herself the chance to do so.

Gemma D – strengths and areas for development

SUBJECT	STRENGTHS	AREAS TO WORK ON
Science	Works well when she is feeling settled and calm.	Taking her turn to contribute in class discussions – listening respectfully to others.
Mathematics	Algebra. Gemma seems to have a real feel for this.	Homework, concentration, doing as she is told!
English	Presentation skills, her diagrams are neatly drawn and labelled.	Application to the set task.
German	Speaking and listening. She has a good accent and is confident in speaking out in class.	Punctuality and persistence.
Humanities	Good recall of information.	Finishing tasks. Staying in her seat (and in the classroom!).
Design Technology	Gemma's graphic skills.	Concentration. Motivation. Working quietly.
Art	She seems to enjoy this subject. She has produced a good 'still life' drawing. She showed real persistence in working on this until she was completely satisfied.	Staying calm when things don't go quite as she wants them to.

SUBJECT	STRENGTHS	AREAS TO WORK ON
Music	Puts a lot of effort into this lesson. She shines when presenting to the class.	More of the same; keep up the good work!
PE	Good at expressive dance – she could become a reasonable gymnast with a bit more effort.	Having the correct kit. Working as part of a team.
PSHE and Tutorial	Gemma often surprises me with her knowledge. She can show real empathy to classmates (and me!).	Staying focused on the task. Making sure others see her good side. Developing the skills for working in a group.

Supporting parents

(KS 9, 13, 21)

In many situations, it may be the parents you are providing the support for. Following through a programme of changing behaviour with a child is a daunting task and requires a huge amount of input from parents in following the plan and sticking to their part of the deal.

They will need constant support so that they remember the overall goal and don't become sidetracked by responding to behaviour that is not part of achieving the main goal. Parents also have to fight against reverting to previous ways of dealing with their child's behaviour. Any materials you can produce to remind parents will be very valuable. It could be sticky notes to put on the fridge saying things like:

- Is this helping to achieve the goal?
- Just one behaviour at a time
- Explain everything
- Praise every wanted behaviour
- Be consistent.

Find out if there is a network in your area where parents who are dealing with challenging behaviour can be in contact. If not, think about starting one.

Relaxing

(KS 25)

One of the ways in which you can support children and young people is to offer strategies to help them to manage their own behaviour. Learning to relax is one of the valuable ways that challenging behaviour can be reduced. Not all young children will be able to use the techniques, but older children and young people can master using deep breaths to calm down and relaxing generally to get rid of tensions and stresses. Older young people may also be able to use the muscle relaxing techniques described on the following page. Calming and soothing music may be the order of the day to accompany relaxation, but for many young people, chilling out listening to music not usually thought of as relaxing may work better!

Relaxation can reduce challenging behaviour

Abdominal breathing

A simple way of encouraging the mind and body to relax is to practise abdominal breathing. It is generally accepted that people who are anxious and under stress breathe in a shallow way, from their chest, whilst those who are more relaxed breathe more slowly and deeply, from their abdomen. Practising abdominal breathing is an excellent way of relieving stress and anxiety and encouraging calmness and relaxation. It is a simple technique to learn and to practise, and is useful to offer as advice to someone who is feeling distressed, anxious or stressed.

1   Place one hand on your abdomen just beneath your rib cage.

2   Inhale slowly and deeply through your nose feeling the air going as deep as possible into your lungs. You will know if you are breathing from your abdomen as your hand will rise. The chest will only move slightly. If your chest moves or rises whilst your abdomen falls or does not move, then you have not done it correctly and should try again. It is important that your abdomen rises as you breath in.

3   Pause following the breath in, then exhale slowly through your nose or mouth. Exhale fully and allow your whole body to relax and become loose and limp.

4   Repeat. In order to feel calm and relaxed you should try 10 slow full abdominal breaths, keeping breathing smooth and regular.

Maximum benefit is reported by people who maintain five minutes of abdominal breathing on a daily basis. This is also a useful exercise that can be undertaken at any time when people feel the onset of distress, stress or anxiety.

Progressive muscle relaxation

Another useful way of encouraging people to relax in order to minimise their distress is to use a very simple technique of progressive muscle relaxation. This is very useful for people who become very tense as a result of stress or anxiety, which can result in muscle tightness in the shoulders and neck or tension headaches, backaches and tightness around the jaw and eyes.

Before commencing progressive muscle relaxation it is important to ensure that you are in a quiet setting where you will be undisturbed. You may want to play soothing gentle music in the background. Ideally relaxation should be practised on an empty stomach before meals. You will need to loosen any tight clothing and take off shoes, contact lenses, watches, glasses, etc.

You should assume a comfortable position, your entire body should be supported, lying down on a sofa or bed, provided you will not fall asleep, or sitting in a reclining chair. Once you are sitting or lying comfortably in a quiet and relaxing atmosphere, then you should follow these instructions.

1   Start by taking three abdominal breaths, exhaling slowly each time.

2   Clench your fists, hold tightly for 7 to 10 seconds, then release for 15 to 20 seconds.

3   Tighten your biceps by drawing your forearms up towards your shoulders, hold as before for 7 to 10 seconds, then release for 15 to 20 seconds.

4   Tighten your triceps (the muscles on the undersides of your upper arms) by extending your arms out straight and locking your elbows, hold as before and then relax.

5   Tense the muscles in your forehead by raising your eyebrows as far as you can, hold and then relax.

6   Tense the muscles around your eyes by clenching your eyelids tightly shut, hold then relax.

7   Tense your jaw muscles by opening your mouth widely to stretch the muscles around the hinges of your jaw, hold and then relax.

8   Tighten the muscles in the back of your neck by pulling your head back as if you were going to touch your head on your back, hold and then relax.

9   Tighten your shoulders by raising them towards your ears, hold and relax.

10 Tense the muscles around your shoulder blades by pushing your shoulder blades back as if you were going to touch them together, hold and relax.

11 Tighten the muscles of your chest by taking inner deep breaths, hold for 10 seconds and then release slowly.

12 Tense your stomach muscles by sucking your stomach in, hold and release.

13 Tighten your lower back by arching it up, hold and relax.

14 Tighten your buttocks by pulling them together, hold and relax.

15 Squeeze the muscles in your thighs down to your knees, hold and relax.

16 Tighten your calf muscles by pulling your toes towards you, hold and relax.

17 Tighten your feet by curling your toes downwards, hold and relax.

18 Scan your body to see if you can find any particular area that remains tense: if there is a tense area, simple repeat the tense and relax cycles for that group of muscles.

19 You then need to imagine a wave of relaxation spreading throughout your body starting at your head and penetrating every muscle group all the way to your toes. The entire muscle relaxation sequence is likely to take you between 20 and 30 minutes and you should enjoy that relaxing process and making that time for yourself.

For maximum benefit the exercises should be done on a daily basis, but they can also be used in response to having been in a particularly tense or stressful situation.

Test yourself

1 What is the most important part of any behaviour change programme?

2 Which professionals should be engaged with a behaviour change programme?

3 What kind of approach would a psychodynamic therapist take to changing behaviour?

4 What kind of approach would a therapist from the interactionist school take?

5 Why is praise so important?

HSC 326c Enable children and young people to recognise and understand their behaviour and its consequences

Causes

(KS 2, 26)

Having looked at some of the reasons why children and young people behave in a challenging way, we need to look at some of the causes – the 'triggers' for the behaviour.

Remember

Causes and reasons are not the same thing.

Naturally, every child and young person is different, and they will react to situations differently. Circumstances that will trigger challenging behaviour in one child will not do so in another.

It is important that you look at the causes for each individual child. The most effective way to approach this is likely to be a combination of observation and discussion. As you work alongside the child or young person, it will become clear what or who seems to trigger outbursts of unwanted behaviour. Your observations need to be confirmed through a conversation with the child or young person in a one-to-one session. You will need to use all of your communication skills, including active listening, to make sure that the child or young person feels secure and comfortable with you.

How to support children and young people

(KS 2, 14, 15, 22)

It is helpful if you can encourage a child or young person to look at their behaviour by working with them to 'replay', as far as possible, the events which led up to the most recent incident of challenging behaviour. Try to look at three or four incidents at least and see if there is a pattern emerging. There usually is.

You must do this at the appropriate level of communication for the child. The approach with a 6-year-old might be to plan an activity around 'things that make us happy and things that make us cross'. This will give you an opportunity to explore some of the 'cross things'. The activity could be painting or cutting out or it could be a game of putting things into baskets, giving names to stones or balls before putting them in a happy or cross basket. You can then talk about each of the items as you go.

With a young person you may sit down with them to make a chart, showing the behaviour, the incident, what happened immediately before it and the circumstances surrounding it. There is an example on the next page.

Pete's behaviour chart

When	Behaviour	Who	Where	What	Mood prior
Saturday morning	Verbal abuse, very angry, kicked over coffee table	Charlie, Marie, Mark	Main lounge	Asked Mark to borrow jacket – Mark refused	Happy – looking forward to night out
Thursday evening	Verbal abuse, pushed Charlie against wall	Charlie, Marie, Dave	Kitchen	Wanted ice-cream for pudding, none left, Charlie eaten it all	Fed up – boring day at school
Tuesday morning	Verbal abuse, angry, smashed dressing table mirror	Alone	Bedroom	Phone call from ex-girlfriend – does not want to get back together	Grumpy – first thing in morning

Taking this table as an example, this might mean that you can sit down with Pete, use the process of drawing up the table as a time to talk about what led to the incidents and then try to find any common factors or patterns in the finished table. Patterns can be based on:

- people present
- place
- mood
- trigger
- type of behaviour
- time of day.

Looking at the table for Pete, you could suggest that he look at the triggers. In each case it has been a disappointment – some apparently minor, some quite significant – but each has provoked similar behaviour. Pete's behaviour is usually similar – verbal aggression and damage to the immediate environment; in one incident there was a threat of physical violence.

In Pete's case, it does not look as if it is a particular person who triggers his behaviour, nor does it seem to be a particular mood or a place. Of course, this is only looking at three occasions; in reality, you will be likely to look at quite a few more before you can see patterns emerging.

Active knowledge HSC 326c pc 5, 6, 7

Ideally, this should be done with an individual you work with who is presenting challenging behaviour. However, if this is not possible, you can work with a friend or colleague and use examples of any type of behaviour – it doesn't matter if it is happy, sad, scared or angry. Work with someone to produce a table like the one shown for Pete, using at least six occasions. Complete all of the sections and then look at the patterns you can see. Make notes about the patterns and then try to see the possible causes or triggers, making notes, with explanations. If you have done this with an individual you are supporting, use what you have learned about human behaviour to make some notes on what you think some of the underlying reasons for the behaviour may be.

Facing up to consequences

(KS 20)

One of the difficult tasks you can face when dealing with challenging behaviour is making sure that a child or young person understands that there are consequences which result from what they do. For example, if they are living in a residential setting with other young people, and others are being placed at risk from violent or aggressive behaviour, then ultimately it may be that they are not able to remain.

Similarly, in a setting such as a supported living environment, someone who is aggressive and disruptive may ultimately be asked to leave.

There are inevitably tensions when young people share living space; this is true of families so it is inevitable that young people without the close bonds of a family will have issues when they live together. However, there is a difference between tensions and others being at risk, and if challenging behaviour is placing other vulnerable young people at serious risk, then it cannot be allowed to continue. Sometimes it is hard to decide between the rights of an individual young person and your responsibilities to others you support, but the question of risk to others is always the decider.

Depending on the circumstances in which young people are living, the consequences of their behaviour may involve losing friends or family. It could involve disputes with neighbours or criminal proceedings: unacceptable anti-social behaviour can result in the kind of restrictions on freedom imposed by an anti-social behaviour order (ASBO) or a custodial sentence in the case of serious criminal activity.

Challenging behaviour can also have devastating effects on people close to the child or young person, and you will need to help them to look at and face up to the effects of their behaviour on other people that they care about. It is not easy to face the fact that your behaviour frightens your mother or worries your girlfriend, but as young people mature, they need to be able to take responsibility for their behaviour.

The law says that children from the age of 10 understand the difference between right and wrong and must take criminal responsibility for any illegal behaviour. Many children of this age do not fully understand the consequences of their actions and, whilst they can see an immediate and direct consequence, it is harder for them to think about some of the 'knock on' effects and broader consequences.

Your role is to make sure that older children and young people are aware of what could happen as a result of their behaviour. Sometimes, becoming aware of consequences can be a motivation for young people to deal with their behaviour: if they are able to realise that they are at risk of losing their home or people they care about, then they may decide that this is the point to do something about the behaviour.

Other help

(KS 21)

Your role is to support children and young people; you are not a therapist, psychiatrist or psychologist – nor should you try to be. However, there are some children and young people who will need more specialist help than you can give in order to understand their behaviour. You will need to discuss with them, their parents and the team the options for seeking further help, either through CAMHS or through their social worker.

 My story

Hi, I'm Jacob. I'm 17 and I live in a hostel – that's sort of halfway between care and being out on your own. I've been in care since I was 10 – there's only my gran, and she's away with the fairies, got no idea if I've been to see her not, so there's no point, is there? Anyway, now I'm working I don't have much time. I've got a really great job working for an IT company, and they said they'll give me more training and all that. But I'm telling you about this because it wasn't always like that. When I first left school I had a few different jobs – I met some right planks, honest I did, but if any of them would like, tell me what to do, I just felt as if they was picking on me. It was like as if because I'd been in care they didn't think I was good enough – or something. I don't really know where my head was. Anyway – I kept on walking out. Adam was really positive. He said I could deal with this and that he was sure that I could get a job, if I just got better at dealing with like being criticised. He explained that you could have 'constructive criticism' – that's when people make suggestions about what you could do better – and that this was different from people finding fault or saying you was doing something wrong. We made a plan about how I was going to get a job and keep it. It looked OK when we planned it out. All the others in the hostel helped out too – it was like everyone really cared – especially Adam. I had to listen to stuff that my mates in the hostel said and not get mad. It was hard at first, but I did try dead hard because I knew I was going nowhere if I didn't. And now – here I am – good job and going prosspects. What do you mean, I've spelt that wrong? Are you saying I can't spell? Are you saying I'm illiterate? It's OK – I'm only joking – but see – six months ago that would've been for real!

Dealing with challenging behaviour

(KS 5, 14, 15, 25)

This unit is about supporting children and young people to manage their own challenging behaviour, but it is important that you have the ability to deal with potentially violent or aggressive behaviour and to defuse a situation. This is not an issue of safety for you if you work with very young children; you may end up with a bruised shin (but if you get bitten by a distressed young child, that must receive immediate medical attention as human bites can become badly infected.) It is potentially a safety issue if you work with older children and young people.

You need to be able to judge when a situation is developing and when a child or young person is starting to show behaviour that may place themselves or others at risk. If you can intervene in the early stages, it is often easier to defuse and calm a situation.

Physical effects of strong emotions

There are definite and measurable physical effects caused by strong and powerful emotional responses. It is useful to be aware of these physical effects of emotion, as they can often be an early indicator of a potentially highly charged or dangerous situation. The physical effects of strong emotion can be any or all of the following:

- pupils dilate, the eye lids open wider than usual, and the eyes protrude
- speed and strength of the heart beat is increased
- blood pressure is increased and blood is forced outwards towards the surface of the body – this is clearly noticeable in flushing of the face and neck
- the hair can stand up causing goose pimples
- breathing patterns will change, this can be either faster or slower
- the lung function alters to allow up to 25 per cent more oxygen to be absorbed
- more sweat is produced – this can be often identified as a 'cold sweat'
- the salivary glands are inhibited – the dry mouth feeling

- digestion is affected – the gastric fluids are reduced and blood is withdrawn from the digestive organs
- increase in adrenaline – reinforces all effects and increases blood clotting.

This reaction of physical responses to strong emotions prepares humans for 'fight or flight'. This is a basic human response to a situation in which we are placed under threat, in which the body physically prepares us to fight or run away. There are other very noticeable effects in children and young people who are in a highly emotional state. They will often have what appears to be increased energy: for example, they don't speak, they shout; they don't sit or stand still, they will run or walk about; they will slam doors and possibly throw furniture or objects around.

There are situations in which the additional energy and strength that result from powerful emotions can be extremely valuable and essential in preserving life. There are many stories about people performing heroic feats of strength or endurance when in the most severe emotional situations, for example, in a house fire or an accident or some other life-threatening situation. Another apparent effect of strong emotional responses is a temporary lessening of the awareness of pain, again this is often seen where people have acted regardless of severe injury on the battlefield or in an accident or other emergency and it is only when the immediate threat has passed that they subsequently become aware of their injuries.

Recognising the signs

When you have a close working knowledge of a child's behaviour over a period of time, it becomes easy to identify when they are becoming angry or distressed: you will find that you have become well 'tuned in' to their behaviour and can recognise the small signs that indicate a change in mood. However, you will not always be in a situation of knowing the child or young person, or you may be dealing with challenging behaviour from a parent or even a work colleague. There are some general indications of anger or distress that you can use in order to take immediate action. Here are the things that you are most likely to notice:

- *changes in voice*: it may be raised or at a higher pitch than usual
- *changes in facial expression*: this could be scowling, crying, snarling
- *changes in eyes*: pupils could be dilated and eyes open wider
- *body language* would demonstrate agitation and people may adopt an aggressive stance leaning forward with fists clenched
- the *face and neck* are likely to be reddened
- there may be *excessive sweating*
- *changes in breathing patterns*: they may breath faster than normal.

A risk to themselves

Anger is not always directed at others: children and young people can turn anger inwards to be directed against themselves. You may be faced with a situation where a distressed, hurt and angry young person makes it clear to you that they intend to harm themselves. Where this is the case, you have a responsibility to take immediate action in order to protect the young person.

It is never acceptable for you to comply with a request from a young person to assist them in harming themselves or for you to allow them to deliberately harm themselves. If you are faced with such a request you must immediately report it to your manager and arrange for emergency assistance to assess the risk.

An assessment of risk of self-harm needs to be a specialist one in the first instance: you must not make a judgement about the likelihood of a young person harming themselves unless you have specialist knowledge and training. You may be able to contribute valuable information to support the assessment process, but the decision is in the hands of Child and Adolescent Mental Health Specialists (CAMHS).

Responding to challenging behaviour

(KS 5, 6, 7, 8, 9, 10, 25)

Your organisation will have a policy and procedures about responding to challenging behaviour and the extent of any sanctions you can use or actions you can take. You must act in line with the policies and procedures of your organisation. These will vary, but are likely to include most of the following.

- Your objective is to defuse and de-escalate the situation. First, defuse by making sure that any triggers are removed, or the child or young person is removed from the trigger.
- Do not allow an audience if possible – this is not a spectator sport, and audiences can often make children and young people feel threatened and more aggressive.
- If you are alone, simply instruct other children and young people to leave; if you have a colleague, ask them to remove those who do not need to be there.
- Do not become aggressive yourself; appear calm (even if you're not!).
- Make sure that you are between the young person and the exit – move if necessary.
- Speak in a calm, clear voice, without shouting.
- Do not make prolonged eye contact.
- Keep a relaxed posture, sitting if possible; if not, stand in a relaxed way, not full on to the young person.
- Make sure that the young person has their own space.
- If the young person is in a public space, try to move them to somewhere private.
- It is essential that you appear to be in control – remember that the young person needs someone to be in control because they're not, and that is frightening for them.
- Do not get involved, or respond to arguments or verbal abuse, but encourage communication – ask the young person to tell you why they are angry, show that you have understood.
- De-escalating requires that you provide a non-challenging situation, so do not threaten or issue an ultimatum – once you have done so, you have created a win-lose situation which can only escalate.
- Calm, clear communication and a demonstration of understanding and recognition of the causes of the anger and distress are the keys to de-escalating the situation.

Physical interventions

Physical intervention should only ever be used when there is no other alternative and all other approaches have been tried. Any physical interventions should be recorded in an incident book (as always, with numbered pages). The report must include:

- time, date and location
- young person concerned
- staff member concerned
- any witnesses, children or staff
- details of the incident and what de-escalation was attempted
- details of the physical intervention used
- information as to how the young person responded to the intervention
- how the incident was resolved.

You should not attempt to physically intervene in a violent situation unless you have been specially trained. If you feel that training would be useful for you, raise the issue with your manager.

All physical interventions must be on the basis of the minimum possible intervention necessary in order to remove the risk, and must be within local and national policy guidelines.

All organisations should have a plan for physical interventions, so that there is an understood approach which all staff use, everyone is trained in the techniques that can be used, and risk assessments have been carried out as far as possible. The intervention that may be used can range from stepping in front of a young person, barring their way, guiding by the arm or with a hand in the middle of their back, holding if absolutely necessary to avoid risk or damage to the young person or others.

Recording

Recording any incidents of challenging behaviour is vital. It is especially important if physical intervention has been necessary, but it must be done for any incident, regardless of the level.

Your organisation will have procedures and you must follow those in relation to the information you need to record and the format in which you do it. Procedures will vary, but they are likely to include the following.

1 Date, time, location
2 People present
3 Full description of incident, including what led up to it
4 Any interventions, physical or verbal
5 How the situation was resolved
6 Views of the individual concerned
7 Views of any other individuals involved or as witnesses
8 Implications for management of behaviour
9 Recommendations for next steps.

Remember that the information you are recording is subject to the Data Protection Act, so if you want to make recommendations for general policy issues or for organisational approaches, you will need to prepare a separate document, which does not identify individuals.

Recording is also very useful for individuals who are working to manage their challenging behaviour. If they, and you record any incidents, the records can be used to review progress towards targets and to check if there are problems, or targets are being missed.

The impact on you

Do not underestimate how upsetting it can be to deal with a young person who is displaying very strong and powerful emotions. Sometimes children's stories or experiences can be very moving and it is inevitable in such circumstances that we compare their situations with our own. This may make you feel very grateful for your own circumstances or it could have the effect of making you feel guilty, if you feel that you have a particularly happy situation compared to a child in appalling circumstances.

Feeling concerned, upset or even angry after a particularly emotional experience with a child is perfectly normal. Even if this is a day-to-day occurrence, as it is for many staff who work in specialised units, there will still be particular situations that will get to you and distress you.

You should not feel that the fact that you continue to have an emotional response after a situation is over is in any way a reflection of the quality of your work or your ability as a childcare professional. After dealing with any challenging or emotional situation, most people are likely to continue to think about it for some time afterwards. You should discuss it either with your line manager or another person you find supportive, but always follow the principles of confidentiality if you are talking to anyone other than your manager. If you do find after a period of time that you are not able to put a particular incident out of your mind or you feel that it is interfering with your work, with either that child or others, then there are plenty of sources of help available to you, both within your work place and outside it. You will need to talk to your line manager or supervisor to ensure that you have access to any help that you need.

The distress of children, whether it takes the form of anger or sadness or worry or anxiety, will always be

Your line manager or supervisor should be able to ensure that you have access to any help you need

upsetting for the person who works with them; but if you are able to develop your skills and knowledge so that you can identify distress, contribute towards reducing it and offer effective help and support to those children who are experiencing it, then you are making a useful and meaningful contribution to the provision of quality care for children.

Test yourself

1 Why is it important to identify triggers to challenging behaviour?

2 Why do people need to identify boundaries?

3 You need to appear calm when dealing with challenging behaviour – why?

4 Why is it important to plan the management of challenging behaviour?

HSC 326 UNIT TEST

1 Name three different approaches to understanding challenging behaviour.

2 What is the basis for most psychological theories?

3 What is the difference between reasons and causes?

4 Why is it important for people to understand the consequences of their behaviour?

5 What are the factors that have to be balanced when dealing with the effects and consequences of challenging behaviour?

Don't forget to refer to the evidence opportunities grid (see pages 357–375) for more ideas for suitable evidence for your NVQ.

Glossary

Accredited	Known to have expert knowledge in the subject concerned. The source is credible and previous experience has proved its information to be correct.
Caucasian	The technical term used by scientists, in law, etc. for referring to white people.
Cogent	Clear, logical and convincing.
Cognitive development	The development of intelligence, conscious thought and problem-solving ability which begins in infancy.
Ecomap	A diagram that uses lines to show what the different relationships in a family are like: weak, strong, stressful, etc.
Genogram	A diagram that uses symbols and lines to show the relationships in a family over three generations, giving a visual overview of the family as a whole.
Hazard	Something that could possibly cause harm.
Non-verbal communication	A way of communicating without words, through body language, gestures, facial expression and eye contact.
Palliative care	Care given to those with conditions that cannot be cured, usually terminal illnesses. The care aims to improve quality of life and lessen symptoms, but cannot actually combat the condition itself.
Pedagogue	A teacher or education specialist.
Personal development	Developing the personal qualities and skills needed to live and work with others.
Professional development	Developing the qualities and skills necessary for the workforce.
Reliability	A piece of research shows *reliability* when the results would be repeated if someone else were to carry out the same piece of research in exactly the same way, so the research can be depended on and trusted.
Risk	The likelihood of a hazard causing harm.
Risk control measures	Actions taken in order to reduce an identified risk.
Secure unit	A residential placement where the children or young people are locked in, or prevented from leaving.
Social pedagogy	Education with a focus on the child as a whole person, aiming to support their overall development as well as their academic education.
Socially clean	Clean enough to be acceptable socially, but not 'clinically clean', i.e. you could not carry out any sort of clinical contact in this condition. For hands, it means you could shake hands with someone, but not operate on them. There are three levels of clean: socially clean, clean and sterile.
Validity	A piece of research shows *validity* when the conclusions drawn from it are consistent with the results, consistent with the way in which the research was carried out and consistent with the way in which the information has been interpreted.

Evidence Opportunities Grid

How can I find evidence to show that I am knowledgeable and competent?

The evidence you collect will need to prove that you can do effectively whatever the performance criteria state. This is best done by planning observations with your assessor to show them your practice. If they cannot see you doing this, you might need to write a case study based on what you do or would do. You can sometimes ask someone who has seen you do this well to write up what you did and sign it (your assessor may be happy for you to write it up and get this person to sign it).

You must also prove that you fully understand the underlying reasons (knowledge) which underpin your practice (what you do).

This is harder to demonstrate in practice and how much you will need to write about these will depend on how much time your assessor has for oral questioning and discussion.

It is important that you remember that the knowledge which you need to demonstrate is in relation to your job role – that may mean you have to have some understanding of a child or young person's circumstances before they came to the setting in which you work, and also an insight into their next placement, or the support that will be available to them and their family if that is at home. Without this it is difficult to work effectively.

For almost all units you will need to show the knowledge identified below, and for most units most of the knowledge you need to show is very similar; you just need to make small additions relevant to specific units.

For this reason it is sensible to see how you can cover more than one unit with each bit of evidence. This is known as holistic assessment and once you get the hang of it, it will reduce repetition and also help you to see the whole picture rather than a unit-by-unit version.

Knowledge which is common to most units includes:

- values, which include such things as:
  - partnership working
  - placing the child at the centre of all you do
  - actively supporting children and young people
  - managing dilemmas
  - your own views and values and how they impact on the work you do
  - equality and diversity
  - challenging discrimination
  - rights (including the UN Convention on the Rights of the Child).
- legislation, which will always include how you work with parents (or when you will not):
  - organisational policies and procedures, which include codes of conduct
  - accountability, particularly in personal behaviour in respect to policies, legislation, standards, etc., as well as recording and reporting
  - National Minimum Standards/Ofsted standards which relate to your job role

- theory and practice (as well as practice theory which will be different for each unit) which relate to:
  - accessing information
  - involving children and young people in planning and decision making, including ways which are appropriate to the age and understanding of the child
  - human growth and development
  - identity and self-esteem
  - the effects of loss and change and the importance of stable relationships.

You will need to look at the performance criteria in each element of each unit you have chosen **and** the knowledge specifications too.

Please note that the format for Unit HSC 33 is different from the others and is covered separately.

To help you to reduce the repetition, each unit has a colour code relating to its colour in the book and where criteria overlap you will see a number of different colour codes in the third column.

31	Promote effective communication for and about individuals
32	Promote, monitor and maintain health, safety and security in the working environment
33	Reflect on and develop your own practice
34	Promote the well-being and protection of children and young people
36	Contribute to the assessment of children and young people's needs and the development of care plans
38	Support children and young people to manage their lives
39	Support children and young people to achieve their educational potential
310	Work with children and young people to prepare them for adulthood, citizenship and independence
316	Support the needs of children and young people with additional requirements
319	Support families in their own home
323	Contribute to childcare practice in group living
326	Contribute to the prevention and management of challenging behaviour in children and young people

Suggestions for how you can provide evidence of both competence and knowledge

Although the performance criteria are set out in boxes which show you how you could get more than one performance criterion about the same topic in the same piece of evidence, remember: many boxes will link together. For example, if you are communicating with a child or young person, you may also be considering their health and safety, additional needs, behaviour and self-esteem, and thinking about the policies of the setting at the same time.

We do all these things together all the time – you do not need to repeat this for every unit separately. You need to show clearly where this evidence is. You can do this by making sure the performance criterion or knowledge specification is shown, then just make sure that it is clear in your index (cross-referencing it to any relevant units and criteria). If you do this, then the assessor, internal verifier and external verifier will be able to find it easily and there will be much less repetition.

Evidence	What could it show?	Link to units
Recording and sharing information	Explain/show your assessor how you know about this child's/young person's communication needs and preferences, how you keep records and when you have shared this information with others in the team. You should be able to demonstrate that you: ● can access information about the child/young person – this could be from others/from reports/from transition paperwork/from observations/from applying theory of developmental stages (HSC 31a 1) ● understand confidentiality (all units KSE Legislation/Policies) ● understand safe storage and accessibility of information, Data Protection Act (all units KSE Legislation/Policies) ● understand sharing information in e.g. Looked After Children reviews/case conferences/child protection issues/risk assessments/health records, etc. and with whom they can be shared.	HSC 31a pc 4 HSC 31b pc 10 HSC 31d pc 1, 2, 3, 4, 5, 6, 7, 8 see also HSC 326c pc 10, 11
Interaction with a child/young person	Show your assessor how you interact with a child or young person. Show that you: ● made the most of the environment to assist the communication ● used an appropriate level/pace and tone ● positioned yourself in a non-threatening and attentive way which facilitated communication ● checked understanding, both yours and the child's (where appropriate), and changed approach if necessary (used paraphrasing and reflecting back techniques, especially if this was a difficult, sensitive or complex issue) ● cleared up any misunderstandings between yourself and the child/young person which arose during the interaction or were present before this interaction started (HSC 31b 7) ● effectively responded to pre-speech and non-verbal communications, listened effectively ● used pauses and silences effectively, especially if this was a difficult, sensitive or complex issue ● observed and responded to the reactions of the child/young person and supported them to deal with the effects of the content, especially if this was a difficult, sensitive or complex issue when they may have been angry, upset or even violent (HSC 31b 6, HSC 31b 7) ● took appropriate action to reduce any risk to yourself or others as a result of the child's reaction (particularly in difficult, complex or sensitive issues) by asking others to leave or calling for assistance or leaving the room in accordance with policies and legislation (HSC 31b 7) ● used any additional aids and techniques to assist the interaction such as: ■ BSL ■ Makaton ■ 'Switches such as Big Mac's' ■ Symbols ■ PECS ■ Text to talk (HSC 31a 2, HSC 31a 6, HSC 34b 3 part). If this was an interaction in which you communicated a difficult, complex or sensitive issue, this will also cover HSC 31b 3, 4, 5 and 6 – if it was not you will need to add this to the report which you give to your assessor.	HSC 31b pc 1 HSC 36a pc 3, 4 HSC 31b pc 7, 8, 9 HSC 31b pc 2, 3, 4, 5
Different ways of communicating with other key people	Describe how to identify the different ways of communicating with other key people. You could explain how you: ● might adapt what you say to talk to a worried parent/carer, an upset friend of a child/young person or someone with a communication difficulty e.g. hearing/autism ● talk to parents on the phone ● talk to the health visitor/social worker/GP/dentist/school staff ● adapt to changing needs when communicating … and explain why these changes in your communication are important.	HSC 31a pc 3 HSC 31c pc 3
Get help or advice when having difficulties in communicating	Explain, show or tell your assessor how you get help or advice when having difficulties in communicating with individuals in their preferred way. You could explain how you would: ● seek help from a more experienced person – perhaps a key worker/social worker who knows the child well ● use an interpreter ● use a translator – mechanical or human ● use a telephone translator service if available to you ● use speech and language therapists' advice ● use a health visitor … and explain why you would be doing this (link it to policies too) (HSC 31a 4).	HSC 31a pc 4a

Seek advice on how to handle a possible reaction to a communication exchange	Explain how you would seek advice on what to say and how to handle a possible reaction. Show that you know: • when to seek help • where to seek help • your own limitations • the policies of your organisation • the possible response of the child/young person with whom you re working (HSC 31a 5).	HSC 31b pc 9 HSC 31a pc 4b, 5
Effectively communicate difficult/sensitive or complex issues AND	Report on (or use a witness statement or even an observation) an interaction which has been used to communicate effectively difficult, sensitive or complex issues – perhaps when: • a child is moving on to a new residential placement • when they are changing school/classes/units • when they have come to respite care unwillingly • they have been accused of something at school or by the police • someone or a pet has died or been hurt • plans they had made need to be altered • their key worker is changing • they have a body odour or foot odour problem • discussing how their care plan was working for them – which parts were working best, which parts needed changing and changes in circumstances which affect the care plan – this could be moving into an adult placement/leaving care/having gained sufficient skills confidence to become more independent/needing support from Youth Offending Team/parental circumstances changed. What policies/procedures or legislation would you have considered and how would you record this interaction – who could access it? (HSC 31d 1, 2, 4, HSC 31 KSE)	HSC 31b pc 1, 2, 3, 4, 5 also HSC 36c pc 2a, b, c, d
Arrange the environment to assist and support the interaction	Think about the way the furniture and 'equipment' were positioned in respect to: • 'power' • available support • light • sound/noise • other barriers to communication. You could consider support from others in this interaction – an advocate/friend who you were sure the child or young person was comfortable with, or the use of pictures/dolls/puppets/drawing or writing materials/photographs to support the interaction or stimulate interest (especially when assessing needs, wishes and preferences).	HSC 31b pc 2, 3, 4 also HSC 36a pc 4, 5
Support to communicate using their preferred method Explain your role in making sure that the child or young person can use any of these methods effectively.	Explain/show your assessor how you help children to decide how they want to communicate taking into account their level of development and understanding and how you help them to use any of the following methods effectively: • speech – sentence structure/vocabulary used to help them to understand its impact • sign BSL/Makaton • using hearing aids • symbols/pictures/photos • texts • advocates • translators • in writing • phone • email • use of switches • voice-activated software • computer-generated sounds • showing • pointing • puppets/toys • chat rooms.	HSC 31c pc 1, 2, 3, 4 also HSC 34a pc 1 HSC 36a pc 3, 4
Communication – by chosen method including those who are non-verbal or use pre-speech	Explain/show that you know how to communicate – both listening and 'speaking': • use specific aids e.g. PECS • interpret BSL/Makaton and show how to simply sign back etc. • build relationship with others to assist gradually in communication • use non-verbal/behavioural cues in relation to health and well-being.	HSC 31c pc 1, 2, 3 also HSC 36a pc 3 HSC 34b pc 3
Overcoming barriers to communication	Explain/show how you can help children or young people to engage with others and to overcome barriers to communication and inappropriate responses through: • discussions • using specialist aids	HSC 31c pc 4 also

	watching for trigger signs of distress, anger or frustration and intervening before the behaviour becomes unacceptable ● providing suitable space, appropriate support and a suitable environment ● providing alternatives – writing, drawing, photos, etc.	HSC 34b pc 1
Recording changes which have arisen	Explain/show/talk to your assessor about how you record changes in the condition and care needs, support needs and conflicts which have arisen in relation to the children/young people in your care. Link this to things such as: ● care plans (may be known as IECPs ICPs but will be individual care plans/programmes for each child/young person) ● daily 'diaries' or records ● individual action plans ● reports to social services ● reports to parents ● feedback to team ● referrals to child protection ● 'contact' books ● accident, injury or incident recording systems ● LAC (Looked After Children) reviews. Link all these to internal policies and procedures, legislation and guidance (could be: Children Acts 1989 and 2004/Data Protection Act 1984 and 1998/Health and Safety at Work Act 1974 (plus future additions)/Mental Health Act 1983/Care Standards Act 2000/National Minimum Standards where appropriate.	HSC 31d pc 1, 2, 3, 4, 5 also HSC 32 HSC 33 HSC 34c pc 9, 10, 12
Involve children with their records and the safety and security of these	Explain/show/talk to your assessor about how you involve children with the records and reports concerning them, and how and why you ensure the safety and security of these records and reports. Include: ● how and where you write the report – with or without the child/young person – why? ● details of an effective environment for such involvement of the child/young person – time/place/language used/mood of child or young person/your approach ● reasons for not involving the children – perhaps level of understanding due to learning disability or age (babies or toddlers)/increased anxiety affecting health/autism ● sharing content with but not leaving a copy of the document with a child or young person – when/why you would do so ● maintaining confidential storage ● providing relevant access to records. Link all these to Data Protection Act/Human Rights Act/UN Convention on the Rights of the Child; internal policies on involving children with decision making; reporting and storage of information; confidentiality and who has access to information; National Minimum Standards.	HSC 31d pc 7, 8 HSC 32
Safety and security	Write a case study which shows that you understand the needs of children and young people and which legislation contributes to the safety and security of children and young people (and the people who work with them). Think about which health and safety legislation you comply with when you are working in the residential setting in relation to: ● who you report potential hazards to and why ● why there are fire and evacuation procedures and how often you practise them in your setting and why ● why CRB checks and induction training are so important ● why it is important not to leave confidential information or photos where they can be accessed by unauthorised people ● how you dispose of waste/soiled pads and nappies safely and why. ● Maintaining the privacy and dignity of individuals in an emergency (e.g. fits, accidents, evacuations during night time or bath time, etc.) ● How you support individuals and help them to follow instructions in an emergency (how you speak, behave, use the tone and pace of your voice or specific communication aids.	HSC 32a pc 1 HSC 32b pc 1 HSC 32c pc 1, 4, 5, 6, 7 HSC 31b pc 3 HSC 34 pc 3
Visitors	Explain/show/talk to your assessor about: ● why there is a routine for visitors to the setting ● how you use this to ensure that only visitors who are authorised or wanted gain access to the children and young people ● how you ensure that you keep visitors safe.	HSC 32a pc 2, 3 HSC 34c 6b

Accident/incident report	Complete an accident/incident report for your setting. If you have done this or secluded or restrained a child, get a senior person who witnessed you using the correct policies and procedures for your setting to sign that you have done so. You should be able to write this yourself and quote the policies, legislation (including RIDDOR) and guidance (e.g. National Minimum Standards) which applied to it, and then get a more senior member of staff to sign to say that you did this accurately. Your own assessor or another may be available to record this as a direct observation.	HSC 32a pc 5b, 9 HSC 32c pc 7 also HSC 31 HSC 34c pc 12
Risk assessment	Explain/show/talk to your assessor about how you plan to manage the risks connected to a new setting or for an activity off site or with new people or in a change of venue. Again, you need to explain which legislation/regulations/policies or guidance (e.g. NMS) you are considering. Remember to include people, places and equipment and also plans for if something goes wrong – particularly if you are working with children and young people who have behaviours which can present a challenge. There is always a potential risk in relation to child protection for anyone who works with children and young people – make sure that any work you produce includes reference to keeping children and young people as safe as possible, but also recognises the needs for young people to take measured and assessed risks as part of growing up.	HSC 32a pc 5b, 9 HSC 32b pc 1, 3c also HSC31 HSC 34c pc 1, 2, 3, 4
Moving people and objects	Show by case study or, better still, through a direct observation that you can use the theories of safe manual handling and that you know which regulations cover this. This could be shown through: ● getting equipment from a shed to use outside/moving tables/benches etc. ● transferring children from one place to another ● assisting children or young people to exit a swimming pool, etc. ● moving boxes or even Christmas trees!	HSC 32b pc 3a
Storing and using hazardous substances and medications	This is easy to evidence in an observation, but it is possible for you to write it up as a case study too. Try to make sure when you plan an observation with your assessor that you include it. You need to show that you know how to store and/or use: ● kitchens (utensils and cleaning fluids/cleaning cupboards (polish, bleach, etc.) ● medicines/medicine cupboards or trolleys (both over the counter medicines and prescribed) should be included The assessor needs to know that you are aware of the legislation, policies and guidance about this.	HSC 32 pc 4, 5a, 7a HSC 34c pc 1, 2
Using correct protective clothing or equipment	Again try to make sure when you plan your direct observation that you have the opportunity to use protective clothing/equipment, or if that opportunity does not arise that you can explain to your assessor why you would use protective clothing/equipment.	HSC 32a pc 7b, 7c HSC 316 additional needs
	This should include dealing with and disposing of: ● bodily fluids ● soiled linen ● 'sharps', e.g. syringe needles ● minimising risk of other types of cross-infection.	
Using specialist equipment	Explain or show that you are 'safe' when using specialist equipment, e.g. ● hoists ● minibuses which carry wheelchairs ● travel systems for babies etc. ● mobility aids ● physiotherapy aids ● any electronic aid. Make sure you explain how you do the following as appropriate: ● read, follow and keep instructions ● update your training ● do risk assessments etc.	HSC 32b pc 3b also HSC 316
Raising awareness of health and safety with the children and other staff, parents or other carers	Explain/show/talk to your assessor about how you are raising awareness of health and safety with the children and other staff, parents or other carers. This could be through: ● personal contact in play – boundaries ● routines for running baths/washing hands/using toilet	HSC 32a pc 8 HSC 32b pc 5

	• using and storing equipment/games and toys	**HSC 32c pc 5**
	• traffic safety/use of crossings/seat belts in vehicles/exiting buses	**HSC 34 pc 1**
	• blowing noses and disposing of tissues	
	• stranger safety	
	• substances which are safe and not safe	
	• avoiding involvement in the aggressive behaviour of other children and young people	
	• personal safety in relation to physical and sexual abuse	
	• personal safety in relation to financial abuse	
	• using electronic equipment	
	• giving out phone numbers/addresses	
	• chat rooms.	
First aid	You are likely to have done a recent first aid course. It may be useful and also could be evidence if you create a small and simple pocket-sized information book which you can carry in your pocket with key words about potential accidents. You could then discuss this with your assessor. If you are not a qualified first aider you should know what the policies and procedures expect you to do and be able to explain this to your assessor.	**HSC 32c pc 1, 2, 3, 4, 5, 6**
Actively promote the rights and individuality of children and young people	Explain to your assessor how you actively promote the rights of children and young people in your work setting, putting them at the centre of everything you do. A good way to do this may be to write down all the things you do and the reasons you do them for the following: 1. Treating everyone equally (not the same) and not discriminating against them so that they have a similar opportunity to gain similar experiences (e.g. water aerobics in a hydrotherapy pool or swimming in local public pool). Not excluding them for any reason unless it is on a behaviour support plan or the care plan.	**HSC 34a pc 5, 6**

	2. Ensuring that you treat and value each child or young person as an individual in your day-to-day work, and respect their diversity, culture and values, including
	  • choices – clothes/music/activities etc.
	  • beliefs – religious and non religious
	  • size, shape and physical appearance
	  • language skills
	  • upbringing or socialisation
	  • interpersonal skills/team work skills.
		HSC 34a pc 2, 4

	3. Ensuring that all children have their rights to privacy and dignity met:
	  • own room, inviting others to enter
	  • private time
	  • able to talk privately to parents/befrienders (if needs permit)
	  • personal hygiene routines/facilities/procedures/policies
	  • sanitary equipment stored in girls' rooms
	  • cultural needs/prayer routines
	  • confidentiality.
	Link to:
	• Human Rights Act 1998
	• UN Convention on the Rights of the Child 1990
	• policies in your setting
	• National Minimum Standards.
		HSC 34a pc 3

Active support to maximise independence and take age-related responsibilities	Explain/show/talk to your assessor about how you actively support children to maximise independence and take age-related responsibilities. This could be through: • encouraging decision making and choices on a range of topics • supporting self advocacy • shopping/saving/having a bank account • travelling independently • solving disputes with others • developing strategies to manage own behaviour (linked to behaviour support plans/care plans) • supporting to be involved in youth/student/children's councils • sexual relationships • leaving the setting	**HSC 34a pc 7, 8** **HSC 34b pc 2, 5**

	<ul><li>communicating their needs, views, preferences and aspirations about:<ul><li>their emotional, physical and social well-being</li><li>their cultural and spiritual well being</li><li>their education, talents and interests</li><li>their relationships with parents, families and carers</li><li>what they want to achieve</li></ul></li><li>understanding risks connected to their choices, etc.</li><li>preparing for adulthood, independence and citizenship</li></ul>	
	Communicate with children, young people, parents, families and carers on their talents, abilities, beliefs and educational aspirations.	HSC 310a pc 2 HSC 39a pc 1
Challenging discriminatory practice of others	Explain/show/talk to your assessor about how you do this or how you would do this if it arose. Include:<ul><li>why it is important to challenge the discrimination/poor practice of others</li><li>how you would/could do it if it were an individual</li><li>how you would/could do it if it were widespread practice.</li></ul>	HSC 34a pc 8
Help to know how to make complaints	Explain/show/talk to your assessor about how you would make sure that children and young people know how make a complaint and how they can get support for this; also that their parents, families or carers know how to challenge and complain about the child or young person's assessment.	HSC 34a pc 6d, 9 also HSC 36a pc 11
Seek help and advice from others	Explain how you seek help and advice from others when:<ul><li>you are having difficulty in supporting the equality, diversity, rights or responsibilities of children and young people</li><li>you are working with young people to assess their needs and equip them for adulthood, citizenship and independence.</li></ul>	HSC 34a pc 10 HSC 310a pc 1
Self-esteem/belonging	Explain/show how you work in a positive way with children and young people to raise their self-esteem/sense of belonging and to help them to develop trusting relationships. This should be apparent across all observations, and it will cover the knowledge required for putting the child at the centre of all planning and decision making. It will reflect your own values and links closely to equality and diversity. It is likely that you can include here dilemmas relating to the difference between your views and those of the child or young person as well as those in relation risk. This could also link with managing behaviour.	HSC 34b pc 4 HSC 34c pc 7 Common knowledge HSC 326
Working with parents or families or carers to help them to understand the needs, views, preferences, aspirations and expectations of children and young people	Explain or show this through:<ul><li>contact books for respite care</li><li>school reports for residential schools</li><li>joint working prior to re-integration of children in foster care</li><li>joint working with young mothers</li><li>young carers support</li><li>phone calls home (by staff) for residential care</li><li>encouraging children and young people to share these</li><li>encouraging (self) advocacy at lac reviews/educational reviews</li><li>advocacy at lac reviews/educational reviews</li><li>key workers.</li></ul>Include helping them to understand any factor that may present a risk of harm or abuse to children and young people (this will change as they grow and develop):<ul><li>people</li><li>places</li><li>behaviour.</li></ul>	HSC 34b pc 6 HSC 36a pc 7 HSC 34 pc 5 HSC 36a pc 7
	Communicate with children, young people, parents, families and carers on their talents, abilities, beliefs and educational aspirations	HSC 39a pc 1 HSC 36b pc 3
	Explain how you help parents, families or carers to understand the care plan for the child or young person and accept where the child's views of needs and preferences may be different or developing, and how the final plan is agreed and how it is reviewed.	HSC 36c pc 3, 4, 5 Links also with much of HSC 316

Partnership/interagency working	Explain how you share the promotion of life chances and well-being for the children or young people in your setting with other agencies, e.g. ● GP ● speech and language therapists ● hospital ● continence advisors ● dentist ● physiotherapists ● optician ● respite care ● dietitian ● youth offending team ● counsellors ● child protection teams ● psychologists ● education (home tutors/schools) ● psychiatrists ● social services (social workers) … and why they are important in promoting the life chances for the children and young people.	HSC 34b pc 7
Protection for children and young people	Explain how you manage access to videos/DVDs/the internet/books and the media. Explain/show how you monitor this and how you make judgements when it is not appropriate depending on age and understanding. Link this to National Minimum Standards/internal policies.	HSC 34c pc 3
Trusting relationships	Explain how you help children and young people to develop trusting relationships with you so that they can express their needs, views and preferences about all kinds of things, and their fears, feelings anxieties and concerns, without fear of ridicule, rejection or retribution.	HSC 34b pc 1 HSC 34c pc 8
Boundaries	Explain how you set and maintain safe, consistent and understandable boundaries for the children and young people in your setting in relation to: ● acceptable behaviour ● if wishes/preferences cannot be met in care plan ● implementation of care plan. Link to policies and National Minimum Standards.	HSC 34c pc 4 links to self-esteem also HSC 36b pc 3
Unwanted behaviour – taking action	Explain how you take action when children or young people with whom you work are likely to become involved or are involved in offending/offensive behaviour, or are subjected to the offending or offensive behaviour of others. Examples may include: ● borrowing without returning ● devaluing beliefs ● borrowing without permission (with understanding) ● frightening behaviour ● shouting ● stealing ● throwing things ● damaging property ● bullying ● swearing ● self-harm ● spitting (deliberate) ● reckless but not offensive behaviour. ● unfair criticism	HSC 34 pc 6, 7

Signs and symptoms of danger, harm and abuse, and procedures	Explain (this is unlikely to be able to be assessed through observation) the signs of:
	● danger:
	  ■ people
	  ■ places
	  ■ substances
	  ■ activities
	  ■ peer pressure
	● physical/emotional harm or **neglect**
	● physical/emotional/sexual **abuse**
	● emotional effects of all aspects of abuse
	● range of possible behavioural signs of abuse – physical, sexual, emotional, financial.
		HSC 34 pc 9

Reporting and recording suspicion or disclosure of abuse and legal requirements for future investigations/court	Explain when and how you report and record any suspicion or disclosure of abuse. ● To whom do you report and why? Why is one person the named person for child protection in each setting? ● What must you include regarding when/where and who was present when the abuse was seen/heard/disclosed? ● What must you **not** do when a child or young person is disclosing? ● What **must** you do when you realise that a child or young person is about to disclose, or if they try to get you to promise secrecy? ● How quickly should you pass on the information? You may also be able to link this to evidence in your workplace **but** this should only be **signposted, not** included in your portfolio.	HSC 34c pc 12

Your needs when involved in disclosure	Explain how you would seek support when you have been involved in a disclosure/child protection situation. Explain the role of your supervisor/line manager/named person for child protection. Again, this may be evidenced through records in your work place, but this should only be signposted, **not** included in your portfolio.	HSC 34c pc 11

Roles and responsibilities in relation to care planning	Explain/show that you know what your role and responsibility is and which parts are the roles and responsibilities of others in relation to:
	● asessment of the child or young person's needs, wishes and preferences relating to their care plan (usually managed by their local authority)
	● assessment relating to the child or young person's day-to-day care plan (internal to the setting and often known as an individual education and care plan or something similar) where you are that person's key worker
	● assessment on a day-to-day basis where you are not that person's key worker – sometimes a new person sees a child or young person from a new perspective
	● feeding back on short, medium and long term health and care needs – to whom/when/how – making sure that you have taken into account:
	  ■ the child or young person's views
	  ■ your views
	  ■ the views of parents/family as well others within and outside the organisation (if appropriate) This could be feedback about going to a football club/scout group/religious meetings/music group etc.
	● participating in reviews – lac or educational reviews
	● developing and implementing care plans
	  ■ Recording and reporting significant changes
	  ■ Recording and reporting significant changes
	  ■ Helping child/young person and others involved to identify and monitor changes to needs/circumstances/preferences – perhaps through team/key worker meetings/reviews and importantly in one-to-one discussions with child at a level appropriate to age and understanding, including pre-verbal and non-verbal children and young people
	● reviewing care plans:
	  ■ What is your responsibility e.g. in a LAC review – how can you contribute to revising and implementing any changes to the care plans?
	  ■ What responsibility does your immediate manager take?
	  ■ What is the Head of Care's responsibility (for some foster care placements this may be your immediate line manager)?
	  ■ What responsibility is taken by the local authority?
	
	Link to UN Convention on the Rights of the Child, internal policies, National Minimum Standards, Children Act.
		HSC 36a
		
		Also common knowledge: placing child at centre
		
		HSC 36a pc 8, 9
		
		HSC 36a pc 2
		
		HSC 36b pc 1, 5, 6, 7, 8, 9
		
		HSC 36c pc 4
		
		HSC 36b pc 1, 3, 4, 5, 6
		
		HSC 36c pc 1, 8

Access and review information	Explain or show that you know how to access information about the different dimensions of children and young people's lives and review this information: ● children and young people's case files ● LAC reviews. ● key worker reviews ● team meetings.	HSC 36a pc 2, 10 Also link to common knowledge: storing and using information and Data Protection Act
Conflict	Explain/show how you follow organisational policies if there is conflict about your feedback or observation.	HSC 36c pc 6
Children and young people's clothes, appearance, environment and pocket money	Explain or show your assessor how you support children and young people to: ● communicate their needs and preferences ● take care of and manage ● make choices in relation to their clothes, their appearance, their environment and the spending (or saving) their pocket money. This will include how you: ● arrange, organise and decorate their environment so that you meet their needs and preferences and respect their right to privacy ● give advice (if they want you to) on clothes and appearance ● support them to choose, shop for and buy their own clothes ● help young people who find managing their pocket money difficult.	HSC 38a pc 1, 2, 3, 4, 5 Link to UN Convention on the Rights of the Child, Human Rights Act

Developing talents, interests and abilities	Explain or show your assessor how you support children and young people to develop their interests, talents and abilities so that: ● they develop a positive self-image and so self-esteem rises, ● they take part in activities to extend their interests, talents and abilities which are appropriate to their age, level of development and circumstances, e.g. joining a football or swimming club, having singing lessons, making Christmas cards for friends, gardening, dog walking for a rescue centre, going to Sunday school, church or joining a choir ● you discuss with their statutory sponsoring authority if there is any funding to support these activities or where possible provide them with the necessary resources from your setting's budget ● you help children to see how they could use these interests, talents and abilities to better their life chances – e.g. get a sought after job, get an opportunity to be part of something special, improve their CV, etc.	HSC 38b pc 1, 2, 3, 4, 5 Link to self-image/self-esteem Links to HSC 39
Recreational activities	Explain or show how you invite other children to participate in recreational activities in which the children you work with are interested and how you support these children and young people to become their friends (bearing in mind their protection and restrictions which may be relevant). You might consider sharing lifts/meals/encouraging them to join trips, etc.	HSC 38c pc 7
Specialist support	Explain or show how you could/do support young people to access support, advice or information (including material/organisations) which helps to help them to understand aspects of independence/citizenship/ adulthood: ● housing – letting agents – access for people with disability/response to those not in work ● adult placements – options ● continuing education and training – benefits and options ● cooking – manageable menus ● budgeting – managing bank accounts/meetings with advisors ● counsellors – understanding own reactions ● moving around – public transport ● voting rights ● rights to sexual relationships/marriage (both homosexual and heterosexual) ● understand and evaluate the support materials, and identify those which any which may be discriminatory ● basic skills training for literacy/numeracy if appropriate Show or explain how you do/would use specialist help – such as: ● occupational therapist to assess specialist adaptations for independent living ● dyslexia assessment and possible laptops/software ● Disability assist ● gateway to work ● counsellor ● family therapy ● behaviour support/Psychologists ● financial ● basic skills.	HSC 310a pc 3, 4, 5, 6 HSC 310b pc 7
Skills and abilities required to become adults and effective citizens	Explain or show how you work with young people to identify skills, abilities, rights and responsibilities which help them to become effective citizens when adult, e.g. ● the financial implications of being independent or semi-independent – paying bills, paying rent, making choices about food/clothes/equipment which is based on income – this could include budget management at any level where the young person has an understanding of money, managing a bank account, how to pay bills ● how to find a place to live, including responsibilities for rent – this could include looking through papers/letting agents details – skills could include working out travel times to access work or college ● the opportunities for further education and the possible longer-term benefits this might have – how to apply for an apprenticeship/full- or part-time course ● getting up independently (where appropriate) ● basic healthy eating principles and practising buying ingredients and cooking simple menus (where appropriate) ● how to use bus and train timetables ● the need to move on from children and young person placement to an adult placement and manage the change – particularly relevant to young people who have lived in residential schools for many years	HSC 310 pc 1, 2, 3, 4

	<ul><li>consequences of not complying to society's rules – difference between internal 'sanctions' and police involvement, and not fitting in because of behaviour</li><li>options in relation to conflict – looking for win-win outcomes/walking away/not getting 'sucked in' managing own behaviour so that potential for conflict is minimised.</li><li>understand what is socially acceptable behaviour in terms of hygiene/noise/language etc.</li><li>understand how the government works and how get a vote</li></ul>Link these to Children Act, Pathway Plan.	
Impact of personal experiences and behaviour	Explain how the experiences and behaviour of children and young people who could or do use your workplace can affect their ability to become effective citizens and responsible adults. This might include:<ul><li>difficulties in trusting others</li><li>difficulties in forming close or permanent relationships</li><li>difficulties in choosing friends who value them</li><li>difficulties managing their aggression</li><li>difficulties in voicing their opinion</li><li>difficulties in personal care</li><li>difficulties with change</li><li>obsessional behaviour</li><li>echolalia/speech difficulties</li><li>elective mute</li><li>difficulties with those in positions of perceived authority.</li></ul>	HSC 310b pc 4
Risks of harm, danger and abuse in adulthood	Explain or show how you would use:<ul><li>articles in teenage magazines</li><li>newspapers</li><li>TV programmes, especially soaps/docusoaps</li><li>DVD/videos</li><li>music</li><li>pictures</li><li>holiday brochures</li><li>posters</li><li>photographs</li><li>health education literature</li><li>care plans</li></ul>to initiate discussions on the positive aspect of citizenship and any associated risk of danger, harm and abuse.	HSC 310b pc 5
Communicating on educational potential	Show or explain to your assessor how you show young people and children that you have listened and taken account of:<ul><li>their view</li><li>their experience to date, which may be significantly different from person to person</li><li>their expertise – looking at their skills across a range of areas</li><li>any difficulties they are facing</li><li>their perceived strengths – sometimes this may be an unrealistic view and you may need to gently respond</li><li>their educational aspirations and responding to changes in these (remembering that these will change – often regularly).</li></ul>	HSC 39a pc 2, 3, 4 HSC 39b pc 1
Achieving potential	Show or explain how you help children and young people to examine what they want to achieve in their lives and how you actively support them to use their skills, talents and abilities to help them to reach their goal. This will include:<ul><li>identifying talents and interests</li><li>suggesting ideas on how they can develop them</li><li>enabling them to make links with clubs/organisations</li><li>liaising with schools, FE colleges, Connexions, etc.</li><li>enabling them to gather information on careers and look at realistic pathways etc.</li><li>supporting them to prepare for interviews</li><li>supporting their applications</li><li>encouraging attendance</li><li>encouraging realistic time spent on homework (not nagging!).</li></ul>	HSC 39a pc 6, 7 This follows on from HSC 39a pc 1–5 which are linked with HSC 31

Support needs and targets to access educational and recreational opportunities	Show or explain to your assessor how you: ● encourage children and young people to communicate any difficulties (education based) they are having ● identify extra support to help them to overcome these difficulties (human, electronic and other resources) ● plan short-, medium- and long-term goals ● work in a joined up way with others to make these goals more likely become a reality. This could include: ● organisational skills – remembering to do or take things ● learning or remembering ● relationships with teaching staff which affects learning ● relationships with peers which affect learning ● behaviours which affect learning ● support from specialist staff in school ● support from people at home, wherever home is ● support in the use of equipment – computer/memory sticks/football boots/art materials etc. ● physical support – change of glasses/school uniform/lunch money/sanitary needs met etc. ● planning – making sure that necessary equipment is taken on right days/homework is completed on time/arrive on work experience on time, etc. ● support to meeting goals by breaking the pathway into smaller bite-sized sections – helping children and young people to make connections between taking appropriate equipment and performing better e.g. ■ remember football boots (short-term targets) ■ get into school team (middle-term targets) ■ go for trails for county team (long-term targets) ■ Play for Exeter City! (ultimate targets) and listen and respond to how the child or young person feels about this. ● Working with parents/family/carer so all are supporting the child or young person in a 'joined up way'. ● Helping them as they move along the pathway to make realistic choices about what is possible and what needs to happen to make the outcomes likely. How you encourage children and young people to look for creative solutions to help them in their educational needs and preferences if resources are not available – perhaps re-structuring activities to meet their learning style, or providing audio input where concentration is less developed, or work shadowing, etc.	HSC 39b pc 2, 3, 4, 5, 6, 7 and 8 (educational) HSC 38c pc 1, 2, 3, 4, 5, 6 (recreational)
Give positive feedback and support to help reach educational potential	Explain or show your assessor that you have: ● given the child or young person the agreed support and also positive feedback on their efforts ● encouraged others who care for them to do the same ● given enthusiastic feedback (you may have celebrated their success in some way which is appropriate to their age or level of understanding, e.g. a treat/special recognition, particularly one which involves other).	HSC 39c pc 1, 2, 3, 4 Links to self-esteem ECM Enjoy and achieve Also links with communicating in preferred way
Monitor and review plans for reaching educational potential	Explain or show your assessor that you have worked with the child or young person to: ● identify things which may undermine their educational efforts and help them to address these (could be attendance/attitude/friends/planning etc.) ● help them to set realistic aspirations about their future educational prospects, based on monitoring their progress and make sure that you help them to see how this affects their life chances ● Help them to negotiate, agree and implement any necessary changes that need to made to any educational programmes or plans.	HSC 39c pc 5, 6, 7, 8, 9

Conbute to the assessment of specific developmental levels and support needstri	Explain or show how you contribute to the assessment of support needs for children and young people with additional requirements by:
	• working with others (including the child) to contribute to identifying how the child or young person's needs can be assessed – this could be by using:
	  ■ a formal assessment package (range here is huge: dyslexia, hearing, vision, mobility, independence, reading, etc.)
	  ■ observation
	  ■ feedback from all key people (including child or young person)
	• actively supporting the child or young person (and parents, families and carers too) so that they understand what is going to happen in an assessment and why it is being done, and that you value their input on their needs, views and preferences:
	  ■ this could be through discussion/demonstration/DVD/video support/in writing (in many residential settings the contact with parents/families and other carers may also be done formally through written communication by the family's social worker
	  ■ you consider the expertise, experience and culture of both the children/young people and their parents/families and carers and adapt how you work accordingly.
		HSC 316a pc 1, 2, 3, 5

	Show or explain how, during the assessment, you support the child or young person so they: • understand what is happening • are at ease in the situation. In some cases you may have to support the person doing the assessment if the child has additional needs which are not usually seen in this circumstance, e.g. a child with autism having an eye test, or a child with cerebral palsy having a dyslexia assessment, so that they understand the expertise and experience or culture of the child.	HSC 316a pc 5, 7
	Where there is likely to be disagreement (perhaps home/school or setting/school or setting/home) you have thought about this and had discussions with your line manager about how this will be managed, and are fully updated on any policies in your setting which might relate to this.	HSC 316a pc 4
	Show or explain how you do assessments and how you record them.	HSC 316a pc 6, 8
Support the implementation of support activities	Explain or show how you implement programmes or support activities to meet the needs of children and young people with additional needs by: 1. identifying resources: could be to improve skills, e.g. PECS cards or specialist mobility aids, or to help mange risks, e.g. leak-proof pads for swimming pools for those who have poor or no bowel control 2. looking at options which are available to meet the identified needs and work with the children/young people and others concerned in their care to find options which best meet their needs, wishes and preferences. You will need to show how you balance their need and their preference and how you help them to understand this.	HSC 316b pc 1, 2, 3
Carry out, monitor and record activities to support additional needs	Explain or show how you: • carry out the agreed activities • observe and monitor how well they work • record any problems, including changes in the needs/wishes or preferences of the child/young person • feed this back – **seeking help** if you are out of your depth or beyond your comfortable level of competence or your own personal or emotional needs are affected (e.g. in situations following significant abuse/life limiting conditions/smearing/elective vomiting etc.).	HSC 316b pc 4, 5, 6, 7, 8

Contribute to evaluating programmes and support activities	Show or explain how you:
	1. observe and analyse the impact of programmes and support activities:
	  • how do you know if these are helping?
	  • what is working?
	  • what needs to be improved?
	2. get parents/families and others to do the same
	3. check that the programme is still meeting the wishes and preferences of the child/young person.
	4. take part in reviewing the programme against the intended outcome e.g. consistently using PECS reduces the frustration of the child and so reduces incidents; using pads in the pool stops leakage and so enables another child to continue swimming.
		HSC 316c pc 1, 2, 3, 4, 6

Changes to programmes and support activities	Explain or show how, if changes have to happen, you support the child/young person and other key people to understand: • the changes • the timing • the people involved • the resources which will be changed.	HSC 316c pc 7

Reviewing your support	Explain or show how you get objective feedback on **your role** in supporting the child/young person with additional needs (from child/young person, families and others). Part of this could be in supervisions and appraisals, but how do you get the child's (or in non-residential settings the family's) view on **your** role – not the role of the team?	HSC 316c pc 5
Prepare to visit families in their own homes	Show or explain how you find out as much as possible about the family, their culture, their background and the issues which they are facing, e.g.: ● the family structure and local support available ● children at which school ● religious beliefs ● cultural practices ● housing ● transport links. Work out the gaps in your knowledge and understanding of the family's situation and try to 'plug' these. You may need some input on: ● medical needs – understanding certain conditions (physical, learning disabilities or mental health) – research via internet of non-specific information from health centre ● educational needs – newly recognised specific conditions affecting learning, e.g. PDA etc. Look at all the information and reach a **preliminary** view on the issues facing the family and how you can help in addressing some of these: ● how prepared are you before you visit? ● have you an outline idea and plan? You work alongside other workers both within and outside your organisation to produce a plan for your initial visit. ● Have you talked to others who know the family or the area or have experience with similar situations? ● Have you considered social services, education, health and voluntary organisations? ● How did you approach these people? ● How did you find out directions and know that you could arrive on time for your visit? You communicated with the family in an accessible way to prepare them for the visit: ● you used a language which they understood ● you used vocabulary which they understood ● you gave them clear information so they were informed and comfortable ● if necessary, you organised for an interpreter to make the arrangements and accompany you ● you used talk to text technology if appropriate ● you gave clear information on who you were and if anyone would be accompanying you, so they knew what to expect.	HSC 319a pc 1, 2, 3, 4, 5
Liaising with families and others to identify and support families' needs	Show or explain how you provide active support to help families to identify and explain their own needs and how you manage it if their perception of their need is different from yours. This could be about personal values/cultural values or a range of confusion regarding the significance of information. Work with the family and others (both within and outside your organisation) to find out about resources which are available and what the options are. This could be looking at a balance between using human resources to support, or providing physical resources, or assisting financial support/structures through liaising with others. Know your role and responsibilities in the arrangements to support the family and know your role. What is your role, where does your role start and stop and how do you manage the grey area where your role overlaps that of others? Show that you have thought through how you will manage any potential problems and conflicts.	HSC 319b pc 1, 2a, b, c, d Links to HSC 32 Communication
Support individuals and family to function more effectively as a family unit	Show or explain how you do this by: ● ensuring that they are clear about the your contribution in supporting them and how your work with them fits into a bigger picture of support: ● your boundaries and when you are intruding on their rights and responsibilities ● referring the family to others ● working with others	HSC 319c pc 1, 2, 3, 4, 5

	<ul><li>supporting them in identifying and making the changes to function more effectively as a family unit:<ul><li>not promising what you cannot deliver</li><li>dealing with or challenging discrimination within family members</li><li>building and evaluating relationships</li><li>considering factors which cause risk</li><li>considering the type of support for disabled children</li></ul></li><li>encouraging them using support networks</li><li>helping them to address problems which arise due to the diversity of views of the family members:<ul><li>using theories of how families function effectively</li><li>understanding theories on power and its potential use and abuse</li><li>using theories to resolve conflicts</li><li>using strategies for handling aggression</li></ul></li><li>Praising successes and giving constructive feedback.</li></ul>	
Contribute to planning and implementing a daily living programme for children and young people	Explain or show how you always:<ul><li>consider the age, level of development and understanding of each child or young person when planning or implementing daily activities</li><li>consider and are flexible in how you meet each child or young person's needs and preferences</li><li>balance the needs of the group with the needs of the individual.</li></ul>Possibilities for evidence:<ul><li>planning trips</li><li>cooking</li><li>'treats'</li><li>allocation of rooms/units</li><li>tv programmes and videos watched in common spaces</li><li>life skills/personal care routines</li><li>communication methods</li><li>acceptable noise levels</li><li>access to kitchens/higher risk areas</li><li>independent travel</li><li>general independence.</li></ul>	HSC 323a pc 1, 2 Links to HSC 31
Contribute to reviewing a daily living programme for children and young people	Explain or show how you:<ul><li>participate in assessing the strengths and weaknesses of the provision's programme by contributing:<ul><li>at team meetings</li><li>at personal supervision</li><li>through key worker meetings</li><li>through reports, etc.</li></ul></li><li>Take part, and encourage children and young people to meet with you and other staff regularly, both in groups and individually to share their views and plan activities – perhaps through:<ul><li>key worker meetings</li><li>'house meetings'</li><li>'councils'.</li></ul></li></ul>	HSC 323a pc 4, 5
Use handovers to contribute to continuity of care	Explain or show that you use handovers effectively to contribute to continuity of care provision, by:<ul><li>listening to the contributions of others</li><li>sharing your views with others, even if they seem less than willing to listen</li><li>reporting accurately on progress/issues</li><li>sharing information which helps others to understand the 'mood' of the children and young people at that moment and any factors which are affecting this.</li></ul>	HSC 323a pc 6 Link to HSC 31
Work with groups to promote individual growth and development	Explain or show how you work with the group to promote individual growth and development by:<ul><li>supporting a positive and appropriate culture such as respecting privacy, allowing each a chance to express their views, listening and valuing each other's differences</li></ul>	HSC 323b pc 1, 2 HSC 323c pc 1a, 4

372

	<ul><li>helping the children or young people to be involved in identifying, implementing and evaluating group work activities that they feel would be helpful to the group – could be:<ul><li>activities which help team building</li><li>routines for cooking</li><li>organising BBQs</li><li>fund raising</li><li>planning activities for Christmas/bonfire night/birthdays</li><li>holidays</li><li>clearing up after activities</li><li>visits</li><li>celebrations of any kind.</li></ul></li></ul>	
Balance positive outcomes for individuals in 'friendship groups' and the group as a whole	Explain or show how you work with small 'friendship groups' and the group as a whole so that all children and young people have the opportunity for positive outcomes.<ul><li>How do you work with the child or young person who seems not to fit in?</li><li>Who has completely different interests from others in the group?</li><li>Who is at a different stage of development either physically, intellectually, socially or emotionally to others in the group?</li><li>How do you help to minimise any adverse affects to children and young people which are as a result of belonging to either friendship groups or the group as a whole – perhaps in response to peer pressure?</li></ul>	HSC 323b pc 3, 4, 5
Make group care a positive experience	Explain or show how you work with the children and young people in the setting so that:<ul><li>conflict, tensions and crisis are addressed looking for win-win solutions</li><li>risk of harm, danger and abuse is recognised and action is taken</li><li>you work constructively with group dynamics looking for win-win outcomes</li><li>the children and young people are involved in decisions about group care and how this can be improved (perhaps through key workers or maybe through a 'council' approach)</li><li>you record and report on the effects of this provision in accordance with confidentiality agreements and legal and organisational requirements.</li></ul>	HSC 323c pc 1b, c, 2, 3, 5, 6
Setting goals and boundaries for behaviour	Explain or show how you work with children, young people and others involved in their care to: set goals and boundaries which are understood by the child/young person and are achievable for them. This will usually be evidenced by being involved in working together with others in:<ul><li>planning a behaviour support plan</li><li>monitoring a behaviour support plan</li><li>reviewing a behaviour support plan</li><li>changing or modifying it as necessary (using feedback from those within and outside your organisation (this could be the child/young person, schools, clubs, groups, counsellors, psychologists, family, respite carers, etc.).</li></ul>You may also be a key worker who links with the family or supports other carers who are not as familiar with the behaviour support plan as you and will therefore need to help them to consistently apply it, even if the behaviour is challenging. Explain or show how you ensure that the goals and boundaries contribute to the social, emotional and physical well-being of children and young people. You will need to show that you understand that if the behaviour continues it will be detrimental to the child/young person's development, and sometimes to the development of other children or young people in the setting.	HSC 326a pc 1a, b, 2, 3, 4, 6, 7
Role modelling	Explain or show that you understand the importance of:<ul><li>role modeling in terms of your own behaviour (you could link this to the theories of Albert Bandura) and that your behaviour complies with boundaries set for the children and young people</li><li>always behaving in a calm and controlled manner when handling incidents of unwanted behaviour.</li></ul>	HSC 326a pc 5
Patterns and 'triggers'	Explain or show how you minimise unwanted behaviours by reducing the events and patterns which trigger them by:<ul><li>ensuring that you provide sufficiently varied and attractive activities</li><li>applying fair and consistent rules and boundaries – both day to day and person to person</li><li>diverting unwanted behaviours by changing activity or mood/attitude when you see the first signs</li><li>ensuring that children and young people do not become frustrated (not heard/not asked/not included)</li></ul>	HSC 326b pc 1, 2 HSC 326c pc 5, 6, 7

	• ensuring that children and young people are not bored – activity not stimulating or challenging/not age appropriate/not in tune with preferences of the child or young person (TV programme/music/video etc.). Show that you know and understand the patterns, factors and triggers which lead to unwanted behaviours by: • supporting the children and young people to identify the triggers and patterns which cause their behaviours • observing what happens and talking to the child/young person to help them to see what happens • reading previous notes, asking previous key workers/social workers about known patterns or triggers which cause or contribute to unwanted behaviour.	
Looking for positives	Explain or show how you support children and young people and those who care for them to look for the benefits of positive behaviour rather than focusing on the negative. This should include: • expectations of behaviour which are appropriate to the age, ability, level of development and understanding of the child or young person • highlighting and praising positives – trying to use a minimum of 3 positive highlights of behaviour following 1 negative highlighted behaviour model • sharing positive aspects of behaviour with family/carers and others to improve the child or young person's self-esteem and set an expectation for future behaviour.	HSC 326b pc 3, 4, 5, part 6
Constructive feedback for unwanted behaviour	Explain or show how you will, at an appropriate time and in an appropriate place, discuss unwanted behaviour and help the child or young person to accept some constructive supportive feedback – always remembering to make sure they understand that it is the behaviour not themselves which is unwanted. Also show how you use naturally occurring opportunities to raise awareness of positive and negative ways to handle situations – sometimes watching soaps on TV can be a way of doing this.	HSC 326b pc part 6 HSC 326c pc 8
Interventions	Explain or show how you handle incidents of unwanted behaviour by using appropriate methods of interventions at the appropriate time to support children and young people to cease the unwanted behaviour.	HSC 326c pc 1, 2
Sanctions	Explain or show how you explain to children and young people: • when and why sanctions have been applied following unwanted behaviour • that this is consistent with the policy of the organisation • that this is in response to the unwanted behaviour not a personal response to themselves.	HSC 326c pc 3, 4
Restraint	Explain or show how you understand the legal and organisational policies on the use of physical restraint, that you would: • use it only in circumstances where the child or young person was a significant risk to themselves or others • and **never** as a form of punishment • and **never** as a display of power. You will also need to show that you understand your role and responsibilities if restraint is used in your setting and how this is recorded and reported	HSC 326c pc 9
Procedures for reporting and recording incidents of unwanted behaviours	Explain or show how you apply the policies and procedures of your organisation in respect of recording and reporting incidents of unwanted behaviour. This should also include any: • verbal abuse (racist comments, threats, bullying) • physical abuse (assault, damage to property) • illegal behaviour • withdrawals • seclusion • restraint (already covered above).	HSC 326c pc 10, 11

UNIT HSC 33 ONLY Reflect on your own practice	Write or draw annotated diagrams which you can use to discuss with your assessor what is required to be a competent, effective and safe practitioner in your setting who provides active support for individuals and key people. You need to include what your strengths are and areas that need developing in terms of: ● Skills and knowledge (Do you know why you do the things you do in the way you do them? Or is it that you have always done things in that way? ● Your attitude and behaviour – if you were outside looking in at you working, would you always be happy with what you saw. Most of us have good days and bad days and our behaviour can irritate others at times. What would you see? ● Your values and beliefs – do these affect your work in any way? This is about more than religious beliefs; it is your whole value system. It can even include not swimming with a key child because you are not comfortable with your own body image. ● However well you practise it is unlikely that you do everything with the same level of competence. Which bits of the job are you excellent in? Which bits do you know you are not so confident in? ● What about the work products – reports/form filling/preparing for reviews etc.? ● Evidence of research.	HSC 33a pc 1, 2
Take action to enhance your practice	Explain how you go about getting constructive feedback on your practice from: ● the children and young people ● your supervisors ● your peers ● outside agencies (as appropriate). Create a personal development plan which you monitor during a 3-month period to show that you are developing. Ask others to feed back on your plan and see if they agree.	HSC 33a pc 3, 4 HSC 33b pc 1, 2, 3, 4

Index

This index is in word by word order. Pages in *italics* indicate figures and diagrams.

compensation 143, 187
complaints, care plans 166, 237
computer records 42
conduct disorders 329
confidence 131–32
confidentiality 39–41, 43, 144, 291–93
continuing professional development 104, 106–7, 108–10, 112
Control of Substances Hazardous to Health (COSHH) 59–62
cooking 251–53
corporal punishment 124, 125
Criminal Records Bureau 55
cultural differences 32, 296

D
daily living 311–13
Data Protection Act (1998) 42, 294, *295*
de-brief evaluation 339
deafness 26–27, 34, 259, 266
decision making 164–65, 319
development 11–13, 157–59
developmental activities 271–82
developmental checks 259–61
diagnostic assessment 262, 266–67
diet 251–53, *252*, 303
differences 23, 25, 32, 95, 296
direct payments 240, 280
Disability Discrimination Act (1995) 69
disabled children
    aspirations 208, 210
    assessment 259–70
    clothing 176–77, *177*
    communication with 26–29, 31–32, 34–35
    developmental activities 271–82
    discrimination 95
    leaving care 238
    stereotyping 7
discipline 124, 125, 186–87, 341
disclosure of abuse 138
discrimination, causes 95
diseases, reporting 63–64
disposable gloves 70
distress 29–30, 86–87, 328–29
domestic skills 303
Domestic Violence Crime and Victims Act (2004) 147

E
e-mail communication 39, 43
Early Support 262
early years 205, 206
ecomap 290, *292*
education 158, 202–8, 240
Education Act (2002) 147, 204
Education Reform Act (1988) 203
electrical injuries 84–85
emergencies 74–87, 147, *148*
emotional abuse 137
emotional development *11–13*, *158*
emotional disorders 329
emotional needs 129, 154
emotions
    of care workers 20–21, 144–45, 354–55

and clothes 175
    effects of 14–15, 352–53
    responding to 15, 16–19, 29–31, 86–87
empathy 19
employees/employers, responsibilities 51, 57, 68
employment 184–85, 241
encouragement 129, 130, 192, 196–97, 210, 226, 278
epileptic seizure 81–82
equipment, safety and use 67, 68, 72, 276–77
evacuation procedures 77
evaluation of progress 280–82, 339–40
evidence-based practice 110, 298
evidence of competence 357–76
expectations 275
eye contact 3, 5, 6, 17

F
facial expressions 3, *3*, 4, 5
families
    involvement 222, 268–69, 299
    relationships *159*, 160–61, 289–90, 302–3
    responsibilities 301
    structure 285–88
family, *see also* parents
Family Assessment model 298
family group conferences 162–63
Family Law Act (1996) 288–89
family learning 223–24
faxed information 38–39, 43
feedback 103, 225–26, 278, 339
'fight or flight' response 14, *15*, 352
filing records 42, 47–49
financial support, care leavers 238–39, 240–41
fire extinguishers 75–77
Fire Precautions (Workplace) (Amendment) Regulations (1999) 74
fire safety 74–77
first aid 77
    see also health emergencies
formal assessment 264–69
fractures 82–83
Freedom of Information Act (2000) 42
friendships 198

G
General Social Care Council 92, 127
genetic factors, and behaviour 334
genogram 290, *291*
gestures 3, 5, 6, 25, *26*
gifted children 188–89, *189*
Gillick ruling 41
goals
    aspirations 132, 207–8, 211–12
    for behaviour 336
    developmental 272, 274–76
    evaluating 281
government, UK 247
groups 245, 306, 315–16, 317, 321–24

H
hair 67, 72, 180–81
hand washing 71, *71*